Women Who Invented the Sixties

Women Who Invented the Sixties

Ella Baker,
Jane Jacobs,
Rachel Carson,
and Betty Friedan

Steve Golin

University Press of Mississippi / Jackson

The University Press of Mississippi is the scholarly publishing agency of
the Mississippi Institutions of Higher Learning: Alcorn State University,
Delta State University, Jackson State University, Mississippi State University,
Mississippi University for Women, Mississippi Valley State University,
University of Mississippi, and University of Southern Mississippi.

www.upress.state.ms.us

The University Press of Mississippi is a member
of the Association of University Presses.

First printing 2022
∞

Library of Congress Cataloging-in-Publication Data

Names: Golin, Steve, 1939– author.
Title: Women who invented the sixties : Ella Baker, Jane Jacobs, Rachel
Carson, and Betty Friedan / Steve Golin.
Description: Jackson : University Press of Mississippi, 2022. | Includes
bibliographical references and index.
Identifiers: LCCN 2022019443 (print) | LCCN 2022019444 (ebook) | ISBN
9781496841469 (hardback) | ISBN 9781496841476 (epub) | ISBN
9781496841483 (epub) | ISBN 9781496841490 (pdf) | ISBN 9781496841506
(pdf)
Subjects: LCSH: Baker, Ella, 1903–1986. | Jacobs, Jane, 1916–2006. |
Carson, Rachel, 1907–1964. | Friedan, Betty. | Social movements—United
States—History—20th century. | Nineteen sixties. | Women political
activists—United States—Biography.
Classification: LCC HN59 .G656 2022 (print) | LCC HN59 (ebook) | DDC
306.0973/0904—dc23/eng/20220701
LC record available at https://lccn.loc.gov/2022019443
LC ebook record available at https://lccn.loc.gov/2022019444

British Library Cataloging-in-Publication Data available

For Elaine, Josh, Jenny, and Clara

Contents

Part 3: The Sixties

Acknowledgments

I'm grateful, first of all, to Barbara Rambsy and Linda Lear for their scholarly and comprehensive biographies of Ella Baker and Rachel Carson. I also relied on Daniel Horowitz's study of Betty Friedan and on Peter Laurence's study of Jane Jacobs. These four scholars made my work possible. The scholar to whom I owe the greatest debt is Charles Payne, whose work on Ella Baker, SNCC, and Mississippi not only informed but inspired me.

I want to acknowledge the archivists at the Schomburg Center for Research in Black Culture, the John J. Burns Library of Boston College, the Beinecke Rare Book and Manuscript Library of Yale, and the Schlesinger Library of the History of Women in America of Radcliffe. I thank the librarians at my own public library in Glen Ridge, NJ, and Mark Jackson, librarian at Bloomfield College, who over many years found everything I needed.

Early on, during the writing, I benefited from feedback I received from Katie Keeran, Marlie Wasserman, and Nelson Kasfir; they pointed me in the right direction. Ron Aronson, Bill Caspary, and Nancy Wolcott read my first draft and challenged me to rethink what I was trying to do and how I was doing it. I'm grateful to them and to Michal and Lynne McMahon, Susan Sailor, and Tom Miles, who, from time to time, listened deeply and encouragingly while I read a chapter aloud.

Alice Golin read the first and last draft and the ones in between. Drawing on her expertise as a writer of fiction for children, she pushed me to write more clearly and effectively. Throughout, she gave me suggestions regarding my narrative strategy and my publishing strategy. And that was the least of what I'm grateful for. Without her, I not only wouldn't have been able to complete the book; I wouldn't even have started it.

Introduction: Four Women

Rebecca Solnit wrote a short essay, "Three Who Made a Revolution," in 2006. The three were Jane Jacobs, Rachel Carson, and Betty Friedan. I was struck by her point that their most influential works appeared at virtually the same time: Jacobs's *Death and Life of Great American Cities* in 1961, Carson's *Silent Spring* in 1962, and Friedan's *The Feminine Mystique* in 1963.[1] Working independently, in separate fields—urban studies, environmental studies, women's studies—Jacobs, Carson, and Friedan made an immediate and lasting impact, transforming the way the public, as well as future scholars, approached urban renewal, chemical agriculture, and male domination. The three books seemed connected to one another and to the moment of transition from the 1950s to the 1960s.

But it wasn't until some years later, when I thought of adding Ella Baker, that I became excited about a research project. Baker had fascinated me for some time, since I read Charles Payne's book about the organizing in Mississippi of the Student Nonviolent Coordinating Committee (SNCC).[2] Baker added diversity—Jacobs, Carson, and Friedan were white; Baker was Black—and sharpened the focus to activism. She was a lifelong activist who made herself an expert on how to build movements from below and was the key person in the founding of SNCC in 1960. As I studied *Death and Life* and *Silent Spring*, I realized they too were activist works, intended to build popular movements for change. Jacobs wanted to stop the destruction of neighborhoods, done in the name of progress. Carson wanted to stop the destruction of nature, also done in the name of progress. Friedan was a little different. She did not write *The Feminine Mystique* with the intention of building a popular movement; she did not become an activist in, or a leader of, the women's movement until three years after the book. Nevertheless, her book attacked the direction of historical change, protesting against the growing tendency to reduce women to housewifery. I began to see the founding of SNCC and the three books as successful interventions in history.

The four women had different histories and trajectories. Ella Baker was dignified, private, questioning, profound. She was born in Virginia and grew up in rural North Carolina. She came to New York in 1927, after graduating from college. In New York, she became an organizer and a student of organizing, learning to distrust top-down organizations and leaders who were celebrities. When the student sit-ins against lunch-counter segregation broke out in the upper South in 1960, Baker was ready to turn them into a mass movement for equality in the Deep South. She immediately saw the need for a group of dedicated young organizers who would build from the ground up. She saw, in short, the need for SNCC, and moved, effectively, to make SNCC happen, calling a conference of student activists and protecting their autonomy. Together, she and they created SNCC. She helped young people in SNCC become organizers by listening to them, patiently and deeply. In turn, SNCC organizers listened to local people in Mississippi, and helped them become leaders.

Jane Jacobs was curious, playful, funny, down to earth. She was born in Scranton, a middle-sized city in eastern Pennsylvania, and came to New York a year after graduating from high school. In New York, she discovered her place—Greenwich Village—and her calling: to defend neighborhoods against so-called urban renewal. Falling in love with the diversity, small scale, and density of her neighborhood in the West Village, Jacobs became a champion of her neighborhood and of all neighborhoods. Top-down planning made cities better for automobiles and worse for people. Changing the direction of urban history was integral to her *Death and Life*. She did not want readers merely to understand how cities worked or why they were in decline. She wanted citizens to take pleasure in their cities and to make them more pleasurable—to reverse the decline.

Rachel Carson was idealistic, transcendental, indignant, prone to depression. She was born in Springdale, a destroyed industrial town in western Pennsylvania. Whereas Jacobs enjoyed examining the wheels of locomotives in Scranton's train station, Carson loved to walk with her mother in the unspoiled hills outside Springdale. She loathed cities and avoided them as much as possible, settling in Maryland and Maine. She became a marine biologist and an author of best-selling books about nature, especially the sea. Carson deplored the destruction of the land by commercial civilization and offered the unspoiled ocean as comfort and cure. But in *Silent Spring*, she pivoted from flight to fight, making a direct attack on the spraying of DDT. In her quiet, reasonable way, she became a rabble-rouser, trying to provoke readers of *Silent Spring* to act, for the robin's sake and their own. She wrote because she wanted citizens to make a lot of noise while they still could.

Betty Friedan was tempestuous, combative, hungry, ambitious. Born in Peoria, Illinois, she came to New York after college and spent most of her adult life in the New York area. For almost a decade, she worked full time as a reporter for the labor press, covering strikes and other forms of class struggle as a partisan of radical labor. But when she was laid off, she suffered a career and political crisis. After a decade of not-very-successful freelancing, she wrote *The Feminine Mystique*, a critique of what American culture was doing to girls and women. She exposed the post-WWII consensus— women were happiest as homemakers, serving their families—as propaganda aimed at reversing the progress of women. She was not trying to start a movement when she wrote the book; she was only naming a problem. Yet her act of naming would prove as disruptive as the interventions by Baker, Jacobs, and Carson.

My book is about these four interventions. When Baker founded SNCC (1960), and Jacobs wrote *Death and Life* (1961), and Carson *Silent Spring* (1962), and Friedan *The Feminine Mystique* (1963), they were protesting against the direction of historical change and seeking to alter or even reverse that direction. Baker did not think the Brown decision of 1954 would, by itself, improve the lives of Black people. Only a mass movement of Black people could do that. When she helped start SNCC, she was deliberately shifting the direction of protest away from the legal focus of the NAACP and the moral focus of the Southern Christian Leadership Conference, toward a bottom-up movement for economic and political equality. When Jacobs, in *Death and Life*, and Carson, in *Silent Spring*, critiqued the bland assurances of the experts that a little destruction was the necessary price of progress, they hoped for nothing less than to reverse the direction of historical change. Friedan, in *The Feminine Mystique*, argued that the mystique was a kind of counterrevolution against the progress that women had made; she saw her book as a step toward restoring the revolutionary project of feminism.

Baker, Jacobs, Carson, and Friedan "invented the sixties" in the sense that their interventions, from 1960 to 1963, inaugurated a decade of radical thought and action. Defying the association of protest with Communism that characterized the 1950s, they helped bring that fearful time to an end. All four women attacked the experts who promoted passivity; all four encouraged ordinary people to trust their own instincts. Critical of established leaders and institutions, including leaders of reform, Baker, Jacobs, Carson, and Friedan fostered a democratic upsurge from below.

As women, they were outsiders in their chosen fields. Baker worked effectively at high levels of the civil rights movement—in the NAACP and then the SCLC—but was held back by top male leaders from exercising her full authority. Jacobs was treated as an amateur in urban planning, meddling in matters beyond her domestic sphere. Although Carson was able to become a scientist, she was barred, as a woman, from most field and lab work. Friedan knew, in advance, while writing, that she was going to be ridiculed because she was taking women seriously. Being outsiders nevertheless gave them an advantage. They were able to question assumptions that limited the vision of leading men in their fields. They brought fresh eyes; they saw not only what was wrong but new possibilities of change.

They were good listeners. Baker listened to Marxist theorists in New York and to uneducated Blacks in the South; over the years, she developed a method of organizing that was based on listening. Carson listened to scientists who were concerned about the effects of pesticides and to birdwatchers who were observing those effects. Jacobs listened to social workers, neighborhood people, and other activists, all of whom she gratefully acknowledged. Friedan listened, more briefly but crucially, to housewives who knew that something was wrong with their lives but were unable to say what it was.

Part I situates each woman in the 1950s. Cold-War anti-Communism seemed regressive and repressive to Baker, Jacobs, and Friedan. The highly touted progress of the fifties was frightening to Jacobs, Carson, and Friedan: the highways, cars, and urban renewal; the better living through chemistry; the cult of the happy housewife. But they did not experience the 1950s as only a bad time. Especially as the decade went on, they glimpsed new possibilities. Baker experienced the Montgomery Bus Boycott of 1955–56 as tremendously exciting and hopeful and soon moved back down South to be part of the action (chapter 1). In 1956, Jacobs began to speak publicly about cities; in 1958, she became deeply involved in a protest to protect Washington Square Park (chapter 2). Carson, responding to protests against the spraying of pesticides in 1957, changed the direction of her work from celebrating nature as refuge from commercial civilization, to attacking a major industry that was destroying nature (chapter 3). Friedan, gathering information from the fifteenth reunion of her class at Smith College in 1957, began to develop a theory about what American culture was doing to women (chapter 4).

Part II is about their responses to the problems and possibilities of the 1950s, which I call their interventions. Baker seized the moment of the lunch-counter sit-ins of 1960 to create SNCC (chapter 5). Jacobs, with *Death and Life* (chapter 6); Carson, with *Silent Spring* (chapter 7); and Friedan, with *The Feminine Mystique* (chapter 8), intervened with books. Jacobs and Carson immediately became national movement leaders; Baker, who already was a leader, assumed her rightful place on the cutting edge. Friedan, three years after her book appeared, also became a movement leader.

There were many protests in the 1950s—against racial segregation, against discrimination of various kinds, against economic inequality, against urban renewal, against McCarthyism, against the nuclear build up. But the movements that took off in the early 1960s were qualitatively different. They were sustained, not momentary; they were national, not just local; they changed public opinion, instead of being marginalized. Part III examines the bottom-up and democratic movement against racial inequality led by Ella Baker's SNCC, especially in Mississippi (chapter 9), and the bottom-up and democratic movement led by Jane Jacobs and her neighbors in the West Village (chapter 10). Rachel Carson turned the attacks mounted against her by chemical companies and their allies in 1962 and 1963 into a means of bringing visibility and focus to the emerging environmental movement (chapter 11).

Part III then follows the movements into the middle and later 1960s, when they began to interact. The women's movement took off, a tremendous explosion of energy from below. Friedan became the recognized leader of one branch, while the more radical and youthful wing of the women's movement emerged out of—and against—SNCC (chapter 12). Friedan wrestled with the young women in the radical women's movement and with the consequences of her own celebrity; Jacobs, in her last American battle, was able to draw on a decade of radical civil disobedience (chapter 13).

The epilogue follows the women and the movements into 1970 and beyond. Carson was dead, but the environmental movement that she helped shape won an early victory in 1970. Jacobs's urban movement, in its struggle against building major highways through cities, appropriated a key idea from the environmental movement. Capitalism emerged as an issue for the environmental movement, and for Jacobs, Baker, and Friedan, each of whom reacted differently.

Historians have grappled with the sixties, especially the transition from the fifties to the sixties. Daniel Horowitz's *On the Cusp* examines "the microlevel" of the Yale class of 1960. Horowitz mentions the founding of SNCC during their last semester and an article by Friedan months after they graduated, but acknowledges that it was not until later in the 1960s that the issues of race and gender emerged clearly in the consciousness of his classmates. He gets so close to his classmates' experience, and his own, that he cannot fully see the changes.[3] David Halberstam, in *The Fifties*, takes the opposite approach. Halberstam explores stirrings that led to the sixties, including Friedan's writing of the late 1950s, and succeeds in complicating the conventional view of the fifties. But he stands so far back that he is left with generalizations about "forces" that some-how came together and exploded in the 1960s.[4] Fred Kaplan's *1959* takes the middle ground, locating 1959 as the "pivotal year" of cultural and social "break-throughs" that prepared the "upheavals" of the sixties. Kaplan mentions Baker's founding of SNCC in 1960. However, by trying to analyze emerging changes "not only in culture, but also in politics, society, race, science, sex, everything," he can only touch lightly on any particular change.[5]

David Farber, reviewing Robert Cohen's biography of Mario Savio—which treated Savio respectfully as a radical thinker and activist—reflects on the his-toriography that has expanded the sixties, including transnational approaches and especially the long sixties approach, which stretches the sixties back to WWII. The aim, which he shared, was to put the sixties in historical context; when he taught, he would begin his course in "The American Sixties" with the New Deal. In the review essay, Farber acknowledges the cost of this long six-ties approach: "We have lost 'the Sixties.'" He wants to return to an older tradi-tion that focused on the disruptiveness of the sixties, as Cohen's biography did, and to narrow his course to "The Radical Sixties."[6]

Like Farber's course, this book treats the sixties as a time of radical thought and action. The book focuses on four interventions. It traces their origins in the later 1950s, closely analyzes their manifestations in the early 1960s, and explores their consequences in the later 1960s. What Baker, Jacobs, Carson, and Friedan did, from 1960 to 1963, radically changed how people thought and acted. We are still living through those changes.

Part I

The Fifties

1

Ella Baker: Activists' Activist

Ella Baker, 1962, photograph by Danny Lyon. Courtesy of Ella
Baker Center for Human Rights.

A Radical Sense of Equality

Ella Baker probably knew more about building movements from below than
anyone in America. After graduating from college in 1927, in North Carolina,
she moved to Harlem, where she learned from intellectuals who talked class
struggle and from union organizers who practiced it. She combined class with
race, looking for seeds of future uprising in all those excluded from power

and status: Blacks, workers, women, young people. Her whole approach was based on grass-root struggle and confrontation.

She was immediately excited to be in New York, as Jane Jacobs would be eight years later, but not for the same reason. It was not the streets or neighborhoods that excited her, but the ideas. "New York was the hotbed of—let's call it radical thinking. You had every spectrum of radical thinking. . . . We had a lovely time! The ignorant ones, like me, we had lots of opportunity to hear and to evaluate whether or not this was the kind of thing you wanted to get into. Boy, it was good."[1] As she listened, she decided what to get into. Listening was never passive for her, never opposed to acting.

Early on, she waitressed in Greenwich Village, near Washington Square.

> My first discussion on communism was from a Russian Jew. . . . I would go down in Washington Square Park. I liked to smell the fresh-turned earth, and they used to plow up and plant new grass or flowers or something. And I was just standing there enjoying, I guess indulging my nostalgia for the land. And he began to talk, and I listened. . . . He wasn't too keen about the Soviets. He was basically approving the concept, but highly critical of the implementation of the concept so far as the Russian Revolution was concerned.[2]

In Harlem, she met other anti-Soviet Marxists as well as Marxists who were pro-Soviet. "And that was always food for me. I didn't care so much about the socializing as the exchange of ideas."[3] From Communists and other Marxists, she took the emphasis on social and economic equality but rejected the authoritarianism. She was developing a radical sense of equality.

Listening to Marxists during the Depression, questioning them, Baker developed an understanding of class that deepened her understanding of race. She was not going to be satisfied with helping talented Black individuals rise to the top of American society. "When I came out of the depression, I came out of it with a different point of view as to what constituted success," she explained. "I began to feel that my greatest success would be to succeed in doing with some people some of the things that I thought would raise the level of masses of people, rather than the individual being accepted by the establishment."[4]

Baker took a series of jobs to pay the rent, but her real work was organizing. Talking with radicals in Harlem and in Greenwich Village, working with the Brotherhood of Sleeping Car Porters and militant CIO unions, organizing coops in New York and NAACP chapters everywhere, she was learning how to build movements from below. Organizing involved slowing down, getting to know people, listening to them, encouraging them to listen to one another's experience and tackle their common problems. Traveling for the Young Negroes' Cooperative League (YNCL) during the Depression, she honed her organizing style. "It will be more than a barnstorming tour," announced the YNCL. "Miss Baker will spend at least two days in your community, studying with you your problems, organizing groups where there are none, pointing out from the experiences of others what plans to make and what steps to avoid."[5]

From 1940 to 1946, she worked for the national NAACP as an organizer and then as the director of branches, visiting local branches all over the country. Her emphasis was on organizing one's own community. When she went to Albany, New York, in 1941, she was disappointed with the local NAACP for not addressing inequality in Albany's schools. "The blacks who graduated from high school were all in a C track," not in college prep. But the Albany branch "was not concerned about that, hadn't done anything at all about that.... In fact, they were always talking about the poor people down South."[6] When she was elected president of the New York City branch of the NAACP, in 1952, she moved the office uptown, to Harlem and focused the chapter's work on challenging school segregation in New York. She believed in organizing around your own issues: that's where you could do the most, learn the most, grow the most.

In 1941, she experienced the NAACP national conference in Houston as deadening. After the conference, she recommended that the "session used by staff members might evoke greater response from delegates if, instead of staff members making speeches, several delegates be designated to talk out of their own experience."[7] The proper role of leaders was to help others find their voice. Most leaders emphasized their speaking ability. Baker emphasized listening, drawing people out, helping them discover their power.

When she traveled to NAACP branches, her assigned job was to increase membership. "You go in and speak one night and you have a big mass meeting and you say, 'How many are interested?' and so you get the membership, but you haven't trained them, you haven't provided them with the strength to resist what's coming." To mitigate the NAACP's top-down structure, she created leadership conferences, actively involving participants instead of lecturing at them. "We began having these regional conferences where people had dialogue and those in the so-called leadership roles were subject to questioning."[8] In her bottom-up organizing, people developed a sense of their own power by questioning authority, including the authorities in their own protest organizations.

Organizing in the 1930s, 1940s, and 1950s, she subverted hierarchy. When she was organizing for the NAACP, she went where people were, whether considered respectable or not: "pool rooms, boot black parlors, bars and grilles."[9] In Birmingham, she "spent the morning visiting barber shops, filling stations, grocery stores and housewives."[10] She never looked down on people. In her view, an elite education could be a handicap, because you might imagine you were better or smarter than others. There was an NAACP lawyer whom she regarded as an exception. "I think he was a Harvard man, but that wasn't in his way. He wasn't blocked by being a Harvard man."[11] Subservience was no better than elitism. Walter White, the head of the national NAACP, often went to Washington. Too often. "Unfortunately, he . . . felt the need to impress government people. He had not learned, as many people still have not learned, that if you are involved with people and organizing them as a force, you didn't need to go and seek out the Establishment people. They would seek you out."[12]

She was drawn to class conflict, especially when the labor struggle and the Black struggle converged. During the 1930s, she worked with, and was inspired by, the Brotherhood of Sleeping Car Porters, the first Black union to win recognition. "This was one of the first—I call it mass organizations that surfaced during that particular period. . . . The NAACP had come into existence and had already been institutionalized. The Urban League had been institutionalized. But the Brotherhood of Sleeping Car Porters was different."[13] To be institutionalized meant you might not be open to the new thrust from below. She was excited by the growth of CIO unions, which, in contrast to the established and institutionalized AFL unions, were aggressively organizing unskilled workers, Black and white. "The CIO began to send people down south, and you'd run across them, and frequently they found their only companionship in the early stages with somebody like people who were part of the NAACP."[14] She met CIO organizers in Mobile, when she was recruiting and fund raising for the NAACP. And in Newport News: "The CIO is moving in, organizing everything," she wrote in 1942. "I wish I could stay here several months. It is just the time to do a real piece of organizing for the NAACP, but as usual, I can only linger long enough to increase the membership by a few hundred and collect a few dollars." Frustrated in Newport News by the NAACP's business-as-usual approach, she took the opportunity to study mass organizing. "I am rushing to a CIO meeting."[15]

In 1946, she left her vice-presidency of the national NAACP because it was too cautious, too focused on legal strategies, too afraid to risk confrontation, too top-down. She remained a leader of the New York branch. But she knew that merely ending legal segregation was not her goal. She was emerging in her own right as a leader of a vital current of radical democratic thought and action on the cutting edge of the civil rights movement, committed to the rising of the masses, not to opening opportunities for the Black elite.[16] What she learned in New York about class as well as race put her at odds with the national NAACP. "Many times there are other groups, especially in the New York area, that are much further advanced, further advanced in terms of dealing with social issues that affect the whole population than the N.A.A.C.P. which was concentrating primarily on race."[17] No longer confined by the NAACP model of organizing, she was free to respond to the new possibilities of uprisings from below.

Montgomery

The Montgomery bus boycott of 1955–56 seemed to be that uprising. "The poor people down South"—so often objects of condescension—were in the lead.

> Here you have a situation historically unthought of and unpredicted, where thousands of individuals, just black ordinary people, subjected themselves to inconveniences that were certainly beyond the thinking of most folk. Where they would walk: old women and maids who ran the risk of losing their little income would walk, if they got there, rather than ride the buses. Now this meant you had a momentum that had not been seen even in the work of the N.A.A.C.P. And it was something that suggested a higher potential for widespread action through the South.[18]

Could the uprising in Montgomery be extended throughout the South? The boycott "suggested that there could be a much wider extension of this mass-type action which carried with it a certain amount of confrontation."[19] Unlike most civil rights leaders in the 1950s, Baker welcomed confrontation. The challenge for her was "How does this get carried on?"[20] The NAACP was the only existing organization with local chapters throughout the South. "The question arose in respect to mass action—does the N.A.A.C.P. lend itself to mass action or . . . will it continue its program of legalism?"[21] The NAACP's preferred approach was through the courts, whereas her preferred approach was through organizing and confrontation. "Court decisions, however favorable, become meaningful only as they are implemented by people making use of them."[22]

For Baker, the Montgomery boycott of 1955–1956, rather than the Brown decision of 1954, was the turning point in the civil rights movement. She played no direct role in starting the boycott and was as surprised as anyone. But her long-standing emphasis on uprisings from below caused her to value the surprise. "Here you had a social phenomenon that had not taken place in the history of those of us who were around at that time." And she knew two people who had started the boycott, "two people who had functioned with the N.A.A.C.P. over the years and they were Mrs. Rosa Parks and E. D. Nixon." It was Nixon, the leading Black activist in Montgomery, who chose Reverend Martin Luther King Jr. to be the spokesperson. "Martin was not the initiator or the real spirit behind the Montgomery movement. The initiator . . . was E. D. Nixon. And why was he ready? He was part of the original effort of organizing the Brotherhood of Sleeping Car Porters."[23]

Baker saw Nixon as a bridge between the labor organizing of the 1930s and the civil rights organizing of the 1950s. She understood Nixon's historic role, because she was a bridge too. Much of what she brought to the civil rights movement of the 1950s she learned during the 1930s in New York, when she was active with the Brotherhood, and in the consumer cooperative movement, and—inspired by militant CIO unions—in worker's education.[24]

Nixon headed the Montgomery NAACP branch; Parks was active in it. In 1946, Parks attended one of Baker's NAACP leadership conferences in Atlanta. They met again a month later, in Jacksonville, when Parks participated in another leadership conference. After that, when Baker visited Montgomery, she would stay with Parks. Parks considered Baker "a true friend—a mentor."[25] Baker praised Parks as "a kind person, whose kindness didn't have class lines." Baker despised class prejudice as much as racial prejudice. It was ridiculous to look down on people when you wanted to build equality. Some NAACP branches served as social clubs for the black elite. But Parks was not like that. "In many Southern cities at that stage especially, there were very sharp class lines in terms of what you had and how much 'education' you had. But she had none of that."[26]

Baker longed to be part of the action in Montgomery. In February 1956, in the third month of the boycott, she wrote to a northern friend with uncharacteristic emotion and misspelling. "I came as near as shouting as I ever did when you told me what had been done to stimulate immediate and direct economic aid to the Monthomery [sic] bus boycott. For I too am chafing at the bit to be down there as part of the struggle; but since I can not I am concern [sic] that we on this end build strong supply lines for those on the actual line of battle."[27] Chafing at the bit: it would be four long years before she would feel fully involved in the southern struggle. Meanwhile, she did everything she could to support and extend the mass movement.

In May 1956, Parks came north and toured Harlem with Baker, raising money for the boycott, and Baker helped organize a mass rally at Madison Square Garden, where Parks and Nixon spoke.[28] Meanwhile, Baker strategized with two radical friends in New York: Bayard Rustin, a black civil rights organizer, socialist, and pacifist, who was close to A. Philip Randolph; and Stanley Levison, a Jewish activist and fundraiser who was close to the Communist Party. "There were three of us who talked into the wee hours of the morning in terms of, how do you develop a course that can enlarge upon the gains or the impact of the Montgomery bus boycott."[29] Together, Baker, Rustin, and Levison created a group, In Friendship, to direct northern financial resources to grass-roots organizing, not only in Montgomery, but also elsewhere in the South.[30]

When the boycott ended in victory, Baker and Rustin traveled to Atlanta, hoping to turn the Montgomery boycott into the beginning of a mass uprising throughout the South. Along with others who did not share their radical egalitarianism, they founded the Southern Christian Leadership Conference (SCLC). Did people at that founding meeting think that the SCLC would be a democratic or a hierarchical organization? "Well," Baker explained, "the thinking about the nature of the organization would vary with the people doing the thinking. Those of us who preferred an organization that was democratic and where the decision making was left with the people would think in one vein," but "a majority of the people who were called together were ministers." They were preachers, not organizers. "They functioned largely in the church vein; that if you had a meeting and you preached to the people, the people would go out and do what you said to do." Could the ministers build on the democratic thrust of Montgomery? "Basically your ministers are not people who go in for decisions on the part of the people."[31]

Martin Luther King Jr. was the head of SCLC. In Baker's view, the mass movement in Montgomery created King. "The movement made Martin rather than Martin making the movement. This is not a discredit to him. This is, to me, as it should be. The only discrediting factor would be if this contradicts his own assessment of who made whom."[32] When she helped found SCLC, she was hoping King understood that real power comes from below and that the new southern-based organization which he now headed could "provide a mass base for action. Hopefully. . . . Of course, you couldn't be sure."[33]

Needing an executive director, SCLC hired a minister. When he failed to get the organization up and running, Baker was hired as acting executive director. She already knew that SCLC was not going to be a good fit for her. She would be a woman in an organization dominated by men—men who, as ministers, were used to women in supportive and subordinate roles. Had she been in fact the only woman in the founding meeting of SCLC? "I don't know. I didn't look around me to see. I wasn't even in it as such. Somebody's got to run the mimeograph machine."[34]

She was not comfortable with her role in the new organization, nor with its structure or strategy. But she was so committed to building on the momentum from Montgomery that despite her misgivings, she went to work for SCLC.

> Unless something were done whatever impetus had been gained would be lost, and nobody else was available who was willing or able to do it. So I went because to me it was more important to see what was a potential for all of us than to do what I might have done for myself. I knew from the beginning that as a woman, an older woman, in a group of ministers who are accustomed to having women largely as supporters, there was no place for me to have come into a leadership role.[35]

She moved from Harlem to Atlanta in January 1958, to set up the office of SCLC. "I went down with the idea of not spending more than six weeks there, giving myself a month to get the thing going, and then two weeks to clean it up. I stayed with SCLC for two and a half years, because they didn't have anybody."[36] Trying to build on the momentum of Montgomery, from a distance, had been frustrating for her. So she went south, and ran the office and programs for SCLC as its acting executive director and became more frustrated. She knew more about organizing than King, who was still in his twenties; she would have liked to mentor him. But no woman was allowed to play a leading role in SCLC. Although women played major roles in the Montgomery boycott, Baker was the only woman of any importance in the organization that came out of the boycott, and she was hired not to lead, but to run the office for a while, until a minister could be found to take over as the real director.[37]

Her frustration boiled over when SCLC commemorated the boycott. "The [third] anniversary of the Montgomery boycott was being celebrated, and the handbill that was circulated didn't say practically anything about the movement or what the movement stood for, what it had done or anything, but was simply adulation of the leader, you know, Dr. King."[38] The ministers and the media narrowed the story of the popular uprising in Montgomery into the story of one man. His elevation as an individual above the mass was exactly the opposite of what Baker believed in. And to have the individual raised up in connection with a mass action, where so many ordinary people had walked and fought and sacrificed, was intolerable to her.

She probably wondered what she was doing in Atlanta. She certainly was not succeeding in keeping alive the democratic spirit of Montgomery. But she was a fighter. She confronted King. Why was the anniversary celebration all about him? "'Why permit it?' He said, 'Well, I don't want to. The people want to do this.' So, Martin wasn't one to buck forces too much, at least at this stage."[39] To her, Martin Luther King Jr., in 1958, was not the kind of leader who encouraged people to claim their own victories and feel their own power. Instead, he allowed them to ascribe their gains to him.

Baker soon realized that the SCLC, like the NAACP, was not going to build on the momentum of Montgomery. She wrote back to Rustin and Levinson that SCLC was failing "to develop and use our major weapon—mass resistance."[40] Nevertheless, she stayed on, deepening her extensive network throughout the South, building on her contacts from her NAACP days, hoping for an opportunity to do more within the framework of the SCLC to encourage local leadership. And she tried to jumpstart SCLC, almost by force of will. In October 1959, she wrote to the leaders, spelling out the steps they should take "for developing the crusading potential of S.C.L.C." Barely containing her frustration, she urged them to search out "indigenous leaders, especially in the hard core states." By hard-core states, she meant the black-belt states in the Deep South. As indigenous leaders, she cited a minister in Jackson, two people in Greenville "who could be useful in visiting other areas of the State," and a deacon and a young priest in Mound Bayou who were helping people register to vote. Mound Bayou, Greenville and Jackson were all in Mississippi. She was trying to direct SCLC where it should go: "This seems to offer a means of expanding voter registration in Mississippi."[41]

She was not content to stop there. In the memo, she urged the ministers of SCLC to work harder at voter registration, to "participate in house to house canvassing. . . . If initiated and accepted by the leadership of S.C.L.C, it is quite possible, I believe, to commit 1,000 leaders to give eight hours a month, to work directly with the people in their communities." SCLC could spearhead "a vigorous movement, . . . involving masses of people."[42] Baker's memo shows that in late 1959 she was looking to create an organization of local activists to go house to house and unleash a mass movement in Mississippi. It was almost as if she could envisage the voter registration movement that would transform Mississippi in the early 1960s but didn't yet know how to get there.

Why Did the Students Listen to Her?

Less than four months later, there was a new uprising from below. On February 1, 1960, four college students sat-in at a Woolworth's lunch counter in Greensboro, North Carolina. Baker didn't start the Greensboro sit-in any more than she started the Montgomery bus boycott. She was actually less connected to the four Greensboro students—two of them were members of a local NAACP youth group that she helped start back in 1943[43]—than to Nixon or Parks. But this time she was in a position to help build exactly the kind of movement that she had been working toward since she heard the news of Montgomery. This time, she could use her position in SCLC to go beyond SCLC.

As a student of mass movements, she anticipated that the initial sit-in would spread. "When they first sat in at Greensboro from ANT [North Carolina Agricultural and Technical College], I recognized that the probability was that other schools would follow."[44] In fact, the movement grew faster than even she expected. "All of us were unprepared for the speed with which the sit-ins escalated."[45] As sit-ins leapt from college town to college town in North Carolina, and then to other college towns and cities in other southeastern and border states, Baker experienced the same excitement she felt at the news of the Montgomery boycott. Again, she saw leadership emerging from below and recognized the possibility of a mass uprising throughout the South. The difference was that this time she was nearby, in a southern-based organization with resources. "I was glad to be there when the sit-ins started, because then I was able to reach out and be of some effect in terms of the emerging students."[46] This time, she pulled the activists together, organizing a conference, giving them the time and space to find their own way.

How did she do it? How did her strategic thinking and mode of organizing enable her to reach the young people? Why did they listen to her? They didn't know her. Why would they trust her? And she was fifty-six, even older than their parents. "She was much older in terms of age," acknowledges John Lewis, a leader of the Nashville sit-in, "but in terms of ideas and philosophy and commitment she was one of the youngest persons in the movement."[47]

Her ability to connect with the young people began with her admiration. She admired their courage in the face of hostility and violence. "When the kids began to sit in, and set, and took it, none of us who were older who had a streak of humanity could fail to find some way of identifying with it." She was particularly impressed by their sense of their own rights. "My generation didn't have the nerve to do it, maybe. But they did. They acted as if they believed that this was their right and they weren't asking for any favors, in the sense of won't you please."[48]

As Rosa Parks exhibited no class prejudice, Ella Baker had no generational prejudice. She never patronized the students for being young or criticized them for being naïve. "I didn't change my speech pattern and they didn't have to change their speech pattern. But we were able to communicate."[49] An adult supporter of civil rights later complained that she herself was not able to connect with the young people because of their brashness. Baker responded: "Maybe some of us were willing to forego manners to replace the lack of militancy that we had found in the old." When the other woman insisted she wanted both activism and manners, Baker responded: "Well, you can't have everything."[50]

The fact that the young people were not like her, that they had thoughts and did things she hadn't thought or done, made them more, not less, attractive to her. As she got to know them, she became even more impressed. "Here were these youngsters who not only were willing to take the kinds of stands that I might have suggested but they had gone even beyond that."[51] Instead of looking down on the students for being inexperienced, Baker saw their youth as an advantage. They were not afraid. They didn't back away from confrontation, unlike the older generation, which was "primarily a silent generation. People who had not been accustomed to protest. People who had not voiced their opinion. They had been under the impact of the McCarthy period."[52]

She realized immediately how crucial it would be for the students to remain in control of the movement. "My basic hope from the beginning was that it would be an independent organization of young people. I thought they had the right to direct their own affairs and make their own mistakes."[53] She wanted to help them develop their capacity for leadership, "rather than having it taken away from them in terms of 'leadership' or credit."[54] In the early 1930s, as a leader of the Black cooperative movement, she promoted the leadership of young people.[55] In 1959, she insisted: "The participation of women and youth in the Southern civil rights struggle must be promoted."[56] And when now, in February 1960, young people took the lead, she was ready and willing to offer her services.

The young people had never heard of her. Her decades of quiet and effective organizing work for cooperatives and the NAACP and SCLC had not resulted in a national reputation. She flew beneath the radar of the media. This was a disadvantage, if she wanted fame and followers. But it was an advantage for engaging in serious dialogue with young people. She did not feel confined by her role as acting executive director of SCLC. She could listen to the young people; she could appreciate what they had done; she could recognize what was hopeful and new. Instead of talking down to them, she could respond to their potential for leadership.

Asked later how she was able to help the students, she began, modestly, by pointing to the fact that she was there. She was able to help them form their own organization "not because of any unusual capacity that I had that others did not have, but, you see, where I was placed."[57] Also, she was able to help because she knew the area, including the colleges, and was able to make personal connections. "When something popped up in Raleigh or Durham or Greensboro or someplace in Virginia, these were areas I knew about."[58]

> I grew up in the area. I had been involved in student activity because I spent eight years in boarding school. And then I had been able to place a couple of young students, young friends, or advised them where to go to school; and I knew a lot of people throughout North Carolina especially, and so as names surfaced, it would refresh memories of maybe their mother or their father or somebody related to them or a place that I had been in terms of meetings of various kinds.[59]

She didn't know the students, but she knew some of their mothers and fathers. She also knew, through SCLC, some of the young ministers who had rapport with the students. And she knew a young dean at Shaw University in Raleigh, where she had been a student, thirty-three years earlier. After learning that no facility in Greensboro was available for the weekend she picked for the conference, she decided to bring the students to Shaw.[60]

In the urgency of the moment, she drew on all she had learned through her decades of organizing and studying mass action and facilitating social change.

> It was very obvious for one who had been knocking around, as news stories broke, that one group was not in touch with the other group. There was not too much communication except as sisters who were in one school would call their brother or their cousin or whoever else there was in another school. . . . But there was nobody trying to structure a gathering that would provide for all of those who were interested to come together and sort of sit down for a while.[61]

Those who were sitting in, separately, needed to sit down together. And not just the youths who were already protesting, but also "those who were chafing at the bit, as it were, to be a part of it."[62] They were chafing at the bit, as she was when she watched Montgomery unfold. Some adults, watching the sit-ins, wondered how they could attach the energy of the students to their own organization. Baker knew, very early on, that she wanted to bring students together, face to face, so they could find their own way.

Her experience in the 1930s, 40s, and 50s enabled her to recognize the potential of the sit-ins and to grasp the need for coordination, so the students could get to know one another and strategize together. Her experience in SCLC was particularly important because she learned that SCLC would not be a good fit for the students. Martin Luther King Jr. was not ready to organize a mass uprising. "I had been working with him very closely, so I knew some of the potentials that were not there. And so I, with my particular bent toward young people, not because I felt they were going to embrace me with open arms because very few of them knew me, but I felt that I could at least stand in between those who would want to co-opt the idea, and so I suggested that a meeting be held."[63]

As SCLC's executive director, Baker invited the students to Shaw for the weekend of April 16–18. King suggested that she preside at the opening session, but she declined to do so. She preferred to listen. Throughout the conference, she did a lot of listening. Because she listened to the students, they listened to her.

> People aren't willing to get up early in the morning and sit down and talk with kids or talk with young people, sit up late at night and talk with them, or let them agonize—deal with them when they are agonizing with something that is bothering them. They miss the chance. . . . And so when the meeting was over, when the conference was over, they come to look for the old lady who is around there still, because the other party is somewhere else.[64]

Julian Bond, who was sitting-in at Atlanta, came to the Shaw conference. Baker struck him as older, dignified, almost severe. "She was not the kind of person I would call Ella. I would call her Miss Baker. She always wore suits, and she was well in her middle age when I met her. So she was not somebody you joked or laughed around with. She was right on the edge of being stern." Yet from that first meeting and all the subsequent meetings of SNCC, he trusted her, because she was a different kind of leader.

> She never said, "Do this." But she always was able to pose questions to you that made you think about alternative ways and end up with a solution that involved some kind of democratic process involving everybody. So that if four or five of us were sitting here, she would ask what everybody thinks. . . . She wouldn't tolerate someone coming in and saying, "Okay, here's what we're going to do." It had to be talked out among us all. It took us forever to make decisions. But when we made them, you had the feeling that everyone had their say. It might not be the decision you wanted, but at least you got to say something about it, to argue your point of view.

She was not one of them, one of the young people, someone you called by her first name. But to Bond, she embodied the principle that "you couldn't fight for democracy without being democratic." It would become SNCC's guiding principle: "Your method and your goals had to be the same."[65]

Diane Nash, a leader of the Nashville sit-in, also came to Shaw.

> I remember receiving the invitation to attend the conference that would bring
> together student leadership from many campuses where sit-ins were going on. Ella
> Baker saw how important it was to recognize the fact that the students should set
> the goals and directions and maintain control of the student movement. I never
> had to worry where Ella Baker was coming from. She would speak her mind hon-
> estly, and I turned to her frequently, because she could emotionally pick me back
> up and dust me off. . . . Her participation as a person some years older than we
> were could really serve as a model of how older people can give energy and help
> to younger people, and at the same time not take over and tell them what to do.[66]

Like Bond, Nash emphasized Baker's democratic style of leadership, her
ability to help the young people forge their own direction. Unlike Bond,
however, Nash experienced Baker as nurturing, not only to the organization,
but also to herself as an individual. Perhaps Baker tried especially hard to
support women and encourage them to become leaders in the movement. Just
the example of Baker's own leadership style, so calm and confident and clear,
made Nash think: "I'd love to be able to make contributions like that."[67]

Baker was able to help the students find their way at Shaw because she had
no agenda of her own, no overriding ego. "I think that got over to them, in
the original meeting. Because they knew that the meeting came into being
because I did it. But they also saw that I made no effort to become a leading
figure in the meeting. And so they began to have that kind of confidence, and
so they felt they could trust me."[68] After Raleigh, back in Atlanta, she did the
little things to keep the organization going: compiling a mailing list, typing,
writing, phoning, fundraising. "They had been able to rely on me to do what
they could not do . . . at the moment, in terms of the nitty-gritty work that
had to be done. So they were willing to listen."[69] It would have been almost
unimaginable for a male leader to do this kind of work in 1960.

Because she did not try to take over, because she did not have an oversized
ego, because she was willing to do the nitty-gritty work, and because she was
willing to listen—in short, because she was a woman leader, though she would
never put it that way—they listened to her.

Woman Leader

Activism was Baker's career: being an activist, fostering activism in people,
helping them foster activism in others. What kept her going during four

decades of organizing, through all the starts and stops, the frustrations and disappointments? Certainly not the money. An interviewer, impressed by her frequent consulting with many organizations, told her that he wanted to be like her. "Well, I suggest that you not follow what I'm doing, especially if you want to make some money. You can forget it, just forget it."[70] And it wasn't the fame. "I set up the office of the Southern Christian Leadership Conference in 1958, but you didn't see me on television, you didn't see news stories about me. The kind of role that I tried to play was to pick up pieces out of which I hoped organization might come."[71] What sustained her was "the belief in people. The right of people to expect those who are older, those who claim to have more experience, to help them to grow. It's a simple type of thing."[72]

Ella Baker put nurturing people first. She was a woman leader, not a leader who happened to be a woman. She herself did not consider her gender to be important, one way or the other.[73] But she was sharply critical of the way most male leaders thought about leadership. Attracted to the media spotlight, they were often in love with their own eloquence; they tended to lecture, to speak down to people whom they thought of as followers; they wanted women in the background, performing the necessary supportive tasks. Her difference was a cause of conflict in SCLC. James Lawson, a young activist minister in Nashville and mentor to many student activists, knew King and Baker well. "Martin had real trouble with having a woman in a high position."[74] Andrew Young, a minister from Alabama who joined SCLC while Baker was there, described her as a "determined woman" and observed: "The Baptist Church had no tradition of women in independent leadership roles, and the result was dissatisfaction all around."[75] Baker explained the conflict in similar terms. "I had known, number one, that there would never be any role for me in a leadership capacity with SCLC. Why? First, I'm a woman." [76] Worse, she was a woman who expressed her opinion as an equal. "Baptist ministers have never been strong on dialogue."[77] And "I was difficult. I wasn't an easy pushover. Cause I could talk back a lot—not only could but did. So that was frustrating to those who had never had . . . a woman who knew how to say no."[78]

Her manner and age exacerbated the conflict. She looked everyone—male or female—directly in the eye. She didn't flirt; she was not a sex object. "I was too old to create any interest on a man-female basis." Flirtation might have taken the edge off the clash between the ministerial ego and an outspoken woman. But she was as incapable of flirtation as of adulation. It wasn't just King who was not comfortable with her. Most ministers in the leadership of SCLC were uncomfortable with her, and they limited her role. She could have represented the organization in the way that executive directors of other organizations did; she could have been "the spokesman. But they couldn't tolerate having . . . a lady, and an old lady at that. It was too much for the masculine and ministerial ego."[79]

Another thing wrong with her was her way of thinking about organization. Between her and the men around King, there were differences in orientation,

> differences in terms of whether or not you really ought to have a leader-centered movement or a group-centered leadership. . . . Instead of trying to develop people around a leader, the thrust, in my direction, should be that the first consideration is to try to develop leadership out of the group and to spread the leadership roles so that you develop—in other words, you're organizing people to be self-sufficient rather than to be dependent upon the charismatic leader.[80]

A leader-centered group depended on its charismatic head. A group-centered leader encouraged horizontal ties between members, insisting that they work through their differences in a democratic way and helping them become increasingly independent of herself. Baker saw the alternatives as lecture or dialogue, a hierarchical organization or a democratic one, SCLC or SNCC.

Baker's different way of thinking about leadership, which was a cause of conflict in SCLC, would become a ground of community in SNCC. Through dialogue and democratic decision making, young people in SNCC became better at listening and at treating people with respect. That's how they were able to organize in the Deep South. A charismatic leader could call a demonstration. But actual organizing, sustained over the long haul, only happened when many people developed their own powers to the point of being able to make decisions and learn from their mistakes.

SNCC would be effective in Mississippi, Baker explained, because SNCC organizers behaved toward local people with the same democratic respect with which, in SNCC, they learned to behave toward one another. "So, in the first thrust [SNCC] made in electing to go into the hard-core, Black-Belt areas, this also carried with it a conviction that had come out of our dialogue of developing people; organizing them for their own leadership rather than getting them mobilized to be dependent upon some extraneous, or outside, or imported leadership."[81] SNCC organizers would not tell people in Mississippi what to do. In SNCC meetings, the young activists were involved "in the decisions that affected their lives." In Mississippi, they would begin "to operate on that basis of people being involved in decisions that affected their lives."[82] They would treat local people the way they had learned to treat one another.

Charles Payne, in his groundbreaking 1989 article on Ella Baker and in his terrific 1996 book on SNCC in Mississippi, emphasizes Baker's distinction between mobilizing and organizing. What SCLC later did in Birmingham and in Albany, however important and necessary, was mobilizing. "What SNCC did in rural Mississippi, Alabama, and Georgia was organizing." The important question was what people learned. "How many people show up for a rally may matter less than how much the people who organize the rally learn from doing so." Payne contrasts "the more traditional conception of leadership as moving people and directing events" with Baker's concept of "leadership as teaching." He follows Baker's thinking about leadership through to its conclusion. "If growth toward self-sufficiency is the point, then there may be times when people will have to be allowed to make 'wrong' decisions. . . . That was why Ella Baker tried to avoid exerting too much influence on the decision making in SNCC."[83]

Baker's radical democratic vision made no exceptions for Martin Luther King Jr. or anyone else. Her challenge to King is still challenging for historians. Baker is now recognized as a major figure in the Black freedom movement, especially since the appearance in 2003 of Barbara Ransby's definitive biography, *Ella Baker and the Black Freedom Movement: A Radical Democratic Vision* But even Ransby and J. Todd Moye, author of a more recent biography of Baker, protect King against her criticisms.[84] By contrast, Charles Payne, in his older study of organizing in Mississippi, sides with Baker in her criticism of King's leadership style and his preference for mobilizing over organizing.[85] In telling of the clash between Baker and King, I follow Baker and Payne.

Leadership as teaching, says Payne: Baker was, originally, supposed to be a teacher. Her mother expected her to teach when she graduated from college; teaching was the best an educated Black woman could hope to do. Baker rebelled, fled to New York, worked odd jobs, and began organizing. As an organizer, increasingly confident of her skills, she became, finally, a teacher. Not a lecturer. She was a teacher who questioned and dialogued, who nurtured the individual and the group, who challenged young people to listen to one another, to make the decisions, to become fully human.

According to Baker, a leader might sit quietly in the back of the room, listening. Leadership of this kind was not a function of charisma, but rather of connecting with people, recognizing their achievements and their potential for greater achievement. A woman leader, with a different conception of leadership, she was able to nurture individuals and an organization. She fostered the democratic culture of SNCC, out of which grew the young organizers who would transform Mississippi. A democratic leader responded to others and was frequently led by them, as Baker was led in 1956 by women who walked and in 1960 by students who sat. Her relationship with Rosa Parks exemplified this idea of leadership. Baker was Parks's teacher at the leadership conferences. And then Parks was, in effect, Baker's teacher, when she refused to get up from her seat in the bus and triggered the mass movement in Montgomery.

Under Baker's guidance, SNCC became an organization where, as Julian Bond put it, "you couldn't fight for democracy without being democratic." For democratic activists everywhere, she remains the model of a different kind of leader.

2

Jane Jacobs: Playful Activist

Jane Jacobs, chairman of the Committee to Save the West Village, at a press conference at Lions Head Restaurant at Hudson and Charles Streets, 1961. (Library of Congress.)

Playing

Jane Jacobs liked to go "Hitch-hiking with the Fish." She and her husband, Robert, began taking coastal adventures in 1946. Once, they went to Tangiers, a fishing port in Chesapeake Bay, hoping to catch a boat to islands and obscure coastal places.

"No way to manage such a thing," said all the knowledgeable landsmen and hotel keepers along our route in Maryland.

"No problem at all," said the fishermen on the Tangiers docks. "Be here at four tomorrow morning."[1]

Jacobs laughed at people who told her that it couldn't be done, that the only way to go was by "orthodox mail boat."[2] She listened to fishermen, whose knowledge was rooted in daily experience. She wasn't yet focused on what would become her great subject: densely populated cities. On the contrary, this unpublished 1954 piece is about thinly populated villages. But she was already skeptical of orthodoxy.

And skeptical of cars. "Naturally, you cannot take a car along." Put your bike on the bus or train. "The impressions received during an automobile trip and the impressions received from a more intimate bicycle-and-fishing trip are so different as to seem hardly descriptive of the same place."[3] She was skeptical of planning too. "One of the nicest things about a coastal hitch-hiking trip . . . is that it takes almost no advance planning. In fact, there is very little of it you could plan if you wanted to."[4]

She was told, by landsmen, that superstitious fishermen didn't take women abroad. "Like other disheartening 'information' about our prospects, given us by landsmen, this is an objection we have never run into where it counts—on the docks."[5] Thinking for herself, seeing for herself, following her curiosity, always pleased Jacobs. So did meeting people, talking to them, playing with them. On coastal trips, she and Robert sometimes camped, but they mostly found lodging. "Camping as a regular thing on a coastal trip cheats you out of much companionship with the people where you have landed. You would miss playing poker with the doctor and the postmaster in the back room of the Chesapeake House."[6] Playing with people was the point. If the play was slightly disreputable—like back-room poker—so much the better.

She played all her life. Learning to read in school was fun. After that, she was bored, "reading secretly with a book under the desk."[7] She frequently got into trouble. "I would break paper bags in the lunch room and make explosions and I would be sent to the principal."[8] Sometimes she organized mini-rebellions. "It was as if she sought trouble for the sheer delight of it," says Robert Kanigel, who comes closest among her biographers to capturing her playful spirit.[9]

An eighth-grade classmate describes her as "a free spirit, clever, hilariously funny, and fearless" and remembers "the only escalator in the city at the time. Jane, to the half fright and half admiration of her followers went up the down staircase of the escalator. No mean feat because the steps were not too wide and they were always crowded."[10] Bored in high school, she got poor grades and had no interest in going to college. After high school, she studied stenography and worked as assistant to the editor of the woman's page at the *Scranton Tribune*; just for fun, she created an advice column, writing pseudonymous letters asking for advice and more letters lambasting herself for giving bad advice.[11]

Scranton was a modern city, reaching its peak population of 143,000 in 1930. In addition to the escalator, there was an electric streetcar system, and trains. "I used to like to go to the railroad station in Scranton and watch the locomotives. I got a big bang out of seeing those locomotives and those pistons that moved the wheels." She was especially interested in the way the older locomotives invited you to see their mechanism. "They were painted in a way to show you how they worked." Newer locomotives "had skirts on them and you couldn't see how the wheels moved and that disturbed me."[12] As an adult, she would enjoy removing the skirts, or decent draperies, from things, revealing how they worked.

When she was nineteen, seeking adventure and work, she moved to New York. The city was so much more complex than Scranton; there was so much more to examine. She would go up on the roof of her apartment building and watch the garbage trucks making their rounds. "I would think, what a complicated, great place this is, and all these pieces of it that make it work."[13] When she was twenty-four, she published a piece on manhole covers in NYC, explaining how to decode them for clues to the world of electricity, gas, and steam hidden below.[14]

She was living with her sister Betty in Brooklyn, looking for secretarial work in Manhattan. It was the Depression, but she was not depressed. In the morning, she would go for interviews. In the afternoon, she would explore whatever neighborhood her interview landed her in. "Or if I had already looked around I would spend a nickel on the subway and go arbitrarily to some other stop and look around there." She was playing this game one day where it brought her to Greenwich Village. "I just liked the sound of the name: Christopher Street—so I got out at Christopher Street, and I was enchanted with this neighborhood, and walked around it all afternoon." The variety, the "scale of things," the "craftsmen's shops" delighted her. "I rushed back to Brooklyn. And I said, 'Betty I found this place where we have to live.'"[15]

Five years after graduating from high school, she enrolled in Columbia's School of General Studies, "taking whatever I pleased, mostly in natural sciences (I found I passionately loved geology and zoology). . . . For the first time

I liked school and for the first time I made good marks." But Barnard College, Columbia's sister school, didn't like her playing.

> After I had garnered, statistically, a certain number of credits, I became the property of Barnard and once I became the property of Barnard I had to take, it seemed, what Barnard wanted me to take not what I wanted to learn. Fortunately, my high school marks had been so bad that Barnard decided I could not belong to it.[16]

Subverting established rules was one of her favorite forms of play. When she was young, her boss at a trade journal regarded her as a troublemaker because she questioned his authority. When she was middle-aged, and famous, interviewers asked how she would improve schools.

> If I were running a school, I'd have one standing assignment that would begin in the first grade and go on all through school, every week: that each child should bring in something said by an authority—it could be a teacher, or something they see in print, but something they don't agree with—and refute it.[17]

Jane Jacobs, like Ella Baker, believed in questioning authority. They were instinctively democratic and never saw a hierarchy that they didn't want to up-end. Trusting ordinary people, rather than those who manage and control people, they went to disreputable places that were normally off limits to respectable women. Baker did it because she wouldn't let traditional class or gender restrictions get in the way of her organizing, whereas Jacobs did it for fun.

Jacob's angle of vision, like Baker's, was bottom up. She was working at a State Department magazine in 1952, and the FBI inquired into her beliefs. "I believe in control from below and support from above," she wrote, contrasting her view with the Soviet view of "control from above and support from below." Challenging the government's Cold-War assumptions, she defiantly asserted her right to register in the left-wing American Labor Party in 1947 and to continue doing so in 1948 and 1949, when many considered it subversive. "I felt that the issue of my right to do something which was not illegal, to defy the pressure of fear. . . , was a vital issue," she told the government. "I still feel that way."[18]

And that is the fundamental difference between Jacobs and Baker. Jacobs insisted on exercising her individual right to register for whatever political party she wished. Baker was fighting for the right of Blacks as a group to register to vote in the first place. They were both freedom fighters, but they did not mean the same thing by freedom. Jacobs experienced freedom primarily as liberty, Baker, as equality. Baker was less concerned about her individual freedom and much more concerned about the collective freedom of Blacks. She fought for African Americans to have the rights, as Americans, that Jacobs was born into, the rights that the American Constitution of 1787 guaranteed white people. Jacobs *liked* the Constitution; in 1941, she edited an admiring book about it.[19]

In New York, she supported herself by temporary secretarial jobs and occasional pieces for magazines, until she found steady work writing first for a trade journal, and then for the State Department. In 1952, she got a better job, with more opportunities for play. *Architectural Forum* was in Rockefeller Center and she rode her bike to work from Greenwich Village, where she lived with Robert. Her writing assignments at *Architectural Forum* gave her the chance to learn firsthand about planning and urban renewal. Robert, an architect, taught her to read architectural blueprints.[20] Learning to read buildings was fun, like learning to read books in first grade.

It was a job that gave her opportunities to question authority. She visited new housing projects, making up her own mind about them. And she visited other cities, meeting their architects and planners, questioning them. At first, she was an enthusiastic supporter of the new urban redevelopment, financed by Title I of the 1949 Housing Act. The only thing that bothered her was that urban planning was top down, weakening democratic control by the community.[21] As she examined cities for herself and questioned the experts, her doubts grew. In this way, trusting her curiosity and following her instincts, she fell into her real work. She became an antiexpert on cities.

In 1956, she spoke at a conference on urban design at Harvard. She was substituting for her boss and was nervous; she was not used to public speaking. She had no formal credentials, not even a college degree, and was addressing architects and urban planners. But she was still bursting paper bags. What makes a city vital? Little businesses.

> The stores themselves are social centers—especially the bars, candy stores, and diners. A store is also often an empty store front. Into those fronts go all manners of churches, clubs, and mutual uplift societies. These store front activities are enormously valuable. They are the institutions that people create, themselves.[22]

By contrast, big modern developments built according to the latest planning ideas were sterile. In a housing development in East Harlem, there were few signs of life.

Some settlement house workers fine-tooth-combed that development of 2,000 people to find where they could make easy-going contact with adults. Absolutely the only place that showed signs of working as an adult social area was the laundry. We wonder if the planner of that project had any idea its heart would be in the basement.[23]

Mocking architects and planners. At a conference of architects and planners. At Harvard. What could be more fun?

Perhaps, mocking architects, planners, and businessmen in the pages of *Fortune*. After her positive reception at Harvard, *Fortune* asked for a piece on downtowns. In "Downtown Is for People," she advocated play, contrasting the life of a thriving downtown—the "magnetism" and "exuberance," the "gaiety, the wonder, the cheerful hurly-burly"—with orderly city planning: stable, symmetrical, dignified, and dead. "We are becoming too solemn about downtown. The architects, planners—and businessmen—are seized with dreams of order." She pointed to plans for downtown San Francisco, Pittsburgh, Cleveland, Kansas City, Little Rock, and Nashville. "They will be spacious, parklike, and uncrowded. They will feature long green vistas. They will be stable and symmetrical and orderly. They will be clean, impressive, and monumental. They will have all the attributes of a well-kept, dignified cemetery."[24]

She continued this funereal theme in a talk at the New School for Social Research, in Greenwich Village, in April 1958. She called the plan for Lincoln Center "a piece of built-in rigor mortis." She knew she was being provocative. Lincoln Center was supposed to be one of New York's crown jewels. "It is planned entirely on the assumption that the logical neighbor of a hall is another hall. Nonsense. Who goes straight from the Metropolitan Opera to a Philharmonic concert and thence to the ballet?" In place of the ideal of planned order, she pointed to the actual, organic, messy order of urban life. "The logical neighbors of a hall are bars, florist shops, non-institutionalized restaurants, studios, all the kind of thing you find on West 57th Street or along Times Square or generated by the off-Broadway theaters down here in the Village."[25]

Jacobs loved mixing high and low, opera and bars, the modern project and the basement laundry. It was a kind of play. But in this talk at the New School, something else was happening, something new. She was beginning to think and talk like an activist.

She didn't speak as a neighborhood activist at Harvard or in the *Fortune* article, where she asserted that urban renewal could be beneficial, if there was only more consultation with neighborhood people. If planners and builders created renewal plans and ran them by citizens, the citizen with "an observant eye, curiosity about people, and a willingness to walk" would be the "ultimate expert" on one question only: "Will the city be any fun?" Working with the planners and architects, citizens would "adapt the rebuilding machinery."[26] In the *Fortune* article, "rebuilding" was not yet a dirty word.

But in the talk at the New School, just months later, she was angry. "Our slum clearers, housing officials, highway planners and semi-public developers have been . . . destroying New York's variety and disorganizing its economic and social relationships just as swiftly and efficiently as rebuilding money can destroy them." And again: "Our rebuilders have no idea what they are destroying, and they have no ideas of repairing the damage—or making it possible for anyone else to do so."[27]

The anger was because of Robert Moses's plan to ram a four-lane highway through Washington Square Park. To Moses, cars were modern, efficient, serious; they embodied twentieth-century progress. His plan for Washington Square dated back to the 1930s, after he became parks commissioner. He didn't consult people in the Village, who opposed his initial plan when they found out about it, forcing him to temporarily back off. "Our plans were blocked by stupid and selfish people in the neighborhood," he complained publicly.[28] By 1948, he'd quietly gotten approval from the Board of Estimate for a four-lane highway through Washington Square Park. It was a minor part of his master plan for the city, which included superhighways around and across Manhattan. The road through Washington Square would extend Fifth Avenue through the park, linking his planned expressway across midtown Manhattan with his planned expressway across lower Manhattan.

In 1952, Moses received the funding to go ahead, and the protests intensified. In 1955, Jacobs signed a petition and wrote a letter, but she was still only peripherally involved. In 1957, however, in a talk at Cooper Union, she cited Moses's plan to illustrate how poorly he and his allies understood the difference between failed neighborhoods and healthy ones.[29] By 1958, she was a leader in the struggle and was thinking through its implications. In the New School talk, she mocked Moses.

Planners who respected the city and its potentialities would not only attempt to learn from the Village—and there is much to learn from it—but they would certainly protect such an asset to the city from needless blight.

But instead we find that Mr. Moses the Commissioner of Parks, Mr. Moses the Slum Clearance Chairman, Mr. Moses the City Coordinator of Construction, and Mr. Wiley the Commissioner of Traffic are all in cahoots, determined that the heart of this community, Washington Square Park, shall be made a parkway so it can carry an arterial stream of traffic.[30]

Still playful, she imagined Moses in cahoots with himself. But she was less detached now than in the Harvard talk or *Fortune* article. For the first time, she was digging in and fighting back. "Because Greenwich Village is still an effective, functioning community, we are going to defeat this attempt at vandalism and get Washington Square Park closed to all but emergency traffic. We have to."[31]

It was a transitional moment for Jacobs, as she moved from criticizing the worst excesses of urban renewal to resisting urban renewal itself. In this talk at the New School, in April 1958, she was almost but not quite there.

> In the place of bulldozer unplanning, we will have urban renewal planning, much more sensitive to exactly what is cleared out of an area, what is left in, what is put back and why. The West Side Urban Renewal Study of the City Planning Commission, which is to be released this Wednesday, is our first small portent of this approach.

She was still hoping for something good from New York's Planning Commission, still thinking urban renewal might be reformed, but not for long. In the margin of her copy of the typescript of the New School talk, next to her optimistic words about urban renewal planning and the Planning Commission's small step forward, she scrawled "Haw!"[32] She was laughing at herself, at her naiveté. She stopped believing in urban renewal and the Planning Commission. She never stopped laughing.

In 1971, looking back at the endless struggles against top-down urban planning, she acknowledged that "fights like these are an outrageous imposition on the time and resources of citizens." How could this tremendous expenditure of time and energy be justified? What would make these incessant fights worthwhile? Her answer circled back to where she began. "The way to make all this absurdity tolerable is not only to decide to win if one is embroiled at all, but also, it seems to me, to have a bang-up good time in the process, and a satisfying vengeance against the rascals at the end."[33]

A good time in the process: even in struggles that involved the death or life of her community, perhaps of her city, Jane Jacobs insisted on the importance of play. She became a street fighter, taking conflicts out of hearing rooms into the street and bringing the street into the hearing room. She tasted the joy of defeating bullies like Robert Moses, the David-vs.-Goliath pleasure of satisfied vengeance. She learned to focus on winning, even when it meant not being nice to nice people. But she never stopped playing.

In her writing and activism, play was means and end, method and point. Ella Baker felt she was carrying a race on her back. Rachel Carson felt she was carrying the whole world of living organisms on her back. Betty Friedan would come to feel she was carrying half of humanity. But Jane Jacobs felt free to play.

Apprentice Activist

Three decades after Baker listened to a radical in Washington Square Park and savored the smell of earth, Jacobs led a fight to save the park. To her, the park was a place where her three children played. And a playground for adults, who used it "inventively and exuberantly." Musicians, dancers, sunbathers, talkers, readers, and tourists transformed the fountain basin into "a theater in the round . . . with complete confusion as to who are spectators and who are the show."[34] The diverse people who used the park made it what it was. Now they were fighting to protect it. Much of what Jacobs learned about fighting, she learned in the battle over the park.

She learned from more experienced fighters. In *The Death and Life of Great American Cities*, Jacobs praised two mothers for their unconventional thinking about the proposed highway through Washington Square Park. Most protestors hoped to preserve the status quo. Facing automobiles and experts, progress and planning, they aimed at a draw. They did not imagine that they could actually make the park better.

> However, two daring women, Mrs. Shirley Hayes and Mrs. Edith Lyons, were less conventional in their thinking. They took the remarkable intellectual step of envisioning improvements for certain city uses, such as children's play, strolling, and horsing around, at the expense of vehicular traffic. They advocated eliminating the existing road, that is, closing the park to all automobile traffic— but at the same time *not* widening the perimeter roads either.[35]

Hayes and Lyons defied the logic of the male heavyweights of the Planning Commission and the Traffic Commission, and the heaviest weight of all, Robert Moses. These experts knew that closing Washington Square Park to cars without widening alternative routes would cause a traffic mess and that the Villagers would be sorry. Except that it didn't, and they weren't.

Hayes and Lyons began the fight in 1952, when the initial funds were allocated to begin building Moses's four-lane road through the park, and there was an article about it in the *New York Times.* "Shirley Hayes was the person who showed me" the article, explained Lyons; "she was in the park with her boys. I was in the park with one of my children."[36] Hayes and Lyons organized other mothers. Hayes summarized: "A few women got together to say no, no, no."[37] The Board of Estimate halted work on the road. "Protests from all corners of the Village, and particularly from the mothers of the community, defeated the plan," concluded the *Times.* "The plan, envisioned by its sponsors as an improvement both ornamentally and functionally, had the effect of enraging those who used the park most, the women, who on a fair day, spend hours there with their children."[38]

Hayes and Lyons weren't satisfied. They wanted a ban on all traffic through the park, even the buses that took the existing narrow park road. According to Jacobs, they "sat in the park with their little kids and wondered ... why you had to have additional roads for traffic around Washington Square at all."[39] Moses also wasn't satisfied. He was used to local protests and used to overriding them; he believed he embodied progress, and protesters were "selfish and shortsighted."[40] His highway through the park would be doubly progressive, not only enabling automobiles to move more efficiently through the city, but also giving cachet to the new housing that developers were building south of the park, replacing the 10 blocks that he had already razed.

Hayes and Lyons appeared to have little chance. The wealth, power, and authority were on the other side: Moses, planners, elected officials, bureaucrats, and the park's biggest neighbor, New York University. But the two women had some advantages. They had a vital interest in the outcome, because they and their kids hung out in the park. Unlike NYU, they didn't need favors from the city government. And as mothers, they were outsiders; excluded from decision-making circles, they didn't have to be reasonable. Hayes and Lyons rejected the alternatives that the powerful, reasonable people offered. "And they were considered crazy women who just didn't understand the facts of life. 'Isn't this just like a woman to think this way' was the attitude."[41]

The stalemate lasted five years, until late 1957, when Moses rejected the various compromise solutions and decided it was time to push Fifth Avenue through the park as a four-lane highway. This was when Jacobs got deeply involved. Like Hayes and Lyons, Jacobs valued "children's play, strolling, and horsing around"; like them, she refused to accept the top-down logic that started with prioritizing automobile traffic and ended with sacrificing kids and play. Now her new role as public critic of urban planning began to dynamically interact with her even newer role as street fighter.

From Hayes and Lyons, Jacobs learned that protest from below might transform the established reasonable alternatives. From Ray Rubinow, a foundation executive, she learned the value of creating an ad-hoc group focused on the issue. Rubinow and Hayes formed the Joint Emergency Committee to Close Washington Square Park to Traffic, and Rubinow invited all Villagers to join. Jacobs recognized that without an umbrella group, protest bogged down in bureaucracy. "All the established organizations in the community had their own important concerns on which they focussed. Most of them should logically have been our natural allies, but . . . they had to go through time-taking procedures, more often than not at infrequent meetings, to debate and pass resolutions."[42] The Joint Emergency Committee bypassed the bureaucratic procedures of existing groups and appealed to anyone who didn't like Moses's plan. That was Rubinow's idea. "His solution, which was wonderfully practical, was to have an umbrella organization that was only about this particular issue."[43]

Rallies, petitions, and a single-issue group might slow Moses down. To stop him, the protestors had to become as tough as he was. Robert Jacobs woke Jane up one night and explained that he had figured out how to use politicians, instead of being used by them. Normally, candidates made promises; active citizens rallied to their preferred candidates; someone got elected; and the promises got broken. As Jane put it, "elections were not being used to reinforce democracy and to get constituents what they wanted, but were being used in the opposite way, to undermine."[44] Robert's idea was to force the politician currently in office to act *before* the election.

In practice, Robert's approach meant working with the Tammany Hall machine of Carmine De Sapio, rather than with the insurgent reformer Mike Seymour, who was running for state assemblyman. Compared to the machine candidate, Jane acknowledged, "Mike Seymour was more independent-minded, and he had been in favor of closing Washington Square Park to all but emergency traffic for a long time. He was one of the first fighters on this. He was a very good fighter. He believed in this. He had every reason to expect and hope that he would get the support of others who felt like him. The trouble was, he was not in power. The people who were in power were De Sapio's machine."[45]

She discussed Robert's idea with the Joint Emergency Committee, which threw its support not to Seymour but to his machine opponent—on the condition that De Sapio use his power to stop Moses's road before the election. De Sapio's intervention was a "trump card" in the fight against the roadway, observed the *Times*; "Mr. De Sapio, who lives in Greenwich Village, was responding to pressure from Village organizations," which "demanded a verdict before Election Day."[46]

Four days before Election Day, 1958, a Washington Square ceremony commemorated the victory of the moms over Moses. Instead of ribbon cutting, there was ribbon tying, symbolizing the closing of the road. Lyons and Rubinow and the child of an activist held one end of the ribbon. De Sapio and Mary Jacobs (Jane and Robert's little daughter) held the other end.[47] The threatened increase of traffic around the park never materialized; drivers found other routes or took public transportation. Moses lost. The mothers won.

Mike Seymour lost. "He was outraged at this. He felt it was immoral. I don't think he ever changed his mind since," said Jacobs, almost forty years later. Seymour was "important as an alternative, an election alternative." He gave plausibility to the pressure on De Sapio, but the Joint Emergency Committee chose to win. "As far as I know this was the first instance in which a citizens' group, a citizens' movement, deliberately and—some people thought cold-bloodedly—used an election for their purposes and their cause, instead of letting the election divide and shatter them."[48]

Jacobs did not take Seymour's anger personally. She explained to an interviewer in 1962: "I made my choice according to my own priorities; the partisans [i.e., Democratic Party reformers like Seymour] made theirs. I respect both choices—we need the pressurers and we need the partisans too." The interviewer, however, suggested Jacobs had "manipulated" the political process. Jacobs, who embraced the hurly burly of urban politics as she embraced the hurly burly of urban life, pushed back against the word "manipulated." "We believe in self-government, and that means politics. So I wonder why we devise such awful words for its operations—like we do for sex."[49]

Jacobs emerged more tough-minded and radical from the Washington Square fight. She saw Moses as more of a symptom of the problem rather than the cause. Moses himself was not corrupt, in a strict financial sense, but the system that gave him the power to reward developers was corrupt. She told the *Times* in 1959 that firing "Mr. Moses would help—but not much." The problem was that Title I "hands great chunks of the city over to officially anointed barons, [and] makes city rebuilding . . . into a monopolistic-set up for the favored few. Whether their motives are pure or greedy is beside the point."[50]

Years later, she remembered Moses speaking at a hearing, railing against the opposition to his road through the park. "There is nobody against this—*nobody, nobody, nobody*—but a bunch of, a bunch of *mothers!*"[51] Like Hayes and Lyons, Jacobs dared to think like a mother. In 1950s America, there was nothing more ridiculous.

By contrast to the mothers, most NYU faculty behaved sensibly. They did not like Moses's plan for the park, which served informally as their campus, but they did not openly oppose it. During the fight, many offered private encouragement. Jacobs asked: "Well what about you, will you speak?" But they answered: "Well no, it wouldn't be prudent"; their employer wouldn't appreciate it. Of course, that's precisely why it would have been useful for faculty to speak, because they could have contradicted the administration of NYU, which did indeed speak for the university in support of Moses's plans. Beyond the strategy and tactics that she learned in the Washington Square fight, Jacobs learned to loathe the logic of the cowardly and reasonable lions of the university—"What a bunch of hypocrites! What a bunch of cowards!"[52]—and to embrace the logic of the brave, crazy moms.

As an activist, Jacobs gratefully acknowledged the lead of others: the intellectual leap of Hayes and Lyons, the wonderfully practical solution of Rubinow, the hard logic of her husband. She learned most from Hayes and Lyons, who dared to put people before cars. Jacobs had wanted to do that too.[53] But she had no idea how to do it. Hayes and Lyons did. Their unconventional thinking contained the germ of a theory about how American cities could become great, a theory that *The Death and Life of Great American Cities* unpacked and elaborated. In crediting the two women by name in the book, Jacobs acknowledged their contribution not only to the victory, but also to her theory.

Writing as Activism

Jacobs's writing and activism merged from 1958 through 1961. Her book was protest; her protests were research. The Washington Square victory, in 1958, showed that Moses was not as powerful as he seemed. *Death and Life*, written from 1959 to 1961, showed that his claim to authority was groundless. Literally. He began with a lofty ideal and deduced down to actual cities. *Death and Life* began with life on ground level—vital, playful, anarchic—and worked up from there. Robert Fishman, in his wonderful essay on the struggle to save Washington Square Park, views *Death and Life* as the translation of that struggle into urban theory. *Death and Life* "vindicated Shirley Hayes's original intuition that saving the park for her children and her neighbors' children was somehow more important than all Moses's megahighways."[54]

Death and Life was about how to see as well as how to fight. Jacobs learned about fighting from Hayes, Lyons, Rubinow, and Robert. From other activists—Ellen Lurie and William Kirk—she learned how to see.

Lurie was a young social worker at Union Settlement. Working at *Architectural Forum*, Jacobs read, and sometimes edited, Lurie's reports on the devastation caused by urban renewal in East Harlem. People who really want to improve a neighborhood, Lurie wrote, "must be humble, for even the poorest, most unsavory-appearing community has elements of unique vitality which must be recognized, ferreted out, and saved."[55] Lurie's respect for poor people and poor communities appealed to Jacobs, in contrast to the disrespect shown by Robert Moses and city planners.

Kirk, who was Union Settlement's director, tried to get people to pay attention to what was going so wrong in East Harlem. In 1955, he visited *Architectural Forum* to talk to Jacobs's superiors. But it was Jacobs who listened and decided to hang out with him in East Harlem, so that she could learn to see what he saw. At the height of the Washington Square struggle, in July 1958, Jacobs applied to the Rockefeller Foundation for a grant. She told the foundation that she wanted to write a book that would let the reader experience what she experienced when she walked around the streets of East Harlem with Kirk.

> In fact, the way I began looking at the city in this fashion—hunting for evidence of how people use it—was a result of being walked around East Harlem for several afternoons by William Kirk.... I hardly knew what he was driving at, at first, but the accumulation of detail and incident soon began to make pretty exciting sense, and opened my eyes to other things in other places. This is the process I will try to duplicate in the reader's mind.[56]

The Rockefeller grant enabled her to take a leave from *Architectural Forum* and begin full-time work on *Death and Life*. In the book, she quoted Lurie twice, and acknowledged Kirk with characteristic generosity. "The basic idea, to try to begin understanding the intricate social and economic order under the seeming disorder of cities, was not my idea at all, but that of William Kirk, head worker of Union Settlement in East Harlem, New York, who, by showing me East Harlem, showed me a way of seeing other neighborhoods."[57]

Writing to a friend in 1959, she was precise about what she learned in East Harlem.

> I began to see that the most important thing in life in East Harlem was relationships of all kinds among people—that these relationships, many of them very casual, were the means of keeping the peace, of assistance in time of trouble, of squeezing some fun and joy out of the slum.... I saw that many people in East

Harlem were of true importance in their circles and had the dignity that comes of having some mastery, however little, on their environment.

But urban renewal destroyed all that. "These relationships were wiped out in the projects . . . and so was the dignity and responsibility."[58]

In addition, Jacobs learned to see from men who were blind. Edmund Bacon, the leading planner in Philadelphia, showed her a block crowded with poor Blacks from the South. She saw adults sitting on stoops and kids playing in the street. "Obviously they were very poor people, but enjoying themselves and each other." That was not, however, Bacon's point. To demonstrate the improvement planning makes, he showed her his nearby housing development. "Everything was new but the streets were deserted. There was no one around. Everyone was over on the other, older street." She questioned him about this: Why did people desert his improvements? He said: "They don't appreciate these things." She was shocked by his arrogance.[59] "I didn't have any credence in him any more," she said. "So I made myself my own expert."[60]

She also went to see Ed Logue, who was the Robert Moses of New Haven. The most important thing she learned in New Haven, however, concerned another city.

> He said that the best thing that could happen to San Francisco would be another earthquake and fire. . . . And I was appalled at this. I had been to San Francisco and I thought it was [a] wonderful place. He was serious about it, he thought all that should be wiped out and built new.[61]

The "Death" in the title of Jacobs's book was not abstract. It was grounded in her experience of what Moses was doing to East Harlem, what Bacon was doing to Philadelphia, and what Logue would do to San Francisco, if he could.

In Boston, she met architects who lied about the West End. Two architects admitted privately that buildings they examined in the West End were well built and beautifully detailed. But in their public function, they condemned the neighborhood as a slum and called for its destruction. "They could justify it because urban renewal was a greater good, so they would bear false witness for the greater good."[62] For Jacobs, by contrast, the end never justified the means; she would never falsify the facts in the name of progress. "We do not consider community destruction as progress, no matter how shiny or clean it looks," she said in 1957.[63] In 1962, she insisted that if "planning is good for human beings, it shouldn't keep hurting them in the concrete and helping them in the abstract."[64]

The more she talked with established experts, the more she learned to trust her own instincts. And the more she developed her own view, the more she realized that planners and architects were not her audience. They were not open to new ideas. Her audience was the citizens themselves. The experts claimed to know better than ordinary people. Their profoundly antidemocratic view shaped, dialectically, her own radically democratic vision. Like Ella Baker, Jane Jacobs came to believe that change came from below. After her book was published, she was on a panel about public housing and urban renewal with Logue and other experts, and she was direct, as always. "The last people in the country who are going to try anything new are the people professionally concerned. The change will come from outside. Meetings like this are going to accomplish very little. Change is rapidly coming from resistance and disenchantment of citizens."[65]

A few months later, she described how she reached this conclusion. At Harvard in 1956, speaking to planners and architects, "I got a big hand and I overcame my stage fright, but it didn't help. All they got out of it was 'put in a grocery store.'" Her article on downtown for *Fortune*, "was applauded, too, and everything went on as before." Unlike the Harvard talk or the *Fortune* article, *Death and Life* was intended for citizens, to stimulate their activism. The book encouraged citizens to trust their experience and mistrust the experts. "Citizens have to force change," she said on her book tour. "Often they are told they're selfish. It is not being selfish when you want to protect your neighborhood."[66]

When people saw their park or home or neighborhood destroyed, they grieved. They felt sad because something had died. But they felt even worse because they had been taught that progress was good and they shouldn't be sad.

> People *do* have feelings; they express them in every way they can, even while they are being ridden over roughshod. But they're intimidated by experts who tell them what they feel is selfish and ignorant, and unfortunately they are willing to believe it—to believe that there is even something disreputable about their grief.[67]

Her mission, in *Death and Life*, was to encourage citizens to trust their thoughts and feelings to the point where they would be able to act on them before something died.

In 1960, while she was writing the book, her activism became more personal. She was tucking her older son, Jimmy, into bed on a Friday night. "We are going to lose our tree," he said. A few adults had asked surveyors on Hudson Street what they were doing, but the surveyors were vague. Jimmy, like his mother, was genuinely curious. Responding to him, the surveyors explained that five feet were going to be cut off the sidewalk. To give cars more room, the Manhattan borough president was going to narrow the sidewalk and widen the street. But Jacobs knew the wide sidewalk provided a buffer against traffic on Hudson Street and made the street livable for kids and grownups.

Saturday morning, Jacobs and her kids wrote a petition and took it to the printer on the next block. The printer said he wouldn't be able to print it for a few weeks. A child explained that the petition was to save the sidewalk in front of the print shop. The printer said he'd have the job done in an hour.[68] The Jacobs children and other neighborhood children collected signatures.

> The people on Hudson Street who had been involved in the Washington Square battle knew a lot about techniques now, including the children—maybe even especially the children who had learned all about getting petitions around, getting signatures for petitions, and responsibly delivering them. The children, in fact, were much more successful in getting petitions signed—both the Washington Square ones and then later the sidewalk ones—because of the McCarthy era. Lots of grown ups were still afraid to sign petitions. They were afraid that they would automatically be associated with dangerous radicals or something. But when you see a nice little kid who sincerely wants to save his park or sidewalk . . . it's hard to resist such sincerity and idealism.[69]

About 1,000 people signed the petition. Many sent letters to the borough president. A delegation went to see him. Nevertheless, there was a lot of pessimism. "Oh it's all decided. You can't fight city hall."[70] The borough president was legally entitled to widen streets without consulting the people who lived there. The contractor was already chosen; money and jobs were in play. The sidewalk had to be sacrificed because the streets had to be widened because cars needed more space. It was city policy and national policy: cars before people.

But the protesting adults and kids of Hudson Street were not alone. They were part of a larger network that had formed in the battle over Washington Square.

> Connections that we had made in the Washington Square battle were very important. We now knew—way over in our more obscure neighborhood of the Village—we now knew people in other parts of the Village—and people who could accomplish things and knew their way around. One of these, a very

> wonderful citizen of Greenwich Village was Tony Dapolito, who had a bakery on
> Prince Street. It was a good bakery. . . . When he saw we were helping ourselves
> with petitions and how concerned we were, he pitched in, too. And it was owing
> to Tony's help that we quickly got to the right people in the city government to
> talk to and to send delegations to, and actually got the scheme stopped.[71]

The emphasis on the necessity of both street protest *and* political savvy was
typical of Jacobs. And typical was the merry note amidst serious struggle: it
was a good bakery.

Techniques and networks developed in the struggle to save Washington
Square Park from 1952 to 1958 made it possible to save the Hudson Street
sidewalk in 1960. Victory led to victory. And again to victory: "It was the next
year that we had to save the whole neighborhood. And it was very important
that we had this fight about the sidewalks. . . . It turned out to be a great les-
son, that we could win."[72] The fight to save the West Village, which began in
1961, would be incomparably harder than the fight to save the sidewalk. But
Jacobs and many of her neighbors had already learned how to fight city hall.

From 1956 to 1961, Jacobs learned both on the job and in the neighborhood,
through research and through movement building. Everything she learned—
from visiting East Harlem and living in the Village; from talking to planners
and experts in New York, Philadelphia, New Haven, and Boston; from fighting
to save the park and fighting to save the sidewalk—she put in the book. Even
the fight to save the West Village made it into the text, as a footnote that she
added after sending off the manuscript.[73]

The Death and Life of Great American Cities flowed out of a current of
late 1950s activism into the great river of 1960s activism. More than anything,
Jacobs and her book embodied a new attitude, at once playful and subversive.
Readers who had been taught that progress required them to sacrifice their
selfish pleasures, that the automobile was savior and planners its high priests,
that protest was Communistic, spent time with a woman who was not afraid.
Jane Jacobs helped usher in sixties' attitudes and activism by laughing, playing, thinking, writing, protesting, and inviting everyone to join.

Looking back, decades later, she thought *Death and Life* succeeded.

> A lot of people already knew the things that I was writing about from their own
> experience of life. But they had been taught to mistrust their own experience in
> favor of what the experts said. I think my book gave heart to a lot of people to
> trust what they knew. Before, if they fought city hall, they were told they were
> being selfish. The book helped people feel less guilty.[74]

Still later, she took pains to explain that if the book helped people, people helped the book. Neighborhood people were regarded by experts as "old fashioned and selfish--troublesome sand in the wheels of progress. . . . This book turned out to be helpful ammunition against such experts. But it is less accurate to call this effect 'influence' than to see it as corroboration and collaboration."[75] By corroboration, she meant: I confirmed in the book what you already knew in your gut. By collaboration, I learned from you; we wrote it together.

3

Rachel Carson: Reluctant Activist

Rachel Carson on her deck in Maine, 1961. (Linda Lear Center for Special Collections and Archives, Connecticut College.)

Nature as Refuge

In 1956, when Jacobs burst on the scene with her Harvard talk and Baker was longing to be near the action in Montgomery, Rachel Carson was already the author of three best-selling nature books. Confident in her direction as a writer, Carson was assured of an adoring audience and confirmed in her sense of providing comfort and cure.

In her first book, *Under the Sea-Wind* (1941), she was optimistic: puny humanity, a latecomer to the natural world, could not destroy nature. "The ocean is too big and vast and its forces too mighty to be much affected by human activity."[1] *Under the Sea-Wind* depicted human history as insignificant. Kingdoms rose and fell, but the life of the ocean went on.

To stand at the edge of the sea, to sense the ebb and the flow of the tides, to . . . watch the flight of shore birds that have swept up and down the surf lines of the continents for untold thousands of years, to see the running of the old eels and the young shad to the sea, is to have knowledge of things that are as nearly eternal as any earthly life can be. These things were before ever man stood on the shore of the ocean and looked upon it with wonder; they continue year in, year out, through the centuries and the ages, while man's kingdom's rise and fall.[2]

Her language was elevated, reverential, reassuring. Nature offered a spiritual retreat from advancing commerce and civilization. So did nature writing.

Humans were selfish; commerce was heedless. Catching mullet, fishermen threw other, smaller fish on the beach to die. But gulls and crabs ate the discarded fish, recycling them. "For in the sea, nothing is lost. One dies, another lives, as the precious elements of life are passed on and on in endless chains."[3] The balance of nature was too powerful for the fishing industry, for any human enterprise, to destroy. In 1938, reviewing a book that praised nature and Hitler, she recommended the book, ignoring Hitler.[4] For Carson, all kingdoms—including Hitler's—were nothing compared to natural history, especially the history of the ocean.

In contrast to the ocean, the land was vulnerable. She knew, from experience, how commerce could destroy the country. She had grown up in western Pennsylvania, in a rural area not far from Pittsburgh, and watched as the lands and rivers of her youth, which she loved, were ruined by industrial pollution.[5] Her secular creed was that the land was mortal, corrupted by mortals, but the sea was eternal. "I am much impressed by man's dependence upon the ocean, directly, and in thousands of ways unsuspected by most people," she wrote, summarizing her second book, *The Sea around Us*. "These relationships, and my belief that we will become even more dependent upon the ocean as we destroy the land, are really the theme of the book."[6]

The Sea around Us, published in 1951, was a huge bestseller and won the National Book Award. (Only then was the 1941 book republished, becoming a bestseller in its own right.) Carson was gratified that people took comfort in the book. She received mail

from all sorts of people, from college presidents to fishermen, and from scientists to housewives. . . . They suggest that they have found refreshment and
release from tension in the contemplation of millions and billions of years—in
the long vistas of geologic time in which men had no part—in the realization
that despite our utter dependence on the earth, this same earth and sea have no
need of us.

History was the story of "man with his vanities and greed," but the story of
the sea offered a healthier perspective, one which could lead us away from the
tendency "to plan for our own destruction."[7]

Her language was more urgent in 1951. World War II, especially the development and use of nuclear weapons, crystalized her sense of the destructive
power of humans. A decade later, looking back at how she became an activist,
she would point to World War II as the turning point.

In the days before Hiroshima I used to wonder whether nature—nature in the
broadest context of the word—actually needed protection from man. Surely
the sea was inviolate and forever beyond man's power to change it. Surely the
vast cycles by which water is drawn up into the clouds to return again to the
earth could never be touched. And just as surely the vast tides of life—the
migrating birds—would continue to ebb and flow over the continents, marking
the passage of the seasons.

But I was wrong.[8]

In *The Sea around Us*, she approached WWII indirectly. The Laysan rail,
a flightless bird—"a charming gnomelike creature" with "a voice like tinkling
bells"—was endangered by commerce. Ships brought rabbits ashore, and the
rabbits destroyed the balance of nature on Laysan. The last rail on the island
died around 1924. But fortunately, in the 1880s, a ship brought some Laysan
rails to Midway, where they survived. Until WWII: "During the war in the
Pacific, rats went ashore to island after island from ships and landing craft.
They invaded Midway in 1943. The adult rails were slaughtered. The eggs were
eaten, and the young birds killed. The world's last Laysan rail was seen in 1944."[9]

Rats and humans: a lethal combination. In *Under the Sea-Wind*, she told
a different rat story. She was observing the rising tide on a North Carolina
beach at dusk. "A rat, crafty with the cunning of years and filled with a lust for
blood, had come down to the water." Digging up terrapin eggs from the sand
and "snuffling and squeaking in excitement," he sucked out the yolks. Then
he spotted a baby terrapin. "Engrossed in gnawing away the thin shell of the

terrapin, he did not notice how the tide was creeping up about him and running deeper around the hummock. It was thus that the blue heron, wading back around the shore of the island, came upon the rat and speared him."[10]

Carson didn't intervene. She watched the heron intervene.

That was in 1941, before the war. Shocked by the destructiveness of the war, she became less sanguine that nature could take care of itself. At a benefit for the National Symphony Orchestra in 1951, she suggested that "symphony orchestras that present and interpret the music of the ages are not luxuries in this mechanized, this atomic age. They are, more than ever, necessities."[11] Nature writing, like classical music, restored man to his better self. In this way, by restoring balance to humans, nature writing could help restore the balance of nature.

Her role in this secular religion was to describe the beauty of nature. But what if humans were unable to see? "In the western world our thinking has for many centuries been dominated by the Jewish-Christian concept of man's relation to nature, in which man is regarded as the master of all the earth's inhabitants," she later explained. "I have pointed out some exquisite creature of the jade pools to a chance companion. 'What is it for?' he may ask, and he is obviously disappointed if I can't assure him that it can be eaten or at least made into some bauble to be sold in a shop."[12] The human tendency to treat nature as raw material for exploitation posed an ever-greater threat.

In her day job, as a senior editor and biologist at the US Fish and Wildlife Service, she watched with increasing distress as corporate interests gnawed away at federal regulations.[13] To her, the election of Eisenhower in 1952 seemed to tip the balance of forces decisively in favor of commercial development and destruction. The success of *The Sea around Us* made it financially possible for her to write full time, and she resigned from her job. Leaving the government, she was now free to criticize it.

In an angry letter to the *Washington Post* in 1953, she denounced the new administration, detailing its crimes against nature, pointing to "the proposed giveaway of our offshore oil reserves and the threatened invasion of national parks, forests and other public lands" and the firing of the head of the Fish and Wildlife Service. "For many years public-spirited citizens throughout the country have been working for the conservation of our natural resources. . . . Apparently their hard-won progress is to be wiped out, as a politically minded Administration returns us to the dark ages of unrestrained exploitation and destruction."[14] For the first time, Carson publicly sided with conservationists against the government and the commercial interests that dominated it.

Addressing nearly 1,000 women journalists in 1954, she deplored "the destruction of beauty and the suppression of human individuality in hundreds of suburban real estate developments where the first act is to cut down all the trees." The same greedy behavior could be seen "in proposals to invade the national parks with commercial schemes such as the building of power dams. . . . Is it the right of this, our generation, in its selfish materialism, to destroy these things because we are blinded by the dollar sign?"[15] Sounding like Jane Jacobs, Carson told the women journalists about a plan for a highway through a park in Washington DC. "Now they propose to run a six-lane arterial highway through the heart of that narrow woodland valley—destroying forever its true and immeasurable value to the city and the nation." Unlike Jacobs, however, Carson was not trying to protect city life, but on the contrary, to protect nature from the city. The park was "a place where one can go, away from the noise of traffic and of man-made confusions, for a little interval of refreshing and restoring quiet—where . . . a veery sings in the green twilight."[16]

Carson delivered this pivotal critique of the destructiveness of unrestrained capitalism to an audience of women. "Women have a greater intuitive understanding of such things," she explained in the talk. Also, professional women, like the journalists, understood how hard it was to be a professional woman. She told them how, in 1949, she wanted to join a voyage of discovery on the *Albatross*, a boat owned by the Fish and Wildlife Service. Like Jacobs, who wanted to catch a ride on a fishing boat in 1946, Carson ran into resistance.

> It was decided finally—and I might have had something to do with originating the idea—that perhaps I could do a better job of handling publications about the *Albatross* if I had been out on her. But there was one great obstacle. No woman had ever been on the *Albatross*. . . . Among my male colleagues who had to sign the papers, the thought of one woman on a ship with some fifty men was unthinkable. After much soul searching, it was decided that maybe *two* women would be all right, so I arranged with a friend, who was also a writer, to go with me.[17]

What could an ambitious woman do, in 1954, but joke about the obstacles put in the way of practicing her profession?

In fact, Carson's whole career as a scientist had been shaped and limited by stereotypes of women. When the Fish and Wildlife Service hired her in 1936, she was just the second woman to work there in a non-clerical job. In the beginning, she signed her articles "R. L. Carson," because "we have felt that they would be more effective . . . if they were presumably written by a man."[18] Although she rose quickly from assistant to associate to full aquatic biologist, she was excluded from most lab and field work, because she was a woman. When she became famous as the author of *The Sea around Us*, she ran into the same stereotype. "People often seem to be surprised that a woman has written a book about the sea. This is especially true, I find, of men. Perhaps they have been accustomed to thinking of the more exciting fields of scientific knowledge as exclusively masculine domains."[19]

Male scientists kept the exciting work for themselves, leaving the care of daily life to women. "But the notion that 'science' is something that belongs in a separate compartment of its own, apart from everyday life, is one that I would like to challenge," she said in 1952. "We live in a scientific age; yet we assume that knowledge of science is the prerogative of only a small number of human beings, isolated and priestlike in their laboratories."[20] There were few women in the priesthood.

Carson herself could not escape the obligations of domestic life. During the 1950s, she took increasingly burdensome care of her ailing mother and her ailing niece and her niece's son. "I am not being a writer at present," she complained.[21] Women—including ambitious working women like Jane Jacobs and Betty Friedan, who had three children each—were in charge of the children. Women who did not have children often felt forced to take on maternal duties. Ella Baker felt obliged to adopt her niece. When Carson's niece died in 1957, Carson adopted her son, who was five. Her extensive domestic duties interfered with writing. "It seems so silly to be spending my time being a nurse and housemaid." In effect, she needed a wife. "What is needed is a near-twin of me who can do everything I do except write, and let me do that!"[22] It is hard to imagine any male best-selling author finding himself burdened in this way.

But being a woman was also connected to her strength. Her contemporary, Barbara McClintock, who won a Nobel Prize for her work on the genetics of maize, argued that in order to understand an organism, you must have a feel for it; you must be able to "hear what the material has to say to you."[23] Rachel Carson had a feeling for the veery and terrapin. She employed the empirical methods of science; she was careful to get her facts right and acknowledge when the facts were not yet known. But she did not pretend to be neutral. During the 1950s, Carson increasingly took sides against those who, in their arrogance and greed, did not care for nature and would not take care of it.

In contrast to the masculine ideal of the priestly scientist dissecting nature in his lab, Carson was drawn to the ecological approach of understanding the complex interrelations between different life forms. That's why lab work was useful, but never enough. She needed to be out in nature, observing life where it occurred. In her third book, and third bestseller—*The Edge of the Sea*—she described wading off the Florida Keys and meeting a basket star, a relative of a starfish. "I stood beside it, lost to all but its extraordinary and somewhat fragile beauty. I had no wish to 'collect' it; to disturb such a being would have seemed a desecration." Walking on a Georgia beach at night, she saw a small ghost crab. "I was filled with the odd sensation that for the first time I knew the creature in its own world—that I understood, as never before, the essence of its being."[24]

The Edge of the Sea, in 1955, offered an alternative to the dominant idea of progress. Progress in the 1950s was usually seen in terms of cities and cars, suburbs and highways, industry and technology. Carson's idea of progress was rooted in the way that life—especially life in the sea—extends, expands, triumphs.

> As long as the currents move on their courses there is the possibility, the probability, even the certainty, that some particular form of life will extend its range. . . . It is one of life's mysteries that most of the participants in this cosmic migration are doomed to failure; it is no less mysterious that their failure turns into success when, for all the billions lost, a few succeed.

She watched a sea cave at low tide. A fish swam in and became "almost a symbol of modernity," compared to the ancient sponges that lined the cave. "And I, in whose eyes the images of the two were beheld . . . , was a mere newcomer whose ancestors had inhabited the earth so briefly that my presence was almost anachronistic."[25]

But though humans were mere newcomers, they were fully capable of destroying the caves and shore. Carson began to feel she could no longer stand by. "Within the long cycles of the earth what we do probably makes little difference; yet within the restricted cycle that is completed within one person's life the shore can never be itself once man has 'developed' it," she wrote late in 1957.[26] The shore was being developed so quickly that she tried, unsuccessfully, to buy a piece of the Maine coast, to preserve it. She also considered the possibility of writing a book about the need to save unprotected shore, "an appealing idea, as giving me a chance to *do* something and a place to say what I want to say, for certainly I can give only a small part of the *Holiday* piece to being a Cassandra."[27]

In that *Holiday* piece, about the shore, she briefly mentioned her central concern.

> The shore might seem beyond the power of man to change, to corrupt. But this is not so. Unhappily, some of the places of which I have written no longer remain wild and unspoiled. Instead, they have been tainted by the sordid

transformation of "development"—cluttered with amusement concessions, refreshment stands, fishing shacks—all the untidy litter of what passes under the name of civilization.[28]

Jacobs might enjoy those fishing shacks and the other untidy enterprises; unlike Carson, she took pleasure in the human, disorderly, and commercial. For Carson, the commercial development of the shore was a symptom of a civilization that had lost all reverence and restraint—of a progress gone mad.

By 1957, she had outgrown nature writing. She no longer wanted to comfort. She was looking for a way to agitate. Her fundamental vision—nature vs. civilization—never changed, but since WWII it had grown increasingly dark, and the need to speak out, to intervene, had grown more compelling. In the end, turning from flight to fight, she wrote a book where she could be Cassandra. This final book would not be about the shore or the ocean. *Silent Spring* would turn back to the embattled land.

Among Activists

Late in 1957, Carson learned that fourteen residents of Long Island, New York, were suing the federal and state government. They were trying to halt the aerial spraying of gypsy moths and mosquitoes with a chemical pesticide, a chlorinated hydrocarbon known as DDT. No chemical was ever sprayed so heavily or so widely. The United States Department of Agriculture—which was oriented toward industry—was pushing DDT as a miracle chemical. Compared to previously available chemical pesticides, DDT was cheaper, killed more bugs, lent itself more easily to aerial spraying, and, in early tests, appeared less toxic to mammals.[29]

But to Marjorie Spock, who practiced organic gardening for years and was at the center of the Long Island case, DDT was the toxin that destroyed the garden that she and Polly Richards created. Spock was a progressive educator and younger sister of Benjamin Spock, the pediatrician. Carson got in touch with Spock, wanting to know more. Spock sent Carson documents from the case and included a personal note: "I think you know how grim this struggle with the U.S. government and the whole chemical industry is going to be."[30] Carson didn't know but was going to find out. As an activist, she was a neophyte. Spock and Richards were to Rachel Carson what Shirley Hayes and Edith Lyons were to Jane Jacobs: women more experienced in struggle, who would take her under their wing and mentor her. She would need all the help she could get.

The correspondence with Spock was the turning point for Carson. She had always fought the battle indirectly, pointing to the sea as proof of the healing power of nature. Now she pivoted and faced the enemy. Joining the battle over DDT, putting herself on the line, she led the charge against unrestricted commerce.

Carson's concerns about the destructiveness of DDT went back to WWII, when it was used by the US military to prevent disease.[31] Very quickly now, her concern moved from the periphery to the center. Spock and Richards later described what happened.

> Rachel went into high gear at once. Every few days came a new letter discussing an article or clipping, inquiring into the background of some fact we had called to her attention, or asking to be put in touch with this or that witness from our lawsuit. She began to correspond with every independent scientist who knew some facet of pesticides. When she got dizzy writing, she telephoned.[32]

In 1957, government and industry were waging three simultaneous chemical wars: spraying gypsy moths with DDT, including on Long Island; spraying elm trees with DDT, especially in the Midwest; and spraying fire ants with dieldrin (a newer chlorinated hydrocarbon, with properties similar to DDT), in the South. These assaults had triggered protests by some citizens, including birdwatchers and a few wildlife biologists. Carson identified with the protests against pesticides in a way that she never identified with a protest.[33] She began thinking in terms of a book about chemical pesticides. In mid-1958, she contracted with Houghton Mifflin to write a book whose working title was "Man against the Earth."

Spock and Richards, who had put together a formidable team of scientific experts to serve as witnesses, gave Carson access to these experts, who became crucial to her emerging network of scientists opposed to pesticides. Spock suggested seeking further evidence on the effects of pesticides from hunters and fishermen, and Carson reached out to old contacts, "left over from my days in Fish and Wildlife; I am trying to sow more seeds of discontent."[34] In 1959, she asked Spock for another kind of help. As citizens heard of the Long Island case, they often wrote Spock, describing their own experiences with aerial spraying. Carson asked Spock to pick out the best letters and send them to her, to give her book "not only interest but authenticity." She also asked Spock to let her know of other cases against government spraying that were in the courts. "I am sure you know of many more cases than I do but the information I have suggests that there is a groundswell of protest."[35]

Being part of a groundswell of protest, sowing the seeds of discontent, was new for Carson. She was transformed by the struggle, and she transformed it. Inspired by the protests, she wanted to focus them, deepen them, broaden them. In a letter to Spock at the end of 1958, she referred to "our present crusade."[36] In 1959, during the first appeal of Spock's case, she asked: "If the decision is against us, will you still attempt to carry it further?"[37] Our crusade, against us: Spock, Richards, and Carson were now in the same struggle. Soon Carson learned that the Long Island case was lost, and it lost again on appeal. (Spock later explained: "The government ran rough shod over anyone who got in the way of the new technology. They brushed us off like so many flies."[38]) Spock and Richard's legal strategy was not enough. Carson saw her own contribution as extralegal, indeed as political. Her new book was designed to intensify the citizen protest against chemical pesticides and force the government to limit their use.

It was clear that this book, unlike her first three books, would be fiercely attacked. Her closest friend tried to stop her from writing it. Dorothy Freeman had sent Carson a fan letter in 1951, after reading *The Sea around Us*. They began to correspond and then meet, becoming emotionally dependent on one another. Carson dedicated *The Edge of the Sea* to Freeman and her husband. But what Dorothy Freeman loved about *The Sea around Us* and *The Edge of the Sea* was that they were beautiful books, books that provided an escape from the ugliness of modern life. The new project would directly confront that ugliness and, Freeman feared, inevitably become caught up in it.

Distressed by her friend's reaction, Carson responded by explaining her new direction.

I suppose my thinking began to be affected after atomic science was firmly established. Some of the thoughts that came were so unattractive to me that I rejected them completely, for the old ideas die hard, especially when they are emotionally as well as intellectually dear to one. It was pleasant to believe, for example, that much of Nature was forever beyond the tampering reach of man. . . . But that does no good, and I have now opened my eyes and my mind.[39]

Freeman was not persuaded. Later in 1958, Carson took up the thread. "I know you are not happy about my project." She pleaded with Freeman to accept her activist turn, on the grounds that she could do no other. "Knowing what I do, there would be no future peace for me if I kept silent." Freeman was unpersuaded. Carson wrote yet again, promising to limit the length of the project and the time devoted to it, "so I can soon be free to move on into happier projects."[40] It was not a promise she could keep.

Clarence Cottam, a wildlife biologist and friend, also warned Carson that her new book would be received very differently from her three bestsellers. Cottam publicly raised questions about the long-term effects of DDT as early as 1946, when he and Carson worked in the Fish and Wildlife Service. By 1957, when Carson learned of the massive spraying of dieldrin in the South, Cottam was already a vocal critic of spraying fire ants.[41] By 1958, Carson and Cottam were allies and co-conspirators, who liked, respected, and needed each other. She sent questions, and he sent answers, and she sent drafts based on his information, to make sure she had it right. Thinking of the powerful interests that opposed their work, he wrote: "I am sure you will render a great public service, although I shall predict that your book will not be the best seller that *The Sea around Us* has been."[42]

Carson told Cottam of her plan to minimize her public exposure while preparing the book. "As you know, the whole thing is so explosive, and the pressures on the other side so powerful and enormous, that I feel it far wiser to keep my own council [sic] insofar as I can until I am ready to launch my attack as a whole."[43] Her description of the book—"my attack"—was similar to the first sentence of Jacobs's book: "This book is an attack on current city planning and rebuilding." Like Jacobs, Carson saw her book as aggressively taking an existing struggle to a new level.

Whereas Cottam took public stands on specific issues, Carson collected, analyzed, and synthesized all the latest information. Cottam knew much more than Carson about the damage caused by pesticides. She learned quickly, however, and soon was sending him information as well. When she received a letter from the Northwest about the consequences of chemically spraying hops, she sent word to Cottam about it.[44] This was how news traveled along the network. It *was* news, because Carson didn't merely assemble what scientists already knew about pesticides. With industry and government rushing ahead, spraying different pests in different parts of the country, the side effects were beginning to be observed and analyzed by activists of all kinds. It was a rapidly evolving field, and Carson, with her relentless focus, made herself an expert.

She learned quickly because she was good at asking questions. In her work at the Fish and Wildlife Service, she questioned local fisherman, hunters, wildlife-refuge personnel, and scientists. Now she questioned the scientists she knew from her government service (like Cottam); the scientists she found through Spock; librarians, congressional aides, and clerks in the Government Printing Office; and birdwatchers, fishermen, and hunters. She asked birders and other amateurs what they were seeing in their own locales. She asked government employees for explanations, more contacts, and restricted files. Some were willing to help because they themselves were already engaged in the struggle. Others were willing to help because they had read and admired her books about the sea. In this way, through asking and listening, she transformed herself into a leader of the burgeoning protest.[45]

All four women in this book were skilled questioners and listeners. Baker listened to social critics, student activists, and local people; she was more likely to lead by questions than by a speech. Jacobs listened to social workers, to local people, to her husband the architect, learning to see what they saw. Even Betty Friedan, who was perhaps not as good a listener, would make her most important discoveries by questioning housewives about their lives. Carson listened to local people, scientists, and nature. "Instead of always trying to impose our will on Nature we should sometimes be quiet and listen to what she has to tell us."[46]

The local people to whom she listened were often women: engaged, active citizens organized in garden clubs, humane societies, and especially Audubon societies.[47] Carson, an avid birder herself, was a longtime board member of her local (Washington area) Audubon Society, who had gone on trips with committed birders and joined them in fighting to protect the habitats of birds. Early in 1958, Olga Huckins—an energetic Audubon Society member in Massachusetts, and a friend—published a letter in the *Boston Herald* against DDT spraying and sent Carson a copy: "We picked up three dead bodies the next morning right by the door. They were birds that had lived close to us, trusted us, and built their nests in our trees year after year."[48] Birders like Huckins took the effects of spraying personally. Long part of Carson's social life, birdwatchers now became part of her political life.[49]

Nationally, the Audubon Society was cautious. An established and respectable group, a government lobby led by men, it hesitated to lead the struggle. The national president did urge President Eisenhower to halt gypsy moth spraying. And National Audubon advised a change in federal rules: instead of the public having to prove that a chemical was unsafe, the chemical companies and government should have to prove that it was safe.[50] But the burden of activism fell on local and state Audubon Societies and on the dedicated women and men in them. Many of the early observations of the destructiveness of pesticides—and most of the scattered protests against them—were by birders. In 1947, residents of Princeton, NJ, protested the experimental use of DDT on elms, because it was killing birds. In 1957, the Illinois Audubon Society protested against spraying on behalf of birds; there were similar protests in Wisconsin.[51] Protests by birders, however—like protests by mothers against urban renewal—were dismissed as sentimental and unscientific, indeed as feminine. One prominent wildlife biologist admitted, years later—after it became clear that the women were right—that he initially ignored their protests because they were only housewives.[52]

Carson questioned an official in the Food and Drug Administration about bird kills, but he did not take her seriously. Needing help, she turned to one of Spock's scientific experts, George Wallace, an ornithologist at Michigan State. Wallace was studying the effect of the massive spraying of elms with DDT on his campus. Intended to kill Dutch elm disease, the spraying was not saving elms, but it was killing robins and other birds. Carson explained to Wallace: "The sprayers and their allies adopt such a loftily scornful attitude about birds (a man very high in Food and Drug said to me: 'What if a few meadowlarks have stepped in this poison dieldrin and died?') that I want to build up this part of the material with every bit of factual evidence available."[53]

Wallace told Carson about his theories and put her in touch with midwestern birders, who were accumulating the data. Through Wallace, she found Dixie Larkin, a birder, an antispraying activist in Wisconsin, and a founding member of the local environmental group. In the summer of 1957, before Carson became involved, Larkin warned the Wisconsin Society for Ornithology about DDT and—as chair of a group of Wisconsin citizens opposed to spraying—wrote to a state official: "The D.D.T. spraying for controlling the Dutch Elm Disease has caused an increasingly heavy toll of birds," killing not only "the migrant species, that are with us in the spring and fall, but also the familiar summer residents."[54] When Wisconsin finally agreed to hold hearings, in 1960, Larkin and her friends were there. "Mrs. Larkin, and several others . . . insisted on stringent control of aerial spraying," reported a local paper." Supporters of spraying were there too, and there was a lively debate. "We're accused of trying to save every bird," argued Larkin. "But the elm sprayers are trying to save every tree and . . . [the] cost of spraying will increase from here to eternity."[55]

Carson asked Larkin for help. "Like you, I have "bushels" of material on literally every aspect of this problem, so it may seem strange that I want still more. However, in dealing with the subject of the tragic destruction of bird life I find that many people . . . respond more to actual experiences and observations of people like yourself, than to laboratory experiments or the findings of professional biologists."[56] Larkin, Huckins, Spock, and other local activists inspired Carson's emerging activism and fed her material she used in the book. In *Silent Spring*, she would acknowledge "vast indebtedness to a host of people . . . who first spoke out against the reckless and irresponsible poisoning of the world . . . and who are even now fighting the thousands of small battles that in the end will bring victory."[57]

Carson loved birds the way she loved the sea. When she was not at the shore, birds connected her to nature. During spring migration, she got up early, hoping to see the warblers passing through. "One could sense that birds 'speak' to you more than plants," her agent wrote, after reading a draft of the chapter on birds. "Silent Spring," originally the title for the bird chapter, grew to encompass the book as a whole. As Carson reminded Freeman, "I told you once that if I kept silent I could never again listen to a veery's song without overwhelming self-reproach."[58]

In Carson's correspondence, some news of birds was for pleasure (warblers, veeries) and some for battle. "I am sure you have seen the recent newspaper reports on the decline of the eagle, attributing the obvious sterility to spraying," she wrote to Spock.[59] She learned from the Florida Audubon Society that "the Bald Eagle is dying out in Florida but a movement has been started to protect it."[60] Carson didn't start that movement—Charles Broley, an amateur, was carefully tracking the decline of eagles in Florida and connecting the decline to DDT—just as she didn't singlehandedly start the larger environmental movement. She was inspired and helped by Broley and Larkin, Spock and Huckins, Cottam and Wallace, and many other activists.[61] Like Baker and Jacobs, Rachel Carson was becoming an activist among activists, one who took the energy of limited protests and helped transform them into a powerful national movement.

Her own emerging activism was mainly through her local Audubon Society. In March of 1959, her local group sent a protest to Agriculture Secretary Ezra Taft Benson, denouncing a Department of Agriculture propaganda film about the benefits of spraying fire ants. "The threat of the fire ant is insignificant compared with the serious and long-lasting damage inflicted by your efforts to control it." Carson wrote most of the protest, yet was able to keep her name off of it.[62] By avoiding publicity, she was protecting the book, until it was ready. She was also postponing, as long as possible, the inevitable ugliness.

The pace of her protest was quickening, however. The next month, April 1959, she wrote to the *Washington Post*, responding to a piece that reported fewer spring birds and attributed the decline to a harsh winter. Carson said the decline was not temporary, and it was not caused by weather. The cumulative effects of fifteen years of spraying, starting on a small scale and recently accelerating, was the cause of decline. She concluded:

To many of us this sudden silencing of the song of birds, this obliteration of the color and beauty and interest of bird life, is sufficient cause for sharp regret. To those who have never known such rewarding enjoyment of nature, there should yet remain a nagging and insistent question: If this "rain of death" has produced so disastrous an effect on birds, what of other lives, including our own.[63]

The idea that what was happening to birds could happen to you, that spraying was bad for people too, would become a key argument in her book.

In June 1959, she came more into the open. Plans for spraying Japanese beetles reached her own area in Silver Spring, Maryland. "Fortunately," she told Spock, "there are probably enough people in the area who have misgivings about it, so that we can put a stop to this program, but we may have a fight on our hands." She distinguished between Spock's legal situation and her own in Silver Spring. "We are lucky that this is merely a local organization and not the state or federal government because apparently we can, if necessary, stand on our rights of preventing trespass on private property."[64] At the meeting, she spoke for fifteen minutes. "I really hit hard on the few points I gave and was delighted by the reception of my facts," she reported to Spock. "I felt like this was a fair little test of the reception that may be given the book."[65] Clarence Cottam had warned that the book would not be a bestseller. But the response to her talk suggested that there might be great receptivity among citizens to the book's arguments.

A week later, Carson lent her name and expertise to a battle over the spraying of mosquitoes in Lincoln, Massachusetts. Paul Brooks, her friend and editor, asked for help. "Enclosed is your weapon," she wrote back, enclosing a letter, signed by her, that he read at a Lincoln town meeting.

Insect populations very quickly develop resistance to chemical sprays. . . . We have killed off or endangered fish, birds, and other wildlife, contaminated vegetables and fruit, damaged shrubbery and flowers, and introduced poisonous chemicals into soil and water supplies. After all this, we find that the mosquito has the last laugh, for while we have been progressively poisoning our own environment, the mosquito has been breeding a superior race composed of individuals that are immune to chemical attack.[66]

The citizens of Lincoln voted four to one against spraying. The argument Carson made in the letter—that insects tend to develop resistance to chemical pesticides—was the argument that would, when the book appeared, be especially awkward for the chemical companies.

In the fall of 1959, she spoke for 30 minutes to officials from regional Audubon, ornithological, and natural history societies. In the Q and A, a forester challenged her on the practicality of suddenly stopping spraying. She agreed with him. "I think it would be fine if you could. I doubt that it is possible from the practical standpoint, but I do think that one great trouble . . . is this desire for the quick and the easy way of doing something, without any consideration of the consequences." [67] Her exchange with a Michigan Audubon official was more contentious. "All unknown to anyone there, he proved to be an employee of the Dow Chemical Co." With the man from industry, there was no common ground. "However, I think that I was able to take care of him." [68]

From 1959 to 1961, local activists—in Long Island, Silver Spring, Milwaukee, Lincoln, Illinois, Florida, and elsewhere—were feeding, and being fed by, her efforts. Whereas her scientific allies were men, these local activists were mostly women. Robert Musil, in his book about Carson and her sister activists, points out that the deepest influences on her were women. Women, beginning with her mother, taught her to love nature and birds; women professors nurtured her imagination and writing; women constituted her activist networks; women were her most intimate friends, helpers, and supporters. Now famous women rallied to her. In 1962, before the first installment of *Silent Spring* appeared in the *New Yorker*, Agnes Meyer, owner of the *Washington Post*, threw a lunch party for Carson, invited a number of prominent women, and gave each woman a copy of the proofs of the book. One of the women, head of the National Council of Women, invited Carson to address the council. [69]

By now, even Dorothy Freeman was coming around to accepting the book. "I'm glad that before publication you have come to understand not only why it is important to me, but to the world," Carson wrote Freeman at the beginning of 1962. "People are ready for the book, and need it now. I, too, think that a couple of years ago would have been too soon. But now I know that there are many, many people who are eager to do something and long to be given the facts to fight with." [70] *Silent Spring* was intended as a weapon for people to use in the fight against the chemical companies.

Genteel Subversive

Decades later, Mark Hamilton Lytle was teaching about ecological thinking at Bard College. His students helped him see just how radical Carson was. They emphasized that she not only took on the powerful chemical industry—this Lytle already appreciated—but that she also insisted on the right of citizens to know what was being done to their planet and to themselves. "I finally realized that Rachel Carson, so genteel and proper in her personal life, was a subversive." Lytle went on to write *The Gentle Subversive*.[71] Subversive fits her perfectly. But gentle doesn't. She was too angry to be really gentle. Rachel Carson was more genteel, in manner and dress, than Jacobs or Friedan, or even Baker, but she was at least as angry as any of them.

In Silver Springs, in 1959, a local man visited her, hoping to dissuade her from speaking at the community association. Patronizingly, he told her she was an alarmist. She countered with case histories. He dismissed them, and her. "She was furious," says her research assistant, who was there. "No one, seeing her response that afternoon, could have called her gentle."[72]

Carson channeled her anger into writing *Silent Spring*. "One of my delights in the book will be to take apart Dr. Wayland Hayes' much cited feeding experiment." As chief toxicologist of the United States Public Health Service, Hayes was the leading medical defender of DDT and the key government witness in the Long Island case. Hayes fed DDT to prisoners in Atlanta, as an experiment, and concluded that they were fine, and DDT was safe. Carson wanted to expose his methodology, which involved no follow-up with the prisoners and so had nothing to say on the crucial question of DDT's long-term effect.[73] Carson was angry at Hayes for dismissing the complaints of the prisoners. In the book, she cited British case histories of DDT's harmful effects on humans and pointed to the very different paper of which Hayes was lead author: "Despite this evidence, several American investigators conducting an experiment with DDT on volunteer subjects dismissed the complaint of headache and 'pain in every bone' as 'obviously of psychoneurotic origin.'"[74]

But Carson didn't let anger get in the way of her effectiveness. She rode the anger, instead of acting it out. When Spock sent her a new article lauding the benefits of pesticides, she responded gleefully: "I doubt that I shall be able to resist the temptation to tear it to pieces in my book." She added: "I have been having similar fun with that dreadful A.M.A. editorial on cranberries."[75] The cranberry crop was contaminated by spraying of chemical herbicide. Carson attended a public hearing on cranberries, late in 1959. Arthur Flemming, secretary of health, education, and welfare, had recommended suspending the sale of cranberries. The industry and its supporters, including the American Medical Association, were fighting back. "Flemming certainly went way up in my estimation; he handled the whole thing with such quiet dignity and courtesy, but they didn't ever put anything over on him!" she reported to Spock. "At the conclusion of a speaker's statement, he would gently pick up the very thing I'd been hoping he would demolish."[76]

Carson felt the temptation to demolish bad science, to tear it to pieces; it would be fun. But as an author, she controlled the temptation. Like Fleming, she had to be disciplined and dignified because she was engaged in an intensely partisan battle. Like Jacobs, she had decided to win. Unlike Jacobs, Carson sacrificed the fun. Her anger, if it showed, would be used against her and the book. "I have to admit that I have taken on this venture in a crusading spirit," she wrote to a scientific ally, "but I am trying to set the whole thing in perspective and make no statements that are not thoroughly supported."[77]

Out of a disciplined commitment to winning the war, she avoided unnecessary battles with the chemical industry and the government scientists who served as its apologists. Any mistakes she made would be used against her. Spock forwarded scientific claims about pesticides causing a decline in whitefish, but Carson responded that whitefish were already in decline when she was at the Fish and Wildlife Service, "long before the use of DDT." Because she and Spock were engaged in a struggle with powerful opponents, it was important to get their facts right. "There are so many clear cut examples of the harmful effects of insecticides that we should all guard against the temptation to raise this problem in cases where the connection is on such shaky grounds."[78] She made the same point, more sharply, in a letter to Paul Brooks. "Too many people—with the best possible motives—have rushed out statements without adequate support, furnishing the best possible targets for the opposition."[79]

Her own determination to be disciplined was reinforced by two of her closest allies. Clarence Cottam, when he read a draft of the entire manuscript, responded he was going to hold her to a higher standard.

> Your writing is superb. I am certain you are rendering a tremendous public service. Yet, I want to warn you that I am convinced you are going to be subjected to ridicule and condemnation. . . . Facts will not stand in the way of some confirmed pest control workers and those who are receiving substantial subsidies from pesticides manufacturers. Some of the operational people of the Department of Agriculture likely will be the loudest in their condemnation of your book and charge you with inaccuracy and lack of information. Because of this opinion, I am going to be more critical of your manuscript than I otherwise would be.[80]

Marie Rodell, her agent and friend, cautioned her that the book needed to seem detached, objective, and balanced. Rodell pointed to a phrase in Carson's draft concerning "the 'enormously profitable' chemical industry and its reluctance to give up its profits." Rodell wanted Carson to avoid sounding as if she was out to get the chemical companies. "The references to and comments about the chemical companies need to be phrased very carefully not to set up a counter-reaction in the readers. We must at all costs avoid giving anyone the opportunity to yell 'crank.'" [81] Rodell recognized that to win the battle for public opinion, it would not be enough to be right. To win, *Silent Spring* would need to anticipate the counterattack, by seeming calm, objective, factual, scientific—anything but furious.

Carson joined the struggle out of anger at what humans were doing to nature. "The beauty of the living world I was trying to save has always been uppermost in my mind—that, and anger at the senseless brutish things that were being done." [82] Increasingly, however, she extended her caring, and her anger, to humans. In the beginning, it was a tactical choice: readers who didn't care about birds would care about themselves and their children. But as she immersed herself in the emerging literature on the long-term effects of DDT, she became even angrier at the possibility that it caused cancer in humans.

Through Spock, she contacted Dr. Malcolm Hargraves, whose work at the Mayo Clinic focused on the link between chemicals and leukemia. At the end of 1959, she explained to her editor how her thinking about cancer had evolved.

> Until recently, I saw this as part of a general chapter on the physical effects on man. Now it looms so terrifically important that I want to devote a whole chapter to it—and that perhaps will be the most important chapter of the book. To tell the truth, in the beginning I felt the link between pesticides and cancer was tenuous and at best circumstantial. . . . But now I feel that a lot of isolated pieces of the jig-saw puzzle have suddenly fallen into place. [83]

Soon she had personal reason to be angry. In April 1960, she had surgery for a tumor on her breast, but the surgeon was reassuring. In December, she learned that he lied. "I now know that I was not told the truth at the time of my operation," she wrote to Brooks. "The tumor was malignant, and there was even at the time evidence that it had metastasized, for some of the lymph nodes also were found to be involved. But I was told none of this, even though I asked directly." [84] Cancer did not stop her. If anything, it galvanized her. As she fought for the right of citizens to know the facts, she was angry that she had not been told the facts. As she critiqued the patronizing assurances of industry spokesmen and government scientists, she was angry at her doctor for having patronized her. As she wrote of the growing evidence of a connection between cancer and the spread of pesticides in the environment, the cancer was spreading in her own body.

The two struggles—with the chemical companies and with her cancer—were not in fact entirely separable in her mind. In April, when she had the surgery, she wrote Spock: "I am giving details to special friends like you—not to others. . . . I have no wish to read of my ailments in literary gossip columns. Too much comfort for the chemical companies."[85] When her new doctor, in December, was honest with her, she was grateful. "I appreciate . . . your having enough respect for my mentality and emotional stability to discuss all this frankly with me. I have a great deal more peace of mind when I feel I know the facts, even though I might wish they were different."[86] The new doctor did not treat her like a hysterical woman. He told her the truth about her cancer, as she was going to tell citizens the truth about pesticides and cancer, even though they might wish the facts were different. It was, in both cases, a question of respect.

Many citizens, including activists, thought of pesticides and herbicides as poisons. So did Carson, at the beginning; *Silent Spring* began—in Dorothy Freeman's disapproving phrase—as the "poison book."[87] As Carson got deeper into her research, she began to think differently. "I suspect that the great hazard is not so much toxicity as genetic and carcinogenic effects," she wrote Spock in 1960.[88] Her suspicions were prescient. She died too soon to know that research would prove she was right. It's easy to see that large doses of DDT are directly, and immediately, toxic to the central nervous system. But indirectly, and in the long run, even small doses of DDT affect hormonal balances, which can cause reproductive failure.[89] This takes time to see, because the connection is invisible. The bald eagle was declining not because it had been sprayed but because small residues of DDT that were concentrated in the food chain caused the eagle's eggshells to become too thin to be viable. The carcinogenic effects of chemical pesticides also take time to reveal themselves.

In her earlier books on sea and shore, Carson located herself in the conservationist tradition. Conservationists wanted national parks and bird sanctuaries set aside, to protect nature from the encroachment of commercial development. In the vision of Teddy Roosevelt, or even a younger Carson, capitalism and nature could flourish, side by side. The massive spraying of DDT revealed to her the inadequacy of this approach. On the one hand, DDT spread throughout the ecosystem, making illusory the protection of areas of unspoiled nature. On the other hand, massive spraying of DDT made obsolete the distinction between protecting nature and protecting people. At this juncture, the old conservation movement morphed into the new environmental movement. Carson was right there, at the moment of transformation, fighting to protect not unspoiled islands but the environment as a whole.[90]

In *Silent Spring*, Carson married the conservationist tradition, which focused on nature, to the public health tradition, which focused on people. In the cancer chapter, she told of a housewife who sprayed her basement heavily with DDT to get rid of spiders. After spraying, she felt sick, "with nausea and extreme anxiety." When she felt better, she sprayed again. Now she had fever, joint pain, swelling in one leg, "general malaise." Carson was angry that no one took the woman's complaints seriously. "When examined by Dr. Hargraves, she was found to be suffering from acute leukemia. She died within the following month."[91]

Rachel Carson had wanted to escape from history. She didn't consider herself an activist, as Baker did; she didn't enjoy battle, like Jacobs. But because she believed that commerce was winning, she intervened in history, deliberately and decisively. Carson and her allies showed that it was impossible to saturate our environment with synthetic chemicals without them blowing back on us. Her critics, from 1962 to the present, have claimed she valued nature more than people; she ignored the fact that spraying killed birds but saved humans. There was some truth in this caricature of Carson. She began her research on chemical pesticides out of a concern for birds and nature. But the activist who wrote *Silent Spring* became transformed in the process and ended up fighting to save us too.

4

Betty Friedan: Discouraged Activist

Betty Friedan, 1960. *World Telegram & Sun* photo by Fred
Palumbo. (Courtesy Library of Congress.)

That Was the Story

Betty Goldstein was a reporter for the *Federated Press*, a news service for labor
papers. In 1946, there was a one-day general strike in Stamford, Connecticut. "I
got off the train at Stamford and into a taxi with the writer and photographer
covering the story for 'Life' magazine." The three journalists asked the cab
driver to take them to the town center, but he didn't want to drive through

the crowds in the street. The men from *Life* pressed him. "The question was repeated, the Yale accent persuasive, a little impatient underneath—'We'll pay you. You won't lose by it. It'll be worth your while.'" The driver refused.

In the evening, on the train back to New York, Goldstein again ran into the two men from *Life*. "That taxi driver was an idiot," one said. She countered: "Maybe he'd rather be in the strike." They "looked blank; it hadn't occurred to them." She asked how they'd spent the day. They had stopped by the demonstration briefly, toured the manufacturing plants, talked to the owners, and found a machine running. "It wasn't a general strike at all," they concluded. "They were triumphant about this."

In turn, they asked about her day.

> Well, I'd gone to the demonstration, talked to the workers, gone out to see the picket line and the soup kitchen, and spent the afternoon going into the stores and talking to ordinary people of Stamford—shopowners, salesmen, people in the streets.
>
> "How could you get the truth that way?" they asked cynically. "Probably everybody you talked to was for the strike."
>
> "They were," I said, "that was the story."[1]

The story was solidarity: shop owners, salesmen, and workers of all kinds supported the strike. While the men from *Life* listened to the manufacturers, Goldstein listened to working- and middle-class people. She listened as well, between the lines, to the cab driver. Like Ella Baker, Jane Jacobs, and Rachel Carson, Goldstein was good at listening. She listened less patiently to the men from *Life*. Their class assumptions and class blindness were part of her story for the *Federated Press*. They felt superior to the people of Stamford, whose solidarity did not move them. They thought they could buy the cab driver. She connected the Yale accent to their inability to grasp the new thing that was happening. Like Baker, she thought having an elite education could be a handicap.

When their story appeared in *Life*, they conceded the strike was effective. "Factory workers, painters, bakers, musicians, barbers, and bartenders sang, cheered, danced and listened to speeches by union leaders." But they recalled that one machine: "strictly speaking, it was not a full-fledged general strike." In their view, the strike was frivolous—"Everybody had a grand old time."— and destructive: "The demonstration succeeded in breaking up a public negotiation session between union and company officials."[2] Their version of the one-day general strike in Stamford contrasted with hers. They looked from the top down, Goldstein from the bottom up.

Less than two weeks later, she was in New Jersey, observing an electrical workers' strike in Bloomfield. "The whole town was with the United Electrical Radio & Machine Workers (CIO) strikers . . . as they marched 5,000 strong from the Westinghouse & General Electric picket lines to the old Town Green." She noted that over half the marchers, including strikers and strike supporters, were women. In Bloomfield, as in Stamford, her story was solidarity.

> The parade was headed by an escort of friendly policemen wearing no arms, no nightsticks. . . . At the Green, Local Legion Commander Edward P. Harrington told the strikers they were soldiers—"not the killing kind, but soldiers in a new fight." Ninety percent . . . supported the strike, he said, adding: "We're a strictly Republican town, but we're not anti-labor."[3]

The American Legion, Republicans, police, on the side of striking workers? In 1946, American unions were at their peak of power and confidence. Workers struck more in 1946 than in any other year of American history. The Stamford general strike was the first of five general strikes that shut down American cities during the year. In Bloomfield, white-collar workers and small businessmen followed the lead of unionized blue-collar workers. Goldstein interviewed the local president of the United Electrical Workers (UE), who explained that the wage gains won by unionized workers benefited the townspeople. "'They know it's the union that's made the whole town prosperous.'"[4]

Betty Goldstein believed the labor movement that emerged from the Depression and WWII was so dynamic that it was lifting all boats. Baker similarly viewed the postwar labor movement as driving progress for middle-class as well as working-class people. In 1947, Baker was in Bethel, Georgia, launching a membership drive for the NAACP. She told her Black middle-class audience that "the fight for unionization concerns the businessman, the doctor, the lawyer and other professional folk, because they cannot exist except with the money made by the working man."[5] Baker, Goldstein, and many other left-leaning people saw the postwar labor movement as crucial to the hope of building a more equal and just society.

Goldstein celebrated labor's strength and ridiculed its enemies. On the 100th day of the Westinghouse strike, she went to Wall Street to observe the picket line outside Westinghouse's office. A worker from the Bloomfield plant brought her two little boys, "while 13-year-old Marguerite danced around the sidewalk giving out leaflets." One bystander took offense. "'Imagine, children wearing out their good shoes on a picketline,' sniffed a well-dressed passerby, settling her fur piece more comfortably around her neck."[6] To Goldstein, there was no solidarity between upper-class and working-class women. On the contrary, there was a world of difference—socially, politically, morally—between the dancing girl and the disapproving woman with the fur, who was as blind as the journalist from *Life*. The main dividing line in Goldstein's world was not sex but class.

The moment of 1946, when many progressive people shared Goldstein's enthusiasm for working-class power, did not last. Very soon, the Cold War set in. Communist-led unions, including the UE, were purged from the CIO. The world around Betty Goldstein changed, but she did not. When the *Federated Press* downsized as a result of Cold-War pressures, and she lost her job, she was hired by the *UE News*. She married Carl Friedan in 1947 and had a son in 1948. Her commitment to the labor movement and to her career as a labor reporter was unaffected by marriage or motherhood. After a year's paid maternity leave, she returned to her full-time job at *UE News*. Her commitment was professional, political, and personal.

By 1952, she was a veteran journalist who had worked full time for the labor press for nine years. In the *UE News*, she criticized the CIO for joining the red-baiting and for no longer being radical. The CIO agreed to a wage freeze during the Korean War. How did this freeze affect working people? Again, Goldstein contrasted a rich, out-of-touch woman with struggling workers. Her tone was harsher now.

> The wife of a Wall Street and Washington big shot recently ordered a $10,000 diamond-studded necklace for her poodle. . . . But the Browns of Trenton, N.J., can't afford beef and fresh vegetables anymore and haven't been able to buy any new clothes in almost a year on the $55 a week that's left in Leland Brown's paycheck from Westinghouse after taxes. . . . That is what equality of sacrifice means under our new war economy.[7]

Goldstein was an investigative reporter, discovering class conflict below the surface of American life. "These are true stories which we uncovered during our investigation into what [wage] 'stabilization' is doing to people's living standards."[8] As she later explained, "In my years after college as a reporter for the labor press, I learned to pierce through the fog of words and even of psychology to the grubby economic underside of American reality."[9]

Sometimes an investigative reporter went undercover. Baker once posed as a domestic worker looking for employment during the Depression, to expose the exploitation of Black maids and illuminate their need for a union of their own.[10] Goldstein also went undercover. In 1944, she infiltrated a meeting of a new right-wing group that hoped to divide white-collar from blue-collar work-ers. "In a luxurious suite of offices in a swank building off Wall Street," she man-aged to get near the leader, who was on the phone. "'We must appear struggling at first,'" he said, meaning it was necessary to hide their funding. "He put down the phone, turned to a tall dark woman wearing expensive furs and jewels sit-ting beside his desk. She murmured: 'I can promise you $5,000 to begin with.'"[11]

This woman with expensive furs and jewels who funded right-wing plots in 1944 was a precursor to the fur-clad woman sniffing at the pickets in 1946 and the Wall Street wife buying her dog a diamond necklace in 1951. To Goldstein, these women were embodiments of a class system that privi-leged rich men and their idle women at the expense of working women and men. As a student at Smith College, Goldstein supported the right of maids to organize. Aware of women's issues, she helped classmates get abortions.[12] But women's issues, for her, were subsumed under the paradigm of class. There were working-class women, including maids, who were exploited and needed unions. And there were rich bitches who wore expensive jewels and furs and didn't give a damn, or worse, who actively opposed the struggles of working women and men.

The labor movement was the way to advance the rights of women, Betty Goldstein believed. Jane Jacobs similarly believed at the time that unions were the way to get equal pay for women. In a 1943 article for the *Herald Tribune*, Jacobs celebrated the millions of women who were getting good jobs during the war. Meanwhile, she tried to unionize the secretarial staff at the trade jour-nal where she worked; she was especially interested in organizing the women.[13]

To Goldstein, working-class power supported the right of working-class women not only to equal pay but also to childcare. She asked Ruth Young, an official of the UE, why women in wartime industry took off more time than men. Young explained that a woman worker was responsible for her children and home as well as her job. "Women as individuals can't solve these problems," Goldstein concluded. Only the government could provide childcare for working mothers, and only the labor movement could push the government to do it.[14]

Goldstein viewed big business as the enemy of women workers. Before WWII, one of her Smith professors, a woman, compared the men running American women's magazines to Nazis: both wanted to push working women back into the home.[15] Late in the war, covering a convention of the National Association of Manufacturers (NAM), Goldstein observed businessmen patronizing women workers. There was "a salute to 12 outstanding war work-ers, including . . . several pretty blond and red-headed women wearing light blue denim overalls. They were given a rising ovation before the convention settled down to the day's business." The women were patted on the head and dismissed. "A few hours later, the NAM went on record with a new solution for postwar unemployment: ' . . . women should go back home.'"[16]

Goldstein researched and wrote a pamphlet about women workers, published in 1952 by the UE. Industry paid women less than men, claiming women were "young, temporary workers," who were waiting to get married and willing to "work for pin money." But according to government data, half of women workers were thirty-five or older and 93 percent helped support themselves and their family. The truth was that corporations opposed equal rights for women because they wanted to continue to exploit them. "The public acceptance of women's equality would mean the loss of a huge source of labor they could segregate and exploit." Goldstein contrasted the celebration of women as consumers with their exploitation as producers. "In advertisements across the land, industry glorifies the American Woman—in her gleaming GE kitchen, at her Westinghouse Laundromat, before her Sylvania television set. Nothing is too good for her—unless she works for GE, or Westinghouse, or Sylvania."[17] The best hope, for women as for men, was working-class solidarity. That was Betty Goldstein's story for over a decade.

In 1941, she spent the summer between her junior and senior years of college at Highlander School in Tennessee, where the CIO held training sessions. At Highlander, Goldstein studied radical unionism. "Applause followed a brief speech by the wife of a Ford worker, who said: 'I have only one thing to say about the union coming to our plant. Before, he came home tired. Now he doesn't.'"[18] Two years later, Goldstein wrote to Highlander, explaining that, as a graduate student in psychology at Berkeley, she felt she was missing out on the struggles of the day. She had worked on her junior high and high school newspapers and been editor of her college paper. Could Highlander find her a full-time job as a labor journalist? With help from Highlander, she got the job at *Federated Press*. Her hometown newspaper in Peoria noted that Goldstein gave up her fellowship at Berkeley because "she wanted to work in the labor movement—on the labor press."[19] She did not fall into this work; she chose it, and for over a decade she embraced it. It was her story.

Looking Back

Later, in the 1970s, looking back at the loss of faith in the radical labor movement, Betty Friedan recognized that anti-Communist repression had been crucial. In her astute telling, political counterrevolution led to domesticity.

"Security" was a big part of what began to happen in 1949. "Security," as in "risks," was in the headlines, as in atomic secrets, Communist espionage, the House Un-American Activities Committee, loyalty oaths, and the beginning of the blacklists for writers. Was it unconscious political retreat that so many who had talked so bravely, and marched, suddenly detoured to the security of the private four walls of that house in suburbia—everything that was "bourgeois."

Women who hoped to change the world retreated to the home. "Having babies, the Care and Feeding of Children according to Doctor Spock, began to structure our lives. It took the place of politics."[20]

For many progressive women, the outbreak of the Cold War was a turning point. But not for Betty Goldstein. Until the UE let her go in 1952, she continued to work full time in the radical labor movement, signing her articles Betty Goldstein, leaving her son in the care of a nanny. Anti-Communist repression didn't scare her away from radical unions and politics. Nor was she deterred from her career in labor journalism by postwar propaganda about what wasn't feminine. She gave up on class struggle only after the UE let her go. At that point, the story of working-class solidarity began to seem meaningless, and she felt lost.

In 1952, for the first time, she was home, with two children, no job, and no graduate degree because she dropped out of Berkeley to work in the labor movement. Writing as Betty Friedan after 1952, she tried to publish pieces in popular magazines. She still saw herself as a writer but lacked a compelling story to tell or a place to tell it. Today, when we think of her, we think of the new paradigm of gender: gender as a way of seeing. But during the 1950s, she did not yet have a new way of seeing. She was between paradigms, groping for a way forward. She no longer believed in working-class solidarity as a vital force driving history forward. She did not yet believe in women's solidarity as a vital force driving history forward.

Later, when she looked back in the 1970s from her vantage point as a leader of the women's movement, the meaning of her career in the labor movement shifted. Women's issues, no longer subsumed under class issues, exploded the paradigm of class. Women were oppressed even in the radical labor movement. "I remember now a funny feeling, almost of recognition, when on a routine assignment involving a strike at a major electric plant, most of whose workers were women, I discovered that women seemed to be discriminated against not only by the company but in the union. But no one was interested."[21] When she was fired by the UE in 1952, after she got pregnant again, she tried calling a meeting to protest. Again, no one was interested. "The other women were just embarrassed, and the men uncomprehending."[22]

At the time, she was bewildered. Only when she looked back through the lens of the modern women's movement did she see that her life as a labor journalist was circumscribed by unwritten rules. Only then did she realize how angry she was.

> It was somehow your fault, *pushy* of you, to want that good assignment for your-self, want the credit, the by-line, if the idea, even the writing, had been yours. *Pushy*, too, if you felt rejected when the men went out to lunch and talked shop in one of those restaurants where women were not allowed—even if one of these same men asked you out to lunch, alone, in the other kind of restaurant, and held your hand, or knee, under the tablecloth.[23]

After the UE let her go, she needed a new direction. But the double standard that shaped her career in the labor movement continued to vex her. Worse: it was inside her. She signed up for a seminar in how to write for quality television. But she was "assistant den mother in the Cub Scouts. . . . To take the bus into the city on time, I'd have to skip my den mother duty every other week. I did it twice, and had such a guilty asthma attack—and writer's block on the TV script—that I simply resigned the seminar, honor and professional opportunities not-withstanding."[24] The guilt never went away. "So, twenty-five years later when that grown-up boy is having trouble with his girl . . . [and] says his insecurity in love is all my fault, I still feel the pains of the guilt caused by leaving my first baby with a nurse when I went back to work."[25] When she looked back through the lens of the new paradigm that she helped to create, she saw that the powerful 1950s' consensus about women's roles damaged even an ambitious woman like herself.

After 1952, feeling lost, Friedan began exploring her roots. In freelance pieces, she revisited her past as a girl in Peoria, as a student at Smith, as a young mother. Maybe by looking back, she could find clues to how to move forward.

She began with Smith. Members of her class, the class of 1942, filled out a questionnaire for the 10th reunion. She studied the results. Seventy-eight percent wanted a Republican to become president. Yet "we read Marx and Lenin and Stalin in college—prescribed by our professors." Friedan's ostensible point in the piece (which, at the height of McCarthyism, she was unable to publish) was that a liberal education exposed students to radical ideas but did not make them radical. Her underlying, less reassuring point was about the fate of her professors. "Sooner or later almost any of them might be called before an investigating committee."[26] The generation of professors that criticized capitalism did not succeed in reproducing itself. In 1952, their former students were anything but radical.

When she looked back at her experience of becoming a mother, she defended her choice to continue her career after her son was born in 1948. "I Went Back to Work," published in 1955 in *Charm*, explained how she knew she would return to work after her year-long maternity leave; the knowledge helped her stay sane—and was therefore good for the baby. "If I had planned to stay home permanently when Danny was born, I might have had an unconscious resentment of him."[27]

This article in *Charm* was transitional for Friedan. It did not, like her later work, mention guilt toward her son because of her ambition. And it retained a commitment to social and economic equality, like her earlier work. "I was lucky in being able to take a year's maternity leave and still hold my job. If all working women could do that I think it would be better for them and for their children." Most working mothers were forced to choose between their job and their kids. They didn't get long maternity leaves and couldn't afford quality childcare. For Danny, she hired "a really good mother substitute—a housekeeper-nurse . . . who really loves him." But her individual solution was not available to most women. "This is the most difficult problem for working mothers to solve and one that is virtually impossible for some because of the expense." For a solution, she looked further back: "The best solution was the excellent day nurseries which the government financed during the war for the children of working mothers."[28]

Friedan, in 1955, hadn't forgotten what Ruth Young of the UE explained during the war: individual women couldn't solve the problem of childcare. Strong unions, including the UE, pushed the government to provide day nurseries. The UE also provided her year's maternity leave; it was part of her union contract. But when she got pregnant again, the UE fired her. The role of unions in fighting for child care was part of the old story, the story she no longer found compelling. As she looked for a new story, Friedan became less interested in unions and the working class. Increasingly, she focused on middle-class women.

Daniel Horowitz highlights the importance of this change. Betty Goldstein "was the labor journalist" who wrote under that name even after marriage. Betty Friedan began to use her married name only when she began writing freelance pieces. The change in name and venue suggests a discontinuity, a break. "Now she was writing not as an observer of lives very different from her own but as a witness of lives and issues that she knew first hand." Horowitz emphasizes Freidan's gain when she began writing about women like herself.[29] But it's equally true that there was a loss, in the gradual disappearance from her work of women unlike herself—working-class women, including the housekeeper-nurse, the mother and daughter who picketed Westinghouse, or the maids at Smith.

As her orientation shifted toward the middle class, she wrote about a middle-class activist in Peoria, her hometown. Once Harriet and Betty "marched in front of the graduating class, valedictorians together. We left Peoria together for Smith College, headed for New York together afterwards, I to write, Harriet to do research." In Greenwich Village, they imagined changing the world. "But we never thought of doing it in Peoria. . . . We were ashamed to admit we even came from Peoria." Harriet married a man from Peoria, went back home, and had four children. "You Can Go Home Again" described Friedan's surprise when she visited Peoria in 1954. "I found Harriet sitting at her big dining room table—exuberantly doing research!"[30]

Harriet was analyzing the school budget, digging for dollars that could be used to restore kindergarten. "At teas and potluck suppers and over the phone, she got her figures to other mothers so they could write letters to the newspaper that wouldn't just be 'women talking.'" The mothers forced the Board of Education to restore not only kindergarten, but also art, music, sports, and libraries. "Remembering our bull sessions in Greenwich Village, Harriet grinned: 'in Peoria, it's not just talk. If you want to do something, you can do it.'"[31] Not just talk, not just women talking: Harrriet and Betty knew that in the 1950s women were routinely dismissed as chattering lightweights.

In fact, it wasn't just talk in Greenwich Village, where Shirley Hayes, Edith Lyons, and other mothers were already battling Robert Moses over Washington Square Park. Or in other New York neighborhoods, where mothers were fighting for improvements in predominantly Black schools. ("In the early '50s the protesters were mostly women," Baker observed.[32]) Even in Queens, where Friedan was living at the time, there were activist mothers.

It was in Queens that Friedan found another story about a middle-class activist. Wanting a summer day camp for their children, mothers in a big Queens housing project formed a neighborhood committee of eight women, adding Henry Robinson, "in case they needed a man 'to impress people.'" When it was time to hire a director, "they decided a man would be more impressive interviewing, drafted Henry Robinson, and gratefully hired as director the first man with degrees willing to take the job." The camp was awful. No one liked it. Working within the traditional roles—men as leaders, women as followers—hadn't worked.[33] That's when Alice Barsky stepped up. Barsky asked mothers and camp counselors what went wrong, took notes on their responses, and called a meeting. "Maybe we've got to stop expecting somebody to hand us all the answers for our kids," she told the mothers. "This is our chance to be something more than nosewipers and diaperchangers." Henry Robinson quit: "Women! Too much talk, too many meetings, who wants to do so much work!" The camp succeeded. So did Barsky, who was asked to give a speech at a national meeting about children.[34] Friedan titled her piece: "More than a Nosewiper."

Friedan was drawn to women who knew their stuff and acted powerfully. Once she celebrated class solidarity; solidarity between women seemed impossible. Now she was discovering solidarity among women. Alice Barsky organized mothers in the housing project as effectively as Harriet organized mothers in Peoria. Some ingredients of Friedan's later feminism appeared in these mid-1950s pieces about Peoria and Queens. Women were organizing women, discovering their power, becoming themselves. And although husbands, like Henry Robinson, were uncomfortable, there was good news for them, as there would be in *The Feminine Mystique*: a powerful wife was happier, and sexier. "'You couldn't stop her though,' Sid Barsky said. 'I don't even try. It's irritating all right. But I don't know—Alice is sure a more livable person lately. She has on lipstick at breakfast. She even cooks better.'"[35]

Friedan, the former radical, was an activist mother in Queens herself. From 1950 to 1956, in her apartment community, she edited a monthly newsletter, joined a protest, and gave a speech in support of a rent strike. She wrote an article about the community, emphasizing that women dominated the committees and "of course, did most of the work—getting playgrounds built, starting a nursery school."[36] Again women were organizing effectively at the community level.

Looking back at the 1950s, Friedan was struck by the decline of radical activism and the rise of community activism. On the one hand, there were "the schizophrenic and even dangerous politics of the world revolution whose vanguard we used to fancy ourselves"; on the other hand, there was the "surprising effectiveness of the changes you could make happen in school boards, zoning and community politics."[37] However, she was unable to publish the article about her own community. And the pieces about activist mothers in Peoria and Queens were eventually watered down into more conventional stories and published, with changed titles, in *Redbook* and *Parents Magazine*. In the versions that made it into print, the power and solidarity of the women were greatly attenuated.[38] The market for pieces about activist women, even when they were fighting primarily for their children and not for themselves, was limited in the 1950s.

Only when she told the story of middle-class women who were not activists, who were in fact victims, would Friedan become famous.

Friedan's Fifties

In the late 1950s, Friedan began, tentatively, to put together a new story. In 1957, she designed the questionnaire for the 15th reunion of her Smith class, analyzed the responses, and wrestled with the results. She reflected again, as she did after the 10th reunion, on what had happened to herself and her classmates. But this time she went deeper.

She still acquitted Smith of the charge of harming its graduates. "We had problems. . . . But our education did not cause these problems." The problem was "to be a self as well as wife and mother." When they were in college, from 1938 to 1942, they experienced no conflict between being sexy and smart. "The prettiest, most popular girls—not just the brains—were serious about their work." There was no need to choose. "Girls who took their full quota of weekends at Yale also browsed alone, without shame, in the library stacks. We got the most rigorous liberal arts education women could get in this country unhampered by the fear that it was unfeminine to be interested in . . . Einstein, Plato, Bach."[39]

In this piece, which she eventually published, Friedan made no mention of Marx, only Einstein and Plato. On the surface, the piece was about the successful adaptation of her classmates to the housewife role. In their late thirties, she and her classmates were not frustrated or angry. "With every possible appliance from dishwasher to disposal and a cleaning woman once a week (only 12 per cent have full-time housekeepers), we spend four hours a day on housework. . . . But most of us can say frankly that we do not find homemaking 'totally fulfilling' and still say we are 'not frustrated' as suburban housewives."[40]

Nevertheless, it was a disturbing, even subversive piece. Under the reassuring surface ran disquieting questions. How did smart become unfeminine in the years since 1942? Why was it so hard in postwar America to be a self, and a wife/mother? As Friedan pondered these questions, she began sketching a new story, not a celebration about the solidarity of workers or the solidarity of women, but a darker story, an American crime story, a story about what had been done to postwar girls and women.

She was no longer struggling with the contrast between the generation of her professors and her own generation. She was concerned now with the falling off from her generation to the current generation of female college students. The piece was titled: "If One Generation Can Ever Tell Another: A Woman Is a Person Too." She wanted coeds of the late 1950s to prepare for a career beyond the home. She wanted them to get serious now, while they were in college, before it was too late.

In 1959, still wrestling with the piece, she lived with Smith students for a week, as an investigator. She was appalled. Although they dutifully took notes in class, they were not involved in their studies. She worried about them. "Many of us who had no career ambitions in college, have them now. And it's hard, nearing forty, to start."[41] If it was hard for members of the class of 1942 to become individuals, how much harder was it going to be for college girls who did not take their course work seriously, who cared only about being feminine and popular and getting engaged?

By 1961, when she published this piece about the 1957 survey in the *Smith Alumnae Quarterly*, Friedan was immersed in writing a book. The book—*The Feminine Mystique*—began with the survey. "Gradually, without seeing it clearly for quite a while, I came to realize that something is very wrong with the way American women are trying to live their lives today. I sensed it first as a question mark in my own life. . . . It was this personal question mark that led me, in 1957, to spend a great deal of time doing an intensive questionnaire of my college classmates."[42]

At the end of the book, she returned to the survey. Her classmates, she admitted now, were frustrated as housewives. But they were not crushed. "Most of these women continued to grow within the framework of suburban housewifery." The confines of their role did not defeat them. "They set up cooperative nursery schools where none existed; they started teen-age canteens and libraries in schools." This community activism drew on their education and "used and renewed [their] strength of self." Not just Smith graduates: all over the country there were smart, college-educated women, women in early middle age, "fighting their way out of the housewife trap, or never really trapped at all because of their education." They were strong enough to fight back because they had attended college in an earlier age, before girls had to choose between smart and popular. "But these graduates of 1942 were among the last American women educated before the feminine mystique."[43]

Her emphasis, in the book, was that the 1950s were a bad time to be a woman, and a worse time to be a girl. The fifties were a dark age for women who grew up during the Depression and the war, like her Smith classmates, because the feminine mystique—the myth that women were naturally wives and mothers, that career women were unnatural and unfeminine—coerced and seduced many into giving up their careers. But the feminine mystique, in her view, did more harm to younger women, who came of age during the fifties and were never independent in the first place, never knew what it was like to be individuals not primarily defined by their relation to men and children. At least women of Friedan's generation knew what they were missing and were partly able to resist. Younger women never had a chance.

Friedan was the only woman of the four in this book who regarded the 1950s as simply and uniquely destructive. Jacobs and Carson also regarded the 1950s as a bad time. They critiqued the vaunted progress of the fifties, the better living through chemistry and cars. In *The Death and Life of Great American Cities* and in *Silent Spring*, the forces of death dominated the postwar period. But although Jacobs and Carson regarded the fifties as worse than prior decades, the difference was only one of degree. To them, the 1950s continued and intensified earlier destructive trends. Carson knew that the attempt to control nature, to impose top-down order on its diversity, was much older than the fifties. And Jacobs knew that the infatuation with the automobile at the expense of city life originated in the 1920s, when Robert Moses began imposing his vision on New York.

Baker did not experience the fifties as worse than prior decades. She was encouraged by the progress made by Black women and men during the fifties. She was thrilled by the Montgomery bus boycott of 1955–56 and the student lunch-counter sit-ins of 1960. Friedan observed in *The Feminine Mystique*, in passing, that in 1960, while women were at a low ebb, "Negro youth in Southern schools forced the United States, for the first time since the Civil War, to face a moment of democratic truth."[44] Her point was that while others were surging forward, American women were being forced back. Friedan said nothing in her book about women in the southern movement. Because she tended to define women as white, she did not think of progress for Black women as progress for women.

Baker did. She celebrated the achievements of women in Montgomery and was angry afterward that "there were women who had demonstrated a kind of dedication, and who had enough intelligence, and had enough contacts with other people to have been useful, to have found a role to help move people along," but "no role was provided for them." She pointed to a nurse in Montgomery who worked all night yet showed up to demonstrate in the morning. "Now that kind of dedication could have been utilized." Another woman baked and sold pies to raise money for the movement. "That woman may never have developed to the point of being a leader of a workshop, but she could have been integrated into a program and her talents could have

been developed." What happened to these women? "Nothing. That's the tragedy of it."[45] It was a different tragedy than the one Friedan explored, yet not so
different as she imagined.

Where Baker and Jacobs and Carson found continuity between earlier
decades and the fifties, Friedan emphasized a break. To her, the 1950s were
so destructive precisely because they reversed earlier progressive trends. In
The Feminist Mystique, she celebrated the progress women made in the 1920s,
1930s, and first half of the 1940s, attributing the gains in education and careers
to the suffrage movement and the early feminist movement. She saw the fifties as counterrevolutionary, an attempt to reverse the increasing freedom
and equality of women through a new kind of oppression, whereby women
learned to mistrust their own best instincts and to censor their own independent impulses and ambitions.

Some historians have accused Friedan of exaggerating or oversimplifying
the ways popular culture pushed women back and have pointed to her own
activism during the fifties and the activism of many other women.[46] I agree
more with Friedan. What was coming at women in the fifties was terrible:
regressive, repressive, phony. Of course, not all of it was terrible; there are
always contradictions and ambiguities in popular culture. Of course, some
women, including Friedan, found creative ways to assert themselves. People
always do.

Inspired by protest in the 1950s, often protest by women, Baker, Jacobs, and
Carson took it to a higher level. By contrast, Friedan was not able to build
on the pockets of activism she discovered in the 1950s. The women in Peoria
and Queens were activists, but not for women. Women Strike for Peace,
founded in 1961, organized a mass protest in 1962. "It is, perhaps, a step in the
right direction when a woman protests nuclear testing under the banner of
'Women Strike for Peace,'" Friedan acknowledged in *The Feminine Mystique*.
"But why does the professional illustrator who heads the movement say she is
'just a housewife,' and her followers insist that once the testing stops they will
stay at home happily with their children?"[47] Even these radical organizers and
protestors did not challenge the powerful consensus that a woman's first duty
was to her children.

Baker, Jacobs, and Carson found something positive in the 1950s. They
observed currents of grassroots resistance emerging, especially in the late fifties, currents upon which they consciously drew in their work and which they
helped turn into powerful movements. Friedan, when she wrote *The Feminine
Mystique*, did not see her book as helping to create a movement. Her book
focused on the reversal of women's freedom and equality—on the undoing of

women's progress—during the 1950s and on the emptying out of their lives. If Jacobs wrote of the death and life of cities, and Carson of the death and life of nature, Friedan wrote, more simply, of the death of American girls and women.

Friedan experienced the Cold-War fifties as a blighted time, not only because of what was done to women and girls but also because of what was done to women and men who wanted to change the world. As Betty Goldstein, she reported on the House Un-American Activities Committee's attacks on the labor movement and on unions weakening themselves by expelling radicals.[48] Daniel Horowitz points out that she lost both of her reporting jobs for reasons related to the persecution of the Left in the labor movement: although the Federated Press purged itself of Communists and the UE refused to purge itself, both were hurt economically and forced to lay people off. Goldstein knew a number of people who were investigated for being Communists, not only in the radical labor movement, but also at Smith and Berkeley. The FBI kept a file on her. In her community work, like so many other activists of the fifties, Friedan was accused of Communism.[49]

Anti-Communists targeted activists of all kinds, including feminists. Friedan, even more than Baker, Jacobs, or Carson, felt the chill. The repression of radicals and the suppression of women were connected, she thought. "It is probably no accident that the new mystique of femininity coincided with the . . . repression of communism," she wrote in an earlier draft of the book. The feminine mystique was not caused by "McCarthyism and the American political reaction after World war II, but it certainly thrived" in that atmosphere. Historically, "where there has been much concern and battling for freedom and reform, women's emancipation has been advanced. . . . , and in times of reaction, it has receded."[50]

Like Friedan, Baker viewed the witch hunting of the fifties as bad for all movements from below. "Under the impact of the McCarthy period," people became afraid to protest.[51] McCarthyism "silenced large numbers of activists, especially the most radical."[52] Progressive groups began policing themselves. The very name of the Southern Christian Leadership Conference reflected self-policing: "Christian" was added to the name in part to insulate the group against charges of Communism, she noted.[53] In 1958, as acting director of SCLC, Baker complained: "We have no mass movement." And explained that without pressure from the left, established groups had no reason to temper their instinctive moderation. "Because of present restrictions on leftist groups, existing organizations have not found it necessary to compete with them."[54] Anticommunism was so powerful in the 1950s that even Baker blinked. In 1957, serving on the Internal Security Committee of the New York branch of the NAACP, she helped purge Communists from the organization. Later, she recognized that the NAACP and other Black organizations weakened themselves and regretted what she had done. "I followed a national office directive to the letter, and I should not have."[55]

Jacobs was the target of an FBI investigation when she was working for a government magazine. In 1952, the State Department told her to fill out a questionnaire about her personal beliefs and activities. She began by protesting: "It still shocks me, although we should all be used to it by this time, to realize that Americans can be officially questioned on their union membership, political beliefs, reading matter and the like. I do not like this, and I like still less the fear that arises from it."[56] Then she answered the questions about her membership in an "apparently Communist dominated" union and in the leftist American Labor Party.[57] Jacobs was honest in her answers, defending her right to her union and party memberships. But by answering, she strengthened the repressive machinery.

Jacobs was never a Communist and was in fact strongly opposed to Soviet Communism for its restrictions on individual freedom and initiative. She was more at home in America and had less to fear than Friedan, who was Jewish and who had worked for years in the pro-Communist wing of the labor movement. But no one got away with challenging the status quo during the Cold War without being tarnished, directly or indirectly, by the charge of being a Communist. The FBI spied on Baker, on her bank account, her phone bill, her apartment.[58] Even Carson, who had no interest in political ideology and was a revered best-selling author of nature books, was called a Communist when she challenged the chemical companies. The FBI investigated her, monitoring her phone calls. Anticipating attack, Carson in *Silent Spring* played down her debt to Marjorie Spock and other radical activists.[59] Like Baker's decision to help purge the New York NAACP, or Jacobs's decision to answer the State Department's questions about her beliefs, it was a kind of self-policing. Friedan's silence in *The Feminine Mystique* about her decade of labor radicalism must be viewed in this context.

From 1960 to 1962, Baker, Jacobs, and Carson aggressively endorsed protest, defied the fear of speaking out, and ushered in the activist 1960s. Jacobs was glad to see McCarthyism losing its power to intimidate would-be activists. Baker strongly opposed anti-communism in SNCC, acting not as a Communist but as an anti-anti-Communist, because she saw how anticommunism weakened activist groups. Friedan, in *The Feminine Mystique*, took a different but perhaps no less subversive tack. She attacked the fifties consensus at a fundamental point, its suppression of women.

Part 2

The Interventions

5

Ella Baker and the Founding of SNCC, 1960

The Call

Baker's immediate response to the sit-ins that begin on February 1 is to identify the young activists and try to bring them together. To get names, she scans local newspapers and draws on her contacts at colleges. Then she begins phoning activists, asking: "What are you all going to do?"[1] She discovers "little or no communication between those who sat in, say, in Charlotte, North Carolina, and those who eventually sat in at some other place in Virginia or Alabama. They were motivated by what the North Carolina four had started, but they were not in contact with each other, which meant that you couldn't build a sustaining force just based on spontaneity."[2] From decades of organizing, she's learned how to turn spontaneous protests into a sustainable mass movement.

To put the students in touch, she brings them together. In the third week of March, on SCLC letterhead, she sends out a "Call" for a conference. It begins: "Recent lunch counter sit-ins and other nonviolent protests by students of the South are tremendously significant developments." There is "great potential for social change." This emphasis is characteristic of Baker, who is always looking to take protest to the next level. She understands right away that her job—her call, if you will—is to help the student activists find their way beyond sit-ins. Therefore, the question she poses in the Call is: "Where do we go from here[?]"[3]

The Call recognizes the "thoughtful leadership manifested by hundreds of Negro students on college campuses." Baker wants to bring these emerging leaders together, so that, together, they can be thoughtful about the next step. She does not want to tell them what to do or to have other adults tell them what to do. In her radically democratic way, she wants them to talk and listen to one another and figure out where they are going.

She organized many leadership conferences during her years with the NAACP. She knows that a leadership conference is not a demonstration or mobilization, not a show of force in which large numbers are necessary or useful. She asks each campus to send a limited number of activists, because "a leadership conference should not be too large." From the beginning, rather than trying to maximize the number of attendees, she focuses on the quality of discussion between the young Black activists.

One day will not be enough. To give the students time to get to know one another, she allocates a weekend, Easter weekend, April 15–17. To provide them with space, she arranges for them to come to Shaw University in Raleigh. The Call informs students it will cost $6.30 per student for the two nights and six meals. She has already made the arrangements and done the math.

She signs the Call with Martin Luther King Jr.'s name as well as her own. Dr. King is her boss. As acting executive director, she needs him to sign off on the conference and provide the money to fund it—about $800, she figures, including money to help some students with the cost of travel to Raleigh. But she knows that this conference is not going to enhance the power of King or SCLC. On the contrary, she convenes the conference in part out of her frustration with King and SCLC.

In the Call, Baker assures students that the conference will be "youth centered." She feels so strongly about the students playing the determining role in the conference that she is ready to fight with older leaders if they try to annex the new student activists to their own group. "None of the great leadership had anything to do with the sit-ins starting," she later insists. Young people "sat-in, and the movement spread like wildfire. . . . There was a great deal of dissatisfaction among the young that hadn't been articulated with the older leadership."[4] She doesn't want the youthful energy and courage to be co-opted and blunted by older leaders or existing organizations.

She hopes the Raleigh conference will lead to a new organization, independent of any existing group. "It is my hope," she writes on March 21 to a veteran southern activist, "that out of this meeting will come some workable machinery for maintaining affective [sic] communication between youth leaders in areas of recent and future protest activities, and a larger degree of coordinated strategy."[5] At a minimum, communication: southern students will connect with one another at the conference and exchange ideas and experiences with peers. At the maximum, coordination: they will lay the foundation of a new, youth-centered organization. And that is what happens. Out of the conference, the Student Non-Violent Coordinating Committee (SNCC) is born.

Baker is able to help the student activists because she combines a deeply democratic vision with careful attention to detail. The Call itself is the culmination of a painstaking process. On March 2, she issues an SCLC press release, announcing a "youth leadership retreat" for Easter weekend. She cannot yet specify where, "but it is expected to be in either Virginia or North Carolina."[6] From March 7 to 12, she asks hundreds of students and other activists what their thoughts are about the sit-ins. On March 16, she flies to Raleigh, obtaining "an agreement first with the student leadership there for having this meeting."[7] Baker wouldn't think of going ahead with a conference for activists without checking with the local activists.

Raleigh is in the midst of its own sit-in. Glenford Mitchell, student editor of the Shaw University paper, describes how it began. "William Peace hurried into my office. 'Mitch, what are we going to do?' he asked. 'The damned thing is spreading all over the place and we haven't made a move yet!'" It was February 9, eight days after the four students sat-in at Greensboro. That evening, Mitchell and Peace held an open meeting; students from Raleigh's other Black college, St. Augustine, also attended. Together, they decided to sit-in at downtown stores in the morning. Despite short notice, more than 200 students showed up at Woolworths and five other stores. Two days later, there were the first mass arrests of the 1960 sit-in movement—the first in Raleigh, and the first in the South. After the arrests, more students joined the protest and began picketing downtown stores. As adults in the African American community mobilized behind them, the students called for a boycott of the stores.[8]

The Raleigh sit-in typifies the way the movement grew. Students initiated and led. They followed the example of students in other North Carolina college towns but did not coordinate with them. Other than sitting-in, they reinvented all their tactics. "The idea of picketing had not dawned on us," explains Mitchell. After the arrests, "the idea of turning to the general public for support was born, and, along with it, the idea of picketing." After picketing a while, they noticed that sales at the downtown stores were down. "Our new knowledge provided us with a new weapon—the economic boycott."[9]

The strength and limit of the sit-ins, in Raleigh and other cities and college towns across the upper South, is that they were intensely local. Baker recognizes the strength and moves quickly to remove the limit. When she returns to Atlanta from Raleigh, she issues the Call. Then she reports on her trip to Dr. King and to Rev. Ralph Abernathy, the secretary/treasurer of SCLC. In case they have not read her Call closely, or have not taken it seriously, she repeats now, in writing, that "the meeting should be youth centered." She specifies that "adults attending would serve in an advisory capacity, and should mutually agree to 'speak only when spoken to.'" Baker is establishing the ground rules in advance for King, rules that suit her style much better than his because he is a great talker, and she is a great listener. According to her plan, he will address a mass meeting on Saturday night. But the conference will belong to the students. They will make all the decisions at their workshops on Saturday morning and afternoon and at their plenary session Sunday morning.[10]

The tone of Baker's report is unusual from an employee to a boss. Or a lay person to a reverend. Or, in 1960, a woman to a man. Or anyone in the civil rights movement to Martin Luther King Jr. Ella Baker defers to no one. She insists on the ground rules of the conference because she understands what is at stake. She knows she has to protect the students from the good intentions of established leaders. Disappointed in the failure of the leadership of SCLC to organize a mass movement in the South after the uprising in Montgomery, she is determined that the same thing will not happen after the sit-ins.

After reporting to King and Abernathy, she writes to student leaders on each campus, telling them how many delegates they are allotted and asking them "to get together with your fellow student leaders [on your campus] and democratically decide upon your representation."[11] She follows up, a week before the conference, requesting a history of each sit-in: "How, when, and by whom were your demonstrations started?" She wants students to take credit for what they have already done—"Write the story up in your own way"— but also to begin thinking about the future. "What are your plans now?"[12] For Baker, the sit-ins are a very exciting beginning, but only a beginning.

The Conference

At least 124 southern Black students come to the conference. Eighteen of them are still in high school. There are students from eleven southern states, but only a single student from Mississippi.[13] Baker hopes that they will coordinate their protests and launch an assault on racial inequality in all its forms throughout the South, even Mississippi.

Right away, there's a problem. "I had originally thought of pulling together 120–25 sit-in leaders for a leadership training conference—but the rate of spread of the sit-ins was so rapid and the response so electrifying, both North and South, that the meeting ended up with 300 people."[14] The Raleigh conference attracts northern white students, adult civil-rights representatives, and mainstream media, all drawn to the energy of the sit-ins. Northern students, reporters, and civil-rights leaders threaten to encroach on the space that the southern students need to connect with each other and find their own direction. Baker responds decisively to each threat.

"The first step that I took as far as the conference was concerned, was to prevent the press from attending the sessions at which kids were trying to hammer out policy."[15] Before the conference starts, she puts out another press release, informing news organizations that there will be press conferences on Friday at 4 p.m. and on Sunday at 12:30 p.m.—that is, before and after the conference. The media are also invited to attend the Saturday night mass meeting, at which Dr. King will speak. The working sessions—that is, the workshops and the plenary session—will be closed to the media.[16] Publicity is not Baker's aim. She knows "you could not organize in the public press. You might get a lot of lineage, but you really couldn't organize."[17]

She has always been skeptical about organizing in the media. In her long career as an activist, she has avoided the media spotlight. Regarding celebrity as something that usually happens to movement leaders, and usually makes them less effective, she sees King as an example of a media star, too involved in his public image to focus on nurturing protests from the grass roots. She doesn't want the new student activists to get caught up in trying to become famous. Acting on her own authority, before the Raleigh conference begins, she limits the role of the media.[18]

But she cannot resolve by herself the question of the role of northern white students. Fifty-seven northern students, representing Students for a Democratic Society (SDS), the National Student Association, and nineteen northern college campuses, come to Raleigh to be with the southern Black activists.[19] During the conference, some northern students join local Raleigh students in picketing downtown. On Friday, a northern white student is attacked by a southern white man and needs seven stitches. On Saturday, another northern white student is attacked.[20] In a pattern that will be repeated, culminating in the murderous violence against northern volunteers in Mississippi in the summer of 1964, the violence against white people— unlike the violence against Black people—becomes national news.

The presence of northern whites on the picket line is welcome. But their presence in decision making is another matter. As Baker sees it, the problem is that the northern white students are better educated, more sophisticated, and "much more articulate in terms of certain moral philosophies than the

southern students who had come with a rather simple philosophical orientation, namely of the Christian non-violent approach."[21] Full participation in the
conference by northern students may intimidate southern students, depriving
them of the chance to figure out their next step and develop their own philosophy. She can't let that happen.

Early in the conference, she meets with "a small group of students" and with
James Lawson (a young Nashville minister) to develop a schedule whereby
the southern and northern students will meet separately. When at last they do
come together for dialogue near the end of the conference, there is agonizing
over whether to make the separation permanent.

> The decision was finalized that the northern students could not become a part
> of whatever organizational machinery that was set up, that theirs was a sup-
> portive role. We had a good deal of sharp dialogue on that and it became soul
> searching for some, you see, because it wasn't a question of color as much as it
> was a question of retaining the character of a Southern-based movement.

The initial decision of Baker, Lawson, and several students that the southern
students will meet separately at the conference leads to the decision by the
southern students as a whole "that the leadership for the South had to be a
Southern leadership."[22]

This decision—"the first major decision"—made by the students is critical in allowing the sit-in movement to evolve into SNCC. In her mind, it was
right. "I believed very firmly in the right of the people who were under the
heel to be the ones to decide what action they were going to take to get from
under their oppression. As a group, basically, they were the black students
from the South."[23] Southern Blacks must be in charge of the fight against their
own oppression.

She is able to limit the role of the media and to help limit the role of the
northern students. It is harder for her to limit SCLC's role. "The Southern
Christian Leadership Conference felt that they could influence how things
went. They were interested in having the students become an arm of SCLC.
They were most confident that this would be their baby, because I was their
functionary and I had called the meeting."[24] In her Call, and in her report to
King and Abernathy, she insisted that the conference would be student centered. Now she is determined that the decision as to whether or not the students affiliate with SCLC will be made solely by the students themselves.

On Saturday night, SCLC leaders hold a small, adults-only meeting. Baker
listens as several ministers, including King, agree to reach out to students they

know or to other adults who have influence with students, with the aim of making the student movement into the youth arm of SCLC. "This was completely intolerable to me."[25] She is shocked by the assumption that the students could and should be manipulated. "When it was proposed that the leadership could influence the direction by speaking to, let's say, the man from Virginia, he could speak to the leadership of the Virginia student group, and the assumption was that having spoken to so-and-so, so-and-so would do what they wanted done, I was outraged." She has to do something. "I walked out."[26]

The conflict between the SCLC leaders and Baker remains private. King chooses not to press the issue. He thinks the student movement would fit nicely into the structure of SCLC. But he knows how strongly she feels. King tells a younger associate that pressing the issue would be "a little destructive." According to the associate, King doesn't want the conflict "to spew over into a public thing between he [sic] and Ella Baker."[27]

Baker is not the only one who wants the students to maintain their independence. Many southern students oppose annexation by SCLC or any adult group. Two months earlier, when Myles Horton of the Highlander Folk School attended a mass meeting of students in Nashville, he heard students asking adults not to try taking over the leadership of their new movement.[28] Glenford Mitchell, the local Raleigh leader, would insist a few years later: "The southern students have always appreciated and welcomed the support of national bodies, but they cannot and will not countenance intrusion."[29] On Sunday, the last day of the conference, there is an argument between students who don't want to affiliate with SCLC and students who do. The conflict becomes so urgent that the students decide to pause and put the agenda aside. "First, they had to stop and pray and sing some," Baker observes. "Jim Lawson, with his calm, was trying to get them to sing and pray. So they finally, then, came back to the issue. . . . They decided not to become an arm of SCLC, but to retain an independence of their own."[30]

They decide: after singing and praying, the students take another democratic step toward creating their own organization. Baker contributes to their decision not only by her private protest against SCLC's plans but also by what she says publicly at the conference. Her speech has not survived, but right after the conference, she writes an article "Bigger than a Hamburger," repeating the ideas from her speech. Students expressed "apprehension that adults might try to 'capture' the student movement" and "were intolerant of anything that smacked of manipulation or domination." She adds a personal note: "This inclination toward group-centered leadership, rather than toward a leader-centered group . . . , was refreshing indeed to those of the older group who bear the scars of battle, the frustrations and disillusionment that come when the prophetic leader turns out to have heavy feet of clay."[31] Later, she will emphasize the importance of this decision: "SNCC rejected the idea of a God-sent leader," making it possible for the group to evolve into a band of leaders.[32]

Baker's speech at the conference resonates with Julian Bond, who will become a leader of SNCC. "She didn't say, 'Don't let Martin Luther King tell you what to do,' but you got the real feeling that that's what she meant."[33] Her skepticism toward prophetic leaders was connected to a real appreciation of what the southern students had already accomplished on their own. "She insisted that we have something special," remembers Bond. "We had sponta-neously broken out in protest in Greensboro and in Nashville and Atlanta and Birmingham. And she impressed upon us the necessity to keep this special thing separate."[34]

Separate from adult organizations, and separate from northern students: these two separations make SNCC possible. At the end of the conference, the students set up a Temporary Student Non-Violent Coordinating Committee and agree it will meet monthly. Built into the name of the new group is the idea of coordination. "At Raleigh," explains Bond, "as you began to meet these people from all these different sit-in places and you said, 'Oh yeah, I remember reading about what you all did there,' the idea began to seep in that we might be real hell-on-wheels in Atlanta, but if we could coordinate what we're doing in Atlanta with what they're doing here, we would really be tough stuff."[35]

Looking back, three months after Raleigh, the Coordinating Committee recognizes that the biggest accomplishment of the conference was creat-ing a common identity. "This was the beginning in that it was a meeting of people who, up until this time had worked in relative isolation. A gathering in Charlotte had done thus, a handful in Orangeburg had done this, ten or twelve in Nashville had marched, a few students in Frankfort had taken this action, and four freshmen in Greensboro had started the whole thing. Here, at Raleigh, we met. It was that kind of beginning. It was a becoming conscious of 'we.'"[36]

One SNCC or Two?

Combining democratic theory with nitty-gritty practice, Baker enables SNCC to emerge. During the group's first fragile months, she herself coordinates the Coordinating Committee. Why is the new organization located in Atlanta? Because that's where she is. As her job with SCLC winds down, she uses her corner of the Atlanta office of SCLC to do the work of SNCC. Small monthly meetings in Atlanta of the Temporary Coordinating Committee culminate in a large October conference in Atlanta, where the young activists vote to make the organization permanent and begin hiring a few of their number as full-time organizers.

From the beginning, she wants SNCC to go beyond sit-ins. At the Atlanta conference in October 1960, when SNCC drops "temporary" from its name, she suggests the next step. Characteristically, she does it by raising a question.

> You have just heard a review of the success story of the Sit-Ins and it is both logical and mandatory to ask "After the Sit-Ins, What?" This question demands more than answers as to whether the Sit-Ins of last spring will be followed by Kneel-Ins at churches, Wade-Ins at beaches and swimming pools, Stand-Ins at voter registration offices. . . . Even if all those things are done, and I am confident that many of them will be done, there are other answers demanded by the question, "After the Sit-Ins, What?"[37]

To her, the struggle against segregation—of buses in Montgomery in 1956 or lunch counters in the upper South in 1960—is part of the greater struggle for economic, social, and political equality. She is committed, in every sense, to the rising of the masses. She is not aiming at the emergence of a Black middle class. She envisions an egalitarian, classless society in which everyone is free to become fully human. She wants SNCC to organize a mass movement, which will open up the Deep South in a way that sit-ins never can. Ending segregation of public accommodations is "only a surface goal."[38]

Speaking in January 1964, at the height of SNCC's struggle in Mississippi, she will be very clear about this.

> Even if segregation is gone, we will still need to be free; we will still need to see that everyone has a job. Even if we can all vote, but people are still hungry, we will not be free. . . . Remember, we are not fighting for the Negro alone, but for the freedom of the human spirit, a larger freedom that encompasses all mankind.[39]

Grounded in class struggle as well as racial struggle, she aims at full equality for all.

Three months before the sit-ins, she tried to push SCLC to register voters in the Deep South, especially Mississippi. Now, after the Raleigh conference, even before the October conference in Atlanta, she tries to gently nudge SNCC toward Mississippi and voter registration. In the summer of 1960, when Bob Moses comes down from New York to volunteer with SCLC, she drafts him for SNCC and sends him to Amzie Moore in Mississippi. Moore convinces Moses that the vote is the crucial thing, the key to other changes. Moses pushes SNCC toward organizing a massive voter registration campaign in Mississippi, Alabama, and rural Georgia. At a SNCC conference at Highlander School in Tennessee, in August 1961—twenty years after Betty Friedan studied the radical labor movement at Highlander and one year after Baker sent Moses to Mississippi—this new direction meets head on with the original commitment of SNCC activists, threatening to tear the young organization apart. Is it the organization of nonviolent direct action, especially the sit-in? Or is it the organization of political action in the Deep South, especially voter registration?

Some SNCC organizers agree with Moses. But others, including the energized and principled Nashville group led by Diane Nash, are absolutely committed to nonviolent civil disobedience. Whether by sitting-in, or by joining the freedom rides against segregation in interstate buses that the Congress on Racial Equality (CORE) has just launched, the direct actionists believe in putting their bodies on the line against the machinery of segregation. They are suspicious of voter registration precisely because the Kennedy administration is promoting it. These students argue at the August 1961 meeting that the split is irreconcilable. SNCC should become two separate organizations, one to continue and extend the sit-ins and direct action, and the other to pursue voter registration and political action.

At Highlander in 1961, in contrast to Raleigh in 1960, the threat to SNCC comes not from outside but inside. "The worst conference I remember was at the Highlander Folk School," Baker says. "When those who advocated going into voter registration spoke, those who were more highly indoctrinated in the nonviolent approach objected that they didn't want just to go into voter registration. They broke up into a kind of fight—a pulling apart."[40]

Ordinarily, she doesn't intervene, even when she thinks the young people are making a mistake. "I usually tried to present whatever participation I had in terms of questions and try to get people to reach certain decisions by questioning some of the things themselves."[41] She knows people learn more from dialogue than lecture. And she believes, with all the decades of organizing behind her, that people have to participate fully in running their own organizations, talking things through and making their own decisions, including their own mistakes. That's how they become strong and how leaders emerge from within the group, rather than an established leader—someone like herself—imposing decisions in the usual top-down fashion. She believes so strongly in this kind of bottom-up, democratic process that she usually sits in the back at SNCC meetings. "The first time I ever remember having a charley horse in my leg was after thirty hours that I had been more or less sitting in the same sort of cramped position. Because I felt if we had a table, that the first priority would be for the young people to sit there."[42]

But this time at Highlander, with SNCC on the brink, she intervenes. There is too much that can be lost. From the moment the sit-ins broke out, she has had great expectations for the southern students. She knows they are neither experienced in struggle nor sophisticated in political thought. They are young. But that is their great strength. They are not cynical, resigned, or cowed. She sees that there is no telling how far they might go or how much they might accomplish, if they can just have time to learn from one another. And now, at Highlander, as they threaten to tear themselves asunder, she finds a way to help them stay together, completing the action that she took when she brought them together at Raleigh. "I never intervened between the struggles if I could avoid it. . . . But this was a point at which I did have something to say."[43] She argues not for one side, but for SNCC itself.

First, she listens deeply, between the lines. Beneath the polarizing rhetoric, she recognizes that the group committed to nonviolent direct action is feeling defensive. "I think one of the reasons, perhaps, that they were defensive was that the political actionists had developed a much more well congealed plan and they were prepared to argue their position."[44] Even without Moses—who is not in Tennessee because he has already returned to Mississippi—the political actionists are articulate and intimidating. ("We were immensely suspicious of him," Bond says of Moses. "He had a much broader view of social problems and social concerns than we did. We had tunnel vision."[45]) As Baker sensed at Raleigh that northern students might intimidate southern students, so now, at Highlander, she recognizes that political actionists intimidate direct actionists. "This was the old business of groups that are better prepared to advocate their position sometimes engendering a defensiveness on the part of those who are less prepared. So, those who are on the defensive, then, take the step to try to decide to resolve the conflict by saying, 'Well, let's have two organizations.'"[46]

When she speaks, she offers two arguments against splitting. "I certainly felt that number one, historically we had had too much of dividing forces." Usually, she does not dwell on her experience. "But, in this instance I made a little plea against splitting, pointing out the history of organizations among black people and the multiplicity of organizations and the lack of effectiveness as a result of this, to the extent that they decided against it."[47] Nash and the direct actionists listen to her, trusting her long experience as a Black activist. They back away from a split because she has earned their trust by doing everything they need, from planning to secretarial tasks, and by just being there, listening, asking tough questions, nurturing their growth and confidence. They agree to keep SNCC a single organization. But they still aren't happy with political action. [48]

Her second, more decisive argument is designed to reassure the direct actionists. "The persuasive argument, I think, was that once you mounted a voter registration campaign involving mass registration you would have the resistance you were looking for and you could utilize . . . the non-violent approach."[49] Fighting for the vote, confronting the power structure that depends on keeping Blacks from voting, will provoke repression, which will lead to massive nonviolent protest. "If they went into those deeply prejudiced areas and started voter registration, they would have an opportunity to exercise nonviolent resistance."[50] Her first argument against splitting is effective because it is grounded in her experience of Black struggle in the North and South over many decades. Her second argument is even more effective because it is grounded in her knowledge of the Deep South.

Some direct actionists go straight from Highlander to Mississippi, where they join Moses in SNCC's voter registration project. At the end of August, Moses is badly beaten; in September, a black farmer is killed. Organizing voter registration, SNCC activists face violence on a regular basis. "And they began to see that they wouldn't have to abandon their nonviolence. In fact, they would be hard put to keep it up."[51] The long, hard struggle within SNCC is over; there will be no split. "The young people decided—after months and months, weeks and weeks, all night and so forth—recognized that going to southwest Georgia, going down into deep Alabama and Mississippi meant you were going to be faced with violence. So if they compromised, it was largely in terms of the fact that the strength of the movement lay in being together."[52]

Ella Baker makes SNCC possible. She calls the student activists from various southern cities and states to meet at Raleigh; she protects their space from existing organizations and from the media; she supports their decision to form a temporary coordinating committee; she attends to the details of organization in her office space in Atlanta; she sees the young activists through the transition to forming a permanent organization; and she guides the new organization through its early growing pains, gently shaping its approach, mentoring its key leaders, forcefully stepping in to prevent a split when one threatens. Her intervention—from Raleigh, 1960 to Highlander, 1961—changes America.

More than any other individual, Baker helps the student activists become the radically democratic group of organizers who will foster local leadership in Black communities across the Deep South. She plays a crucial role in shaping the first mass movement of the 1960s, the movement that will become the model for many of the radically democratic movements that follow.

6

The Death and Life of
Great American Cities, 1961

City Life

Death and Life playfully confronts the builders of cities, the urban planners who aim to create utopia by tearing down and rebuilding. *Death and Life* finds utopia in the existing city.

> Near where I live is an old open dock . . . , next to a huge Department of Sanitation incinerator and scow anchorage. The dock is used for eel fishing, sunbathing, kite flying, car tinkering, picnicking, bicycle riding, ice-cream and hot-dog vending, waving at passing boats, and general kibitzing. (Since it does not belong to the Parks Department nobody is forbidden anything.) You could not find a happier place on a hot summer evening or a lazy summer Sunday.[1]

In a functioning city, there's room for people tinkering with cars or riding bikes, fishing for eels or sunbathing and waving at boats. So long as you don't hurt anybody, there's no judgment on what you do, no hierarchy whereby some activities are good and healthy and others are bad, unhealthy, or low. If city bureaucrats become interested in the old dock, they will sterilize and deaden it, turning it into yet another approved park, where people are protected from their own low desires. Meanwhile, under the radar of the city bureaucracy, diversity and anarchy flourish.

Only the kibitzing is general, the urban pleasure of observing the scene and commenting on it. Kibitzing? But Jane Jacobs, you are from Scranton,

Pennsylvania; even if people kibitz in Scranton, they don't know that it is the proper name for what they are doing. No, she might answer, I am a New Yorker and have as much claim to the term "kibitzing" as anyone. To be a New Yorker, you don't have to be born or grow up here; you have only to embrace the scene and become part of it.

She liked Scranton, because it was a city, but she doesn't miss it. The freedom of growing up in Scranton is so much greater in New York.

> "I know Greenwich Village like my hand," brags my younger son, taking me
> to see . . . a secret hiding place some nine inches wide between two buildings,
> where he secretes his treasures that people have put out for the sanitation truck
> collections along his morning route to school and that he can thus save and
> retrieve on his return from school. (I had such a hiding place, for the same pur-
> pose, at his age, but mine was a crack in a cliff on my way to school instead of
> a crack between two buildings, and he finds stranger and richer treasures). (85)

Even the trash is richer, more diverse in New York than in Scranton.

Is she nostalgic for that place in the cliff, for the smaller city where she was closer to nature than she is now? Not a bit. Rachel Carson would be. For Jacobs, Greenwich Village is the perfect place to play, for a kid or a grown up. When she thinks of living in a small town, what she thinks about is boredom. But isn't her Hudson Street neighborhood itself like a small town? Not at all. "It is possible in a city street neighborhood to know all kinds of people without unwelcome entanglements, without boredom, necessity for excuses, explanations, fears of giving offense" (62). That's the beauty of a big-city neighborhood: you get the community of a small town without the boredom or invasion of privacy.

In the Village, the simple routines of daily life take on the quality of play.

> The stretch of Hudson Street where I live is each day an intricate sidewalk bal-
> let. I make my first entrance into it a little after eight when I put out the garbage
> can, surely a prosaic occupation, but I enjoy my little part, my little clang, as the
> droves of junior high school students walk by the center of the stage dropping
> candy wrappers. (50–51)

She is giving a little clang to us, waking us up, announcing her theme: on a functioning city street, everyone plays a part. Taking out the garbage, she is taking care of business. Whose business? Only her family's? What about the candy wrappers? "While I sweep up the wrappers, I watch the other rituals of morning" (51).

She has always been interested in garbage. After she moved to New York, she watched the garbage trucks from the rooftop, just for fun, and studied how sewers worked. Now, in *Death and Life*, she describes not only her participation in collecting garbage but also the enjoyment of watching from the dock as trucks dump garbage. "From time to time, a great slushing and clanking fills the air as a sanitation truck dumps its load into a waiting garbage scow. This is not pretty-pretty, but it is an event greatly enjoyed on the dock" (268). Garbage collection involves many people, professional and amateur, working together to make the city a good place to live.

Before she leaves to go to work, she performs a ritual "with Mr. Lofaro, the short, thick-bodied, white-aproned fruit man who stands outside his doorway a little up the street." Mr. Lofaro differs from her in many ways—in body shape, gender, profession, ethnicity, probably education. She is about to go to work, whereas he is already at work. But despite, or rather because of their differences, all is well on Hudson Street. "We nod; we each glance quickly up and down the street, then look back to each other and smile. We have done this many a morning for ten years, and we both know what it means: All is well" (51). Diversity keeps a street safe.

Jacobs treasures the sense of safety on Hudson Street. She raised three babies there. In contrast to the suburban mothers interviewed by Betty Friedan, Jacobs doesn't feel isolated or depressed. "I know the deep night ballet and its seasons best from waking long after midnight to tend a baby and, sitting in the dark, seeing the shadows and hearing the sounds of the sidewalk. Mostly it is a sound like infinitely pattering snatches of party conversation and, about three in the morning, singing, very good singing" (53). In this book that will subvert the field of urban planning, she wants us to know not only that there is singing on her street in the middle of the night, but that it is very good singing.

Planners and architects overlook the little pleasures of urban life. They are not mothers. They have not sat up with a baby and listened to the night sounds of a vibrant neighborhood. "Most city architectural designers and planners are men" who judge the city from on high and find it wanting. Zoning for purely residential areas, they make an urban neighborhood as much like a suburban bedroom community as they can, eliminating small businessmen like Mr. Lofaro. "They design and plan to exclude men as a part of normal, daytime life wherever people live" (83).

The Death and Life of Great American Cities was written by a mother who valued safety and pleasure for herself and her children. In the book, she acknowledges Glennie Lenear, who took care of her kids during the day, enabling Jacobs to be a few blocks away, writing in her studio.[2] Later, she will explain that she wrote the book partly because she was a mother. "When we were raising our children in New York I naturally became concerned about safety and other social conditions and how these are affected by city planning. Such questions led me to write my first book."[3]

Sitting with a baby at night, overlooking the street, she occasionally hears unpleasant sounds. "One night a young man came roaring along, bellowing terrible language at two girls whom he had apparently picked up and who were disappointing him. Doors opened, a wary semicircle formed around him, until the police came" (53). This is a classic Jane Jacobs story. Do what you want on Hudson Street, so long as you do no harm to others. If you pick up two girls, and they're willing, fine; it's between you and them. Privacy is a fundamental urban right. But if the girls are not willing, and you begin to threaten them, then it becomes our business. We form a semicircle around you. We call the police. We restore safety.

And we kibitz about you. "Out came the heads, too, along Hudson Street, offering opinion, 'Drunk . . . Crazy . . . A wild kid from the suburbs.'" Drunk or crazy could explain the young man's behavior. But why the suburbs? If he grew up without a vibrant and diverse community, the young man might never learn right from wrong. In a note at the bottom of the page, Jacobs playfully inverts the cliché about moving to the suburbs to raise kids. "He turned out to be a wild kid from the suburbs. Sometimes, on Hudson Street, we are tempted to believe the suburbs must be a difficult place to bring up children" (53; ellipses in the original).

She knows the city is not for everyone. Some people cannot enjoy the noisy exuberance of a vital city neighborhood. After the book appears, there's a debate between Jacobs and a prominent New York planner. He complains about the noise on his block in Jackson Heights, in Queens. "On early Saturday or early Sunday morning, when I would like to sleep, a horrible garbage truck comes along and wakes me up and makes me sick by the noise it makes collecting garbage from the retail stores." Jacobs is amused. Instead of trying to persuade him of the value of mixed-use neighborhoods, she replies: "I hear other people like you talking, and they object to hearing the sounds of children playing. Actually, anybody so sensitive to noise ought to live out in the country."[4]

She is used to the noise and disorder of children playing. Looking at urban life from a different vantage point than previous urban theorists—from street level, or her window just above—she sees what makes her neighborhood, and other neighborhoods, successful. "A friend of mine lives on a street uptown where a church youth and community center, with many night dances and other activities, performs the same service for his street that the White Horse bar does for ours" (41). She delights in this particular example—a church center serving the same function as a bar—because it tweaks the beaks of moralists and utopians who want to impose their values on city dwellers. The uptown street illustrates her starting point: neighborhoods need diverse activities and diverse people.

A lively city neighborhood, like her own or her uptown friend's, is a wonderful place to live. But it will only remain safe and pleasurable if people actively defend it against the wild boys from the suburbs and the wild men from city hall.

Citizen Activism

In her mind, Jacobs first emerged as a public figure not when she spoke at Harvard in 1956 but earlier, on Hudson Street. During the long battle to save Washington Square Park, a community organizer asked her to help with petitions. She took copies, put them in stores, and collected them.

> As a result of engaging in this messenger work, I have since become automatically the sidewalk public character on petition strategy. Before long, for instance, Mr. Fox at the liquor store was consulting me, as he wrapped up my bottle, on how we could get the city to remove a long abandoned and dangerous eyesore, a closed up comfort station near his corner. (69–70)

She becomes the person who will help with petitions. She didn't plan it that way. Perhaps one reason she was able to be herself at Harvard, despite her nervousness, was because she was already a public character on Hudson Street.

When Jacobs helped with the Park petition, she acted as a citizen on her street, and in the larger community, beyond her street. This is the way citizens are made, and cities. Everyone in the daily dance is already an activist and potentially an organizer. That's precisely why the Village is so good at fighting off the incursions of city planners and city hall. So many people are already involved, in a daily way, taking care of the neighborhood. Picking up candy wrappers or petitioning the city to remove a closed comfort station are on the same continuum. Either way, you're cleaning up the trash. A citizen may find herself, at any time, going beyond her usual part, taking on extra responsibility. She may intervene to break up a fight or protect the helpless. She may call the police or the hospital, or circulate a petition to get an eyesore removed, or become, herself, an organizer fighting against the city bureaucracy. She might write a book.

In describing how she became a public figure, she is as down to earth, as unpretentious, as she is when distributing the petitions. Her earlier, short pieces described how the city worked (like the piece on manholes) or described her own adventures (like the piece on hitchhiking with fishermen). *The Death and Life of Great American Cities* does both. It is a *bildungsroman*. As Jacobs tells the story of the fall and rise of cities, she tells her own story: how she watched the street before she went to work or when up with the baby at night; how she became the petition lady; how she became a leader of the fight to save the park and then the leader of the fight to save the sidewalk. She tells us what she learned, at each stage, and how she learned it. She is not trying to impress us. She wants us to understand that if she did it, we can too.

As her involvement grew, she began attending public hearings. The hearings of the Board of Estimate became a vital part of her education.

> Citizens who wish to speak their minds address the Mayor, the five Borough Presidents, the Comptrollers and the President of the City Council, who sit behind a raised semi-circular bench. . . . I became an addict of the Board of Estimate sessions as a fierce and rooted partisan at just such hearings, and I cannot lose my habit of involvement as some other district's problems are cried out. (405–6)

The men sitting behind the raised semicircular bench in city hall, "like rulers holding court in the manor during medieval days," present themselves as above the battle: their ideal is Olympian. (406) Hers is not. She is a partisan, unashamedly committed to local life. At first, she came to the Board of Estimate only when her ox was being gored. She came to protest, to voice the concerns of her district. She stayed to support the protests of other districts. And this, she believes, is how democracy works: we grow from local concern to concern for other locales. We begin with involvement in our neighborhood, like the dance of Hudson Street and the petition to protect the sidewalk, and we become involved with other streets and other petitions. Involvement is a habit; once you become active, it's hard to stop. There are so many good people crying out their district's problems, hoping somebody will hear.

Attending the Board of Estimate hearings is addictive "because of the abounding vitality, earnestness and sense with which so many of the citizens rise to the occasion. Very plain people, including the poor, including the discriminated against, including the uneducated, reveal themselves momentarily as people with grains of greatness in them, and I do not speak sardonically" (407). These people—working people, poor people, people of color—know more about their neighborhoods than the borough presidents or planners do. They are experts of a different kind. In her own neighborhood, poor people, many of whom are Puerto Rican, "make up a vital part of the web of casual public life. The amount of time they devote to street watching and street management makes some of the rest of us parasites upon them" (281). At the board hearings, poor people from other neighborhoods teach Jacobs about areas of the city she doesn't know. More: they confirm her faith in democracy.

The people in power believe that listening to the cries of citizens would only slow down their own important work. That's why they sit behind a raised bench. The mayor and borough presidents are harder to hold accountable than local elected officials, who often join protests; "if they did not they would never be elected again" (358). The men at the top—whether elected like the mayor or Board of Estimate, or appointed like Robert Moses—are insulated from neighborhoods and dismissive of local protests. "Such protests are discounted as the howls of people of narrow vision standing in the way of progress and higher tax receipts" (288).

The men at the top are powerful because they control public spending. They use their power, systematically, to undermine democracy.

> There are only two ultimate public powers in shaping and running American cities: votes and control of the money. To sound nicer, we may call these "public opinion" and "disbursement of funds," but they are still votes and money. . . . Robert Moses, whose genius at getting things done largely consists in understanding this, has made an art of using control of public money to get his way with those whom the voters elect." (131)

Death and Life calls out the names of those who subvert democracy. It is not a nice book but rather a weapon in the service of democracy. She intends the book as an extension of the battle to save the park.

The next fight—to save the sidewalk on Hudson Street—occurs while she's writing the book and enters the book. "We people on the street . . . were told at first that the plans would not be changed; the sidewalk must go. We needed power to back up our pipsqueak protest" (124–25). We were told: it was not a dialogue. No public hearing was necessary to cut 10 feet off the sidewalk of Hudson Street. The printer ran off petitions; two parochial schools sent petitions home with students; 1000 adults signed them. But they couldn't stop progress. "We were up against a sanctified general policy on street treatment, and were opposing a construction job that would mean a lot of money for somebody, on which arrangements were already far advanced" (124). Theirs was a pipsqueak protest. The Manhattan borough president would not take their petitions seriously unless they could marshal the democratic power of the district of Greenwich Village. "Indeed, a main purpose of our petitions, although not an ostensible purpose, was to dramatize to the district at large that an issue had erupted" (125). By gaining the backing of citizens in the larger Village, who then pressured district officials, the people on the street kept their sidewalk.

Jacobs knows that most people who find themselves in the way of progress are not so lucky. Most streets are not part of functioning districts like Greenwich Village. Most people, on most streets, in most American cities, do not even bother to protest. Knowing they cannot win against money and progress, most people grumble, and submit. And their city dies a little bit more.

City Death

In *The Death and Life of Great American Cities,* Jacobs wants us to fight for our great cities, which are dying. She defines "dead" as "incapable of the constant adjustments, adaptations and permutations that make up the processes of life" (199). Cities began to die a long time ago. Even before modern urban renewal's lifeless projects, many neighborhoods were mortally ill.

> Neighborhoods built up all at once change little physically over the years as a rule. The little physical change that does occur is for the worse—gradual dilapidation, a few random, shabby new uses here and there. . . . The neighborhood shows a strange inability to update itself, enliven itself, repair itself, or to be sought after, out of choice, by a new generation. It is dead. Actually it was dead from birth, but nobody noticed this much until the corpse began to smell. (198)

For living, breathing neighborhoods, you need a mix of old and new buildings, of bars and banks. An area built up all at once does not age and adapt and grow; it just decays, leading to new plans to tear it down and start the sterile cycle anew. Planners tear down the old buildings and put up a whole new neighborhood. Their effort is stillborn. New construction brings high overhead, which limits the type of businesses that can afford to be part of the new neighborhood. "Chain stores, chain restaurants and banks go into new construction. But neighborhood bars, foreign restaurants and pawn shops go into older buildings" (188).

Jacobs is not a preservationist who loves old buildings for their own sake. She is a new breed, an urban ecologist. What interests her is the connection between old and new. Old buildings support different enterprises, which attract different people. City planners try to will new neighborhoods into existence. "But the economic value of old buildings is irreplaceable at will. It is created by time" (199).

City planners believe that having lots of people concentrated in a small area is a bad thing. That's one reason they tear down old neighborhoods. But when Jacobs looks at vital districts—Greenwich Village, Brooklyn Heights, Boston's North End, San Francisco's North Beach-Telegraph Hill, Philadelphia's Rittenhouse Square—she finds high density. On the one hand, high density can be perceived as bad. "On the other hand, people gathered in concentrations of city size and density can be considered a positive good, in the faith that they are desirable because they are the source of immense vitality, and because they do represent, in small geographic compass, a great and exuberant richness of differences and possibilities" (220–21). Urban theorists and planners are repelled by great concentrations of people living on top of one another. "This is a common assumption: that human beings are charming in small numbers and noxious in large numbers." Their solution is that people "should be sorted out and stashed away as decently and quietly as possible, like chickens on a modern egg-factory farm" (220). The same values that inspire modern egg factories—top-down order, homogeneity, standardization—inspire modern rebuilders of cities.

Her deeper point is about ways of looking. You can look up from street level, as neighborhood people do. Or you can look down from the heights of urban theory, as city planners do. They miss the unique, nitty-gritty details that make the difference between a vital and a decaying neighborhood. Despite all their talk of data, they are not really interested in quantifying the mix of high- and low-density buildings in a thriving neighborhood. "It's too hard to generalize about districts like that," says a planner, when she asks about the variations of density in a vital district. He prefers standardization and predictability (204, note). Celebrating uniqueness and diversity, Jacobs grows her own theory organically, working up from successful streets and districts.

Jacobs differs with urban planners on many theoretical points. But the root difference between her and them is emotional and visceral: she loves cities. It is her love for cities that enables her to grasp how they work, as the love of Rachel Carson for birds and crabs and oceans enables her to grasp how they work. After *Death and Life* is published, a reporter for a suburban paper tries to coax Jacobs into making suggestions for improving suburbs. She refuses.

"I don't believe in giving prescriptions unless you love what you're talking about," she explains. "I'm always burned up by people who dislike the city and tell what's wrong with it. It would be just as outrageous for me to do that with the suburbs."[5]

When the book becomes a classic, Penguin puts out a British edition and proposes shortening the title on the cover to "The Death of Great American Cities." Again, she refuses.

> No, it just will not do. It isn't true. It sounds all doom and gloom and the battle lost. Readers who would be put off by the full title but would be attracted by *The Death of Great American Cities* don't want to read what I have to say. They are probably city haters.[6]

Jacobs loves cities and respects the people who live in them. City planners don't respect the intelligence of the people who live in poor neighborhoods. They think they know what is good for slum dwellers: replace the slum with a shiny new project. They see only disorder, squalor, overcrowding. And so, in the name of helping people, they destroy neighborhoods that are capable of healing from within, replacing them with truly hopeless projects. Like the people living in successful neighborhoods, people living in slums are the real experts. "We must regard slum dwellers as people capable of understanding and acting upon their own self-interests. . . . We need to discern, respect and build upon the forces for regeneration that exist in slums themselves" (271).

This is what Jacobs calls unslumming: when the creative and constructive forces inside a slum gradually transform it into a vital neighborhood. Unslumming happens when people begin to choose to stay. So long as the people who *can* leave actually *do* leave, and the only people left are those who—due to racial segregation and poverty—can't leave, the slum gets worse. But when the reverse takes place, when people choose to stay because they like the rituals and uniqueness and begin to feel safe, then unslumming happens. What was once a slum becomes an exciting neighborhood, capable of attracting residents and visitors, like Boston's North End, which was a slum two decades earlier.

Or like the West Village. "My own neighborhood, as recently as the early 1950s, was saved from disastrous amputation only because its citizens were able to fight city hall" (272). (Jacobs doesn't know, as she writes about how the West Village fought off the slum designation in the early 1950s, that her own neighborhood is about to be designated a slum again, and that the fight is about to begin all over again, much more intensely.) *Death and Life* is her attempt to do for American cities what people in Greenwich Village have been doing: fighting against experts, bureaucrats, and planners, fighting for what is vital and growing, fighting to protect and support diversity and the fragile urban ecology.

And fighting against the automobile. Robert Moses and borough presidents and city planners do not merely hate cities. They love automobiles. If American cities are dying, cars are killing them. Or rather, what is killing cities is the vision of making them good places for automobiles. Enabling automobiles to move more easily through Washington Square Park, through Hudson Street, or soon, across lower Manhattan, is the impulse behind much planning. Borough presidents believe that wider streets are arteries of progress. To Jacobs, sidewalks are the real arteries of a city, where most life flows. Playfully, she suggests widening the identical number of sidewalks. "Manhattan alone widened 453 street roadbeds in the years 1955–1958, and its borough president announced that this was only a start. A sensible attrition program . . . would aim—among other things—at widening the sidewalks of at least 453 streets in a four-year period, and would consider this only a start" (364, note).

For her, the difference between what the borough president wants and what she wants is not a misunderstanding or a matter for compromise—of splitting the difference between roads and sidewalk. She titles the chapter: "Erosion of cities or attrition of automobiles" (338). It's either/or: less cars or less life. But if she could, would she widen all the sidewalks right away? No, not even in her dreams. She respects the ecology of the city and knows that change can succeed only if people have time to adjust. "Attrition of automobiles requires changes in habits and adjustments too. . . . It should not disrupt too many habits at once" (369).

Toward residents who need time to adjust to change, Jacobs is compassionate and respectful. Toward the powerful men who love automobiles and hate cities, she is unsparing.

> It is understandable that men who were young in the 1920s were captivated by the vision of the . . . Radiant City, with the specious promise that it would be appropriate to an automobile age. At least it was then a new idea; to men of the generation of New York's Robert Moses, for example, it was radical and exciting in the days when their minds were growing and their ideas forming. Some men tend to cling to old intellectual excitements, just as some belles, when they are old ladies, still cling to the fashions and coiffures of their exciting youth. (371)

She acknowledges that Moses's thinking formed around a new and exciting idea in the 1920s: the Radiant City, articulated by Le Corbusier, with the automobile at the center and freeways connecting groups of skyscrapers with each other. But that's her point: the prince of progress is stuck in the past. In comparing the powerful man astride the city to an old lady who can't let go of the trappings of youth, she is laughing at his claim to masculine domination. Jacobs does not feel the need to be polite, to be nice, to play the game. It's not her game. She is a woman, an outsider who will be dismissed as amateur and mother. Her outsider status gives her the freedom to compare Robert Moses to an aging belle.

The fight to save the sidewalk or the park or the city is a fight against the automobile. In place of living sidewalks, Moses and his allies put deadening highways. In place of vital neighborhoods, or neighborhoods that could revitalize themselves, they put stillborn projects. In place of vital downtowns, they put art centers that are disconnected—by "arterial highways, belts of park, parking lots"—from the daily life of the city. "American downtowns are not declining mysteriously, because they are anachronisms. . . . They are being witlessly murdered" (171).

It is not only New York that is dying. Planners and rebuilders are ruining great cities all over America. There is a brand-new housing project in Cincinnati, with pretty lawns and sidewalks in the front and service alleys in the back. The planners decree that life will be in the front, but life has its own ideas. "All the casual coming and going occurs between the houses and the alleys and therefore, functionally, the backs of the houses have become the fronts and vice versa. Of course the alleys are where the children all are too" (346). How much more pleasurable our housing arrangements would be, she believes, if we began with the women and men, and the children.

Theory should follow life and evolve as life evolves. Her ideas about how to reverse the decline of cities are rooted in the particular circumstances of 1961. She knows circumstances will change. Her prescriptions—for example, for a new way to subsidize housing—are not meant to last forever. "Deliberate, periodic change in tactics of subsidy would afford opportunity to meet new needs that become apparent over time but that nobody can foresee in advance. This observation is, obliquely, a warning against the limitations of my own prescriptions in this book." (335) She is not being humble. She's confident she has discovered key principles about how cities work and key strategies for reversing their decline. But the tactics she recommends are going to become outdated, even—or especially—if they work. Successful neighborhoods may well become, as a result of their very attractiveness, more expensive and less diverse, and therefore less successful. Ideas about how and when to subsidize housing, including her own ideas, must give way to lived experience. Jacobs doesn't want to get stuck in the early 1960s, the way Moses is stuck in the 1920s.

Planners and rebuilders and officials make dead cities. But it takes everyone to create a living city. "Cities have the capability of providing something for everybody, only because, and when, they are created by everybody." (238) It is the emphasis on "by" that is unusual, perhaps unique. Urban theorists and planners claim that their cities are "for" everyone. But who claims that cities could and should be *by* everyone? Isn't it obvious that an elite of planners, builders, and government officials must make, and remake, cities? Not to Jane Jacobs. She is a radical democrat, who loves cities and has faith in the people who live in them. Indeed, her love of cities and her faith in democracy are one and the same. What makes a city great is the participation of its people.

When people take part in the daily ballet, they create their street. When they use the power of petition and protest and the vote to get improvements and protect what works, they create their neighborhood. When they ally with other neighborhoods, and bring power to bear on the borough president or mayor, they create their district. When they ally with other districts, they create their city. It is government by the people, who are the real experts about their streets, neighborhoods, districts, and cities.

She has heard ordinary people, including poor people and people of color, speaking at Board of Estimate meetings and has listened to their voices. She didn't call a conference of neighborhood people against urban renewal, as Ella Baker called a conference for students who were sitting-in. But in a way, *Death and Life* is that conference, bringing together diverse protestors and ideas. In the book, Jacobs is not only an activist but also a strategist of activism. Like Baker, she knows that only the participation of the people, at every level of decision making, can move America forward.

Yet much more than Baker, who feels the pain of racism and the burden to overcome it, Jacobs takes pleasure in the way things are. She feels fortunate to live in a wonderful district, in a great city, in a democratic country, where people can come together to make their communities better. As we fight to save our cities, she doesn't want us to forget that without a working democracy, in our city or country, creative change would be impossible. Our government is accountable; special interests have not entirely corrupted it. "Corruption, chiseling and finagling we can hold down reasonably well, when we choose to. (Think how lucky we are to live in a country where we can do so.)" (334–35). We: citizens of American democracy. She is glad to be one. At the beginning of the 1960s, as she completes *Death and Life*, Jane Jacobs is grateful to be an American.

🦋

Silent Spring, 1962

Public Prosecutor

Silent Spring begins with a simple idea: spraying elms with DDT kills robins and other birds. It moves to a more difficult idea: what we are doing to robins, we are doing to ourselves.

> We spray our elms and the following springs are silent of robin song, not because we sprayed the robins directly but because the poisons traveled, step by step, through the now familiar elm leaf-earthworm-robin cycle. These are matters of record, observable, part of the visible world around us. They reflect the invisible world of life—or death—that scientists know as ecology.
>
> But there is also an ecology of the world within our bodies.[1]

Silent Spring introduces ecology—the biological science that studies the relationship between living organisms and their environment—into general discourse. When the balance of nature is disturbed, insect invasions occur. An ecological approach endeavors to restore the balance, not to drop a chemical bomb on the invaders and thereby disturb the balance even more. The balance in our bodies has also been disturbed. As elms and fields, forests and plains are sprayed with the new chemical pesticides, we do not notice symptoms of disease. Meanwhile, the chemicals accumulate in our fatty tissue and liver, harming us in ways we haven't begun to measure.

Personally, Carson feels more deeply about birds than about us. She loves nature and resents humans for mistreating it. But she recognizes commerce is destroying nature and accepts responsibility for trying to turn the tide of history. And there are not enough bird lovers to do that. To stop the assault on nature, she must disturb and arouse the rest of us.

Silent Spring raises the possibility of human extinction. It invokes the acknowledged threat from nuclear war to help us understand the unacknowledged threat from the chemical war on insects and weeds. "Along with the possibility of the extinction of mankind by nuclear war, the central problem of our age has therefore become the contamination of man's total environment" (8). The threat of nuclear extinction is cited in a subordinate clause because it is already well known; there are ongoing demonstrations against it.[2] Less well known is the threat from chemical war. "The fact that chemicals may play a role similar to radiation has scarcely dawned on the public mind" (211). *Silent Spring* deliberately uses the language of war. "The chemical war is never won, and all life is caught in its violent crossfire." Chemical fallout, like nuclear fallout, is assaulting our genes. As bombs become deadlier, culminating in hydrogen bombs, so too, in "a process of escalation," chemicals become deadlier (8). Carson wants us to demonstrate against the chemical war, too.

What qualifies her to reveal the danger? Where does her authority come from? Her field, marine biology, confers no special authority. She writes about chemical pesticides and herbicides not as a specialist but as a generalist. Her authority comes from seeing the big picture. Unlike chemists, who tend to focus narrowly on short-term results, she looks to long-term consequences. She has another, equally crucial qualification for this work: she is not on the take. Her livelihood is not derived from the chemical industry, directly or indirectly, so she is free to challenge it. Her credentials, in this sense, are negative: not a chemist, not dependent on industry.

In a positive sense, however, her authority derives from the people, who have begun to protest. In the years before 1962, there have been growing but scattered protests against the use of chemical pesticides. *Silent Spring* sides openly with the protestors. In "an era dominated by industry, . . . the right to make a dollar at whatever cost is seldom challenged. When the public protests, confronted by some obvious evidence of damaging results of pesticide applications, it is fed little tranquillizing pills of half truth" (13). Carson magnifies the protests, mainstreams them, and places them on a scientific foundation. Opposing the chemical industry's drive for profit and the government's collusion, she assumes the role of public prosecutor.

Silent Spring tells the story of how robins or eagles, salmon or sage, flourished for thousands of years. "The salmon of the river called Miramichi on the coast of New Brunswick moved in from their feeding grounds in the far Atlantic and ascended their native river. . . . These events repeated a pattern that was age-old, a pattern that has made the Miramichi one of the finest salmon streams in North America" (129–30). But in 1953, DDT was sprayed from the air to kill budworms, because budworms hurt trees that the paper and pulp industry harvests. As a side effect, all the insects died, including insects that salmon eat. None of the young salmon that hatched in 1954 survived. Since then, the spraying of the forest has been repeated year after year, because the budworm—but not the salmon—keeps rebounding.

Carson emphasizes conflict: linear progress versus cyclical time, the paper and pulp industry versus the salmon, commerce versus nature. She wants to alarm us, but also give us hope. Humans are not only destroyers. We have a capacity to learn. In the process of destroying the balance of nature, we are gaining new understanding of that balance. The science of ecology has emerged—science not as power over nature, but as an ally of nature. What's hopeful is that the understanding of ecology, of the interconnections between different life forms, is racing to keep up with the advances of the chemical industry. Embracing the new science, citizens can intervene on the side of life. Humans, who have destroyed the balance of nature, can help restore it. "Man, too, is part of this balance" (246).

Her task, the task of her book, is to hold the chemical industry accountable and tip the balance in favor of the salmon. And of the bald eagle, whose "populations have dwindled alarmingly within the past decade. . . . Something is at work in the eagle's environment which has virtually destroyed its ability to reproduce. What this may be is not yet definitely known, but there is some evidence that insecticides are responsible" (118). No matter how alarmed she feels—and wants us to feel—about the eagle, Carson is careful not to overstate her case. The eagle's catastrophic decline is recent. Studies of that decline are even more recent. The evidence points to DDT, which is absorbed by the fish that eagles eat, and "almost certainly" stored in the fatty tissue of eagles, preventing them from reproducing (122). We can't say for sure. The evidence is still coming in. (Today we know she was right, and the eagle has recovered because she was right.)

Silent Spring is a wonderful mix of scientific caution and moral outrage. DDT is more devastating to salmon and eagles than to insects because insects develop resistance. But we don't know exactly how. "The means by which insects resist chemicals probably vary and as yet are not thoroughly understood" (273). Her point: we cannot wait for perfect understanding. We need to act now, on behalf of life. There is nothing cautious in Carson's willingness to call out the chemical industry and the scientists who do its bidding. Where it would be easy to be cautious, in taking on the industry, she is fearless. Where it would be easy to jump to conclusions, regarding the precise effects of DDT, she waits on the research. Hers is an unusual kind of courage.

She wants to slow down progress, so that nature has a chance to recover. The chemicals pouring out of laboratories give life no time. Time is crucial. There have always been naturally occurring chemicals (calcium, silica, copper) that were harmful to life. Over time, life healed itself. But the human project of conquering nature has released destructive forces that overwhelm life's capacity to heal. "Given time—time not in years but in millennia—life adjusts, and a balance has been reached. For time is the essential ingredient, but in the modern world there is no time" (6).

She frames her book as a critique of the use of pesticides and herbicides. But her stories break the frame, and her big picture keeps getting bigger. *Silent Spring* widens into a critique of man's attempt to conquer nature, a critique of the idea of progress itself. Chemical sprays are simply the most recent and destructive chapter in this larger story. As she recounts how the sagebrush lands of the American West were destroyed, herbicides appear in her narrative as a recent, almost minor, culprit.

> The bitter upland plains, the purple wastes of sage, the wild, swift antelope, and the grouse are then a natural system in perfect balance. Are? The verb must be changed—at least in those vast and growing areas where man is attempting to improve on nature's way. In the name of progress, the land management agencies have set about to satisfy the insatiable demands of the cattlemen for more grazing land. . . . Now millions of acres of sagebrush lands are sprayed each year. (66)

On one side is a balance that evolved over eons between land and sage, and animals feeding on sage, and grass growing beneath it. On the other side is industry—cattle, seed, machines to cut sage, and now chemical sprays to kill it—and government agencies, eager to help the cattlemen and the producers of the seeds, machines, and herbicides.

The science of ecology enables us to introduce natural enemies of pests and to diversify plants. "Even a generation ago no one knew that to fill large areas with a single species of tree was to invite disaster" (117–18). Planting elm trees together made the trees more vulnerable to disease. These are the kinds of mistakes we need no longer make. In that sense, and that sense only, Carson thinks time is on our side. This generation, the postwar generation, the generation that is drastically unbalancing nature, can help nature heal itself. By coming together against pesticides and herbicides, we can heal humanity as well as nature.

There is no individual solution, no place to hide. Not even the far Arctic shores of Alaska. Eskimos eat uncontaminated fish, beaver, caribou, walrus, cranberries, and wild rhubarb. "When scientists investigated the native diet of the Eskimos in this region it was found to be free from insecticides." Eskimo bodies are nevertheless contaminated.

> When some of the Eskimos themselves were checked by analysis of fat samples, small residues of DDT were found. . . . The reason for this was clear. The fat samples were taken from people who had left their native villages to enter the United States Public Health Service Hospital in Anchorage for surgery. There the ways of civilization prevailed, and the meals in the hospital were found to contain as much DDT as those in the most populous city. (179–80)

DDT in the food chain is a public health problem, and the United States Public Health Service is itself contaminated. "For their brief stay in civilization the Eskimos were rewarded with a taint of poison" (180).

Silent Spring acknowledges that the science regarding chemical pesticides is still being created. But we already know enough to confront the chemical companies and the governmental agencies that collude with them. We know, for example, that it's wrong to spray Japanese beetles with chemicals. The beetle, which appeared in New Jersey early in the twentieth century and spread across the country, can be controlled by biological means. It dies when fed milky spore disease. This is not, in 1962, a hypothesis. Fourteen eastern states have done it. Those eastern states are lucky, because they were attacked by the beetle before chemical sprays were available. The eastern states put money up front, waited a year or two for milky spore disease to develop, and learned to live with the small numbers of beetles that survived.

> Why, then, with this impressive record in the East were the same procedures not tried in Illinois and the other midwestern states where the chemical battle of the beetles is being waged with such fury?
>
> We are told that inoculation with milky spore disease is "too expensive"— although no one found it so in the 14 eastern states in the 1940s. And by what sort of accounting was the "too expensive" judgment reached? (98)

Carson exposes the accounting that focuses on short-term benefits and ignores long-term costs. The chemical industry markets chemicals as efficient and inexpensive. In the short run, in the first year, spraying chemicals on Japanese beetles really is cheaper than sickening them with milky spore disease. There are, however, a couple of inconveniences to spraying. The spray kills everything in sight—not only beetles, but also birds and animals. Also, you have to keep spraying every year, more and more, with stronger and stronger doses, to keep up with the resistance that beetles develop. From a profit-making point of view, however, chemical spraying has the great advantage that it has to be perpetually renewed and intensified. Carson appropriates the concept of planned obsolescence, which was introduced into mainstream culture in the 1920s. "Those who want immediate results, at whatever cost, will doubtless continue to use chemical methods against the beetle. So will those who favor the modern trend to built-in obsolescence, for chemical control is self-perpetuating, needing frequent and costly repetition" (98).

Acting as public prosecutor, Carson indicts the enablers of the chemical industry, the scientists who have ignored the promise of natural control and joined the rush for chemical control. Digging deeper, she moves from scientific problems to the problem of scientists. Science, for her, is a way of seeing. If most scientists do not see the consequences of the growing use of chemical pesticides, there must be a scientific explanation for their blindness. Researching the researchers, she indicts scientists who have allowed themselves to be corrupted.

> Most of those best fitted to develop natural controls and assist in putting them into effect have been too busy laboring in the more exciting vineyards of chemical control. . . . Why should this be? The major chemical companies are pouring money into the universities to support research on insecticides. This creates attractive fellowships for graduate students and attractive staff positions. (258–59)

In 1961, in his farewell address, President Eisenhower warned not only of the military-industrial complex but also of the role of funding in pushing university research in a military direction.[3] In 1962, in *Silent Spring*, Carson similarly warns that the chemical industry has subverted science through research grants and fellowships. Although biological control is cheaper, safer, and more effective in the long run, chemical control has become more alluring. Biological control studies "do not promise anyone the fortunes that are to be made in the chemical industry." Many leading entomologists, who should know better, are enthusiastic advocates of chemical control. "Inquiry into the background of some of these men reveals that their entire research program is supported by the chemical industry" (259).

Attacking the chemical industry, Carson realizes she will be attacked. Experts for hire will dismiss her evidence and ridicule her reasoning. She may be sued; she and her agent discuss that possibility while she's writing the book. She has to be cautious in exposing the federal government's collusion with industry. Marjorie Spock's case made clear just how aggressive the government could be, if attacked frontally. Wanting to reduce her legal vulnerability, Carson does not slam the US Department of Agriculture nearly as hard as she would have liked.[4] As a fighter, she knows when to attack and when to dance away.

The Inner Environment

Silent Spring focuses not only on what chemicals are doing to our bodies but also on what the propaganda for chemicals is doing to our minds. Propaganda for chemicals seeps inside us. Advertising and marketing make us stupid, argues Carson, anticipating Betty Friedan. We are manipulated to act against our own interests. Here Carson appropriates the concept of "the hidden persuaders," popularized by Vance Packard in his 1957 book.[5] "Lulled by the soft sell and the hidden persuader, the average citizen is seldom aware of the deadly materials with which he is surrounding himself" (174). And though she uses the standard pronoun "he," Carson, like Friedan, is especially talking about marketing that makes women stupid. It was a housewife who sprayed her basement with so much DDT that she killed herself (228–29).

Experts in the media explain that modern life is better because it's easy to kill any bug or weed. If women, as consumers of products for home and garden, do not participate enthusiastically in the modern age of chemistry, they are made to feel guilty. If they stand against progress, there is something the matter with them. Even if they just stand aside, and don't use toxic chemicals in their garden or kitchen, they are negligent, irresponsible, retrograde. "Gardening is now firmly linked with the super poisons. Every hardware store, garden-supply shop, and supermarket has rows of insecticides for every conceivable horticultural situation. Those who fail to make wide use of this array of lethal sprays and dusts are by implication remiss" (176).

As a result of propaganda, and the ease of killing, farmers as well as housewives are becoming increasingly addicted to chemical pesticides and herbicides. In the early days of chemical spraying, birds died as innocent bystanders.

As the habit of killing grows—the resort to "eradicating" any creature that may annoy or inconvenience us—birds are more and more finding themselves a

> direct target of poison rather than an incidental one. . . . In southern Indiana,
> for example, a group of farmers went together in the summer of 1959 to engage
> a spray plane to treat an area of river bottomland with parathion. (126)

Parathion, an organic phosphate, kills birds, bees, and humans. The farmers wanted to rid themselves of blackbirds, which ate their corn. There was an alternative: they could have planted a variety of corn whose deep-seated ears protect against birds. Killing was simpler. The planes hired by Indiana farmers killed 65,000 birds.

Aerial spraying of farmland is reminiscent of "North by Northwest," the 1959 movie in which a spray plane tries to kill Cary Grant. Carson doesn't refer to the film. But in recounting the history of chemical pesticides, she emphasizes their use against people. In the late 1930s, a German chemist developed organic phosphates as insecticides. The German government realized "almost immediately" they would be useful in killing people, as nerve gas (18). And now, in post-war America, we repeat the cycle. Start by using chemicals sprayed from the air on bugs. Move to spraying birds. And then? The United States began quietly using chemical herbicides, including Agent Orange, in Vietnam just before *Silent Spring* was published, and napalm two years later.[6] Carson would not have been surprised.

Using chemicals to kill is habit forming. Like addicts, we end up doing things that make absolutely no sense.

> We are told that the enormous and expanding use of pesticides is necessary to
> maintain farm production. Yet is our real problem not one of *overproduction*?
> Our farms, despite measures to remove acreages from production and to pay
> farmers *not* to produce, have yielded such a staggering excess of crops that
> the American taxpayer in 1962 is paying out more than one billion dollars a
> year as the total carrying cost of the surplus-food storage program. (9; italics
> in the original)

The Department of Agriculture asserts that as more land is retired from production, the more necessary becomes the "use of chemicals to obtain maximum production on the land retained in crops" (9). This is crazy and contradictory. American taxpayers pay farmers to use less land so that farmers use more chemicals on the remaining land, thereby poisoning the environment and us. Appealing to ordinary citizens over the heads of government, Carson expands and deepens the attempts to limit the chemical spraying of our crops, forests, gardens, and homes. Her job is to clean our minds of the propaganda and help us think clearly about alternatives, so that we can break our dependence on chemicals. Unless we become clean, there is no hope for cleaning up our outer world.

While propaganda is harming our minds, carcinogenic chemicals are harming our bodies. Cancer is on the increase because of the dramatic increase in man-made chemicals in our food, air, and water. "No longer are exposures to dangerous chemicals occupational alone; they have entered the environment of everyone—even of children as yet unborn" (221). Cancer is the punchline of *Silent Spring*. Carson saves the cancer chapter for the later part of the book, building up to it, using italics when she gets there. "A quarter century ago, cancer in children was considered a medical rarity. *Today, more American school children die of cancer than from any other disease*" (221). Is this the world into which we want our children and grandchildren to be born?

As our air, water, and food become saturated with carcinogens, people hope for a cure. But Carson considers this approach too passive. She points to an analogy with the movement against infectious disease. Doctors and citizens launched a successful attack in the late nineteenth century. "Most infectious diseases have now been brought under a reasonable degree of control and some have been eliminated. This brilliant medical achievement came about by an attack that was twofold—that stressed prevention as well as cure" (240). Instead of waiting for a cure, we need to go on the offensive against cancer by preventing the use of carcinogenic chemicals. Research on a cure, or a treatment, is necessary for those who (like Carson) already have cancer. "But for those not yet touched by the disease and certainly for the generations as yet unborn, prevention is the imperative need" (243). It won't be easy, because chemicals have become part of our way of life—and therefore cancer has become part of our way of life.

Many people despair of the long struggle to limit the use of pesticides. They hope the problem will go away, or resolve itself. "The hopeful question is sometimes asked, 'If insects can become resistant to chemicals, could human beings do the same thing?' Theoretically they could; but since this would take hundreds or even thousands of years, the comfort to those living now is slight" (274). Insects become resistant to chemical sprays quickly because they reproduce quickly. Resistance takes many generations to develop. Humans reproduce so slowly that we will continue to poison and kill ourselves. The really hopeful question is not about humans developing resistance in the way insects do, but about whether humans will use our powers of understanding and protest—our capacity for resistance of a different kind—to end chemical spraying.

We put so many chemicals into our air, water, and food that we are changing our bodies. Carson focuses on the damage that chemicals do to cells and
genes. She did not say much about the way chemicals alter hormones, because
the key scientific breakthrough about hormonal disruption was still three
decades away.[7] As we learn what chemicals do to our hormones, we build on
what Carson already taught us—that man-made chemicals are altering the
ecology of our bodies. That's the bad news.

It is also, according to *Silent Spring*, the good news.

> In one important respect the outlook is more encouraging than the situation
> regarding infectious disease at the turn of the century. The world was then full
> of disease germs, as today it is full of carcinogens. But man did not put the
> germs into the environment, and his role in spreading them was involuntary.
> In contrast, man *has* put the vast majority of carcinogens into the environment,
> and he can, if he wishes, eliminate many of them. The chemical agents of cancer
> have become entrenched in our world in two ways: first, and ironically, through
> man's search for a better and easier way of life; second, because the manufacture
> and sales of such chemicals has become an accepted part of our economy and
> our way of life. (242; italics in the text)

We do this to ourselves. We do it in the search for better living through
chemistry. It's no accident that she mimics the industry's favorite slogan. She's
angry and wants us to be angry. Joining the grassroots protests against pesticides, Carson brings protest home to our kitchens and gardens, our food and
water, our minds and bodies, our children and ourselves. The fight that she
joined and briefly led has not gone away. Nor have the issues that she raised:
chemical-based agriculture, the resistance developed by insects, man-made
carcinogens in our environment, the arrogant project of dominating nature.
To a remarkable degree, she set the terms of the ongoing struggle.

Silent Spring and *Death and Life*

Like *Death and Life*, *Silent Spring* is a fighting book. Both books satirize the
enemy. *Death and Life* imagines Robert Moses as an aging belle. *Silent Spring*
mocks the high priests of the religion of progress.

> The chemical weed killers are a bright new toy. They work in a spectacular way;
> they give a giddy sense of power over nature to those who wield them; and
> as for the long-range and less obvious effects—these are easily brushed aside

as the baseless imaginings of pessimists. The "agricultural engineers" speak blithely of "chemical plowing" in a world that is urged to beat its plowshares into spray guns. (68–69)

But even when using ridicule and humor, Carson is not playful. Careful, earnest, sober, grave, she is only nine years older than Jacobs, but she seems much older. For Carson, the stakes are too high for fooling around. Fighting killers, she is dead serious. It is at once her strength and her limitation.

Avoiding the first person, Carson rigorously excludes herself from *Silent Spring*. Jacobs writes playfully, often in the first person, using her own experiences as examples of the experience of ordinary people, inviting us to laugh along with her, to see through her eyes. *Death and Life* celebrates ordinary New Yorkers, from her sister Betty to the settlement-house worker William Kirk. Carson excludes the names of nonscientists from her book, though acknowledging she could not have written it without them. Carson and Jacobs differ profoundly in goal as well as style. Jacobs agrees with mainstream economists that growth is the aim; her argument with them is about how to get there. She is pro-growth. Carson questions the very ideal of economic growth. On this point, the two activists are irreducibly opposed.

Yet each contrasts the organic growth of interdependent life forms, in intricate balance, with the arrogant imposition of order from above. Their thinking converges around the conviction that imposed order is deadly. Both of their titles refer to death. *The Death and Life of Great American Cities* (1961) and *Silent Spring* (1962) examine the death that occurs when experts and authorities deduce down from the idea of progress and the ideal of order, instead of reasoning up from the diversity of existing life forms and the order already implicit in them.

Both books make the invisible visible, revealing the underlying connections between living things. According to *Death and Life*, cities express a hidden order. "Their intricate order—a manifestation of the freedom of countless numbers of people to make and carry out countless plans—is in many ways a great wonder. We ought not to be reluctant to make this living collection of interdependent uses, this freedom, this life, more understandable for what it is."[8] To strengthen the forces of life, and the connections between living things, Carson and Jacobs draw on ecology.

As early as 1950, Carson referred to "an ecological concept" and an "ecological approach."[9] In 1958, beginning research on pesticides, she thanked a scientific ally for introducing her to the latest book of British ecologist Charles Elton, *Ecology of Invasions*. "It cuts through all the foggy discussion of insect

pests and their control like a north wind."[10] Toward the end of *Silent Spring*,
Carson locates the book in a river of thought, the emerging ecological science. Ecological solutions to controlling pests are "based on an understanding
of the living organisms they seek to control, and of the whole fabric of life to
which these organisms belong." Ecological thinking is not new, she knows; it
goes back at least to Elton's first work, in the 1920s. But after WWII, ecological
approaches suffered an eclipse, "a period of drought," due to the enthusiasm for
chemical solutions. "Now at last, as it has become apparent that the headless
and unrestrained use of chemicals is a greater danger to ourselves than to the
targets, the river which is the science of biotic control flows again" (278–79).

Toward the end of *Death and Life*, Jacobs describes the current of thought
of which her book is part. "Cities happen to be problems in organized complexity, like the life sciences."[11] Biological ways of thinking "have become part
of the intellectual fund of our times. . . . A growing number of people have
begun, gradually, to think of cities as problems in organized complexity—
organisms that are replete with unexamined but obviously interconnected,
and surely understandable, relationships. This book is one manifestation of
that idea."[12] Writing a new foreword to *Death and Life*, two decades later, she
says simply: "At some point along the trail [of researching the book] I realized
I was studying the ecology of cities."[13]

Embracing ecology, Carson and Jacobs expose the consequences of the
dominant idea of progress. The superhighway that destroys a neighborhood's
ecology and the chemical spray that destroys a natural ecosystem are products
of an idea of progress that is mechanical and linear, imposed from above on
the diversity and interdependence of life, and rooted in what Carson derides
as "Neanderthal" or "Stone Age" ways of thinking (297). Carson and Jacobs
share the belief that only ecological ways of thinking can reverse the decline
of what each of them loves. What they love is very different, even opposed:
dense urban life on the one hand, unspoiled nature on the other. But they
agree: homogeneity is death. Diversity is life. To Carson, it was a mistake to
plant large areas solely with a single species of tree, making them more vulnerable to disease, and it is a bigger mistake now to spray them with chemicals. To Jacobs, it was a mistake to build up a whole neighborhood at the
same time, so that it got old at once, and it is a bigger mistake now to tear it
all down.

Carson emphasizes that nature needs time to adapt, to heal itself, to create a new balance; massive, repetitive chemical attacks give it no time. Jacobs
emphasizes that neighborhoods need time to grow and adapt. People need
time to develop the ties that make a neighborhood safe, vital, and attractive.

It has to do with the relationships that are formed among people, so they can communicate with each other, so they can work together in an emergency, if necessary, and so they can also enjoy each other. Now, in a place . . . where relationships of this kind are constantly disrupted—don't have time to grow, don't have time to form, don't have time to engender the trust that they need, and the confidence and practice, then you can never get a community that can work.[14]

When people are uprooted by urban renewal or a major highway, their losses are devastating. "Relocated people are destroyed or set back in their social beings, for it takes a long time to get where they were before as social beings in their new neighborhood."[15] Jane and Robert Jacobs bought a run-down house on Hudson Street in 1947 and slowly transformed it. "We did a lot of the work ourselves. We did it as we could afford it. That's different from urban renewal which is done all at once."[16]

Carson, like Jacobs, respects the wisdom of ordinary people. "A glance at the Letters-from-Readers column of newspapers almost anywhere that spraying is being done makes clear the fact that citizens . . . often show a keener understanding of the dangers and inconsistencies of spraying than do the officials who order it" (113). Ordinary people—"the bird watcher, the suburbanite who derives joy from the birds in his garden, the hunter, the fisherman"—know better than the experts because they reason from lived experience. (86) Carson cites farmers who insist—against official denial—that spraying fire ants also kills livestock (167–68).

Like Jacobs, Carson doesn't want ordinary people to feel guilty for opposing the forces of progress. We are not selfish, irrational, or backward when we defend our neighborhoods or our gardens, our cities or forests, our sidewalks or birds. The experts want us to mistrust ourselves and trust them. Jacobs and Carson confirm our misgivings about urban renewal and chemical spraying and encourage us to fight back. They embolden us to trust ourselves and question authority. Separately, side by side, the two women undermine faith in the 1950s' idea of progress and in the experts who propound it.

Death and Life and *Silent Spring* challenge the collusion between business and government. Jacobs and Carson want citizen protest to disrupt the cozy relationship between public officials and private corporations. Their emphasis is different. Jacobs focuses especially on government bureaucrats like Moses, whereas Carson focuses on corporations like the chemical companies. But Carson is also critical of the Department of Agriculture for shilling for the companies and Jacobs is critical of developers who make secret deals with the city bureaucracy. Their underlying point is not so different: for democracy to flourish, the government must not be in bed with the moneyed interests.

Writing and speaking as democratic activists, Carson and Jacobs take pipsqueak protests to a new level, where they cannot be ignored. Like Ella Baker, they inaugurate the activism of the 1960s. Their approach is radical, in Baker's sense of the word: they go to the root of the problem of progress. But their aims are conservative: to restore balance and repair a broken world. Baker, by contrast, is revolutionary. The equality that she hopes to create has never existed. She doesn't want to repair a broken world but to make a new one. And Betty Friedan, despite her hesitations, is also revolutionary.

8

The Feminine Mystique, 1963

Detective

Bringing five housewives together for coffee, Friedan asks about their lives.

> On an April morning in 1959, I heard a mother of four, having coffee with four
> other mothers in a suburban development fifteen miles from New York, say in
> a tone of quiet desperation, "the problem." And the others knew, without words,
> that she was not talking about a problem with her husband, or her children, or
> her home. Suddenly they realized that they all shared the same problem, the
> problem that has no name. They began, hesitantly, to talk about it. Later, after
> they had picked up their children at nursery school and taken them home to
> nap, two of the women cried, in sheer relief, just to know they were not alone.[1]

Friedan contrasts the known quantities of the women's lives with their
invisible suffering. Her account begins with concrete facts. 1959. Fifteen miles.
Four children. Five women. Two cry. But it is really about the opposite: a
problem for which there is no name, a suffering that feels unreal even to the
women who experience it. By actively listening to the women—asking not
just about the facts but about the meaning hidden behind the facts—she helps
them make the invisible visible.

She tells this story early in the first chapter of *The Feminine Mystique*.
She regards it as the key to the book, which will give a name to the problem
that has no name. Like Rachel Carson, who took seriously the complaints of
the prisoners who were fed DDT and the complaints of the housewife who
sprayed her basement, Friedan takes the complaints of these housewives

seriously. Her book will explain what happened to them, or more precisely, what was done to them. This little group that Friedan brings together in 1959 anticipates by almost a decade the consciousness-raising groups of the women's liberation movement. It is a beginning of the end of silence.

Friedan locates herself outside the story. She is a suburban mother too, with three children. But in Westchester, she is a reporter, an outsider, as she was in Stamford during the general strike of 1946. She says on the first page: "My methods were simply those of a reporter on the trail of a story" (7). As a young journalist, she would listen to working women and men. Trying to discover why suburban housewives are disappearing from their own lives, she listens to them. She goes from suburb to suburb, questioning the victims. "I feel as if I don't exist," a housewife tells her (16). "The problem is always being the children's mommy or the minister's wife and never being myself," says another (23). "I just don't feel alive," says a third (17). Not myself, not existing, not alive: it is almost a murder mystery.

Friedan sees herself as a detective solving a crime. As a child, she played girl detective. "This was the era of Nancy Drew."[2] As a young labor reporter, she went undercover. And as an undergraduate and graduate student in psychology, she learned to look between the lines. "That ability to follow leads, clues from many different fields, was invaluable once I truly committed myself to solving this mystery."[3] By this mystery, she means: what is happening to American women and who is doing it to them?

She questions the suburban women, who are the victims. She also questions the authorities. "This is the first clue to the mystery: the problem cannot be understood in the generally accepted terms by which scientists have studied women, doctors have treated them, counselors have advised them, and writers have written about them" (22). Even when listening to male authorities, Friedan tries to hear the voices of American women.

> I found many clues by talking to suburban doctors, gynecologists, obstetricians, child-guidance clinicians, pediatricians, high-school guidance counselors, college professors, marriage counselors, psychiatrists and ministers—questioning them not on their theories, but on their actual experiences in treating American women. (26)

The theories of these professional men are not helpful—are, in fact, part of the problem, the problem that has no name. But they have privileged access to women; they have been told things, even if they didn't really know how to listen. What do suburban housewives tell their doctors, therapists, and ministers? They complain about boredom, about sleeping too much without really being tired, about their husbands. They say they are anxious, blue, depressed, desperate (20–27). Listening between the lines to the condescending theories of male experts, Friedan hears the agonized cries of women.

In recognizing that the pain of the women is real, *The Feminine Mystique* takes an enormous step. Then it puts their suffering in historical context. Before and during World War II, women were becoming increasingly educated and professional. Then came the postwar reaction. After World War II, the professional advances made by American women were halted. More girls began college in the 1950s than in previous decades, but fewer finished, and fewer went to graduate school. Compared to female college students in the decades "before World War II, the Great Divide," more girls dropped out of college to get married in the 1950s, and more got married and became housewives as soon as they graduated (142).

Women not only did not make progress in the fifties; they went backward. In an earlier, less careful draft of the book, Friedan was even more explicit, calling it a "counter-revolution." The feminist movement of the first decades of the twentieth century empowered women to be ambitious, to pursue education and careers. After WWII, "educated women turned their backs on the careers generations of feminists fought to open to them; young women voluntarily gave up the education once considered essential to their emancipation."[4]

How were the gains reversed? She uncovers a deliberate campaign. Almost invisibly, women were coerced into submission. "For fifteen years and longer, there has been a propaganda campaign, as unanimous in this democratic nation as in the most efficient of dictatorships, to give women 'prestige' as housewives" (244). This propaganda campaign is what she calls the feminine mystique. The mystique is viciously antiwomen, all the more so because it pretends to valorize women for having uniquely feminine traits.

The Feminine Mystique quotes *Modern Woman: The Lost Sex*, a 1947 screed against career women by Marynia Farnham and Ferdinand Lundberg. *Modern Woman* openly called for propaganda to get women back in the home. The American postwar project, like the German prewar project, pushed women back into the role of housewife. The form of repression in democratic America was different than in Nazi Germany, but the aim was the same: "to get women back in the home again, not like the Nazis, by ordering them there, but by 'propaganda with a view to restoring woman's sense of prestige and self-esteem as women'" (243).

Friedan criticizes Freudian psychiatrists for reducing girls and women to biology. She's particularly angry at Farnham, a woman psychiatrist who helped legitimize the campaign against career women. Later, Farnham will be exposed in *Rosie the Riveter*, the powerful 1980 documentary about the coordinated propaganda campaign to get women back into the home after WWII. *Rosie the Riveter* effectively extends Friedan's thesis to working-class and Black women who thrived during the war on jobs previously reserved for men, women who are largely absent from *The Feminine Mystique*. But the power of the film comes from the great insight articulated by Friedan: the postwar feminine mystique is not conservative but reactionary, not a continuation of traditional roles for women but a conscious backlash against the gains that women were making toward equality.

She critiques functionalist social scientists as well as the Freudians. Postwar sociologists and anthropologists claim to objectively examine how different social roles function together. Turning description into prescription, what is into what should be, they conclude that being smart and ambitious is a hindrance to femininity—to getting and keeping a man. "By giving an absolute meaning and a sanctimonious value to the generic term 'women's role,' functionalists put American women into a kind of deep freeze—like Sleeping Beauties, waiting for a Prince Charming to waken them" (118). These social scientists bury American women alive.

As a detective, Friedan examines the data on girls dropping out of college; questions expert witnesses; and critiques functionalists and Freudians. She also visits the crime scene. "I saw the change, a very real one, when I went back to my own college in 1959, to live for a week with the students in a campus house at Smith." When she asks students which courses excite them, a graduating senior, a blonde, "looking at me as if I were some prehistoric dinosaur," patiently explains.

> Girls don't get excited about things like that anymore. We don't want careers. Our parents expect us to go to college. Everybody goes. You're a social outcast at home if you don't. But a girl who got serious about anything she studied—like, wanting to go on and do research—would be peculiar, unfeminine. I guess everyone wants to graduate with a ring on her finger. That's the important thing. (144–45)

Visiting other colleges, Friedan finds the same lack of involvement of female students in their studies. She interprets this disconnect as "a defense, a refusal to become involved." In a provocative analogy, she describes students going through the motions: "As a woman who unconsciously thinks sex is a sin is not there, is somewhere else, as she goes through the motions of sex, so these girls are somewhere else" (146).

But why? Why do modern girls resist the excitement of ideas and narrowly focus on becoming engaged and married? When Friedan was a student, from 1938 to 1942, she and her friends didn't have to choose between being smart and being popular. "In my time, popular girls who spent many weekends at Yale were often just as serious about their work as the 'brains'" (146). Smith girls were passionate about learning. Back in the age of the dinosaurs, ideas were sexy. "We used to sit for hours arguing what-is-truth, art for art's sake, religion, sex, war and peace, Freud and Marx" (145). What has changed since then?

A curtain seemed to descend at the end of the 1940s, and the curious, involved, independent girls disappeared behind it. In her earlier draft, she cited a faculty member at Smith, who identified 1949 as the turning point. "The class of 1949 was the last Smith class that felt a sense of involvement in social issues. While former generations would be Freudian one day, Marxist the next, and by the next week scholastic theologians, the present student generation has little of that sense of involvement in social issues."[5]

The Feminine Mystique attacks college presidents and professors for taking "the mystique as the social scientists handed it to them" and imposing it on their female students (149–50). Swallowing the feminine mystique whole, they have becoming "sex-directed educators." Her term is intended to be ambiguous. On the one hand, "sex-directed educators" means that even the top women's colleges are backing away from educating the female sex to its full potential. On the other hand, it means that in place of the old intellectual excitement, there is a new emphasis on sexual satisfaction. "Under the influence of the feminine mystique, some college presidents and professors charged with the education of women had become more concerned with their students' future capacity for sexual orgasm than with their future use of trained intelligence" (148). Being smart becomes the opposite of being sexy.

These college presidents and professors are mostly men, who find "this mystique a positive comfort, a confirmation of [their] own prejudices." But what about female presidents and professors? They are too vulnerable to oppose the trend. The fact that they are college teachers or administrators suggests that they did not put their husbands and children ahead of their careers, which is bad. If they never had husbands and children in the first place, it's worse: "*Modern Woman: The Lost Sex* would forbid them even to teach." Most women educators go along with the new dogma, rather than having "their authority as teachers—and as women—questioned" (150).

The higher culture and higher education direct propaganda at girls and women, telling them to fulfill their destiny as wives and mothers. Looking for more clues, Friedan turns to popular culture. What does a girl or woman learn about herself from popular women's magazines? (Here too, as she noted in the draft but refrains from spelling out in the book, "With almost no exceptions, the women's magazines are edited by men."[6]) The nonfiction in women's magazines recycles *Modern Woman: The Lost Sex*, "ad nauseum" (111). What about the fiction? Working backward, "I went through issue after issue of the three major women's magazines . . . without finding a single heroine who had a career, a commitment to any work, art, profession, or mission in the world, other than 'Occupation Housewife'" (38). Finally, in 1949, in a story in the *Ladies Home Journal* about a girl who loves to fly planes, "I found the last clear note of the passionate search for individual identity that a career seems to have symbolized in the pre-1950 decades" (34). 1949 is the year the Smith professor identified as the last time students felt a sense of involvement, and the year that Friedan, looking back years later, will identify as the turning point in women's retreat into domesticity.[7] Around 1949, the era of independent, ambitious women ended and the era of the feminine mystique began.

Friedan argues persuasively that the feminine mystique is a backlash. She devotes an early chapter, "The Passionate Journey," to documenting the vital, combative, and effective feminist movement in the first half of the century, which broke down barriers and opened doors (73–94). By midcentury, many American women were educated and fully capable of participating in the world. Simultaneously, modern technology was making housework less time consuming, freeing women for more meaningful pursuits. "The basic paradox of the feminine mystique" is "that it emerged to glorify women's role as housewife at the very moment when the barriers to her full participation in society were lowered." When freedom and equality were within reach, a new cultural consensus glorified housework, child care, and sex. "Did the new mystique of separate-but-equal femininity arise because the growth of women in America could no longer be repressed by the old mystique of feminine inferiority?" (229). The new repression and re-segregation of American women is more vicious than the old, because American women were on the verge of real freedom and equality.

The postwar propaganda campaign gets inside women and girls. The blonde at Smith internalizes the propaganda. She believes she would be less sexy if she got serious. She does not need a stormtrooper to hold her back; she holds herself back, and doesn't even know she's doing it. As Friedan explained in the earlier draft, "younger women educated since the war conform so completely to this ideal of femininity that on college campuses today women who take their education seriously . . . are considered freaks."[8]

By confining some of her sharpest formulations to the draft and omitting them from the book, Friedan could be said to be holding herself back. But she knows she is doing it, and why. She knows that her book—because it stands up for women—is going to be attacked, and she is going to be ridiculed.

No female is immune to the pervasive propaganda, no woman or girl is safe. Even the gutsy few who don't stay home when they get married and have children are not immune.

> The most powerful weapon of the feminine mystique is the argument that she rejects her husband and her children by working outside the home. If, for any reason, her child becomes ill or her husband has troubles of his own, the feminine mystique, insidious voices in the community, and even the woman's own inner voice will blame her "rejection" of the housewife's role. (340)

One woman gave up a good job after her husband accused her of wanting to "compete" with him, "to wear the pants." But the woman's drive, her ambition, was too great to be confined to the housewife role. She became successful again, this time as director of a local theater group. One day, when she was at rehearsal, her son was hit by a car. "She blamed herself for the accident, and so she gave up the little-theater group" (347). The feminine mystique shapes the thoughts and feelings of girls and women, making those who resist feel guilty and ashamed.

As Friedan assembles her case, the pieces fit. Social scientists and Freudian psychiatrists warn women of the dangers of competing with men, and educators and popular culture drive the message home. The postwar counterattack against women has killed the drive for equality, resulting in "the mass burial of American women" (351). Escaping freedom, retreating into domesticity, women renounce being fully alive, fully themselves. Friedan sums up her case: "Freedom is a frightening thing. . . . Why should a woman bother to be anything more than a wife and mother if all the forces of her culture tell her she doesn't have to, will be better off not to, grow up?" (195).

And yet, like a good detective, she is not satisfied. "Some months ago, as I began to fit together the puzzle of women's retreat to home, I had the feeling I was missing something." How has the powerful drive for freedom and equality, which goes back a century, been shut down? "The energy behind the feminist movement was too dynamic merely to have trickled dry; it must have been turned off, diverted, by something more powerful." What drives the counterrevolution against women? "What powers it all?" (197).

In college, Friedan and her friends talked of Marx and Freud. As a young labor reporter, she studied Marxian economics at the Communist-sponsored

Jefferson School in New York.[9] Trying now to solve the mystery, she cannot use Freud; his followers are among the perpetrators of the feminine mystique. Instead, she channels Marx. After WWII, to keep the economy growing, women were encouraged to become housewives with an endless appetite for things.

> Why is it never said that the really crucial function, the really important role that women serve as housewives is *to buy more things for the house?* In all the talk of femininity and women's role, one forgets that the real business of America is business. . . . It would take a clever economist to figure out what would keep our affluent economy going if the housewife market began to fall off, just as an economist would have to figure out what to do if there were no threat of war." (197–98; italics in the text)

Writing five years after John Kenneth Galbraith, in *The Affluent Society*, described how demand was created by advertising, and two years after President Eisenhower warned of the insatiable military-industrial complex, Friedan adds her own radical truth: our economy depends on girls growing into insatiable consumers.

Housewives make ideal customers because they are never satisfied. Having given up on their potential for a truly creative and fulfilling life, they are in a permanent state of frustration. The trick, performed so well by advertising, is to turn that frustration into shopping. In the draft, she asks: "Are the roots of the sexual counter-revolution economic?" Whatever the origins, "the new feminine mystique is creating its own economics (as some shrewd advertising men can testify)."[10] In the book, setting aside the question of causality, she stresses the harm caused by advertising men. "The manipulators and their clients in American business can hardly be accused of creating the feminine mystique. But they are the most powerful of its perpetrators" (218).

> Marketing men are criminals.
> The real crime, no matter how profitable for the American economy, is the callous and growing acceptance of the manipulator's advice "to get them young"—the television commercials that children sing, the big beautiful ads almost as easy as "Look, Sally, Look," the magazines deliberately designed to turn teenage girls into housewife buyers of things before they grow up to become women. (221)

Marketers manipulate girls into becoming insatiable customers. Friedan discovers the smoking gun. "I went to see a man who is paid approximately a million dollars a year for his professional services in manipulating the emotions of women to serve the needs of business" (198). Ernest Dichter, head of the Institute for Motivational Research, explains to her how he does it. Friedan, posing as a journalist doing a friendly magazine piece, asks questions and listens, without allowing her anger to show. "Properly manipulated ('if you are not afraid of that word,' he said), American housewives can be given the sense of identity, purpose, creativity, the self-realization, even the sexual joy that they lack—by the buying of things" (199).

Dichter began gathering information about girls and women in 1945, at the very beginning of the postwar era. Feeling no shame, he gives Friedan free access to his reports, based on 300,000 in-depth interviews with women. She paraphrases one conclusion: "In the fifties came the revolutionary discovery of the teenage market. . . . If the pattern of 'happiness through things' could be established when these women were young enough, they could be safely encouraged to go out and get a part-time job to help their husbands pay for all the things they buy" (209). The formerly independent career woman was replaced by the malleable consumer. One of his reports (and this time she quotes) celebrates the disappearance of "the woman who clamored for equality—almost for identity in every sphere of life, the woman who reacted to 'domestic slavery' with indignation and vehemence" (203–4).

Case closed.

Inequality

One of Dichter's reports describes the challenge of selling a woman a new cleaning device. Friedan comments ironically:

> The difficulty is to give her the "sense of achievement" of "ego enhancement" she has been persuaded to seek in the housewife "profession," when, in actuality, according to the survey, "her time-consuming task, housekeeping, is not only endless, it is a task for which society hires the lowliest, least-trained, most trodupon individuals and groups. . . . Anyone with a strong enough back (and a small enough brain) can do these manual chores." (205–6; ellipses in Friedan's text)

The lowly women from trod-upon groups, who clean the homes of middleclass people, are no longer Friedan's concern. She assumes there will always be such women. She is not fighting for the maids, as she did as a Smith student. She wants educated, middle-class, suburban wives to work outside the home and leave the cleaning to those who lack the skills or intelligence for more creative and meaningful work. Friedan's critique in *The Feminist Mystique* of the growing inequality between the sexes presupposes the ongoing inequality between classes.

In the 1940s, watching the daughter of a Westinghouse worker dance on the picket line, she highlighted the role of working-class women in the struggle of working people. The movement she described was a creative expression of people who were pushing back against a class society. That was her story, a story of class conflict. But now, in 1963, she is telling the story of people like herself, middle-class educated women. Her focus shifts from one form of inequality to another.

In 1963, Gerda Lerner is teaching the first academic course in women's history. After reading *The Feminine Mystique*, Lerner writes to Friedan with excitement about "your splendid book." She is moved by Friedan's critique of what American culture is doing to women. "The 'experts' of the feminine mystique have had it their way for far too long." She recognizes that Friedan, like Carson, offers a new way of seeing. "You have done for women what Rachel Carson did for birds and trees." But Lerner also takes Friedan to task. "You address yourself solely to the problems of middle class, college-educated women. . . . Working women, especially Negro women, labor not only under the disadvantages imposed by the feminine mystique, but under the more pressing disadvantages of economic discrimination."[11] Many years later, Friedan will defend herself: "I made no attempt to make my basic study anything other than middle class. My early political experience writing for the so-called working class had taught me that ideas, styles, *change* in America comes from the middle class."[12] By the time she began to research and write *The Feminine Mystique*, the idea that change could come from the working class no longer made sense to her.

Lerner, like Friedan and Ella Baker, was influenced by Marxism and class struggle when she was young.[13] All three learned, early on, to take working-class values, modes of organization, and struggles seriously. For Baker and Lerner, it was never either/or. Baker used the idea of class to deepen her understanding of race. Lerner saw her analysis of class and race as integral to her advocacy for women. She retained her commitment to economic and racial justice, even as she became a founder of the field of women's history and embraced the solidarity of women. But Friedan abandons class analysis when she focuses on women. When she calls, in *The Feminine Mystique*, for women to work outside the home, she discounts the many working-class women who already do so. They are no longer part of her story. When she advises educated women to reduce the time spent on housework and childcare, she assumes that they will hire less-educated women as helpers. Speaking as a woman against the inequality of women, she reproduces the existing class structure.

And she reproduces the existing division of labor within the home. A few years later, young feminists will argue that both house cleaning and child raising should be shared by men and women. Friedan is not so radical in 1963. She assumes that if a professional woman with a full-time career doesn't hire an uneducated woman to do the housework, she must do it herself, in the evening or on the weekend, perhaps with her daughter's help. Her husband should stick to his work.

> "I wish he wouldn't insist on vacuuming the whole house on Tuesday evenings. It doesn't need it and he could be working on his book," the wife of a college professor told me. A capable social worker herself, she had managed all her professional life to work out ways of caring for her house and children without hiring servants. With her daughter's help, she did her own thorough housecleaning on Saturday; it didn't need vacuuming on Tuesday. (242)

Housework is still women's (and girls') work in *The Feminine Mystique*. One reason the book became popular, Joanne Meyerowitz points out, is that it challenged some, but not all, of the popular assumptions about women's role.[14]

Urging suburban women to reject the separate-but-equal feminine mystique, to get out of the home and go to work, Friedan imagines them still responsible for the home and the children in it. She doesn't want men to share equally in cooking, cleaning, or child care. She only wants women to stop pretending that these activities are vital and meaningful. She mocks "a latter-day Einstein's wife [who] expects her husband to put aside that lifeless theory of relativity and help her with the work that is supposed to be the essence of life itself: diaper the baby and don't forget to rinse the soiled diaper in the toilet before putting it in the diaper pail, and then wax the kitchen floor" (237).

Capable women efficiently manage their careers, their houses, their children. But stay-at-home moms expand the housework to fill the time available. Worse, they hover over the kids and make them passive. Inflating her charges against the feminine mystique, piling on the bodies, Friedan blames the counterrevolution against women for all the ills, real and imagined, of the children. "Over the past fifteen years a subtle and devastating change seems to have taken place in the character of American children" (271). Fifteen years since the propagation of the feminine mystique: "I do not think it is a coincidence that the increasing passivity—and dreamlike unreality—of today's children has become so widespread in the same years" (276).

Critiquing what has been done to the mothers, Friedan ends by deni-
grating the children. "Behind the senseless vandalism, the riots in Florida
at spring vacation, the promiscuity, the rise in teenage venereal disease and
illegitimate pregnancies, the alarming dropouts from high school and college, was this new passivity" (274). Even among the rebels: "Their emotional
passivity was visible in bearded, undisciplined beatnikery" (273). Instead of
listening to young people, she relies on stereotypes. Three years after the sit-
ins at southern lunch counters and the founding of SNCC, one year before
Mississippi Freedom Summer and the mass revolt at Berkeley, *The Feminine
Mystique* dismisses young people as hopelessly passive. As expert and pundit,
Friedan does no better than the experts and pundits whom she skewers.

In 1961, Jessica Mitford reported on the activism of the young. "The current
crop of students had gone far to shake the label of apathy and conformity that
had stuck through the fifties." Mitford cited Bay area protests by students against
the House Unamerican Activities Committee and observed the effect of "the
sit-in movement—with its clear-cut goals"—on the conscience, and tactics, of
northern students.[15] Unlike Mitford, Friedan overlooks the independent-minded
student activism at the beginning of the 1960s. She diminishes the young, in
order to highlight the harm that the feminine mystique is doing.

Radical

The Feminine Mystique is nevertheless radical because Friedan listens to
women and takes them seriously. That, in itself, constitutes a fundamental
break with the status quo.

Baker, Jacobs, and Carson were strong, activist women, but they did not
act for women. They were vulnerable to attack because they were women
who raised fundamental issues and insisted on being taken seriously, but they
were dealing with issues that were recognized as serious. Friedan, writing
as a woman for women, lacks even this minimal insulation. As she writes,
she already hears the laughter. "I took the bus into the city from Rockland
County three days a week and wrote at my carrel in . . . the New York Public
Library, and endured jokes at lunch from the professional writers working in
that room because I was writing a book about women, of all things!"[16] Writing
about women was—by definition—less serious. It belonged on the woman's
page, or in women's magazines, or in romance novels. "They thought it was a
big joke, a book about women."[17] To ask women how they felt and what they
thought, to encourage them to find their voice, to write about big questions
from their point of view, is inherently absurd in 1963.

She expects to be ridiculed because women who stand up for women have always been ridiculed. As she makes clear in the book, the laughter is getting louder.

> It has been popular in recent years to laugh at feminism as one of history's dirty jokes: to pity, sniggering, those old-fashioned feminists who fought for women's rights to higher education, careers, the vote. They were neurotic victims of penis envy who wanted to be men, it is said now. In battling for women's freedom to participate in the major work and decisions of society as the equals of men, they denied their very nature as women, which fulfills itself only through sexual passivity, acceptance of male domination, and nurturing motherhood. (73)

This laughter, this sniggering, is the soundtrack for the backlash against women.

The story of that backlash, and what it has done to women, is her story in *The Feminine Mystique*. Describing what happens when she brought five suburban women together to talk about their despair, and explaining how they got that way, is as far as she gets in the book. She succeeds in naming the problem, but it would take many more women coming together to begin to solve it.

The book doesn't point the way forward. "I had a hard time ending that book," she later admits.[18] Her concluding chapter urges educators to encourage young women to fight back. She wants male and female educators who have embraced and enforced the feminine mystique to lead the charge against it. "In almost every professional field, in business and in the arts and sciences, women are still treated as second-class citizens. It would be a great service to tell girls who plan to work in society to expect this subtle, uncomfortable examination—tell them not to be quiet, and hope it will go away, but fight it" (360–61). Tell them: she cannot imagine girls and young women leading the charge.

In her labor reporting, she described what workers were doing—organizing, striking, protesting—to solve their own problems. In *The Feminine Mystique*, however, she describes not what women are doing but what has been done to them. Her book, unlike the books of Jacobs or Carson, is not an activist book. She does not call for women to band together in solidarity, to fight for their rights. She writes as a lone detective on the trail of a great crime, presenting the book as a singular protest not linked to protests by other women. "There was no activism in that cause when I wrote *The Feminine Mystique*," she will later claim, oversimplifying.[19]

The Feminine Mystique is better at analyzing the crime against women than in proposing what comes next. In 1963, Friedan can only imagine individual solutions. Unlike Baker, Jacobs, and Carson, she does not identify with existing protests, foresee an emerging movement, or acknowledge others from whom she has learned. In her book, she tends to suppress her debt to post-war feminists, including Simone de Beauvoir.[20] The central conceit of herself as a lone detective has the effect of magnifying her contribution and minimizing that of others. This is not only an ego thing, but a political choice. Baker, responding to the lunch-counter sit-ins in 1960, defined her role as facilitating changes that were already happening. Jacobs wrote *Death and Life* in 1961 as an activist among activists, taking protest to a new level. Carson drew on networks of citizen activists, hoping *Silent Spring* (1962) would turn scattered protest into a powerful movement. Unable as yet to imagine solidarity between women, Friedan writes as an independent private eye, operating on her own.

Baker, Jacobs, and Carson aimed, in their interventions, at solving a problem. *The Feminine Mystique* only names the problem. Yet that very act of naming is subversive. Friedan questions women and listens to their answers, encouraging them to articulate the truth they've buried deep inside. "The women I have talked to, who are finally listening to that inner voice, seem in some incredible way to be groping through to a truth that has defied the experts" (26). Like Jacobs, she validates the experience of ordinary people against the experts who claim to know what is good for them. Her point, like Jacobs's point, is to learn to mistrust the experts and trust yourself.

Jacobs revealed what, in the name of improving cities, planners were actually doing to them. Friedan reveals what, in the name of improving women, the new educators are actually doing to them. "One senses that these new sex-directed educators do indeed think of themselves as crusaders—crusaders against the old nontherapeutic, nonfunctional values of the intellect, against the old, demanding, sexless education, which confined itself to the life of the mind and the pursuit of truth, and never even tried to help girls pursue a man, have orgasms, or adjust" (160).

Jacobs took the argument one step further: urban planners hate cities; that's why they want to destroy them. Friedan stops short of saying that the experts maim girls and women because they hate them. She is not so angry. Or more precisely, she cannot yet afford to be so angry. She is already too vulnerable because she is taking women seriously and protesting on their behalf. The fact that Betty Friedan tries to moderate her own anger in the book does not reflect a lack of courage. Rather, it is a testament to the power of the ridicule and dismissal that any ambitious and idealistic woman faced in 1963—ambitious for herself and for women generally.

Before the book is published, two popular women's magazines publish excerpts of *The Feminine Mystique*, and many women write to the magazines in gratitude. Friedan is saying out loud what they sometimes think or feel but dare not say. But more women write to the same magazines—four times as many—denouncing Friedan for not understanding that a woman's essence is selflessness; fulfillment comes through sacrifice for husband and children.[21] Even before *The Feminine Mystique* appears as a book, Friedan knows that not only most men but also most women will reject her argument.

Friedan's agent, Marie Rodell, was also Rachel Carson's agent. Rodell worked closely with Carson, helping prepare Carson and the book to withstand the expected counterattack from industry. But Rodell resigns as Friedan's agent before finding a publisher for *The Feminine Mystique*. Friedan thinks Rodell "was threatened by my book, as many women were."[22] The book threatens women perhaps even more than it threatens men because it says women have made a bad bargain, are living a lie, and are afraid to be free.

Carson's fear of counterattack by the chemical industry made her book better. When she wrote *Silent Spring*, she left out everything that was questionable science and specified everything that seemed true but was not yet proven. Unlike Carson, Friedan cannot feel secure in her mainstream identity and is burdened by a radical past. More than Carson, Friedan anticipates the bullying dismissal of her ways of knowing. Publicly identifying as a feminist, she cannot feel secure in herself. Her inner struggle is fought out in *The Feminine Mystique*.

Three years later, Friedan will co-found an important branch of the modern women's movement. Many years later, from the comparative safety of the powerful women's movement that she helped create, she will write, without holding back, of her own anger about her career as a labor reporter.

> It was uncomfortable, unreal in a way, working in that kind of office with "career" still driving you, but having no words to deal with, even *recognize*, that barrier that you could never somehow break through, that made you invisible as a person, that made them not take you seriously, that made you feel so basically unimportant, almost unnecessary, and—buried very deep—so angry.[23]

The women's movement of the late 1960s and early 1970s will enable millions of American women—including Friedan herself—to express their anger at having been made invisible. In *The Feminine Mystique*, Friedan is trying to control her anger and appear more moderate than she is.

And she is between paradigms. The problem that has no name is a new kind of problem. "The women who suffer this problem have a hunger that food cannot fill. It persists in . . . wives of workers and executives who make $5,000 a year or $50,000" (21). To Friedan in 1963, class is no longer a useful tool of analysis; the old story of working-class solidarity is no longer relevant. Yet the new story of female solidarity will not in fact begin to write itself until a couple of years after the publication of the book.

To tell her story of the crime against women in the book, she borrows the language of the movement against racial segregation. "Sex-directed education segregated recent generations of able American women as surely as separate-but-equal education segregated able American Negroes from the opportunity to realize their full abilities in the mainstream of American life" (171). To expose the caricatures of feminists, she draws on the civil rights and labor movements. "The image of the feminists as inhuman, fiery man-eaters, whether expressed as an offense against God or in the modern terms of sexual perversion, is not unlike the stereotype of the Negro as a primitive animal or the union member as an anarchist" (80). The language she needs to name what has been done to women and the authority she needs to speak as a woman for women are not there for her to simply appropriate. Terms like "gender" and "sexism" will be created by the movement and are not yet available.

To give shape to the book, she focuses on the experience of housewives. Some of the material that she uncovers in her research does not fit within that framework. Perhaps that's why this powerful testimony by a psychiatrist, which I found in Friedan's papers, does not appear in her book.

I remember my own days of medical school, getting hung up on the problem of how I can be feminine and still be a doctor. I was one of the first women to be admitted to that medical school, and my professors made me continually self conscious about being a woman. I remember what it did to me, always being singled out, with a sort of chivalry or contempt, in anatomy class, even to present bones[:] "women and children first." You had to react to it, or refuse to react, bristle and get bitter, or try to hide it. There was no way you could win, no way to be comfortable. Some handled it by being hyper feminine . . . and helpless and using their sex in class, some tried to be one of the boys, and some kind of withdrew from the whole thing into a shell, afraid of all men. I remember the relief years later, going back for post-graduate study at another medical school where women had been around long enough to be taken for granted, the enormous relief that I could be myself and be a woman.[24]

To be myself and a woman: Friedan's great accomplishment in the book is to explain how this seemingly simple desire became so enormously difficult for millions of American women. The psychiatrist found relief at the second medical school, where there was a critical mass of women. Friedan's book offers women the similar relief of finding themselves no longer isolated. What happens next will be up to them.

Women will join together to carry the process further, not just identifying the problem, but also supporting one another in a way that transforms it, and themselves, and America. Friedan's relation to that bottom-up movement, when it emerges a few years later, will be complicated. Yet her book's core perception will become a cornerstone of the movement: "Only the strongest, after nearly twenty years of the feminine mystique, can move on by themselves. For this is not just the private problem of each individual woman" (350–51). *The Feminine Mystique* is fundamentally a protest against privatizing unhappiness.

Stephanie Coontz, in *A Strange Stirring: The Feminine Mystique and American Women at the Dawn of the 1960s*, presents moving testimonies from readers of the book. One was thirty-five, with three children, when she took an overdose of sleeping pills. "My doctor sent me to a psychiatrist but he only made me more ashamed of my feelings." The next year the book came out. "I truly believe if I hadn't found the book when I did, I might really have killed myself the next time." Another woman saw a psychiatrist for eight months. Then she read the book. She sent a copy to the psychiatrist, "with a note saying he should read it before he ever again told a woman that all she needed was to come to terms with her 'feminine nature.'" A mother, interpreting the book as saying "you aren't the problem, society is the problem," flushed her tranquilizers. After reading the book, another woman "realized that what I thought might be wrong with me, was in fact, right with me!"[25]

Insisting that the suffering of women must not be psychologized away, Friedan assures her readers that they are right to feel dissatisfied, that they aren't crazy, unwomanly, or selfish to want more. They can and should trust themselves, not their therapists or the other experts who wanted them to adjust to a half-life of domesticity and call it the whole. Just naming the problem was, in itself, a radical action.

Part 3

The Sixties

9

Ella Baker, Bob Moses, and Mississippi

The Transformation of SNCC

When Baker spoke at the Raleigh conference about "More than a Hamburger," she was pointing students beyond lunch counters and beyond the upper South. The students came to Raleigh wanting to expand the sit-ins but continue being students. In their suits and skirts, they seemed like aspirants to the middle class. Looking past their conventional appearance and limited goals, seeing their courage and hope, she recognized their potential for dismantling the very structure of inequality in the deep South. This shift would require another shift, from part-time protesting to full-time organizing.

Many student activists stayed in college after Raleigh and never made the transition to full-time organizing. They were gradually replaced in SNCC by other young people drawn by the energy and courage of the sit-ins and ready to drop out of school, at least for a while, to work full time in the movement.[1] Within a year, they discarded skirts and suits and adopted a new uniform: blue jeans and overalls. Baker explained they "dressed in work clothes in order to identify with those with whom we were working."[2] She never changed her proper style of dress. But she appreciated the way the young students identified with rural people rather than looking down at them. In her demeanor and directness, she modeled a rejection of class snobbery, a refusal to talk down or up. In this way, too, she was SNCC's mentor.

Baker directly influenced SNCC's direction at Highlander when she showed how political action and direct action were complementary. But her speeches—the "More-than- a-Hamburger" speech in 1960 and the Highlander speech in 1961—were exceptions. Baker mostly facilitated the growth of the young people by listening. Charles McDew, a leader of SNCC, explains what Baker taught him. "Somebody may have spoken for 8 hours and 7 hours and 53 minutes was utter bullshit, but 7 minutes was good. She taught us to glean out the 7 minutes."[3] Learning to listen was crucial for the young organizers. There was no other way for them to earn the trust, or benefit from the wisdom, of local people in the rural south.

Courtland Cox, a SNCC organizer, remembers Baker listening.

> The most vivid memory that I have of Ella Baker . . . is her sitting at these SNCC meetings which ran for days—you didn't measure them in hours, they ran for days—with a smoke mask over her nose, listening patiently to the words and discussions she must have heard a thousand times. Most of us can't be patient with ourselves. I mean, for someone else to be patient with us, was probably one of the most important things she was able to bring to SNCC as a group.[4]

Her influence was emotional as well as intellectual. Under her patient leadership, SNCC became a community of young people who respected and loved one another. Through her own example, she encouraged dialogue. At a tense meeting, late in 1963, the young people faced a crucial decision over whether to bring northern white students to Mississippi in the summer of 1964. Mary King, a new staff member, watched Baker.

> Acting as if she needed the information only for her own purposes, she closed her eyes, slowly tilted her head back in thought, and, uttering each word decisively with her flawless diction and cultured voice, said . . . "Let me pose this question again. What is it we are trying to accomplish?" Sensing that this was a watershed decision for us—as indeed it would be for the whole civil rights movement—Miss Baker's searching forced another round of discussion on the reasons for enlisting one thousand white student volunteers. . . . In this process, consensus was reached. I watched as Miss Baker, without being instructive or judgmental, and without even offering her opinion, but using only her nondirective approach, thus gave the final push in support of the plan for the summer project.[5]

The focus of her leadership was to develop leadership in others. She called attention to their power, not to any exclusive power in herself. Asked in 1961 if she would become the executive secretary, she "thought it should remain in the hands of the youngsters."[6] As a result of her low-key leadership style, she was not well known outside of SNCC. Within SNCC, some young people who joined in 1963 and 1964, when the organization was rapidly growing, did not realize the full extent of her influence. Everyone in SNCC knew that Bob Moses was essential to the organizing approach in Mississippi, but not everyone knew how essential Ella Baker was to the organizing approach of Moses.[7]

Because she kept a low profile, historians did not immediately appreciate how much SNCC owed to Baker. In 1964, when historian and activist Howard Zinn wrote *SNCC: The New Abolitionists*, he dedicated the book to Baker. She was "more responsible than any other single individual for the birth of the new abolitionists as an organized group" and was "the most modest" activist he knew. Because of her modesty, not even Zinn was fully aware of the extent of her contribution. He was based in Atlanta, like her, and worked with her. But when he explained in the book how SNCC emerged out of Raleigh, he didn't say that she was the one who protected SNCC's independence. Because she never told him. And when he wrote of the origins of SNCC's move on Mississippi, he didn't say—because she didn't tell him—that she was the one who directed Bob Moses toward Amzie Moore.[8]

Ella Baker and Bob Moses

Moses met Baker in the early summer of 1960. She was still in the SCLC office, but she spent most of her time getting SNCC up and running. He was from Harlem, 25 years old, a math teacher at a private school in New York. In February, he had seen a photo of the determined faces of the young protestors at Greensboro. "The sit-ins woke me up." During spring break, he participated in a sit-in at Newport News. "I joined the picket lines and felt a genuine sense of release."[9] Now, during his summer vacation, he came down to SCLC headquarters, to see if he could be of use. He had heard about Martin Luther King Jr. and SCLC; he had never heard of Ella Baker or SNCC.

Dr. King met with him briefly.

Shortly after my session with Dr. King, Ella Baker . . . made time for me to come in, sit down, and talk with her. She asked me about my upbringing, my thoughts on Harlem, my entrance into the movement. Her interest in me was what struck me; it was in marked contrast to that of Dr. King. . . . Miss Baker was actually talking to me. I felt that this first conversation had seemed important enough to her that she had made time for it; it was not something that she had just squeezed into her busy schedule.[10]

As they talked, they discovered a connection. In the 1940s, in Harlem, Moses, his mother, and his older brother distributed milk for a co-op. Baker had helped organize the co-op. He was moved "to find somebody like that, who was involved in the civil rights movement . . . who also touched on my early life."[11]

This kind of personal connection exemplified Baker's approach.

This style that was so much a part of her would be important to my future work and to SNCC's future work. . . . If you really want to do something with somebody else, really want to work with that person, the first thing you have to do is make a personal connection. You have to find out who it is you are working with. All across the South you could see that in grassroots rural people. That was their style. Miss Baker took this style to a sophisticated level of political work.[12]

Moses came to Atlanta to work with the charismatic leader. He experienced Baker as a different kind of leader. "This was something different from the SCLC version of leadership," he observed. "First, the idea that leadership would emerge in the community and second, the idea of helping leadership grow."[13]

The dramatic climax of SNCC's struggle to transform Mississippi was the Freedom Summer of 1964, but the beginning was this quiet conversation in the summer of 1960 between Baker and Moses. She sent him to Mississippi, Alabama, and Louisiana to look for people willing to come to SNCC's October conference in Atlanta and gave him a list of her personal contacts, developed during her years of organizing for the NAACP, In Friendship, and SCLC. Amzie Moore was on the list. A few years earlier, Baker raised money to support Moore's organizing in Mississippi. She stayed with Moore in Mississippi and worked with him. "I knew the person. I knew he knew the state, and so Bob Moses was able to have an entrée."[14]

Moore put Moses up and showed him around. "Amzie is the best I've met yet," Moses observed in August, "but then I should have known from Miss Baker."[15] Moore told him that gaining the vote was the key to power in Mississippi, because Blacks outnumbered whites in many congressional districts. "Like the sit-ins, Amzie's words slammed into me powerfully."[16] Later, Moses realized his two mentors complemented each other. Baker was expert on the development of local, grassroots leadership; Moore was, himself, that kind of leader. "Amzie provided, sort of, some flesh and bones to Ella's theory."[17]

When Moore and Moses met, Moore was looking for help. He was convinced the existing organizations were not going to register Black voters in Mississippi. Having closely followed the sit-ins, he was hoping the students would do it. Moore, said Moses, is "the only adult I met on this trip who had clearly fixed the students in his sights . . . watching the student movement unfold, waiting for it to come his way."[18] Moore agreed to come to the Atlanta Conference in October. "When the delegates from Mississippi came in," Joanne Grant reported, "they were greeted with a standing ovation. Mississippi was the toughest state, and the students from other areas, already battle-scarred, were paying tribute to the courage of the participants on the newest front."[19] In Atlanta, Moore invited SNCC to invade Mississippi.

The argument within SNCC about whether to commit to voter registration in the Deep South began in Atlanta in October 1960 and lasted until the near split at Highlander in August 1961. Moses was not part of this argument. During the school year of 1960–61, he was back in New York, winding up his teaching obligation, and then, in July of 1961, he was back in Mississippi. "I was happy not to be involved in this debate. Amzie Moore had already convinced me that in hard-core areas of the Deep South, voter registration *was* direct action. And nowhere did this become clearer than in Mississippi."[20]

Mississippi, SNCC's newest front, quickly became its most important. In Liberty, the voter registration drive halted when a local man was murdered; people became too frightened to try to register. But in McComb, in the summer and fall of 1961, something new happened: the movement began to attract young Mississippians, including high school students, and a few became full-time organizers. By the end of 1962, only four of the SNCC organizers in Mississippi, including Moses, were from out of state; nearly twenty SNCC organizers were young people from Mississippi.[21] It was the beginning of the grass-roots leadership that Baker and Moses hoped to develop. The voter registration drive in McComb slowed when Moses and eleven others were sentenced to four months in prison. But now the young SNCC organizers knew they could connect with young Mississippians.

In Greenwood, they learned to connect with older people as well. The older people appeared conservative, passive, resigned. The temptation was to write them off as accommodationists. To work with them, SNCC organizers needed to be patient and inclusive. Here, especially, Baker's influence was decisive. Charles Payne observes that she taught the young organizers that everyone "has something to contribute."[22] Organizing in Mississippi against a closed society, never knowing when the next wave of violence would break, SNCC organizers could not afford to turn down any contribution. And the older people—who were mostly poor—took them in, and fed them, and brought them to the doctor when they were beaten, and gave them money to buy a used car, and space to breathe and prepare for the next encounter with Mississippi terror.

Moses and the other young SNCC organizers learned by listening to local people.

> After all, you can't live as though you're in very real danger every day, every minute; no one can survive like that. The communities we worked in didn't live like that. They knew how to survive, and part of organizing in them was learning from them how to move in times of real danger and how to take advantage of those times when you were not in real danger. Those were the times you relaxed and deepened ties and forged bonds that were not directly connected to any specific political act like going to the county courthouse. You went to church. Or perhaps had a beer at the local juke joint. Or just sat on a front porch and talked.[23]

Leading by listening and developing personal connections, Moses was channeling Ella Baker.

In this way, leadership in Mississippi emerged from below. Fannie Lou Hamer, sharecropper, tried to register, was evicted the following day from the plantation, and became a SNCC organizer and spokesperson. Leadership, Moses explained, could come from a quarter you least expected—from the relatively well off or dirt poor, educated or uneducated, young or old. "You don't have to know in advance who that leadership will be, but it will emerge from the movement that emerges."[24]

SNCC meetings in Mississippi, which Moses facilitated, drew on SNCC meetings in Atlanta that Baker facilitated. Meetings were never merely about getting business done, or getting information across. Meetings were about building a democratic community of organizers, that is, of leaders. Moses did not make decisions. He encouraged people to talk and listen and reach decisions themselves. Worth Long, a SNCC organizer, explained what made Moses so effective, in terms that recalled Baker. "Moses won a tremendous respect for his ability to listen. . . . You would always seek to ask him a question but he would turn it back to the group or to you. He would facilitate a process where you would solve your own problem."[25]

Moses described an early SNCC meeting in Atlanta in almost the same terms as he described meetings in Mississippi. In Atlanta, in August 1960, Baker "came across to [the students] as someone they could trust. And particularly in the fact that . . . the students were running it. I mean she wasn't trying to in any way kind of manipulate the process that they were going through, and which might have been easy to do."[26] In Mississippi, meetings had to shift their focus from being places where there was a person or panel of people presiding, delivering information that the rest of the participants listened to and accepted, and become places where people actively engaged the problems. . . . Sharecroppers and young organizers alike used meetings to figure out approaches to solutions, and ways to organize themselves to effect those solutions.[27]

In Mississippi, Moses and other SNCC organizers put into practice what Baker taught them. When Moses wrote his own history of organizing in Mississippi, he entitled the section on the development of grassroots leadership "In the Spirit of Ella." His name for the chapter on how SNCC survived and took root was "Learning from Ella."[28] Moses explained, again and again, "What Ella Baker did for us, we did for the people of Mississippi."[29]

In Mississippi, far from the Atlanta office and Baker, SNCC became even more like her—committed to developing local leadership, intent on challenging the whole structure of inequality in the Deep South, clear on the distinction between mobilizing people in the short term *vs.* organizing them for the long haul. In the years 1960 to 1964, there was a flowering of the democratic spirit within SNCC. Working away from the media spotlight, like its mentor, SNCC became a powerful force for radical change.

At the end of 1963, Baker addressed a SNCC Conference in Washington DC. She was not expecting to speak, but Jim Forman, SNCC's executive secretary, called on her, and perhaps because she was taken by surprise, she spoke in unusually personal terms. She acknowledged being moved by the applause with which she was greeted: "I almost lose my sense of balance and want to sort of act like a female and cry." She defined what was different about SNCC. First, "it is concerned with not the development of a leader, but the development of leadership." And second, "it goes into the hardcore areas and identifies very closely with people." Then she sketched SNCC's success. "Bob Moses went down into McComb Mississippi, and . . . inspired the high-school students." Living with people and working with people in the poor rural areas, "we have been able to pioneer in a direction that had not been pioneered before." She was glad that SNCC had become an egalitarian, inclusive, democratic community. As a result of its success, SNCC was growing fast. "I am glad to see so many people in SNCC that I don't know them."

But there was danger in success, she cautioned. SNCC staff could be tempted to exclude whites, or control them. She was thinking of the white northern volunteers who would come to Mississippi in the summer. "I can understand, as we grow in our strength and as we flex our muscles of leadership, and flex our muscles from seeing how effective we are, we can begin to feel that the other fellow should come through us. But this is not the way to create a new world." In Raleigh in 1960, she intervened to protect Black southern students from being dominated by white northern ones. Now, at the end of 1963, she pushed the other way. Because the situation, the power balance, had shifted. "I don't think we need to be afraid. Certainly we don't need to be afraid of being taken over." She ended her impromptu talk, as she began, personally and emotionally. "The three years from '60 to '63, out of my fifty-odd years, seem to me to be the best years of my life."[30] Finally she was at home.

Six months later, in the summer of 1964, the Mississippi movement brought its tremendous energy onto the national stage and into the media spotlight. During the summer, northern volunteers helped the Mississippi Freedom Democratic Party (MFDP) organize a freedom ballot, demonstrating how much Black people in Mississippi wanted representation and how little the segregated Democratic Party of Mississippi represented them. Earlier, in the spring, Baker fought off an attempt to set up a national board over the MFDP, which would have limited the decision-making power of local people. Then the young people of SNCC fought off a last-minute attempt to give places in the MFDP delegation to more credentialed, more educated, less active people. Carried on the high of Freedom Summer, the MFDP came to Atlantic City in August to challenge the seating of the all-white Mississippi delegation at the Democratic National Convention, hoping to be recognized as Mississippi's official delegation.[31]

Hubert Humphrey, vice president of the United States, and Walter Reuther, president of the United Auto Workers (UAW), called Moses, Fanny Lou Hamer, and other MFDP representatives to a meeting in Humphrey's suite. Reuther's UAW was no longer as dynamic as the CIO unions that Baker (and Betty Friedan) experienced in the early 1940s. But the UAW was still an essential part of the progressive left, contributing financial support to the civil rights movement. In March, Baker and Moses attended the UAW convention and won Reuther's pledge of support for the MFDP'S upcoming challenge to the all-white delegation. But President Johnson became afraid that if the MFDP delegation was seated, white southerners would leave the Democratic Party, and he might lose the election in November. Johnson pressured Reuther to change his stance. Reuther and Humphrey told the MFDP to give up hope of representing Mississippi at the convention. They offered the MFDP representatives two seats, in token of recognition, and told them who the two delegates would be.[32]

Baker and Moses were furious. "I stomped out of the room," says Moses, "slamming the door in Hubert Humphrey's face."[33] Hamer, who had just electrified the national delegates with her presentation, was also angered by the offer, but less certain about rejecting it. She asked Baker, Moses, and Forman for advice. Each one told her the same thing, which she paraphrased: "Now look, Mrs. Hamer, you're the people living in Mississippi and you people know what you've experienced in Mississippi. We don't have to tell you nothing. You make your own decision." Hamer added: "See, we'd never been allowed to do that before."[34] Hamer and the other delegates from Mississippi chose democratically to reject the Democratic Party's offer.

At Atlantic City, Baker was viewed by influential progressives in the Democratic Party and the civil rights movement as the intransigent force opposing the party's reasonable offer. They wanted to harness the energy of the civil rights movement to push the Democratic Party to reform the system; they correctly perceived her as wanting to radically transform the system from the bottom up. She was not invited to the meeting with Humphrey and Reuther because she did not share their priorities. She explained: "The fact that the liberals and most of the black civil rights leadership were committed *first* to electing Johnson was crucial."[35] She was committed, first and last, to the uprising from below.

Anti-Communism

Mentored by Baker, SNCC became truly radical, a subversive threat to the status quo. "The radicalization of SNCC was foreseen by our godmother, Ella Baker," said Maria Varela, a SNCC organizer in Alabama and Mississippi. Varela quoted Baker: "We are going to have to learn to think in radical terms. I use the term radical in the original meaning—getting down to and understanding the root cause."[36] But "radical," during the Cold War, sounded like Communist. To pose a radical challenge to the status quo, SNCC had to confront the orthodoxy of anti-Communism, including the common practice of identifying Communists and expelling them from liberal groups. Anti-Communism had provided the glue for the conservatism and caution of the 1950s. Again, Baker's influence was decisive. During the fifties, she herself had waffled, helping the New York branch of the NAACP purge itself of suspected reds. Now, as SNCC developed into the kind of organization that she imagined, she moved decisively to protect the young people from the corroding effects of red-baiting.

From the beginning, SNCC was faced with the possibility that it could be infiltrated by Communists. Anyone who seemed different might be a Communist. Bob Moses was a few years older, from the north, well educated, and suspiciously articulate. When he began spending time at the SNCC office in the summer of 1960, two SNCC activists "cornered me, and questioned me in that office about whether I was myself a communist."[37] Julian Bond: "We thought he was a Communist because he was from New York and wore glasses and was smarter than we were."[38] Like all insurgent groups in the early 1960s, SNCC could not avoid the issue of anti-Communism.

Should SNCC police itself, to protect itself from the charge of being soft on Communism? Baker taught not. She encouraged SNCC organizers to work with Anne and Carl Braden, southern white civil-rights activists who were considered to be Communists. Anne Braden recognized Baker's influence.

> You had a new generation of young black people coming into the movement, and gradually a few white southern students coming into the movement . . . who were immediately hit by this red scare, immediately told, at the very first meeting they ever went to, be careful who you associate with. . . . And you see Ella resisted that all along and I think had a tremendous influence with the young people in SNCC in breaking through those fears.[39]

Baker knew anti-Communism would be used to hurt the movement. In the spring of 1963, she warned SNCC staff: "opposition to the civil rights struggle more and more will be conducted under the cloak of national security."[40] She didn't know that the FBI was spying on Martin Luther King Jr., examining the extent of Communist influence on him, hoping to neutralize him, or that the FBI was spying on her. What she did know was that it was impossible to challenge the racial status quo without being charged with Communism, or Communist sympathies, or being the dupe of Communists. As SNCC became more successful and its refusal to police itself became better known, it was increasingly charged with Communist leanings or connections.[41] Refusing to be Communist or anti-communist, Baker and SNCC focused on the struggle for equality.

At the first convention of the Mississippi Freedom Democratic Party, in Jackson on August 6, 1964, Baker addressed the delegates. The bodies of Cheney, Goodman, and Schwerzer, the three young Mississippi Freedom Summer activists who were murdered in June, were found the day before. Even now, with the effects of violence so palpable, Baker emphasized the danger of anti-Communism.

You are waging a war against the closed society of Mississippi. You have not let physical fear immobilize you. And there is that other fear—the fear of communism. The red-smear which is part of the effort of the power structure to maintain itself and maintain its stranglehold. . . . But we have enough sense to know who is using us and who is abusing us.[42]

Bob Moses worried about working with the Bradens. Once, he articulated his fear that SNCC would lose the money from foundations for its voter registration work. Baker replied that what worried her was letting the foundations divide and weaken SNCC.[43] Moses came to agree with her. He recognized Baker as "really a strong force within the organization for opening up the whole discussion," helping "resolve the whole problem about red-baiting, which was clearly there, because you could see it in the treatment I got."[44] In 1963, when several members of SNCC suggested excluding Communists, he advocated "an absolute stand" on SNCC's right "to associate with whom we choose." If SNCC was open and democratic, Communists would be unable to manipulate it. "If we put our cards on the table and we discuss openly what it is that we are about, then I don't see how . . . these people can somehow subvert what we're doing."[45]

Moses spoke at the first large anti–Vietnam War protest, organized by SDS in Washington in April 1965. He focused not on the war, but on the underlying anti-Communism that drove the war. Asking us to not applaud or cheer, speaking calmly and thoughtfully, more like a teacher than a rally speaker, he recalled the United States' invasion of the Dominican Republic, three months earlier; as justification, the American government cited fifty-seven Communists in the popular uprising that overthrew the dictatorial regime. Moses pointed to the assumption behind the rationale for American invasions of the Dominican Republic and Vietnam. Clearly, Communists were not ordinary people, with ordinary human powers. If fifty-seven Communists could subvert and take over a popular democratic uprising, Communists must have superhero powers. He made us laugh and think.[46]

Led by Baker, SNCC broke with the tradition of anti-Communism, with the Cold War, with fear and self-censorship. All the young, insurgent democratic organizations of the sixties, including SDS, followed a similar trajectory, moving from anti-Communism to anti-anti-Communism. Refusing to get caught up in Cold-War issues, they rejected the self-repression of the fifties. In this way, as in so many others, SNCC played a leading role in creating the radical, open, and democratic spirit of the 1960s.

Other activists, independent of SNCC's influence, came to the same conclusion. In Greenwich Village during the fifties, many people were afraid to
protest or sign petitions because they might be called Communist. "How
could all these people turn into such sheep?" wondered Jane Jacobs. But in
1961, when Jacobs and others started the group to save the West Village, something new and "magical" happened. One activist—"he was an artist, and he
thought up lots of our best visual schemes"—was a Communist in the thirties. The group met and decided that was OK; he was OK. Then, a few days
later, an opponent red-baited the group, in the *New York Times*. "He called us
not only selfish, but he called us pinkos. And that would have scared a lot of
people." But the activists had already decided that their movement "was not
an ideological battle at all. It was a battle for a neighborhood. It had all kinds
of people." Instead of getting scared, "everybody laughed."[47] Jacobs knew what
the laughter meant. "I knew that that whole McCarthy business and the fear
that it had engendered was over."[48]

Ella Baker, Jane Jacobs, and other radically democratic women and men
brought the fifties to an end. The new activists learned to not be afraid of
being called red. Laughter dissolved fear in 1961 in the Village and four years
later when Moses spoke in Washington. All over America, people made that
choice, and what we think of as the fifties come to an end.

Ella Baker's Moment

SNCC peaked in the summer of 1964. The radically democratic moment did
not last.

SNCC's strategy of direct action, confrontation, and voter registration
depended on a belief, however fragile, that the federal government, if pushed
hard enough, would do the right thing. Before Atlantic City, many SNCC
organizers were becoming disillusioned with the Kennedy and Johnson
administrations for hesitating to protect them while they risked their lives;
the aim of Mississippi Freedom Summer was to bring northern whites into
the front lines and put more pressure on the government to act. The experience in Atlantic City was a further blow to faith in the Democratic Party
and the federal government, forcing a new look at strategy. Meanwhile, some
Blacks felt that the original idea of a band of southern Black organizers was
being lost because many new staff members were white. Also, as SNCC grew
in numbers and fame, it became harder to operate in the personal and group-
oriented way of Baker and Moses. After Atlantic City, SNCC felt itself in crisis,
and the ways it responded made the crisis worse.[49]

After 1964, SNCC did less grassroots organizing. There was some real organizing in Alabama in 1965. But SNCC's leaders were increasingly relying on
organizing in the media, rather than on developing leadership from below.[50]
Moses left SNCC rather than engage in a power struggle. Baker became less
influential and distanced herself from the organization. The turn toward
Black Power did not alienate her, even when it resulted, in 1966, in the expul-
sion of valued whites. At the Raleigh conference, she facilitated the decision
to exclude northern, mostly white students from decision making because the
southern Black students needed to learn to make decisions by themselves—a
need which now, she says, "has cropped up again in SNCC."[51] Black Power as
Black self-determination made sense. What bothered her was the anger and
bitterness toward whites, including long-time colleagues. It was one thing for
Blacks to want to organize themselves. It was another to call whites honkies.[52]
Though she never attacked SNCC publicly, she remained committed to her
original vision of Black and white, women and men, young and old, rural and
urban, coming together to create an equal world.

The most creative phase of SNCC and of the southern movement was over
by 1965, but the effects continued to ripple outward into other movements
and other groups. Baker understood this. At the end of 1966, although disappointed by SNCCs recent failures in Mississippi, Alabama, and Southwest
Georgia, she observed: "An important part of SNCC's impact has been on
its individual members, who later continue the work in other ways, through
other groups."[53] Interviewed at the end of the decade, she recalled how the
attitude of southern Blacks used to be acceptance of inequality and gratitude
for small improvements. "Thanks to mass action of recent years, which were
generated to a large extent by the student movement between 1960 and 1965,
this tendency toward easy acceptance is definitely changing."[54]

Baker created, in SNCC, a prototype for radical democratic change which
shaped many of the movements of the 1960s. During the sixties, she influenced, in decisive ways, many activists who never heard of her. Today, her
model of developing leadership from below informs the way many organizers think about what they are doing. Increasingly, people on the cutting edge
of movements from below look to Baker as the uncompromising, radical,
and democratic leader who combined racial analysis with class analysis, who
rejected male domination, who was committed to equality in every sense.[55]

10

Jane Jacobs and the Neighborhood Movement

How to Build a Movement

Jane Jacobs mailed off the manuscript of *Death and Life of Great American Cities* early in 1961, three weeks before the fight to save the West Village began. Years later, she was thankful she finished the book before the fight began. "If I'd had to give that much time to the fight, I'd have had to drop the book."[1] Even in retrospect, she would have dropped the book, not the fight! What would have been the point of the book, if she wasn't living according to its principles? What good would it have been to describe the ballet of Hudson Street, if she stood by while the city bulldozed the entire neighborhood? What use was theory, if you didn't put it into practice?

She returned to *Architectural Forum* after completing the book. Before going to work on a Tuesday morning, she was reading the *New York Times*. Mayor Robert Wagner said her neighborhood was "blighted."[2] It would be torn down. "I promptly got on the phone and so did a number of others who read this [announcement] and realized its importance."[3] A number of others: a neighborhood was under attack, and a neighborhood would fight back. "Even if I won a fight with the city to keep my house while all the others were being torn down, I wouldn't stay," she told a reporter. "It isn't the house. It's the neighborhood I love."[4] Like Marjorie Spock and Mary Richards when their garden was sprayed with DDT, Jacobs and her sister activists sprang into action. Unlike Spock and Richards, they would not rely on the courts. They understood, right away that the struggle would be political, that they would have to build a grassroots movement powerful enough to force the city government to back down.

That night, Norman Redlich, a law professor at NYU, invited Jacobs and her husband and Edith Lyons and a few other activists to a private meeting. He also invited heads of civic groups and churches, prominent people who, like him, had been notified of the city's plan a few days earlier. Redlich said that, officially, the plan was to clear out blighted buildings and replace them with attractive, affordable housing. But when he asked friends in the government, they told him the whole neighborhood, a fourteen-block area, was going to be bulldozed. Jacobs added what she knew about urban renewal—how it was advertised initially, and what it actually ended up doing to a neighborhood. As they listened to Redlich and Jacobs, most of the people who had received the early, seductive notice were aghast. Not all. Some still took the promise of urban renewal at face value. But this private meeting was an important first step. The attempt by the city to win over influential people in the area had been neutralized.[5]

Rachele Wall and Ann Lye called the first public meeting for Saturday, four days after the announcement. Wall lived just beyond the border of the area designated for urban renewal; Lye knew a lot about real estate. Local women—in the Village, in Mississippi, and elsewhere—made possible most of the movements from below in the sixties. Lye and Wall "had lots of initiative," Jacobs explained. They convinced their neighborhood association to call a meeting at St. Luke's Episcopal Church, in the area that was to be torn down. Three hundred people showed up. Lye nominated Jacobs as chair of the protest group, which soon took the fighting name of The Committee to Save the West Village. "Already we had, you see, a sort of umbrella organization—thanks to Ann and Rachele—because promptly the people on our borders, on the borders of our neighborhood—understood that this affected them and they joined with us."[6]

In the battle to save Washington Square, Jacobs and other activists learned from Ray Rubinow how to form an umbrella organization focused on a single issue. Now they learned vital lessons from another experienced professional. Wall knew Lester Eisner, who was director of the New York State office of the Federal Urban Renewal Administration. She invited him to go on a tour of the "blighted" neighborhood with her and Jacobs that weekend.

We went into many apartments—the expensive ones, but also the very inexpensive ones—the ones that would have been tagged as slums. And he saw what a fine neighborhood it was, how diverse it was, how neighborly the people were and how happy they were to live there.... This was no Potemkin Village expedition. He went anywhere he wanted. People were willing to let him in anyplace. He met landlords. He met tenants. We didn't say who he was. He didn't say who he was. But he was extremely helpful to us—not in any underhanded way at all—but just by telling us what the law was.[7]

Moved by the vitality and diversity of the neighborhood, Eisner decided to help. He explained the law required that the area be proven a slum according to certain quantifiable criteria: noise level, percentage of abandoned buildings, size of the premises, rent paid, number of occupants, kitchen and bathroom facilities, transience or permanence of the residents. The activists were encouraged. If the city had to prove it was a slum, they could disprove it. This possibility shaped their tactic of rigorously collecting their own data.

Eisner also explained that there had to be some participation by local citizens in the planning. If they made any suggestions or requests, the bureaucrats would check off that requirement and call in the bulldozers. This reality shaped the disciplined refusal of the members of the committee to talk to representatives of the city, until the city removed the designation of "blighted."[8] Of course, the activists wanted to improve the neighborhood: in their newsletter, they emphasized "building up what we already have" as opposed to "destroying the existing neighborhood." All talk of improvement would have to wait, however, until the city agreed not to destroy.[9]

They had one month to make their case. A local man in advertising showed them how to conduct a marketing survey. About twenty people were sitting on the floor of his apartment, late at night, taking notes. "There just weren't enough seats in the apartment to accommodate a classroom. But the blackboard was there, the teacher was there and the determination to learn what to do right was there." Robert Jacobs, the architect, taught them how to determine the condition of the buildings. A sound engineer who lived in the neighborhood volunteered to record sound and compare the noise level to other neighborhoods. People volunteered to go to every apartment in the neighborhood, collecting accurate data. This training took place after work. "We all had jobs and some of us who were working mothers had two jobs, in effect. But ... everybody was in on this. Either their second job or their third job was saving the neighborhood."[10] Jacobs, who now had three jobs, was sleep deprived, but so was everybody else.

Racing to complete the survey, the activists involved the rest of the neighborhood. They translated all leaflets and petitions into Spanish, encouraging Puerto Ricans to join. Shopkeepers allowed posting of the latest news. The children of activists—included the Jacobs's children—delivered petitions to stores, collected them when filled out, and decided when to leave more. Gloria Hamilton, married to an owner of the White Horse Tavern (which "would have been wiped out"), became a leader in the fight. Robert Jacobs went to a bar where longshoremen hung out and told them, and the proprietor, of the threat not only to their bar but also to their church, St. Veronica's, which was nearby. On Sunday, a member of St. Veronica's congregation stood on the steps outside, explaining to people what was going to happen to their church.[11] Now, less than a week after the announcement in the *Times*, there was a movement.

Word of the struggle spread through the Village, and beyond. "We were news just because we were Greenwich Village and newspapers and magazines elsewhere began to take notice that here was an area that didn't meet the criteria of a slum at all—and look, the federal bulldozers were coming after it anyway. That survey that we did . . . [was] worth its weight in gold for showing what kind of an area it was."[12] Ten days after the original announcement, the *New York Times* responded to the growing movement by sending a reporter to the neighborhood. He observed the process of the door-to-door survey, the leafleting in Spanish as well as English, the participation of the kids. "Even small children were campaigning in West Greenwich Village yesterday . . . making posters [and] distributing protest petitions." He saw all the positive energy. But the headline read: "'Villagers' Seek to Halt Renewal."[13] As if resistance to the city's plans was resistance to progress.

On the same day, Friday March 3, the *New York Herald Tribune* sent a reporter to the Village. Her story questioned the dominant narrative of progress.

> Most people look askance at neighborhoods where old men and women sit outside shop doorways and kids play up and down on sidewalks. Frequently they think the best thing to do is tear them down and build a shiny new building.
>
> Mrs. Jane Jacobs lives in a neighborhood like that and loves it.

The reporter went on a tour with Jacobs and saw the buildings that would be torn down, and the resistance. "We couldn't go two steps without children appearing with handfuls of signed petitions," she wrote. "The local printer replenished her supply, and the local coffeehouse proprietor reported on the television show that had filmed their meeting in the shop that morning." The reporter recognized she was witnessing a communal uprising. "Everyone in the neighborhood is working on the Save the West Village Committee."[14]

When the activists finished the survey, on time, they showed Eisner. He was impressed, calling it better than any professional survey he'd seen. The city government was not impressed. The Planning Commission ignored the survey. But officials were not the only, or even the main, audience for the survey. The public was the more important audience. The battle in the West Village was political, pitting the power of people against the power of bureaucrats, planners, and developers. The survey made the neighborhood look good and the Planning Commission look arbitrary, slipshod, and eager to please the developers.

As activists dug deeper into the city's plan, they discovered collusion. "We have all turned into detectives, and are finding out amazing facts about the relationship between the builders and the Planning Commission and Housing & Redevelopment Board," Jacobs wrote during the struggle. "These real-estate grabbers," she said, shortly afterwards. "You'd think that there was oil under the ground here."[15] Developers operated behind the scenes, out of the public's sight, beyond the range of protest. But bureaucrats—like those on the City Planning Commission—were paid by the public, and at least had to pretend to work for the public good. The activists concentrated their fire on them.

Jacobs realized that the "chief weakness" of the planners was the need to keep their plan secret. "Being predators, they instinctively depended on deceit; and being composed of cliques of civil servants and developers . . . , they were under the illusion that they could keep secrets."[16] A few days before the official announcement in the *Times*, the chairman of the city's Housing and Redevelopment Board had given the Women's City Club a preview of urban renewal plans for the year. There were going to be at least seven new projects. But he declined to specify them. "Past experience has shown that such announcements spread alarm and unrest in the affected areas," he said.[17] Robert Moses himself was open about why he wasn't open. "There isn't a project I've been connected with in forty years that would have been built if I had consulted prior to announcing it."[18]

As the Planning Commission and the Redevelopment Board worked best in the shadows, the activists thrived in the light. "We figured honesty and full exposure was the best thing."[19] Like Ella Baker and SNCC, the West Village activists were open about what they were doing.

The City was extremely secretive about all kinds of things. We couldn't be secretive. We had, for one thing, too many people. You can't keep a secret with hundreds of people. . . . And it was still more important that our side should know everything that was going on in this fight. Because each person then could take initiative intelligently when need be, because each one knew just what the strategies were, just what the difficulties were.[20]

Like Baker, Jacobs embraced openness. To Baker, it was a principle of developing leadership from below. Jacobs discovered the way leadership emerged. "The other side was understandably surprised, and so were we when, in crises, scores or even hundreds of us had to improvise cohesively and almost instantaneously; but this in turn was made possible only because so many people were privy to everything known at that current stage of battle."[21]

It is striking how Jacobs's ideas about organizing converged with Baker's. Both women believed that you built your own power through openness and confrontation, rather than going to the powerful people and trying to persuade them. Then the powerful people came to you. "People too often try to 'fix' things at some high level. . . . I don't go for this notion that you can win battles just by getting in with the mayor. What can be fixed can be unfixed so easily," Jacobs said in 1962. "You just make up your mind to win, and if you antagonize a lot of people, well, you do, but in the end they fawn on you."[22]

Independently, Jacobs and Baker arrived at many of the same ideas. They shared a commitment to democracy as the means as well as the end. Popular movements of the early sixties appealed to a shared assumption that America was still a democracy, where citizens ultimately had the power to make politicians do what they were supposed to do. Among activists in Mississippi, in the West Village, and elsewhere, especially during the early years of the decade, there was a belief in the power of honesty, openness, and truth.

The truth was that the city's "renewal" of the West Village was going to destroy a neighborhood that was diverse and vital. The more the Committee to Save the West Village got the truth out—through the survey, the media, petitions, public meetings, and demonstrations—the more cracks appeared within city agencies themselves. "We got lots of information on their plans, which they did try to keep secret. The reason we got all this information and intelligence was that there were so many people in their own offices who agreed with us, and . . . they would always come to us with information. So we always knew what our opponents were cooking up before they were ready to spring it themselves."[23]

The movement proved too powerful for the city. In April, the West Villagers served Mayor Wagner and the other members of the Board of Estimate with a court order, restraining them from designating the area as blighted. Eight hundred demonstrators showed up at the board hearing, to reinforce the court order.[24] In September, on the eve of the primary, wanting to secure reelection more than to tear down and rebuild the West Village, Mayor Wagner surrendered, canceling urban renewal of the neighborhood.

But the plan didn't die. The Planning Commission refused to let it die. Headed by James Felt, a wealthy developer, the Planning Commission announced that it was going ahead, even though the Mayor and—as the Planning Commission admitted—"a substantial majority of the local community" were opposed.[25] In October, at a public meeting at city hall, backed by the police, Felt announced that the Planning Commission met privately and voted to proceed with the demolition. A *Times* reporter was there.

> Angry Greenwich Villagers caused an uproar in City Hall yesterday when the City Planning Commission designated their neighborhood a blighted area suitable for urban renewal.
>
> The villagers, led by Mrs. Jane Jacobs, chairman of the Committee to Save the West Village, leaped from their seats and rushed forward. They shouted a deal had been made with a builder, that the Mayor had been doublecrossed, and that the commission action was illegal.[26]

Felt pounded his gavel and ordered the police to remove disorderly persons from the room. But the police could not restore his authority. When one man was carried out, feet first, others rose to denounce Felt. "You are not an elected official," shouted the activists. "You have made a deal with David Rose." Rose was the developer and builder who was supposed to remain hidden. Speaking to the *Times*, immediately afterward, Jacobs laid out the actual process of urban renewal, highlighting the role of the developer or builder. "First the builder picks the property, then he gets the Planning Commission to designate it, and then the people get bulldozed out of their homes."[27]

The popular movement backed Felt into a corner and he could not recover. But he convinced Mayor Wagner to give him one last chance. He called a meeting of fifteen to twenty West Village protestors and specified that Jacobs could not come. Jacobs found it "hilarious." "Now this was his delusion—that if I was not there that he could manipulate the other people."[28] Without Jacobs, without needing to check with her, the other activists knew what to do. As Felt asked each one what she or he would like to see in the neighborhood, hoping they would suggest improvements and could therefore be shown to have participated, everyone told him the same thing: take away the "blighted" designation. At the end of January 1962, the City Planning Commission removed the designation, and the battle, which had lasted almost a year, was over. Six months later Felt resigned.[29]

Felt's delusion, as Jacobs put it, was to think you could manipulate everyone else if you just get rid of the leader. People in authority imagined that the resistance to them was organized hierarchically, like their own power. The authorities in Mississippi believed, erroneously, that jailing SNCC organizers would crush the movement. Often, confronted with a genuinely democratic movement, people in power don't know what to do and make things worse for themselves. It is a vulnerability of the powerful.

Jacobs, like Baker, understood the power of democratic movements, in which leadership was widely shared. She was an activist among activists, a leader among leaders. But most contemporary commentators gave the credit for the fight to save the West Village to her because she was the most visible figure in the struggle and because her book was published in the midst of the fight. According to the *Village Voice*, "Jane Jacobs looks rather like a prophet. People who have seen her in action . . . rarely forget that clomping, sandaled stride and that straight grey hair flying every which way around a sharp, quizzical face. And she can magnetize a populace into action." The *Voice* added: "The prophet lives by her own book."[30] An admiring magazine editor summed up this view: "She was chairman of the Save-the-West-Village campaign and ran it straight out of the book—and she wrote the book."[31] By the end of the decade, this view had crystallized into dogma: "To Mrs. Jacobs's followers in the West Village urban renewal fight, her book was the city planning bible."[32] She led; they followed. The reality was more interesting.

Some historians, too, have treated Jacobs as the indispensable leader in the fight to save the West Village.[33] She herself consistently made a point of acknowledging the leadership of others. "I get much too much credit for this," she insisted. "There were hundreds and hundreds of people—leaders of all kinds."[34] Writing a biographical sketch of herself, during the campaign, she said simply: "The neighborhood, which has a tremendous sense of city workings, out of experience, rallied to fight the city. I rallied along with the rest."[35] "Oh, I was not even the chief strategist! This was a very joint effort," she later explained.

> That was another of the delusions of the City. They thought that I was the leader of this and that if they could get rid of me that the fight would evaporate somehow. . . . They didn't understand at all how communities worked. They didn't understand at all how movements like this occur. . . . And if I had been removed as the leader there would have been ten other leaders who could come take my place, who knew everything I knew, who had provided a lot of those ideas.[36]

Her insistence that she was one of many leaders reflected her personality. She played well with others. She never had the ego needs of some female and most male leaders. She enjoyed being generous, acknowledging what she learned from other people, sharing the glory. To Jacobs, fighting back was a team sport. In addition, her insistence reflected a sophisticated understanding about "how movements like this occur." Like Baker, Jacobs knew that successful movements only became possible when there were many activists taking initiative. And like Baker, she sensed the perils of being crowned as the indispensable leader by the media. When reporters began to treat a popular movement as the work of one person who inspired people and told them what to do, the leader was in danger of taking herself too seriously. (This would happen to Betty Friedan and many others, later in the decade.) Jacobs deftly avoided the danger by being clear in her own mind, and with the media, that she was one leader among many. She told the *Voice* reporter who wanted to crown her as leader: "If you say I did it, why then people with a cause will think they can't do anything without me."[37]

Limitations

Jacobs began her book tour a month after the victory in the West Village. Wherever she went, she tried to spark local movements against urban renewal. In West Palm Beach, she criticized the new municipal auditorium project. In Ithaca, she denounced the local rebuilding plan. In Pittsburgh, she attacked the new public housing. In a small New Jersey town, she offered mischievous reassurance: "There is nothing in Woodbury as ugly as some of the urban renewal projects I've seen."[38] She addressed herself, everywhere, not to public officials, but to the public. In Milwaukee, a reporter noted Jacobs was pleased that "her book is used by groups fighting planners in Chicago, Philadelphia, Boston, and New York."[39] In Chicago, after condemning the urban renewal plan, she encouraged local citizens: "Resist, resist, resist."[40]

She was regarded, correctly, as a troublemaker. Before her appearance in Philadelphia, her local contact recognized that her time there was limited. "You obviously can't case anything in a few hours, but you could take a quick look at one or two [projects] and raise the question. Might start another row!"[41] Six months later, she pointed to the resistance in Philadelphia, Chicago, Cleveland, and Boston as a first step: stop the bad planning. "This sounds negative, but I think we won't really get things done differently and better until citizen resistance makes it impossible—or too frustrating—to do things as they are being done."[42]

Her book tour and her book encouraged resistance. An observer described *Death and Life*, six months after publication, as "a book that changes history." "No architect or planner can start a project in a city anywhere and pretend he hasn't read or heard of Mrs. Jacobs' book. Of course, he can do things the way they've been done before she started hollering, but he'll have to answer to anyone who comes along, and asks why he hasn't paid attention to Mrs. Jacobs."[43]

Through all the attention she received, she never lost focus. Riding with her through a rundown Philadelphia neighborhood, a reporter asked what she would do if she had the power. She declined to answer; prescribing was what city planners did. "The problems in a place like this are too complicated for offhand suggestions. The first thing would be to learn about the life here."[44] She hollered, and fought, and invited other citizens to join. But she never forgot that it was their love for their neighborhood and city that made them care in the first place. "What really pleases me," she said in Milwaukee, "is the mail from alert, concerned citizens who have much love for their cities."[45]

Her fame grew. In 1964, Lady Bird Johnson invited her to address a Women Doers luncheon at the White House. The subject was Lady Bird's favorite: beautification. Jacobs declined to speak on beautification, which she considered "a superficial, cosmetic idea." She told Mrs. Johnson's press secretary that she would address real urban issues. "I wanted to talk sense to these women," she later explained, "not a lot of inspirational stuff about tulips."[46] When she spoke at the White House, Jacobs was the same as always, playfully speaking truth to power. Since she was in the capitol, she focused on federal power. Federal dollars—for urban renewal, public housing, superhighways—were earmarked for tearing down and rebuilding, not maintaining and improving.

> Let me give an example from my own neighborhood. For years we have been begging for repair and restoration of our park. For years the park has been running down. Last month the city offered to destroy the park and build a new one. Why not use that money, the citizens asked, to restore and maintain the park, and several others besides? The parks commissioner candidly explained that his department is starved for maintenance funds but is relatively well off for capital funds.[47]

Jacobs was herself at the White House: clear, direct, irreverent. But she could not change federal priorities. Federal money continued to flow into tearing down and rebuilding, rather than maintenance. Automobiles continued to be favored over people. Viable neighborhoods continued to be destroyed for federal highways or housing. This was a fight that Jacobs and her allies could not win. The power on the other side was too great, too far from the neighborhoods, too much beyond local democratic control.

Also, the national movement against urban renewal was limited, in numbers and strength, by the fact that it was mostly white. A number of critics fault Jacobs for this.[48] They claim she underestimated how hard it would be for a racially segregated neighborhood to succeed in determining its own fate, as the West Village did. But Jacobs recognized, in *Death and Life*, that it was difficult for Black neighborhoods to "unslum" because most people did not stay by choice; discrimination and segregation forced them to stay. "Segregation and racial discrimination" constituted "our country's most serious social problem.[49] In 1962, she pointed to the unequal impact of urban renewal. "About 80% of the people being pushed around in this country are Negroes."[50] In 1964, at the White House, she informed Mrs. Johnson and her guests that the federal government's policy of destroying and rebuilding cities disproportionately affected Blacks. "Poor people and the Negro are tossed out of their neighborhoods." [51]

Testifying to a Senate subcommittee, late in 1962, she emphasized the structural problem. Black neighborhoods deteriorated because lending institutions refused to loan money for improvement. Redlining was "the single most effective force" preventing Black neighborhoods from unslumming. "I'm not talking about banks and insurance companies that withhold loans because they consider them bad risks," she told the subcommittee. "I'm talking about actual concerted agreement among lending institutions not to loan to certain areas." When Black people moved into functioning neighborhoods, lending ceased, and the neighborhoods were doomed. "They deteriorate because it is impossible to get money for improvements."[52]

She opposed segregation as not only bad for Blacks but for everyone. Diversity of class and race was a core value for Jacobs. At Board of Estimate meetings, she was moved by voices speaking "with passion about concerns that are local but far from narrow"—voices of poor people, "including discriminated against" people.[53] It was "no horror, but healthy and good to have the poor, illiterate, discriminated against races in a neighborhood."[54] Or in a neighborhood school. "The fear on the part of white parents of sending their children to public schools is pure ignorance," she said in 1964. "My two sons are in integrated schools and I think they're darn lucky to be there."[55]

Her daughter also attended a public school, where there were fifty-five Black children from St. Barnabas, a nearby shelter. In the name of ending overcrowding, the City transferred the children from the shelter out of the school at the beginning of the 1963–64 school year. Neighborhood parents protested; they wanted diversity for their children, even if it meant the school was a little crowded. Removal of the fifty-five children, they complained, "will leave an almost lily-white school."[56] That fall, on the first day of school without the Black children, parents picketed. One went further.

> Jane Jacobs, a white parent whose daughter, Mary, was to start 3rd grade at P.S. 41, decided to enter the school and advise the Principal that she was not permitting her daughter to attend until the St. Barnabas children were admitted to the school which they have attended for 4 years. . . . Other parents are joining Jane Jacobs in keeping the children out of school until the St. Barnabas children return.[57]

In February, the parents of P.S. 41 joined a wider struggle against school segregation. Bayard Rustin built on Ella Baker's earlier organizing for integrated New York schools and called a citywide boycott against school segregation. A majority of Black families joined the boycott. But in predominantly white schools, most children went to school. Not, however, at P.S. 41, where a majority of parents kept their children home. Jacobs was spokesperson. "The Board of Education hasn't taken any initiative that has amounted to anything," she told the *Voice*, "so it's up to us to take it."[58] She agreed with Rustin that it would take a mass movement of Blacks and whites, on the model of the southern civil rights movement, to force the City to make the schools more diverse. "We've been chipping away at the problem since 1954, when the Supreme Court declared separate but equal education unconstitutional," she said. "I think we're more segregated now than we were then." "If we could get school integration," she added with almost desperate hope, "it could help break down housing segregation, since choices of residence are often based on where the children in a family go to school."[59]

The attempt to integrate New York schools failed. Institutionalized racism and white resistance proved more powerful than the activists. But it was victory in the battles to save Washington Square Park and the West Village that gave Jacobs and her neighbors the hope and courage to protest segregation in the first place.

One of her fiercest critics at the time worried that the movement against urban renewal might spread to Black neighborhoods. Roger Starr, head of the New York's Citizens Housing and Planning Council and a leading advocate of public housing, attended a Board of Estimate meeting in the early sixties.

> I watched a stout Negro lady, her black coat held together with a big blanket pin, as she arrived at City Hall to protest a city proposal to demolish [her block]. She carried under her arm, as the rationale for her opposition, a copy of Mrs. Jacobs's

book. "We don't live in no slum," she said, "and we don't want to live in no project. We want to stay where we is, but we want it fixed up the way she says."[60]

For Starr, the woman's Black English and the poverty of her attire were proof that she and her neighbors were incapable of knowing what was good for them. For antiracist activists today, the woman's attempt to use Jacobs's book as a weapon to defend and improve her neighborhood suggests there is nothing inherently white or middle class about Jacobs's ideas. The woman's insistence on staying where she was and using *Death and Life* to improve the neighborhood points to a possibility that was largely unrealized in Black neighborhoods facing urban renewal in the 1960s.

Another Black activist, writing fifty years later, took Jacobs's discoveries further. In *Root Shock*, Mindy Thompson Fullilove, a public health psychiatrist, elaborated Jacobs's insight about how community gets built and how it gets destroyed. To clarify what urban renewal did, Fullilove proposed a thought experiment.

> First, imagine Jane Jacobs's street altered in any way you like—change the size of the buildings and their use; reorganize the street—move the subway entrance, relocate the school—and then imagine people making use of it. If you look closely, a sidewalk ballet, albeit different from Jacobs's version, will emerge before your eyes. In this thought experiment, you are observing the degree to which people can adapt to different settings, and not just adapt, but attach, connect. They are connecting not to negatives or even the positives of the setting, but to their own mastery of the local players and their play.
>
> Second, take any setting, and reduce it to shreds. The fundamental geographic points cuing the ballet are now gone. Center stage has disappeared. Jacobs's entry is gone, and so are the stores and the stoop. . . . What you have just imagined is root shock, the traumatic stress from the loss of a person's stage set, lifeworld, mazeway, home.[61]

Building on Jacobs, Fullilove made palpable the trauma that people in destroyed communities suffer. And following Jacobs, she suggested how poor Black neighborhoods might heal themselves. "It was the urbanist Jane Jacobs who provided a vision of the ghetto postsegregation. She argued that, though we call all poor neighborhoods 'slums,' we should distinguish between . . . perpetual slums and unslumming neighborhoods." If Blacks were free to move, some would choose to stay. Their neighborhood, no longer a ghetto, could regenerate itself, becoming neither Black slum nor predominantly-white thriving neighborhood, but a predominantly Black thriving neighborhood.[62]

It is widely assumed today that improving a neighborhood will inevitably lead to it becoming majority white. Together, Jacobs and Fullilove challenge that assumption and suggest the liberating potential in majority-minority neighborhoods, *if* they are allowed to regenerate themselves. Shortly before she died in 2006, Jacobs—who always hated what was being done to Black neighborhoods, and always wanted to be useful—publicly praised Fullilove's book.[63]

11

Rachel Carson and the Bullies

The Attack

The attack on *Silent Spring* began before the book was published. In June 1962, three lengthy installments began appearing in the *New Yorker*. "Pesticides Industry Up in Arms Over a New Book," the *New York Times* announced in July. "The $300,000,000 pesticides industry has been highly irritated by a quiet woman." Carson's previous bestsellers had been inoffensive. "In her latest work, however, Miss Carson is not so gentle . . . [and] the men who make the pesticides are crying foul." Agricultural chemical companies instructed their scientists to go through the excerpts from *Silent Spring* "line by line," noted the *Times*, but "they can find little error of fact." For industry leaders, it was never about Carson's facts. They read the excerpts, correctly, as an attack against pesticides in particular and the chemical industry more broadly. "Our members are raising hell," a trade association said.[1]

The *Chemical and Engineering News* announced: "Industry Maps Defense to Pesticide Criticisms." Some industry leaders told the *News* they wanted to ignore *Silent Spring*; attacks on the book would only add to its sales. But most industry leaders believed that ignoring the book was not a realistic option. They cited the tremendous sales and scientific reputation of *The Sea around Us*, predicted *Silent Spring* would also become popular, and pointed to the fact that it was going to be the Book-of-the-Month Club selection in October and "CBS is considering doing a special TV show on this topic."[2]

They must counterattack. But what approach should they take? Applied Science Laboratories' technical director favored the high road: agree with Carson mistakes had been made and maintain that they were being corrected, thereby protecting the industry's image as benevolent. "It is important that the industry develop a strong image of . . . opposing improper, unsafe and questionable uses."[3] Other scientists and industry insiders told the *News* they wanted to come after her. "The 'Silent Spring' poses leading questions, on which neither the author nor the average reader is qualified to make decisions," insisted a professor of entomology. "I regard it as science fiction."[4] His contention—that these matters of science were beyond the grasp of lay readers and of Carson herself—would become one of the chemical industry's main talking points. And his tone, dismissing Carson as an amateur and her book as science fiction, would become its dominant tone.

The chemical giant Monsanto offered its own science fiction. "The Desolate Year," printed as a pamphlet and widely distributed, imagined what would happen if all pesticides were eliminated. Insects would thrive: grasshoppers, that "awesome plague of the plains;" cattle grubs, "small and ugly organisms that bored through the skin"; potato blight, a "really notorious villain"; "invading fire ants"; "the rasping, blood-sucking lamprey"; boll weevils, "the worst plant-loving demon of them all." "So the farmers planted and cultivated, and too often the harvest was garbage."[5]

Velsicol Chemical Corporation took a more direct approach. Its general counsel, Louis McLean, phoned the *New Yorker*, demanding changes in the installments. In a menacing letter to Houghton Mifflin, publisher of *Silent Spring*, McLean charged that Carson portrayed business as "grasping and immoral" and threatened to sue. The *New Yorker* and Houghton Mifflin refused to back down. So did the editors of *Audubon Magazine*, who McLean threatened because they were going to publish excerpts. Audubon not only published the excerpts from *Silent Spring*, but also published excerpts from McLean's threatening letter to Houghton Mifflin.[6]

The danger in attacking too directly was that the attempt at censorship could make the industry look like a bully. Eschewing Velsicol's direct attack, the National Agricultural Chemicals Association worked behind the scenes. NACA expanded its public relations department and quietly warned magazine and newspaper editors that advertising revenue could decline if they reviewed *Silent Spring* favorably.[7]

Why so much concern about a book? What could a book do? The *News* quoted an officer at Stauffer Chemical Company: *Silent Spring* "may mark the beginning of some serious problems for the chemical industry as well as the pesticide industry." In this discussion within industry, the Stauffer official did not shy away from specifying the nature of the threat. "He feels that if the public becomes frightened about its food supply and general health through 'contamination' by chemicals, governments at all levels will push for unnecessarily increased regulation."[8] A book that became a bestseller could hurt the bottom line.

There was no cost-free way for industry to respond. Ignoring Carson would not work; threatening her publisher only tended to expose the industry; dismissing her evidence was very difficult, because Carson, anticipating attack, had worked hard to get her facts straight. The United States Department of Agriculture, the chemical industry's strongest ally within the federal government, tried to punch holes in her arguments. Byron Shaw, administrator of the USDA's Research Service, was assigned the task but was unable to find much evidence to counter her claims. Orville Freeman, Secretary of Agriculture, hesitated to order an all-out attack.[9]

The strategy eventually adopted by defenders of the chemical industry, when the full book appeared in September, was not cost-free. In its pamphlet, "How to Answer Rachel Carson," NACA acknowledged mistakes were made in the production and marketing of pesticides but defended the integrity of the men and the process. NACA quoted the chief horticulturist at Michigan State University: "The tragedy of Rachel Carson's book is not that she will retard development and use of beneficial agricultural chemicals; it is that she has destroyed the confidence of the public in the men who produce our food."[10] This approach raised the stakes. By arguing that scientists and manufacturers could be trusted to protect the public, and by associating pesticides with progress, industry defenders inadvertently opened to debate the dominant American faith in progress through science, technology, and free enterprise.

A leading agricultural chemical researcher observed that the industrial revolution, which "helped make us a giant among nations," was made possible by an agricultural revolution. And the agricultural revolution, sustained by "dedicated researchers in the United States Department of Agriculture," relied heavily on pesticides. But now "there are some people who are inordinately fearful of pesticides." Spurred by Carson's book, "these people would deny or seriously restrict the use of pesticides. . . . Would they also advocate a return to the horse to pull the plow?"[11] On one side: Carson and her supporters, and on the other, progress, the American century, science, industry, and government.

The chair of the Department of Agricultural Chemistry at Oregon State University expanded the argument that pesticides were essential to the American way of life. After the frontier closed around 1900, chemistry became the new frontier. Mechanized production, fertilized crops, and new crop varieties made possible an intensification of agriculture. These new crops proved vulnerable. "Concentration of relatively few varieties of crops within an area provided an ideal setting for the explosive growth of pests of all kinds." No problem—at least, no problem chemistry couldn't solve. "The development of new organic chemicals for pest control around the time of World War II came just in time." Chemical agriculture became part of the fabric of American life. At his university, ten different departments were developing and testing new chemicals.[12]

This argument was picked up by mainstream media. *Time* attacked Carson as a rabble-rouser, trying to undermine faith in the experts and in the American way of life. She aimed at nothing less than "frightening and arousing her readers," "alarming the non-technical public." Her book was "unfair, one-sided, and hysterically over emphatic." It was true that spraying elms with DDT killed robins "for several years," until DDT disintegrated in the soil. You could argue whether elms were more important than robins. You couldn't argue with the fact that "chemical pesticides are now a necessary part of U.S. Agriculture." Without pesticides, Americans would suffer "recurring famine," instead of having "the happy problem of what to do with food surpluses."[13] Wise citizens would follow the scientists, not the hysterical Carson.

A research-and-development vice president of a chemical company surrounded himself with the multitude of scientists who produced and evaluated pesticides. There are "at least a thousand highly accredited scientists" employed by the pesticides industry. Add to them the hundreds of government scientists—in the Department of Agriculture, the Public Health Service, the Food and Drug Administration—who worked exclusively on pesticides, ensuring their safety. In addition, the National Academy of Sciences and the scientific committees in various states had investigated pesticides and found them safe.

> The allegations in her book would imply that all of the scientists in the areas listed above have either been denied recourse to information available to *her*, or that they have been unable to evaluate it properly—else, why would they not have stopped this senseless slaughter of birds and wildlife . . . this poisoning of themselves and their children?[14]

Why would company scientists, government scientists, and academic scientists poison themselves and their children? By suggesting that the drive to master nature and extract short-term profit was stronger than the desire to protect human life, Carson was challenging the dominant belief system of postwar Americans. DDT's defenders wrapped themselves in the American faith in capitalism, government, and science. Carson's book struck a blow to that faith. The counterattack on Carson showed how radical her book really was.

The *Saturday Evening Post* went after Carson in the same way. She spread irrational fear of the men in charge, undermining faith in science and business. She wasn't just hurting chemical companies. "Implied in the attack on pesticides are the much more serious charges that scientists are ignoring human values." "What it doesn't explain is why an industrialist or a scientist, no matter how grasping, would poison our food and water—the same food and water he himself eats and drinks."[15]

The men who developed and tested pesticides were stung by the way she questioned their integrity. For them, it was personal. The assistant director of Dow Chemical's biochemistry lab conceded that "Miss Carson has contrived what seems to be an accurate and full collection of every type of accident, misuse, question and problem." But she refused "to acknowledge that people involved in research, in development, in the production and use of these substances are aware of the matters she presents and are attempting to do something about these problems."[16] Her emphasis on the corrupting power of money was particularly wounding. A writer in *American Forests* found troubling Carson's view on how money distorted research. "Money is tremendously powerful," he conceded. "But I am not prepared to accept the sweeping implications with which Miss Carson indicts both the chemical industry and those scientists and administrators who direct it."[17]

Academic scientists were angry she attributed their favorable view of pesticides to the amount of money that chemical companies gave to research. The chair of the National Academy of Science's Committee on Pest Control counterattacked. Chemistry "most intimately affected every aspect of our daily life . . . new fibers, new plastics, new medicinals, and new agricultural chemicals." As a result, people lived longer and better. "Benefits, however, have not come without a cost." Pesticides sometimes caused harm; to that extent, she had a point. "I cannot condone, however, the sarcastic and unjustified attack on the ethics and integrity of many scientific workers."[18]

The research director for a seed company blamed her for attempting "to frighten or disturb the existing order. . . . In arousing distrust of those whose duty it is to protect us from impurities and poisons in our foods, Miss Carson has probably done more harm to American agriculture than the European corn borer." Going further. he suggested why she did it. She was "a tremendously popular author. . . . Perhaps she has been too popular; has the need for maintaining income she has enjoyed in past years been the compelling force which led her outside her own field to exploit newer and more sensational topics?" He entitled his piece "CONFIDENCE IN OUR LEADERSHIP: For Sale for Thirty Pieces of Silver."[19] Carson was Judas. She not only did not share the American faith in the leaders of science and industry. She sold them out for her own profit.

Carson was condemned as amateur, do-gooder, rabble-rouser, bird lover, money grubber. Worse: as a woman. "Silence, Miss Carson," was the title of a piece by a member of the National Academy of Sciences, an expert on food production. She should just shut up. Her outlook was "pessimistic." Her book, consisting of "high-pitched sequences of anxieties," had no scientific merit, and would inflame "organic gardeners, the antiflouride leaguers, the worshippers of 'natural foods,' . . . and [other] faddists." She might mislead "the public to press for unwise and ill-conceived restrictions on the production, use, or development of new chemicals," bringing about "the end of all human progress." [20]

In *The Archives of Internal Medicine*, a doctor specializing in nutrition condemned "The Noise of Silent Spring." He, too, wished she'd just been quiet. Virtually alone among her critics, he granted her decisive argument: strains of insects resistant to pesticides would eventually evolve; the advantage gained from spraying was only temporary. Nevertheless, he dismissed her book: "As science it is so much hogwash." And he dismissed her. She was no longer a scientist, objective and above the battle, as she had been in her nature books, but instead was emotional and partisan. "What must be remembered is not that she *was* a scientist but that now she *is* a crusader." As a man, he knew that she was not worth arguing with. "Silent Spring, which I read word for word with some trauma, kept reminding me of trying to win an argument with a woman. It can not be done."[21]

She was an emotional and hysterical woman. You can't argue with a woman. Silence, Miss Carson. Those who attacked Carson tended to highlight her gender. They saw it as a vulnerability. She was not a true scientist, not impartial, not reasonable, not male. Her critic in the *Saturday Evening Post* characterized her as a "retiring single woman," whose arguments were "more emotional than accurate."[22] A federal official wondered "why a spinster with no children was so concerned about genetics?"[23]

The men who ran the economy and the country, who were used to calling the shots, appeared benevolent until challenged. The reaction to *Silent Spring*, like the reaction of the authorities in Mississippi to SNCC, showed the viciousness behind the benevolent mask. But the fury directed toward her demonstrated something else as well. The over-the-top reaction to her book showed that the belief in the guiding wisdom of scientific experts and industrial leaders and government bureaucrats, despite the appearance of evidence-based argument, was based on faith.

Carson not only threatened the bottom line of a major industry. She questioned the 1950s' faith in progress and challenged the experts. They understood that she was subverting their authority. They imagined themselves apart from nature. She called into question their idea of reason, their lack of love for nature, their project of conquering it. Unable to refute her arguments, they attacked her.

Carson's Counterattack

Carson took the attacks in stride. Although she feared criticism while writing the book, when the attack came, in such a vicious and personal form, she proved surprisingly thick-skinned. In contrast to Betty Friedan, who was quite vulnerable to attack, Carson was genuinely tough. Unlike Friedan, she did not have a subversive past and knew her credentials as an American were unassailable. Perhaps she was also too sick to be bothered by personal attacks.

Elaine Tyler May, in her history of the 1950s, emphasizes that the culture of the fifties was still alive and well in the early 1960s: "the cold war consensus," "the ideology of domesticity," "the faith in expertise."[24] Leaving the ideology of domesticity to Friedan, Carson struck an enormous blow against the faith in expertise. In the *New York Times Book Review*, three months after the book appeared, she embraced the accusation of undermining faith in the men in charge. "Until very recently, the average citizen assumed that 'Someone' was looking after these matters and some little understood but confidently relied upon safeguards stood like shields between his person and any harm. Now he has experienced . . . a rather rude shattering of these beliefs."[25]

Responding to attacks, Carson was an effective counterpuncher. Speaking to the Women's National Press Club, with TV cameras on, she observed that the pesticide industry had been pouring out misinformation to repair its reputation and damage her own. "The attack is now falling into a definite pattern and all the well-known devices are being used. One obvious way to weaken a cause is to discredit the person who champions it." Sweeping aside the personal charges, she concentrated on those directed against the book. One reviewer denied that the pesticide companies subsidized academic research. "Now, this is just common knowledge and I can scarcely believe the reviewer is unaware of it, because his own university is among those receiving such grants."[26]

As she fought back, she drew encouragement from the response of citizens, expressed in sales and letters. Within a month of publication, *Silent Spring* went to the top of the bestseller list and remained a bestseller for over six months. Most letter writers were women. Focused on protecting future generations, they told Carson of actions they were taking as a result of reading her book.[27] The letters she received from citizens, telling what they'd done and asking what else they could do, made her think about starting a national organization to fight pesticides.[28] Never a full-fledged activist like Baker, Jacobs, or Friedan, she took pleasure in the emergence of a grassroots movement. Researching *Silent Spring*, she had drawn on protestors like Marjory Spock and Dixie Larkin. *Silent Spring* deepened and broadened the protests. In the short time that she had after the book appeared, Carson encouraged protest and helped build a movement.

In January 1963, she spoke to the women of the Garden Club of America, who were discussing *Silent Spring*; the Garden Club, like the Audubon Society, was becoming a center of resistance. "People are beginning to ask questions and to insist upon proper answers instead of meekly acquiescing," she told the women. "We must continue to challenge and question." The government was not leading; it was part of the problem. "The fundamental wrong is the authoritarian control that has been vested in the agricultural agencies." The answer was democracy and accountability: "public vigilance and public demand for correction of abuses." Citizens must not be passive. "Above all, we must not be deceived by the enormous stream of propaganda that is issuing from the pesticide manufacturers and from industry-related—although ostensibly independent—organizations."[29]

Speaking to the Women's Press Club, she exposed not only industry, but also the American Medical Association. If a patient asked her doctor for information on the dangers of pesticides, the AMA wanted the doctor to refer her to an information kit distributed by the National Agricultural Chemical Association. This advice was part of a pattern of deferring to industry. "When the scientific organization speaks, whose voice do we hear—that of science? or of the sustaining industry?" In Russia, the science of genetics was destroyed by the state. "But here the tailoring, the screening of basic truth, is done, not to suit a party line, but to accommodate to the short-term gain, to serve the gods of profit and production."[30]

In April 1963, "CBS Reports" aired its prime-time special on *Silent Spring*. Two days before the show, the three largest commercial sponsors of the program withdrew. CBS went ahead and gave Carson the last word. There were 10 million people watching. "We still talk in terms of conquest. We still haven't become mature enough to think of ourselves as only a tiny part of a vast and incredible universe. . . . But man is a part of nature and his war against nature is inevitably a war against himself."[31]

More famous than ever, Carson used her fame strategically. She met with the President's Science Advisory Panel on pesticides, formed largely in response to the protests triggered by her book. An agricultural scientist complained that the first draft of the panel's report on pesticides sounded too much like Carson; the Department of Agriculture lobbied unsuccessfully to remove a passage that explicitly praised her work. After her testimony, the panel issued its final report, siding with her, recommending tighter government regulation of pesticides and the eventual elimination of persistent pesticides like DDT. Eric Sevareid of CBS, hailing the report, recognized that Carson and *Silent Spring* had been able "to alert the public" and "build a fire under the Government."[32]

She mustered the strength, in June 1963, to appear before two separate committees of the Senate. She urged them to form an independent agency—with no ties to industry and no conflicts of interest—to protect the environment and regulate pesticides.[33] Her recommendations anticipated the formation, seven years later, of the Environmental Protection Agency.

She died in the spring of 1964, at fifty-six, too soon to see the full flowering of the movement. But Carson and her sister activists put in motion the three-pronged campaign—protest at the grassroots, pressure on Congress, and use of the courts (by Spock) against federal agencies—that would eventually lead to the federal regulation of pesticides and a ban on DDT. The attempt to suppress, distort, neutralize or demonize Carson failed to prevent the emergence of a robust environmental movement or the tougher regulation of pesticides in the United States.

Jane Jacobs and the Bullies

Similar attacks were made on Jane Jacobs. They were not so furious as the attacks on Carson, not financed by such wealthy interests, and not coordinated, but their similarity to the attacks on Carson is nevertheless revealing. Carson and Jacobs identified the forces of death. They blew the whistle, exposing the hoax of progress. Kill the whistleblower: instead of meeting the arguments that Carson and Jacobs made, the bullies made the women the issue.

Robert Moses returned his free copy of *Death and Life* to the publisher, with the instruction: "Sell this junk to someone else." Pointing to page 131, which said that he had made an art of using public money to control public officials, Moses called the book "libelous."[34] His comment anticipated McLean's threat to sue Carson's publisher.

The *American Society of Planning Officials Newsletter* described Jacobs as dangerous. "Mrs. Jacobs has presented the world with a document that will be grabbed by screwballs and reactionaries and used to fight civic improvement and urban renewal projects for years to come."[35] Like Carson, Jacobs encouraged the cranks and crazies. And like Carson, Jacobs was an effective writer, which made her more dangerous. Roger Starr, the New York planner, characterized her view of Greenwich Village as fiction. "But she describes her folksy urban place on Hudson Street (Manhattan) with such spirit and womanly verve that she has made a considerable number of readers believe it really exists."[36]

American City Magazine accused Jacobs of believing she knew more than the experts. She claimed the North End of Boston was a vital neighborhood that was unslumming itself. "It is of no importance that planners classify it as a slum; that the professors at Harvard and MIT send their students there to practice preparing urban-development plans; or that bankers do not care to risk lending money on the property there."[37] The sarcastic tone, characteristic of the reaction against Jacobs, was intended to put her in her place and was strikingly similar to the tone of attacks on Carson. These amateur women, who pretended to know more than the experts, were pied pipers; the uncritical and gullible public was following them toward disaster.

Like Carson, Jacobs created fiction that misled citizens and undermined the authority of the experts. And, like Carson, she did it for profit. When Jacobs criticized Pittsburgh's new public housing, the housing administrator took it personally and responded personally. His public housing project was a paradise "by comparison with the crowded, narrow, dangerous, dirty, rodent and bar-infested streets in . . . Greenwich village." Her criticisms aimed "to provide a market" for her writing.[38] Jacobs herself thought that planners and developers attacked her work because "there just isn't money to be made with my ideas." Her approach gave the power of healing neighborhoods back to the residents. "The people who tear down neighborhoods and then re-build them badly are spending a lot of money. There's no financial profit in letting a neighborhood take care of itself."[39]

But the most vicious attack on Jacobs had nothing to do with money. It came from Lewis Mumford, the senior critic of urban renewal. Mumford had applauded her when she burst on the scene at Harvard in 1956. When she applied to the Rockefeller foundation for the grant to write the book, he wrote a strong letter of support.[40] To her, he expressed excitement about her book project. "This old Master Builder, unlike Ibsen's, likes to hear the younger generation knocking on the door!"[41] But when she came through the door, the old master builder was furious.

Death and Life criticized Mumford's work for being anticity. "Mumford's *The Culture of Cities* was largely a morbid and biased catalog of ills."[42] Asked to respond, he initially declined, dismissing Jacobs as beneath him. "In asking for a comment, you are in effect suggesting that an old surgeon give public judgment on the work of a confident but sloppy novice, operating to remove an imaginary tumor."[43] He waited a year before attacking publicly, while she became "a rampart public figure in the cities movement," with "a sufficiently large uncritical following even among supposedly knowledgeable professors of planning."[44]

His long essay in the *New Yorker* was entitled "Mother Jacobs' Home Remedies." The title continued his medical metaphor, except that she was not a novice surgeon now, just a mother with home remedies. Insisting the city was sick, Mumford invoked Carson. "'Silent Spring' came to the big city long before it visited the countryside." But Jacobs ignored the sickness. "Congestion and disorder" were the normal, indeed desirable, conditions of urban life for her. He denounced "the increasing pathology of the whole mode of life in the great metropolis, a pathology that is directly proportionate to its overgrowth, its purposeless materialism, its congestion, and its insensate disorder—the very conditions she vehemently upholds as the marks of urban vitality." The density that Jacobs romanticized caused carbon monoxide poisoning, pollution, cancer. She was guilty of "sentimentality" and "school-girl howlers," of applying "a homemade poultice for the cure of a cancer." Mumford diagnosed in her "a preoccupation that is almost an obsession: the prevention of criminal violence in big cities." She believed crowded streets and neighborhoods were safer. As a manly man, he knew violence was not the problem. "I speak as a born and bred New Yorker, who in his time has walked almost every street in Manhattan."[45]

Through Mumford's elevated prose comes his horror of the city, with its masses of people living materialistic and disordered lives. There she was, down there with the masses, claiming that they were the source of vitality, that out of their apparent disorder came order, and that he, with his loathing of cities, was part of the problem. It made him want to spank her. To a friend, after writing the piece in the *New Yorker*, he confided: "I can't pretend that I don't enjoy giving her an awful walloping on the soft spot of her carcass that she so carelessly exposed."[46]

Jacobs did not take his attack personally. She liked him.

As far as I was concerned we were friendly. It was very funny. He was furious at
The Death and Life of Great American Cities, absolutely furious. He thought—I
never gave him any reason to think this—he thought that I was a protégé of his,
a disciple. . . . Because he thought that all younger people who were friendly
must be his disciple.[47]

Right after publication of his attack, she invited him to support a protest
(he did); in later years, she continued to read and respect his work.[48] The
problem between them, she believed, was not personal. The problem was that
he hated what she loved. "The great men of planning and its philosophy—
Ebenezer Howard, Corbusier, Lewis Mumford . . .—deplored cities, were dis-
gusted by their streets, and even sought to erase them as much as possible."[49]
When she looked back at her earlier relationship with Mumford, one experience stood out.

We rode into the city together in a car. And I watched how he acted as soon as
he began to get into the city. And he had been talking and all pleasant but as
soon as he began to get into the city he got grim, withdrawn, and distressed.
And it was just so clear that he just hated the city and hated being part of it.[50]

Like Carson, who regarded cities as unnatural, Mumford hated cities. The
difference was that Carson was not trying to prescribe for them.

Mumford's attack on Jacobs was meant to put a presumptuous woman in
her place. Schoolgirl or mother, she was the wrong sex. Men built tall buildings and high theory; women like Jacobs, with their homey ways, should
keep to their own sphere. "Mr. Mumford," she explained, "seemed to think of
women as a ladies' auxiliary of the human race."[51]

In similar fashion, scientists and industrialists—who made no objection to
Carson's writing about the sea—attacked her when she interfered with progress through chemistry. Then she became a disorderly and destructive amateur, a woman who did not know her place. Carson, like Jacobs, was derided
for worrying too much about safety.[52] A critic of Jacobs referred to her as
"Jane"; a critic of Carson addressed her as "Rachel, Rachel."[53] They would never
have referred to a male writer in this way. Jacobs was Mother Jacobs; Carson
was a hysterical spinster. Either way, they were only women, who should not
be allowed to hinder the serious business of men.

Jacobs was attacked, in part, because her ideas interfered with the money
that could be made through urban renewal. Carson was attacked much
more powerfully, because her work directly challenged the profits of a major

industry. Both women were attacked for threatening the cult of expertise. Jacobs and her fellow leaders of the fight to save the West Village exposed the bullies behind the mask of benevolence worn by city bureaucrats and planners. Carson turned the aggression back on the bullies, in her speeches and TV appearances after her book was published, and exposed the chemical industry and its servants. If you were as smart and brave as Carson and Jacobs in the early sixties, you could take on powerful men and win.

12

Baker, Friedan, and the
Two Women's Movements

Ella Baker, SNCC, and the Women's Liberation Movement

Ella Baker and the Student Nonviolent Coordinating Committee created the model for the popular movements that emerged from below in the middle and late sixties. Young activists throughout America were inspired by SNCC's courage, its respect for ordinary people, its insistence on people making their own decisions, its refusal to police itself, and its commitment to organize for the long haul. That's what Charles Payne meant when he suggested that Baker invented the 1960s.[1]

From 1965 to 1970, the largest, most powerful movements from below—the antiwar movement and the women's liberation movement—drew profoundly on the radical democratic spirit of Ella Baker and SNCC. The influence of Baker and SNCC on the leading organization of young antiwar radicals, SDS, is easy to see. The key founders of SDS, Al Haber and Tom Hayden, observed SNCC organizers in action in the South in the very beginning and were galvanized by their commitment to grassroots democracy. Haber, who attended early SNCC meetings, recognized Baker as a crucial influence not only on the Black student movement but on the emerging white student movement as well.[2] Hayden was with SNCC organizers in Mississippi in 1961. "SNCC's early organizing method was based on listening to local people," says Hayden. "We were all influenced by Ella Baker."[3]

Less obvious, at least until Sara Evans published *Personal Politics* in 1979, was the influence of Baker and SNCC on the women's liberation movement. Evans demonstrated that the mass movement for women's liberation, which emerged in the later 60s—radically egalitarian, participatory, open, youthful, and confrontational—was descended from SNCC and Baker.[4] More recently, Linda Gordon showed how the consciousness-raising groups drew on the group-centered leadership that Baker modeled in SNCC. "CR groups were novel but their theory was close to what SNCC's Ella Baker had been enunciating."[5]

Baker consistently fostered leadership by women. As acting executive director of the Southern Christian Leadership Conference, she criticized the ministers for subordinating women, and called for the active involvement of women in the movement.[6] As SNCC's mentor, she encouraged women to assert themselves and become powerful. Baker "cleared obstacles from their way whenever she could," said her biographer, Barbara Ransby. "Her ideas and example influenced not only SNCC in the 1960s, but also . . . the embryonic women's movement of the late 1960s and the 1970s."[7]

In the beginning, SNCC was overwhelmingly male. Like men in other civil rights organizations, men in SNCC expected to lead. In 1961, when SNCC needed a new executive secretary, Baker thought it was too soon for a woman to become executive secretary, "because at that stage I don't know of anyone that was in the group, except Diane Nash, but I didn't think she would have fought the male-female battle that would no doubt have arisen had she been the person to pass the mantle on to."[8] Under Baker's guidance, SNCC became a more women-friendly organization; the male-female balance of power began to change. In 1962, when Martha Prescott Norman helped Bernard Lafayette run a SNCC fund-raiser in Detroit, she was impressed that Diane Nash was the featured speaker. "That Bernard, a minister and excellent speaker himself, chose to focus our work and public attention on Diane reinforced for me the important role women played within early SNCC and how powerful the women were who had cast their lot with the organization. By that time I had heard Miss Baker's ideas floated like gospel."[9]

Baker modeled and facilitated the power of women in SNCC. By 1964, she no longer hesitated to challenge men who tried to keep women back. Lawrence Guyot, a SNCC organizer in Mississippi, made a comment at a SNCC meeting about women needing to step back a little and let the men take charge. "Ella Baker told me: . . . 'You have to learn never, never make the mistake of substituting men in quantity for women of quality.' I haven't done that shit anymore. In fact, I've gone the other way around."[10] Stokely Carmichael echoed Guyot's view. "I would not have been taken seriously as a leader of an organization like SNCC if I had not taken seriously the leadership of women. . . . A woman like Ella Baker would not have tolerated it."[11]

Casey Hayden and Mary King, two young white women, took the crucial next step and sparked the national movement for women's liberation. Hayden acknowledges Baker's profound influence. "So in this way, the women's movement traces back to Ella Baker. She is behind it, as she is always behind the scenes."[12] Hayden met Baker in October 1960 at a SNCC conference and found her "elegant and homey and warm." Baker embodied Hayden's sense of SNCC. "The SNCC of which I was a part was nurturing, warm, familial, supportive, honest and penetrating, radical and pragmatic. I think of it as womanist. I see Ella in all of that."[13]

In 1961–1962, Hayden worked under Baker's direction at the YWCA, where Baker worked part-time, leading discussions on race between young Black and white women.

> I remember Ella beginning our meetings when I got back from a trip [to a college campus] by saying, "Let's see. Now what are we doing here?" She really meant it. In all the arenas in which I saw Ella operate, she always said what she meant. . . . Her approach to people was always fresh. She was interested in everyone and always asked where they were from and about their family.[14]

When Hayden began working full time for SNCC in 1962, she realized that "the value assigned women in SNCC" was due to Baker. "Ella's presence in SNCC defined it in many ways." SNCC organizers rejected hierarchical roles, combining high theory with lowly practice. "I always attributed this integration of intellect and sweat labor to Ella." Baker was the force behind SNCC's democratic commitment to developing leaders from below. "Her notion of the need to raise up new leaders . . . [was] based on years of experience in seeing folks join the leaders' club when they became leaders, leaving their constituents behind."[15]

Mary King took Hayden's place under Baker at the Y in 1962 and became full time in SNCC in 1963. Baker, says King, was "a great listener," whose teaching style was "a series of questions.

> In her resolute and commanding voice, she would query: "Now let me ask this again, what is our purpose here? What are we trying to accomplish?" Again and again, she would force us to articulate our assumptions. . . . She encouraged me to avoid being doctrinaire. "Ask questions, Mary," she would say.[16]

Baker almost never discussed her private life. But she told King that she had married quietly (during the 1930s) and divorced quietly (in 1958). "'I have always been very happy that I didn't change my name,' she said to me. 'I didn't think that I belonged to any man.'"[17] For King and Hayden, Baker was a model of female independence. "Ella was perhaps the most secure, rooted, self-knowledgeable woman I've known," says Hayden.[18] When King and Hayden took the next step, toward women's liberation, they felt that they were drawing on Baker's example and teaching. "Perhaps the most important principle for Miss Baker is that 'you must let the oppressed themselves define their own freedom,'" says King. "Wasn't that in fact what we were seeking to do, to define our own freedom?"[19]

In November 1964, at a SNCC retreat in Mississippi, King and Hayden took a risk. SNCC was struggling to resolve contentious issues about its size, structure, and direction, in the wake of Mississippi Freedom Summer and Atlantic City, and there were many position papers proposing new directions. King and Hayden presented a paper about women in SNCC. Their paper grew out of informal discussions with a few female and male organizers in Mississippi.[20] King wrote the first draft, and Hayden edited it. Baker played no direct role. She wasn't present at the retreat (which, according to Hayden, was one reason the retreat failed.)[21]

King and Hayden took SNCC's critique of racism and applied it to sex roles. They wanted, Hayden explains, "to discern the effects of a system—stereotyping, labeling, and discrimination, wasted talent, separation."[22] They challenged SNCC in terms of its own values—its egalitarianism, its capacity for questioning the dominant assumptions of American society, its cultivation of leadership from below. Hayden and King were driven by the contradiction between the radically democratic ideas of SNCC and the persistent stereotypes of women in the organization. They felt they were channeling Baker's way of raising fundamental questions.

But they submitted the paper anonymously. Like Friedan when she was writing *The Feminine Mystique*, they anticipated ridicule. "Fearing a mirthful reaction, I prepared it secretly, to be presented anonymously," says King. "I did not feel secure raising these questions. My heart was palpitating and I was shaking as I typed it. My fear of a joking response was making me unsteady."[23] The inequality of women seemed so natural and normal that King and Hayden did not feel safe. Three other white women, who played small roles in drafting the paper, chose to remain anonymous for decades.[24] But it soon became known that King and Hayden were the principal authors.

The heart of their paper was a list of eleven examples of male domination. "Any woman in SNCC, no matter what her position or experience, has been asked to take minutes in a meeting when she and other women are outnumbered by men." Two organizers worked together. "Without asking any questions, the male organizer immediately assigned the clerical work to the female organizer although both had had equal experience in organizing campaigns." Even in Mississippi, where SNCC was at its most egalitarian: "Although there are women in the Mississippi project who have been working as long as some of the men, the leadership group . . . is all men."[25]

The final two examples implicitly acknowledged that some women were already leaders in SNCC.

10. Capable, responsible, and experienced women who are in leadership positions
   can expect to have to defer to a man on their project for final decision making.
11. A session at the recent October staff meeting in Atlanta was the first large
   meeting in the past couple of years where a woman was asked to chair.[26]

Hayden and King's point was not that women were servants in SNCC, confined solely to clerical tasks, never allowed to lead. Their point was that women were not equal. They knew that SNCC, which worked so hard to challenge racial stereotypes and encourage Black leadership to emerge, had not made the same effort to challenge sex stereotypes, and so these stereotypes continued to shape the role of men and women in the organization. They wanted their beloved SNCC to make that effort, "so that all of us gradually come to understand that this is no more a man's world than it is a white world."[27]

King and Hayden did not believe SNCC was a worse place for women than other places in the society. Emmie Schrader Adams, one of the women who played a minor role in drafting the paper, is very clear about this. "Which organization in the world before 1965 did not manifest male chauvinism? No one ever said SNCC was in any way worse than the world at large. Indeed, it was quite a bit better."[28] SNCC was a place where women could imagine equality. King says SNCC gave Hayden and her "the nourishment" needed to claim equality: "the political consciousness, boosts to our self-confidence, and encouragement of our native willingness to take risks."[29] Hayden agrees: "It says a great deal about SNCC that we could raise these concerns, hitherto so private, so publicly. Yet, this is what we had learned in SNCC: to raise basic questions with astounding implications."[30]

In the paper, Hayden and King acknowledged that most women in SNCC did not agree with them. "Most women don't talk about these kinds of incidents, because the whole subject is not discussable—strange to some, petty to others, laughable to most."[31] They nevertheless hoped that the paper would open up dialogue. "Maybe the only thing that can come out of this paper is

discussion—amidst the laughter—but still discussion."[32] With so many position papers on seemingly more pressing topics, their paper did not stimulate discussion. A few men, including Bob Moses, expressed support.[33] Most
women, especially Black women, ignored or rejected their argument.

But King and Hayden didn't give up. They tried talking to women one
on one. Hayden reached out to Cynthia Washington, a young Black woman
who had recently assumed a leadership position in Mississippi. Washington
was not impressed. She thought Hayden's protest against inequality didn't
apply to her. "What she said didn't make any particular sense to me because,
at the time, I had my own project in Bolivar County, Miss." Washington dismissed the question of the treatment of women in SNCC as a white woman's
thing. "I remember driving back to Mississippi in my truck, thinking how
crazy they were."

Looking back, in 1977, Washington wasn't so sure. Although it was true she
did the same work as men in SNCC, she was, as a result, invisible as a woman.

> I remember discussing with various [Black] women about our treatment as one
> of the boys and its impact on us as women. We did the same work as men—
> organizing around voter registration and community issues in rural areas—
> usually with men. But when we finally got back to some town where we could
> relax and go out, the men went out with other women. Our skills and abilities
> were recognized and respected, but that seemed to place us in some category
> other than female.[34]

Gloria Wade-Gayles, a Black volunteer during Mississippi Freedom Summer,
also experienced "our invisibility as desired lovers."[35]

In 1964, King and Hayden's critique was of women's public roles in SNCC;
their critique did not reach private, personal experiences, like the one
described by Washington. Only later, when the women's liberation movement
emerged, would an emphasis on personal and sexual experience become
legitimate. In 1964, Washington did not see what Hayden was driving at. "I'm
certain," she says, "that our single-minded focus on the issues of racial discrimination and the black struggle for equality blinded us to other issues."[36]

Many Black women defended SNCC against King and Hayden's criticism
in 1964 and continue to defend it. They see race as key—as more important
than gender. Some employ race to dismiss King and Hayden's critique of
sex roles: King and Hayden, as white women, launched a critique of SNCC
because, as SNCC began to turn toward Black Power, whites no longer had a
major role to play.[37]

Other Black women admit women and men were not equal in SNCC but stress they were not equal anywhere. Annie Pearl Avery organized in Mississippi and Alabama. Her evaluation of the role of women in SNCC is not so different from Hayden's and King's, but her emphasis is much more positive.

> On SNCC projects there was sexism toward women, because this was a way of life for all women. Sometimes, I felt limited because we weren't allowed to drive the cars. At first all the fellows were driving, but they wouldn't teach us how to drive! Eventually, Sammy Younge taught me to drive a stick shift in his yellow VW Bug. The male chauvinism was there, but I don't think it was intentional. It wasn't as dominant in SNCC as it was in SCLC, which Miss Baker told us about.[38]

Penny Patch, who is white, feels the same way. From 1962 to 1965, Patch worked in Georgia and Mississippi. It was the high point of her life. She left SNCC only because Blacks turned against whites—a turn she suffered, understood, and accepted. Later she became active for a while in the women's movement. But the women's movement seemed too white, too unaware of race. For Patch, women's issues literally pale when compared to the injustice faced by Blacks. "Racism for me trumped sexism. Even all these years later, although I have always counted myself a serious feminist, it still does."[39]

> Jean Wiley, who is Black, joined SNCC in June 1964. She felt free and equal.
> I wish to high heaven I had found in my life before, or in the years since, the freedom I as a woman found there. That my gender should prevent me from a role in SNCC was unthinkable. By the time I got to the South, SNCC women were driving the cars and riding the mules, organizing the plantations and directing the field staff, writing the reports and mobilizing the northern campuses. How could it not be so? Ella Baker gathered and mentored us. Fannie Lou Hamer was one of our most eloquent spokespersons. And Ruby Doris Robinson would soon become SNCC's executive secretary. Yes, SNCC was the first and only time in my life that my gender was not a barrier to my aspirations.[40]

Wiley emphasizes the leadership of women within SNCC, whereas King and Hayden stress the ways that stereotypes limited the role of women. In terms of the argument, which is ongoing, they are on opposite sides. But they agree on two fundamental things: by 1964, women were more empowered in SNCC than in the society at large, and Baker's mentoring was a major reason why.

Despite the lack of response, King and Hayden continued to believe they were on to something. One year after failing to stimulate discussion on the inequality of women in SNCC, they wrote a new paper and mailed it to forty young women in the civil rights and antiwar movements. They were going beyond SNCC, beyond Ella Baker. But they still drew on Baker's example and her mentoring. "My having worked with Ella Baker was one of the most important factors in my wanting to share the two documents," says King.[41]

The new paper articulated ideas about inequality that would become central to the women's liberation movement. This time Hayden wrote the draft and King edited it. And this time, they put their names on it: "Sex and Caste: A Kind of Memo from Casey Hayden and Mary King to a Number of Other Women in the Peace and Freedom Movement." Again, they called for discussion about the public roles of movement women, who were forced "to work around or outside hierarchical structures of power." But now they added: "women seem to be placed in the same position of assumed subordination in personal situations too." They had begun to question the very distinction between the personal and the political. It was a big step. "We've talked in the movement about trying to build a society which would see basic human problems (which are now seen as private troubles), as public problems." [42]

Though they were writing as movement women to movement women, Hayden and King never expected women to start a movement of their own. Their second paper, in November 1965, stated that "the chances seem nil that we could start a movement."[43] But by 1967, many young white women in the peace and freedom movements began to give up hope of reform and to create a separate movement of their own. Hayden and King's 1965 "Memo," published in the radical magazine *Liberation* in April 1966, became one of the founding documents of the mass movement for women's liberation. "We hoped that a network would evolve. What developed was far beyond our expectation."[44]

Hayden and King's emphasis on inequality within the movement for equality especially struck a chord in SDS women organizing the poor in northern cities. SDS's Economic Research and Action Projects drew on SNCC's methods of developing leadership from below, which many ERAP organizers learned as SNCC staff or volunteers in the deep South. In the SNCC model, listening was crucial. ERAP women tended to be better listeners than the men and were therefore more successful organizers, but men were the big talkers who dominated national ERAP meetings.[45]

In December 1965, one month after receiving Hayden and King's "Memo," women organizers in ERAP projects organized a workshop for women at a national SDS conference. At the workshop, the young women talked about how they were silenced or marginalized within the movement—in college, in SNCC, in SDS and ERAP. "What we did," wrote one woman, "was trace back our roots, and figure out what made us as we are, and then what are the forms of the ways we are not allowed to fulfill what we could be."[46] This workshop, at the end of 1965, inaugurated the powerful process of women listening to women, which would soon be called consciousness raising.

Listening to one another's stories, finding public threads behind the personal and private stories, the young women at the workshop came up with a radical idea: men and women should equally raise children. They hoped that kids raised in this way would feel free to choose their work instead of allowing stereotypes to shape their choice. These young radical women were talking about work that would transform the society. Sara Evans observed: "Their definition of work reflected a radical rejection of the careerist solution advocated by Betty Friedan."[47]

The new approach of women talking and listening to women spread through SDS. In June 1967, at a national SDS convention, women convened a "Women's Liberation Workshop." They were hoping to reform SDS, as King and Hayden once hoped to reform SNCC. But when young women from the workshop reported the results of their discussion to the whole convention, they were met with hoots of laughter from young men. The derision drove these women toward creating a movement of their own. Alice Echols pointed out that women were pushed to develop their own movement by the increasing turn of SDS, at the end of the sixties, toward hypermasculine posturing. A similar turn toward macho rhetoric and organizing in the media occurred in SNCC. As the youthful movements for civil rights and against the war began to lose momentum and focus, the women's liberation movement, the largest and strongest—most vital, idealistic, democratic, and egalitarian—movement, emerged out of and against SNCC and SDS.[48]

The powerful current of women listening to women in the new movement grew directly from experience in SNCC. At the first National Women's Liberation Conference, in 1968, Kathie Sarachild introduced "A Program for Feminist 'Consciousness Raising.'" For the first time, she defined consciousness raising and argued for its centrality to the women's movement. Beginning as "personal testimonies" and "recognition," consciousness raising culminated in "generalizing [from] individual testimony." She articulated the assumption behind the process: "We assume that our feelings are telling us something from which we can learn . . . that our feelings mean something worth analyzing . . . that our feelings are saying something *political*."[49] Sarachild did voter registration with SNCC during Mississippi Freedom Summer and learned about listening as a mode of organizing. A few years after her seminal paper, she made the connection explicit: "We were applying to women and to ourselves as women's liberation organizers the practice a number of us had learned in the civil rights movement in the South in the early 1960s."[50]

Carol Hanisch wrote a groundbreaking paper in February 1969: "The Personal is Political." Hanish examined the role of consciousness-raising in women's liberation. "One of the first things we discover in these groups is that personal problems are political problems. There are no personal solutions at this time. There is only collective action for a collective solution."[51] Hanisch spent nine months in the Mississippi movement in 1965. In 1970, Pam Allen tried to codify the process of consciousness raising in an influential article titled "Free Space." Allen was with SNCC in Mississippi during Freedom Summer.[52]

No one has traced in detail the influence of Ella Baker on the women's liberation movement. This chapter documents her direct influence on Casey Hayden and Mary King, and her indirect influence on Sarachild, Hanisch, and Allen. The mass movement for women's liberation developed, in decisive ways, out of young white women's experience in SNCC and Mississippi. More than those who joined the Mississippi movement in 1964 or 1965, Hayden and King understood how much Ella Baker shaped that experience.

From 1968 through the early 1970s, in big cities and college towns, young white women created small, decentralized groups that provided a safe space to examine what male domination did to them. Talking and listening to one another, they realized that they had always seen the world, and themselves, through the eyes of men. Now, for the first time, they were learning to see through their own eyes.[53] These participants in the women's liberation movement considered themselves radicals. Linda Gordon pointed out that they borrowed the word "liberation" from revolutionary anticolonial movements, like the one in Vietnam.[54]

Consciousness raising, created by radical young women, proved transformative for many women, including some not so young or so radical. A woman active in the antiwar movement was in her forties when she joined a small group of mothers in Berkeley.

I'll never forget one night, this marvelous woman. She . . . was talking about how while she grew up, she wasn't the stereotypical feminine type, and how this caused her a lot of grief. Then she said, "I realized that it was ok to be a strong woman." Suddenly there was complete silence, followed by shouts of agreement. It was a very exciting moment. People were getting it, right there, in that meeting.[55]

The core assumption of the feminine mystique—forcefulness is not feminine—dissolved when women listened to women. The original group of women that Friedan brought together a decade earlier also experienced the power of listening to one another. The difference in 1969 was that the small groups were part of a movement seeking to transform the society.

Sensing danger to the established society, the FBI infiltrated women's liberation groups, as it infiltrated all uprisings from below in the 1960s. The disorientation of an FBI informant in Baltimore is evident beneath her flat prose. Clearly, something subversive was going on, but it was hard to specify what.

> The women's liberation movement in Baltimore Md. began during the summer of 1968. There was no structure or parent organization. There were no rules or plans to go by. It started out as a group therapy session with young women who were either lonely or confined to the home with small children, getting together to talk about their problems. Along with this they wanted a purpose and that was to be free women from the humdrum existence of being only a wife and mother. They wanted equal opportunities that men have in work and in society. They wanted their husbands to share in the housework and in raising their children.[56]

The FBI was correct to perceive the women's liberation movement as a threat. By 1968, the movement was beginning to transform America.

Betty Friedan and the National Organization for Women

1964, the year of King and Hayden's seminal paper, was also the year of the Civil Rights Act. Betty Friedan explained the importance of Title VII of the Act, which outlawed discrimination by sex. Women, who were "standing still or moving backwards," resumed moving forward.

> This second phase of the feminine revolution began in the United States in 1964 when, in what seemed at first to be a fluke or a joke, sex discrimination in employment was made illegal along with race discrimination. . . . The Congress of the United States erupted in hysterical laughter when Congressman [Howard W.] Smith of Virginia proposed adding sex to the Civil Rights Act.
>
> The new woman emerges, as Congressman Martha Griffiths of Michigan makes the men stop laughing and, with the support of a spontaneous feminine underground in Washington, turns the joke into a reality.[57]

Friedan was not part of the feminine underground that fought to keep women in the 1964 Civil Rights Act. Newly famous as a result of *The Feminine Mystique*, she was initially uncertain what to do with her fame. She responded to the lead of others, especially Pauli Murray, a Black lawyer and professor who fought to keep the prohibition on sex discrimination in the Act and then agitated for enforcement of the law. In October 1965, speaking in New York, Murray recalled how she and other Blacks marched on Washington in 1963 for jobs and freedom and urged women to be ready to march again. "It should not be necessary to have another March on Washington in order that there be equal job opportunities for all. But if this necessity should arise, I hope women will not flinch."[58] Friedan had "almost begun to despair" until she read about Murray's speech in the *New York Times*. "Bringing women into the Civil rights act was not a joke at all," Friedan realized. "It could be the new beginning." She called Murray, who connected her with other activists. Friedan did not start this movement. Rather, she joined it. "I became a member of the feminine underground."[59]

Murray introduced Friedan to Sonia Pressman, the first woman lawyer hired by the Equal Employment Opportunity Commission. EEOC, established in July 1965 to compel compliance with the Civil Rights Act, lacked the muscle and will to implement Title VII. Pressman knew EEOC needed a push and knew, as an employee, that the push had to come from outside. She urged Friedan to take the lead. "Your fame is based on speaking out for women," she told Friedan. "Nobody can fire you."[60] From the beginning, Friedan's leadership was based on her fame.

Pressman explained to Friedan, tearfully, that the country needed "an organization to fight for women the way the NAACP fought for African Americans."[61] Murray similarly urged Friedan to form "an NAACP for women."[62] Friedan, Murray, and a number of other women and a few men founded the National Organization for Women in June 1966. Speaking as NOW's first President, Friedan declared it an "N.A.A.C.P. for women."[63] Later, she acknowledged her debt to other women activists.

> It was in the air that we needed an NAACP for women. There were people in Washington and in the labor movement and in the government, women that had been thinking for much longer than me about women and the need for real equality and the need to break through . . . And they kind of saw that I would be useful in that because I was now quite famous and really looked up to by women for *The Feminine Mystique*. And I had no job to lose.[64]

NOW's Statement of Purpose, written by Friedan with help from Murray, clarified the analogy between NOW and the NAACP. "The purpose of NOW is to take action to bring women into full participation in the mainstream of American society now."[65] Blacks were finally entering the mainstream. But EEOC "has not made clear its intention to enforce the law with the same seriousness on behalf of women." As the NAACP removed barriers that prevented Blacks from rising, NOW would remove barriers that prevented women from rising. "All the women's movement was, or needs to be," Friedan later explained, "is a stage in the whole human right's movement, bringing another group—a majority this time—into the mainstream of human society."[66]

The women's movement led by Friedan and the women's movement triggered by Hayden and King were inspired by the struggle for racial equality. But they drew on very different strands of that struggle. The women's movement led by Friedan modeled itself on the NAACP and saw itself as fighting to extend rights to women, bringing them into the mainstream, so they could rise to the top of American society. The women's movement that grew out of SNCC rejected the very idea of a top and bottom.

When Hayden and King were formulating their ideas about the equality of women, they drew on modern feminism, but not on Friedan. In 1963, they loaned Doris Lessing's *The Golden Notebook* (1962) to Bob Moses and several other male friends in SNCC; they shared Simone de Beauvoir's *The Second Sex* (1949) with the few SNCC women willing to read it. These two key feminist texts were important to the intellectual and political growth of Hayden and King. By contrast, the newest and most popular feminist text did not engage them.

> Betty Friedan's *The Feminine Mystique*, which sent shock waves across American suburbs that same year, seemed irrelevant and marginal to us. . . . It was amazing to us that black women in the United States were not cited once. . . . Friedan's suburban emphasis seemed out of touch with the social and economic issues that concerned us and utterly unrelated to the questions of political and personal self-determination that were beginning to preoccupy us.[67]

Friedan was very aware of the struggle for racial equality. But in contrast to King and Hayden, it was not her struggle. She looked to the civil rights movement for the model of the struggle she would lead. And that model was the NAACP, led by educated and professional people, organized top down, aiming at equal rights and opportunities within the existing society.

She wanted to end discrimination against women so they could compete on a level playing field. Ella Baker wanted to end the competitive struggle and build a cooperative society, one in which everyone could win. Baker was clear about the difference. The basic goal of SNCC, she explained in 1966, was "to change society so that the have-nots can share in it," whereas "the NAACP, Urban League, etc., do not *change* society, they want to get in."[68] Three years later, she distinguished between "the struggle to get into the society, . . . to be part of the American scene," and "the struggle for a different kind of society. The latter is the more radical struggle."[69]

Friedan did not agree. Even in the moderate form NOW embraced, the struggle for the equality of women was inherently radical. "The women's movement was by definition a radical movement—it was going to, had to, bring about radical change in society."[70] She acknowledged that NOW's goal, in the first year, was narrow: to end job discrimination against women. But the means were revolutionary. "Women, for all these years, had done volunteer work and helped organize and support causes of anti-fascism, of the plight of the poor, organizing for everything but women themselves. But now, finally, we were doing it for ourselves—for women."[71] Women fighting for women was the radical step, carrying NOW beyond its initial emphasis on jobs and pay equity and making fundamental changes in American law, institutions, and culture, in areas as varied as employment, education, athletics, and reproductive rights. As Friedan recognized, adding women to the mainstream ended up transforming the mainstream.

In her view, NOW fought for all women, not only educated and professional women. The "Statement of Purpose," reflecting Murray's influence, emphasized the oppression of working-class women, especially Blacks. "About two-thirds of Negro women workers are in the lowest paid service occupations. Working women are becoming increasingly—not less—concentrated on the bottom of the job ladder."[72] During the years of her presidency, from 1966 to 1970, Friedan tried to get working-class women and Black women involved in NOW. In 1966, she went to Detroit, "and I learned about the hassle, the run-around, the intimidation when women tried to speak up for themselves or other women, even in the progressive U.A.W. C.I.O."[73] For a moment, she was listening to working-class women again. Later that year, citing her contacts in Detroit, she pushed back against a young woman who criticized her class bias. "While, in the Feminist Mystique, I did as you noted deal mainly with the situation of the middle-class educated women, I am very well aware of the problem of American women of less education; especially of working women."[74]

NOW was unable, however, to attract working-class women. Unlike SNCC, NOW was not good at developing leadership from below. Local chapters varied, but NOW as a whole remained robustly middle class. Friedan knew this, and sometimes she embraced it. "For the reality of this revolution is that we—the middle-class women who started it—did it for ourselves."[75] Most leaders of NOW were middle-class women credentialed in traditional ways, through educational degrees and/or professional achievements. Conceived as a lobby for women, NOW was a top-down organization.

But not all its leaders were white. Several were professional Black women, including Pauli Murray. Murray had a long history of civil rights activism. In 1940, she was arrested for resisting segregation on a bus in Virginia. In 1947, she and Ella Baker were ready to test segregation in bus travel for the NAACP. "But," Baker explained, "the decision was made that only the men could go."[76] In Murray's experience, Jim Crow was linked to what she called "Jane Crow," and the struggle for the rights of Blacks was linked to the struggle for the rights of women. Friedan recognized Murray as "the black scholar who triggered me first" and "tuned me into the underground network of women."[77]

Yet when Friedan described NOW as the organization for women and the NAACP as the organization for Blacks, she effectively rendered Murray invisible. During the 1950s, unable to get professional work, despite her law degree, Murray was forced to do typing for authors; one author who used her as a typist was Friedan. When they joined together to form NOW, Friedan seemed unaware of their prior relationship.[78] Murray really was invisible. Within a year of co-founding NOW, Murray became disappointed with its decision making, which was undemocratic, and with its membership, which was too white and middle class. Refusing to divide herself into "Negro at one time, woman at another, or worker at another," Murray parted company with NOW in 1967, never breaking entirely with the organization she helped found, but taking her energy and talent elsewhere.[79] Anna Hedgeman, another Black activist who was one of NOW's founders, left NOW in 1968, after trying unsuccessfully to keep the organization focused on women of color and poor women.[80]

Friedan wanted Blacks in NOW more than she wanted working-class women. As president, she contacted prominent women in the civil rights movement and urged them to join, and she even tried to connect with women in SNCC. "I was especially interested in getting black women involved in the South, made special visits to Coretta King, and Julian Bond's sister Jane, and the young women with the afros at the S.N.C.C. headquarters in Atlanta. 'We don't want anything to do with that feminist bag,' one of them said."[81] In the era of Black Power, with its emphasis on restoring the authority of Black men, Black women in SNCC were even less interested in feminism than they were when Hayden and King tried to recruit them.

The radical consciousness-raising groups also had difficulty in attracting Black women. Although young white radical women desperately wanted their movement to be interracial, their appeal to a common sisterhood sounded racist to radical Black women, who experienced race as central to their own identity and felt marginalized by a movement dominated by white women.[82] The decentralized mass movement for women's liberation and the more top-down movement led by NOW remained overwhelmingly white.

NOW's effectiveness as a lobby was limited by the fact that its membership was so middle class and so white. Gerda Lerner warned Friedan in 1963 that Black and white working-class women were crucial to creating equality for women. "By their desperate need, by their numbers, by their organizational experience (if trade union members), working women are most important in reaching institutional solutions to the problems of women."[83] Lerner realized that a women's movement that focused on the experience of white middle-class women and ignored the very different experience of working-class and Black women could not become a majority movement. Like Friedan and Baker, Lerner was influenced by Marxism when she was young. Lerner and Baker never gave up their emphasis on class. Friedan, however, was no longer able to use what she once knew.

In the 1952 pamphlet on women workers that she wrote for the United Electrical Workers, Friedan described "the double bars" holding back Black women workers. "Even more than white women, Negro women have to work to live. . . . But Negro women are barred from almost all jobs except low-paying domestic service in private homes, or menial outside jobs as janitresses and scrubwomen."[84] After 1952, Friedan lost faith in class struggle. As NOW's leader, she adopted the new paradigm of the struggle for equal opportunity. Unlike class struggle, the new paradigm was useful in conferring legitimacy on the aspirations of women. We want what Negroes want. We want in. We don't seek to destroy. We are not un-American radicals. We are reformers, in the tradition of the NAACP and the March on Washington.

One benefit of narrowing the struggle by women to advancement within capitalism was that it avoided associations with Communism. In 1965, a woman wrote to Friedan, urging women to make "determined efforts to free themselves," even though "they may expect hostility from conservative elements politically." She added: "I am not advocating that women become

Communist sympathizers, but I am expecting that progressive women will be so labeled."[85] Having once been a Communist sympathizer, Friedan was well aware of the danger, and she sought to insulate NOW from it. In *The Feminine Mystique*, in 1963, she indicted the American economic system and wondered whether capitalism could survive without exploiting women as consumers. But when she embraced activism, and co-founded NOW in 1966, she narrowed her focus. Eschewing critiques of capitalism, she fought for the right of educated women to flourish within it.

There was an additional narrowing. The experience of women listening to one another, discovering they had the same problem, grounded *The Feminine Mystique*. As NOW's leader, Friedan realized that as the definition of the problem emerged from women talking together, the solution would come from women together. But they had to stop talking. She was a harsh critic of the new consciousness-raising groups. "I saw that nothing was going to happen to most women except talk, words, words, words, unless we organized a movement to change society, as the blacks had done."[86] Disdaining consciousness raising, Friedan's NOW focused on winning important legal battles and reforms. This was the further narrowing. The time for action had come; the time for talking and listening was over.

For Baker's SNCC, the time for listening never stopped. Listening was a form of action; listening was what an organizer did to build connection, participation, and power. The flowering of the women's liberation movement, in the late 60s, took the form of women talking and listening to one another. The mass movement of women that emerged in the late 60s was, in this sense, more in the tradition of Baker's SNCC than of Friedan's NOW. Contrary to Friedan's wish, American women did not stop talking about the problems they had in common. In fact, they were just beginning. The vital, creative, decentralized consciousness-raising groups developed outside of Friedan's NOW, in the other women's movement that descended from Mary King and Casey Hayden and Ella Baker.

As president of NOW, Friedan watched the growth of the radical movement of young white women. In 1967, in notes to herself, she reflected on the struggle of women for equality within SDS. "SDS has had several conferences on woman question." She recognized the anger of the young women—"You give us these typing jobs, don't let us speak at meetings"—and was not at all surprised by the male laughter that erupted.[87] In 1968, she recognized "the rage that was beginning to explode now in women—the ones who . . . had been running the mimeograph machines in SDS and in S.N.C.C."[88] She sensed an opportunity: "I wanted these young radical women in our movement."[89]

But these young radical women were not interested in Friedan's NOW. "We were movement girls, not career women," one explained. "NOW's demands and organizational style weren't radical enough for us. We wanted to build a new society, not get a bigger slice of the pie."[90] Friedan's emphasis on reform, her preference for hierarchical structure, and her hostility to consciousness raising, could not attract the radical young women who were creating a movement of their own, a movement descended from Ella Baker and SNCC.

Yet to fight for their own freedom and equality, young women had to go beyond Ella Baker too. Baker, who was intensely private, did not encourage women to sit around talking about their personal lives. Like Friedan, like many older women (and she was eighteen years older than Friedan), Baker focused on the public roles of women. She encouraged women to be strong, to assert themselves, to assume leadership in the movement. "When the community acted, usually it was some woman who came to the fore," she observed at the end of the sixties, speaking factually, from experience, without exaggeration. "I don't think you could go through the Freedom movement without finding that the backbone of the support of the Movement were women." But in the same speech, she also said: "I have never been one to feel great needs in the direction of setting myself apart as a woman."[91] In her vision, all of us, women and men, Black and white, young and old, working class and middle class, come together to fight for freedom and equality.

By 1968, the leadership of young Black women—many of whom she had mentored—was being attacked and reversed. "This new dialogue that has emanated out of the business of the male having been emasculated by his woman has put an extra burden on the black female, young black female, to not be party to emasculation. So she has begun to take even a much more of a retiring role within the movement than she did in '60."[92] Baker hated what was being done to young Black women in the civil rights movement during the late sixties, but she did not want women to start a movement of their own.

When they did, however, she was there, willing to listen, as always. "I've been involved recently with groups of women, white women," she said in 1968.

> I've never worked exclusively with women because a lot of things about me are not the usual pattern of women-talk and relationship. But these women have been honestly trying to find some answers and to be able to understand what black youngsters are saying, what black people are saying.[93]

Ella Baker began the decade listening to the young people who launched the sit-ins. Now, after SNCC's organizing in Mississippi, after the cresting of the bottom-up movement for civil rights and the emergence of the bottom-up women's movement, she was still listening. She praised the young white women for trying to understand what Blacks were saying. At the same time, she herself was trying to understand the new things the young women were saying. The creative, egalitarian, democratic ethos of SNCC was passing, at the end of the sixties, to the young and radical women meeting in decentralized groups.

13

The Late Sixties:
Jane Jacobs and Betty Friedan

Jane Jacobs, 1968

After successfully defending the West Village, Jacobs led a bigger fight, a fight she tried not to lead.

Father Gerald LaMountain came to see her in the summer of 1962 and asked for help. The young priest of a church in Little Italy, he was leading a struggle against the city's plan to ram a major east-west highway—the Lower Manhattan Expressway (LOMEX)—right through Little Italy. "I suppose it was because he knew that the West Village fight had been won and he thought that maybe some of these seasoned fighters could help him." It wasn't her neighborhood and wasn't her fight. She wanted to say no. "I had a feeling that the city was making not only my life, but everyone's life, absurd by making us spend our precious time and our energy responding to things of this kind instead of doing the work that we wanted to do."[1]

She agreed to attend a meeting, however, and soon learned that the plan for the new expressway was part of Robert Moses's larger plan to ram highways not only up and down Manhattan but also across it. "It was quite clear that the scheme to put the wide roadway through Washington Square was connected to this expressway." So, in a way, it *was* her fight. She recognized "the disaster that it would portend for the Village, as well as the other neighborhoods." The government of New York City—and increasingly, of New York State—was running over citizens who got in the way. "The more I got to know about the expressway, the more hateful I found it—not only for itself and its effects, but for the way it was being done. And therefore, got deeper and deeper into the battle."[2]

Father LaMountain's superiors in the Catholic Church removed him from the struggle. Jacobs became the most visible leader, along with veterans of earlier struggles, including Rachele Wall of the Village and Frances Goldin of the Lower East Side.[3] Together, leading a vast coalition, they defeated LOMEX late in 1962. Then they had to do it again in 1965. In 1968, when Lomex reemerged, Jacobs walked across a stage and the place went wild. As she explained at the end of the decade, protest began with petitions, assemblies, elections. These were seldom enough. Then people moved to civil disobedience.[4] When she disobediently walked across that stage, Jacobs drew on powerful traditions of democratic protest that were forged earlier in the decade—in the Village, in Mississippi, and elsewhere, by hundreds of thousands of activists, many descended from SNCC.

Three years earlier, and 3,000 miles away, Mario Savio disobediently walked across a stage. Acting independently, Savio and Jacobs made similar gestures, with similar results. By comparing the language of their gestures, we view Jacobs in a context beyond New York and beyond the neighborhood movement.

Savio was a Freedom Summer volunteer in Mississippi in 1964. "The thing about the SNCC workers—and that's what really got to me, I think—it was radicalism without ideology."[5] SNCC organizers focused on building power from below, not on Communism or anti-Communism. In Mississippi, Savio learned the distinction between mobilizing and organizing; he learned a style of leadership that centered on the group rather than on the charismatic individual. His biographer explains that "Savio credited this organizing style to Bob Moses (actually, Moses picked it up from Ella Baker.)"[6]

After Freedom Summer, when Savio returned to the University of California at Berkeley, he discovered the authorities had banned civil rights activity from the area set aside for campus groups. Savio and other students defied the ban by setting up a table to raise funds for SNCC. It was direct action, in the southern tradition, and it led to confrontation. The University authorities selected five activists for punishment. Students responded by setting up tables for SNCC and other groups, not in the traditional place for protest, on the edge of campus, but right in front of the administration building. The dean of students ordered the arrest of a student, but hundreds of students surrounded the campus police car and refused to let it move.

The question was whether to continue indefinitely sitting around the police car. Savio favored continuing. Taking off his shoes so as to not damage the police car, he climbed on the roof. For Savio, even at the moment of confrontation, it was important to treat people as ends in themselves, "never as a means only." In June, during the training week in Ohio, when the three civil rights volunteers were reported missing, Savio heard Moses ask volunteers to think about the risks of going to Mississippi before making a final decision; no one would blame them if they decided to return home. Now, from the roof of the car, he channeled Moses: "Nobody who votes 'yes' is better than those who vote 'no.'"[7] The Berkeley students voted to continue. The battle between the administration and what was now the free speech movement raged for the next two months, featuring mass civil disobedience and mass arrests.

In December, the students went on strike. The administration called everyone—students, faculty, staff, altogether about 16,000 people—to a meeting in the outdoor Greek theater. President Clark Kerr, flanked by the department chairs, announced the conclusion: the strike was over; the 800 students who had been arrested would face civil punishment but no additional punishment from the University; some civil rights activities might be allowed on the edge of campus. This decision was presented as a compromise, imposed from above, without discussion, not unlike the Democratic Party's offer to the Mississippi Freedom Democratic Party at Atlantic City, a few months earlier. Savio asked if he could say something, but was denied permission. In front of the 16,000, he walked calmly across the stage toward the microphone. Two university police officers grabbed him and dragged him away. The audience erupted: "Let him speak." Savio was released. Taking the mike, he told students to "clear this disastrous scene."[8] The next day, the Berkeley faculty—forced to choose between the mass civil disobedience of the students and the repressive policies of the administration—chose the students, and the students won.

Savio noticed the physical set-up at the Greek theater. Onstage were "*baronial* chairs and sitting on them were the department heads. The chairs on the chairs . . . were like barons." He found the symbolism of the physical arrangement "beautiful," because it revealed the antidemocratic assumptions of the meeting's organizers.[9] Jacobs, in *Death and Life*, similarly described a Board of Estimate meeting, where the mayor, the borough presidents, the comptrollers and the president of the city council sat behind a raised semicircular bench, "like rulers holding court in the manor during medieval days (406)."[10] Savio and Jacobs were pointing to the reality of hierarchy behind the façade of openness. On April 10, 1968, at Seward High School in Manhattan, Jacobs again observed the physical set up, with officials sitting on stage; the public and the microphone for the public were down below. "The ridiculous thing was that the microphone was turned toward the audience in the auditorium, so that the speaker had to stand behind it, under the stage, and face the audience."[11]

When she spoke, she pointed to the arrangement. "It's interesting the way the mike is set up. At a public hearing you are supposed to address the officials not the audience."[12] The men on stage were not listening and were not going to listen, she explained. The decision to ram LOMAX through had already been made. Before a plan could be approved, New York State rules required a hearing, with a record of public comments by citizens; however, the rules did not require the officials to actually listen. The men on stage were errand boys and should be given a message to deliver to their betters in Albany. A reporter for the *Village Voice* captured what happened next.

> To dramatize their decision not to accept the Expressway, she suggested the residents stage a peaceful demonstration right then and there. So they rose and marched, led by Mrs. Jacobs and Frances Goldin. . . . Elderly couples marched. Catholics and Jews. Italians and Russians. Businessmen and artists. They marched down the center aisle and onto the stage.[13]

As the space designed to separate the audience from the officials collapsed, the officials panicked. The steno-typist, who was recording the official version of the meeting, also panicked. Jacobs watched her jump up and clutch the machine to her chest. "As she danced around like a one armed prizefighter, the tape of the machine she was clutching began to fall out and unroll like a long streamer of confetti."[14] Citizens tore the tape up and tossed it in the air. A policeman told Jacobs that he was supposed to arrest her. She went back to the microphone, like Savio when he adjourned the open-air meeting, and announced that the hearing was over. In fact, it had never happened: "There is no record! There is no hearing!"[15] LOMEX never recovered, and finally died in 1969.

Jacobs playfully sent her mother a *New York Post* article about the arrest, which described her as "the slender 51-year-old author." She circled the word "slender," adding in the margin: "It was worth it to see this! (The reporter interviewed me on a very dark street.)"[16] The *New York* magazine account by her former editor at *Architectural Forum* was equally playful. "On April 10, at about 10 p.m., my friend Jane Jacobs was taken over to the Clinton Street Police Station and booked on a charge of disorderly conduct. Now that was a pretty ridiculous charge: *of course* Jane Jacobs is disorderly—that's her job."[17]

But at the pretrial hearing, a week later, Jacobs was shocked to hear "lies about how I had damaged the stenotype machine." She was upset because, as a former secretary who knew stenography, she respected the machine, and because the charges against her had been upped to "riot, inciting to riot, criminal mischief, and obstructing government administration. Four years in jail. They'd have liked to put me in for it too."[18] Feeling assaulted, she told the *New York Times* that "anybody who criticizes a state program is going to get it in the neck."[19] And she told the *Post*: "I think they are trying to break the spirit of those opposed to the Lower Manhattan Expressway."[20] Her own spirit was unusually low. She later described it as a "real low point."[21]

In 1969, Jacobs and her family left the United States. For the rest of her life, she claimed the bullies of New York City and state had nothing to do with her leaving. She left, she said, because of the war. Her sons, who were eighteen and twenty, intended to go to jail if they were drafted rather than fight in Vietnam. She and Robert wanted to spare them the years in prison. "And so we decided to come to another country." For her, America, itself, had become a bully. "We are just not cut out to be citizens of empire."[22] She also said, "I hate spending money for taxes that go to war goods, expressways, and secret police."[23]

Jacobs regarded the Vietnam War not as a mistake but as immoral: "an enterprise of slaughtering, starving, destroying and uprooting."[24] In October 1967, she had joined the march on the Pentagon. Soldiers in gas masks moved on the protestors. "I was outraged that they should be marching on me, on me, an American." Something broke. "I fell out of love with my country. I know it sounds ridiculous, but I didn't feel part of America anymore."[25] She had been in love. Like Savio and many radical democratic activists in the sixties, Jacobs believed in America. That's why she was so angry, and how America broke her heart.

After the march on the Pentagon, she wrote that a citizen's responsibility was to oppose the war. "If war is an extension of diplomacy, civil disobedience is an extension of self-government." Out of conscience, citizens resisted, and the people in power went mad.

> To those who habitually (often unconsciously) regard most other people as objects to be manipulated or ignored, the evidence of self-propelling integrity out there seems to translate to anarchy, hence is appalling. That, I think, is precisely why innocuous acts of symbolic disobedience—crossing a line at the Pentagon, say—are described as loathsome and why the perpetrators are beaten so brutally.[26]

A month later, she participated in a sit-in against the draft at the Whitehall Induction Center in Manhattan, along with Dr. Benjamin Spock (Marjorie

Spock's big brother) and many others.[27] The police violently attacked the protestors. Jacobs, who was not hurt, was convicted of disorderly conduct and warned that next time she would go to jail. In January 1968, she signed an ad, along with 447 other writers and editors—including Betty Friedan, also worried about her draft-age sons—declaring they would not pay a proposed income tax surcharge, or any tax to support the war.[28] March, write, sit in, refuse to pay taxes: the point was to do whatever you could to end the immoral war. "You know, I don't really blame the predators," she said in 1972, while the war was still raging. "I blame the victims [that is, American citizens] who do nothing. Vietnam would never have been possible without the cooperation of the people who never marched."[29] By that time, she was living in Toronto.

There had been no clear line between Jacobs's play and her activism. She knew much was stupid, or wrong. But common sense and citizen activism might set it right. She could play because she felt at home on Hudson Street, in the Village, in New York, in America. Then she didn't. Two months after her arrest at Seward high school, Jacobs and her family left.

Although the charges against her were later reduced, she chose to remain in Toronto and become a Canadian citizen. Canada was not an empire. "I like paying taxes in Canada where they do not go for war."[30] Canada had another advantage. "One thing that when I moved to Toronto surprised me" was that "there were no ghettos." Racism was built into the urban landscape in America. "It takes an awful lot of effort to make ghettos. And that effort was not expended in Toronto. There was no redlining."[31]

In Toronto, she resumed playing. At a contentious neighborhood meeting, she intervened, calmly explaining why it was good to slow traffic—and more importantly, why neighbors should solve their own disputes rather than turn to planners and politicians. "It was like having Kant come in and speak to your ethics class," said someone who was there.[32] At a demonstration against bulldozing a building, she recalled that Toronto's regulations specified a building could only be torn down if there was a fence around it and suggested that the protestors take down the fence. They did, making neat piles of the planks. The bulldozer couldn't continue.[33] She was still turning bureaucratic rules against the bureaucracy: no fence/no demolition was reminiscent of no tape/no hearing. The neat piles of fence boards recall Savio taking off his shoes before climbing on the police car, and underscore her insistence, and his, that the means be congruent with the end.

Jacobs flourished in Toronto. She joined, and helped lead, a long struggle against a proposed expressway, which the protestors won. Eventually she served as informal advisor to two mayors. "She really enjoyed the activist part," said one mayor.[34] Her great strength was her ability to be playful, even when engaged in a terrific fight. When she couldn't play, when she ran into the power of empire and racism and the prison system, she left America, rather than stop playing. It was America's loss.

Betty Friedan, Late 1960s

Friedan did not believe in playing. Seriousness was the point: women finally being taken seriously, "out from under the jokes and hilarity." That was how she put it in her report as president of NOW in 1968. "We have *begun to change society in reality.*" Her italics emphasized the contrast between NOW and the young radical activists—between "the women of all ages who accept responsibility for the real society" and "the girls who operate as if they are playing childish games. The girls do not understand that we are really doing something here that is changing history." [35] Real, really, reality: her language was earnest, emphatic, scolding. Play was childish. The radical young women who did not follow NOW's lead, her lead, were girls.

Friedan's authority derived from *The Feminist Mystique.* The book made her famous, and the fame made her a leader. As leader, she expected women to listen to her and share her priorities. She tried to impose her priorities on the movement, including ending the safe spaces in which women could talk to women. "The actions geared to concrete breakthroughs against sex discrimination in every field—schools, churches, professional organizations, political parties—must continue until the job is done," she declared. "But the consciousness-raising groups should open to men."[36] Only after Friedan stepped down from the presidency, in 1970, did NOW begin to sponsor consciousness-raising groups.[37]

She articulated, earlier and better than anyone, what America was doing to women. *The Feminine Mystique* showed how postwar culture put married women in an impossible position. If they were working, they were unfeminine, unwomanly. If they stayed home, they suffered the problem that had no name. If they tried to combine work and home, they blamed themselves when something—a serious illness, an accident, a setback—happened to their children. The feminine mystique got inside them, inside their feelings and sense of self, preventing them from being whole.

As an activist, however, Friedan staked out different ground. She focused on practical, legal, institutional change. The resulting reforms were absolutely necessary and important. But her exclusive emphasis on institutional change was in tension with her own analysis of how American culture was eating up women from the inside. She framed the issue as either/or: either winning equal rights for women, or exploring personal experience. She became the foremost proponent of concrete gains for women: affirmative action, child care, equal pay. She became the leading opponent of women talking to women about their experience. "All these navel-gazing rap sessions about trapped housewives . . . wallowing in a soap opera . . . instead of changing the situation."[38] She never grasped the dynamic relationship between talking and acting. Young women talked with one another about sexuality, women's identity, consumerism, anger at men, and women loving women. Out of consciousness-raising groups would come projects—and progress—in women's health, abortion rights, cooperative child care, protection of women against violence, rights for lesbians.[39] In reality, the two women's movements complemented each other. Though participants on both sides were too close to the conflict to see it, the two women's movements, together, were breaking down the barriers to equality for women: psychological, cultural, social, legal.

Friedan was ambivalent toward the young activists. In 1963, in *The Feminine Mystique*, she failed to recognize that an activist generation was launching itself. When, a few years later, young women began to act for themselves, she hesitated. On the one hand, she feared that the energy of the movement would become dissipated by "a lot of . . . consciousness-raising that doesn't go anywhere."[40] On the other hand, "I knew we needed the young, even the most revolutionary of the young, for the women's movement to catch fire."[41] The bodies, the energy, the voices of young women were needed to transform women's protest into a powerful movement. "It needed the emotional verve and style of the young radicals."[42] In 1966, she reached out to student leaders.[43] In 1969, "I said we should make a special effort to bring in the young, new, radical 'women's lib' groups."[44]

At her most radical, in 1970, she called and led a great nationwide one-day strike of women of all ages. But she still insisted on either/or: talk or action, looking inward or looking outward, the personal or the political. "The strike is going to help our whole movement to overcome the wallowing, navel-gazing rap sessions, the orgasm talk that leaves things unchanged." She never agreed with the young women that the personal was political. "This is not a bedroom war. This is a political movement and it will change the politics."[45] She wanted young women to join the movement and march behind her.

Friedan's combative stance toward the young contrasts with Ella Baker's attitude. Throughout the 1960s, Baker never stopped listening to young people because they were driving every uprising from below. Beginning with the sit-ins, she went with the energy, trusting it, concentrating it, deepening it. And when the democratic energy began to seep out of the movement for racial equality, Baker followed the energy. In 1966, when there was a kind of coup within SNCC, resulting in the election of Stokely Carmichael as chair, Baker was critical of the process, but she did not take it personally. "I was fuming but she was calm," said Joanne Grant. "She had abiding faith in young people."[46] In 1968, she was attracted to groups of young white women who were keeping alive the egalitarian and participatory spirit of the sixties. Baker was the rare older leader who encouraged, protected, and followed the lead of young people. Friedan was one of the many established leaders, female and male, who experienced young people—with their tendency to brashness, their readiness to question authority, and their inclination to radicalism—as a threat.

Friedan was particularly disturbed by young women advocating rights for lesbians. "I'd only just begun to realize that some of the best, most hardworking women in NOW were in fact lesbian. But they didn't make an issue of it." The open assertion of equality for lesbians in NOW, by gay women and their allies, was one of the reasons Friedan stepped down from the presidency in 1970. "I was beginning to feel very uneasy about this talk of lesbianism." "There were those murky currents I didn't know how to handle. I didn't want to be a 'straight woman' fronting for a lesbian cabal."[47] "Murky" echoes her language in *The Feminine Mystique*: "the homosexuality that is spreading like a murky smog over the American scene."[48] At a rally for child care and abortion in New York, young women wore lavender armbands in solidarity with lesbians. "It only aroused the creeping horrors in me."[49]

In "An Open Letter to the Women's Movement," in 1975, Friedan denounced the growing assertion of lesbian identity and rights, explaining that a woman who makes love to a woman "just evades the issue. It's something any woman can do without breaking through barriers in the office or school, or threatening those in power. It doesn't require any ability, cost or earn any money, risk or test or change any institution."[50] To Friedan, women making love to women was just personal, not political. It didn't change anything. She never really got the transformational, self-shifting, energy-releasing experience of becoming oneself. "My view, then as now," she said twenty-three years later, "is that one's sexual preference is a private matter."[51] After Friedan stepped down as national president, in 1970, NOW began to defend the rights of lesbians and to recognize lesbian-feminists as an integral part of the women's movement.[52]

Friedan's homophobia was widely shared during the fifties and earlier sixties. In *Death and Life*, Jacobs referred, casually, to a "pervert park," meaning a park where homosexual men went looking for sex.[53] Jacobs, like Friedan, was heterosexual, and she shared the dominant definition of normal. The sexuality of Baker was not so clear. She was extraordinarily private; there were rumors about her sexual orientation, but no one knew whether her close and sustaining friendships with women were sexual or not.[54] Rachel Carson's most intense relationship, with Dorothy Freeman, was filled with physical affection and passionate declarations of love. In 1954, Carson and Freeman burned letters, out of fear that people would think they were lovers.[55] The vicious repression and persecution of homosexuals, in the fifties and sixties, discouraged openness. When the gay liberation movement finally emerged to confront the prejudice and repression at the end of the sixties, Friedan was unable to learn from the young women who advocated equality for lesbians, and fell back on prejudice.

Celebrity

Friedan's inability to listen to people who disagreed with her, including young people, was connected to her celebrity. Only a conscious strategy for dealing with celebrity could enable democratic movements and their leaders to remain open and democratic. Baker, Jacobs, and Carson made that effort. Friedan did not.

Carson saw her celebrity as a necessary evil and a limited resource, to be used strategically. Her fame made it easier for her to contact scientists, bird-watchers, and government workers, all of whom helped her write *Silent Spring*. The attacks on her after the book appeared brought her more media attention, which she turned against the attackers. Neither seeking nor enjoying the media spotlight, Carson used it to help small local protests become a national movement. Jacobs resisted the media's proffered crown, always insisting she was only one leader among many, specifying what she learned from others. She was characteristically clear about her experience of celebrity. "Actually, I like attention being paid to my books and not to me. I don't know who this celebrity called Jane Jacobs is—it's not me. . . . And I just detest it when I'm around somewhere and strangers say, 'Are you Jane Jacobs?' and engage me in conversation in this obsequious way."[56]

Baker developed a critique of celebrity. Working under male leaders in the NAACP and SCLC, in the '40s and '50s, she came to see celebrity as a kind of corruption—corruption not by money, but by fame. She didn't want the star power of Walter White (longtime head of the NAACP) or of Martin Luther King Jr. She wanted to help people discover their own power. Her leadership conferences for the NAACP and her role in founding and leading

SNCC had nothing to do with fame or power for herself and everything to do with enhancing the power of Rosa Parks, Bob Moses, and Diane Nash. She did not want to play king, or queen, of the hill. She wanted to change the game. At Raleigh in 1960, Baker protected the students from the media spotlight. In the later sixties, she was saddened but not surprised when Carmichael and other SNCC leaders began to seek media attention and to perform for the media. "It's the culture we're in," she observed. "When the newspaper people come around, what do they look for? . . . They look for a miracle performer."[57]

Unlike Baker or Jacobs or Carson, Friedan enjoyed celebrity and came to depend on it. In 1973, "in the bleakest month of my own stalled spirit," she went home. She hadn't visited Peoria for almost ten years. No longer NOW's president, she was feeling bruised by ongoing fights with other leaders, including Gloria Steinem and Bella Abzug. As a local girl who had made good, she had been invited to lecture. "I can hardly believe so many people, surely over a thousand, have come out to hear me." Recognizing in the crowd her neighbors, her parents' friends, her kid brother, she realized that Peoria was a vital part of her. "My sense of possibility, whatever it was in me that started women moving, comes from here."[58]

I "started women moving." In 1972, she made a similar claim about "starting our movement six years ago."[59] Six years ago was 1966, when she co-founded NOW and became its first president. Later, she repeated the claim, pushing the starting date back to 1963: "I did not set out consciously to start a revolution when I wrote *The Feminine Mystique.*"[60] I started a revolution. I started the movement. I started women moving. It was the language of celebrity. Although she knew that Pauli Murray, Sonia Pressman, and other members of the feminist underground led her, they faded away when she described her achievement.[61]

Friedan sought the spotlight as positive—as women finally getting their own media attention. After the publication of *The Feminine Mystique*, she received a lot of press. Daniel Horowitz pointed out that it was the first time since she was a student at Smith that Friedan was not subject to male domination, the first time since Smith that she could herself be a star.[62] As a reporter for the radical labor press, she was largely invisible. When she went to report on the Stamford general strike, she experienced the men from *Life* as arrogant representatives of the ruling class. But after *The Feminine Mystique* became a bestseller, she called an editor of *Life*, arranged dinner with him, and was rewarded with a spread in the magazine about her book and herself, complete with photographs.[63]

Because she wrote the book, Friedan was crowned leader by the media. She wore the crown comfortably. "Betty is a star," said a friend.[64] "She gave the mass media what they always look for," explained biographer Milton Meltzer, admiringly, "the star image, an individual they can focus on, the one who projects the ideas of a whole movement."[65] As a star, Friedan moved in a vertically organized world. Writing for mainstream women's magazines in the years after she became famous, she interviewed other famous people, including Pope Paul VI and Indira Gandhi. In 1975, she interviewed Simone de Beauvoir, whose *The Second Sex* had appeared in 1949. For Jacobs, it would have been an opportunity to acknowledge her debt. For Friedan, it was an opportunity to lecture de Beauvoir on the shortcomings of participatory democracy.

> In the women's movement, in the student movement, and, I think, even in the black movement, the argument of elitism has been used to get rid of democratic structure and effective leadership, to manipulate and prevent effective action. This doesn't remove power; it just makes manipulating power easier when there is no structure of clear, responsible leadership.[66]

Friedan conceived two alternatives: either elected individuals exercised top-down power, or unelected individuals exercised top-down power. She could not conceive of leadership arising from below, or, as Baker would have it, of leadership serving primarily to develop leaders from below. Whereas Baker practiced group-centered leadership, Friedan assumed there must be a leader-centered group. But many women were trying to create a new, more egalitarian, kind of group. De Beauvoir told her that among French feminists, "there is a general refusal of what is called the 'star system.'"[67]

Only a conscious effort, like that made by Baker and Jacobs, or an instinctive revulsion against losing one's privacy and becoming public property, like Carson's, could enable prominent movement leaders to avoid becoming corrupted by celebrity. Friedan embraced her media image, as did so many male leaders in the late sixties—of the NAACP and SCLC, of SNCC, SDS and the Black Panthers. If we find her embrace of celebrity more disturbing than the similar behavior of most male leaders, it is because our ideas about leadership are gendered. We expect male leaders to seek fame and glory. What may seem monstrous in a female leader like Friedan seems normal in male leaders.

Bob Moses and Mario Savio were exceptions among male leaders. Like Ella Baker, his mentor, Moses consciously avoided the media spotlight. "Early in Mississippi when I began to get some press, then the reaction of the people I was working with, the staff . . . began to shift, to change how they related to me." They began to see Moses as a little bigger than life, bigger than them, because of what they had been reading about him. "It didn't become big enough in Mississippi and we were able to control it. . . . We really did hold that media space [open], so that it was there when Mrs. Hamer emerged as a person who could fill it."[68] Moses ducked, and Fannie Lou Hamer became the face of the Mississippi movement.

Moses was exceptional in refusing to be macho as well. He led by exposing how vulnerable he was. In June 1964, SNCC staff were wrestling with whether to continue preparing the northern volunteers for Mississippi or to cynically use the volunteers for the publicity that they would generate when some of them would eventually be beaten or killed. In a tense staff-only meeting, in Oxford, Ohio, Moses recalled how afraid he was, at night in Mississippi, whenever he heard a car stop outside. As he spoke, he began to cry. The mood in the room changed. His willingness to reveal his own feelings helped other staff members get in touch with their own deeper feelings.[69] Refusing to be bigger than life, insisting on his vulnerability, Moses was the opposite of a top-down leader. In the critical moment, he didn't preach, exhort, or lift up. He showed how he felt.

Like Jane Jacobs, Moses hated people looking up to him because he was a celebrity. He received more media attention after Mississippi Freedom Summer and resigned from being SNCC's Mississippi director, because he believed other SNCC organizers were depending too much on him. When there was a power struggle in SNCC in 1965, Moses refused to fight. Eventually Carmichael won power. "So that's what happened," said Moses. "Stokely got into the media space and there was something in Stokely that wanted to get into that space. Then, when he did that, he couldn't do what he was doing before. He could no longer organize." Carmichael was a good organizer. But celebrity changes people. "It gets into another mode, which is the mode, which we knew about through King and the other national leaders, which is, you are looking for a media event where you're in this symbiotic relationship with the media. . . . The actual organizing gets lost."[70]

Like Baker, Moses watched as SNCC leaders became caught up in performing for the media, losing sight of the patient, slow work of listening and organizing that made SNCC successful—and famous—in the first place. Moses extended and deepened Baker's critique of celebrity. He recognized that the mass media needed to have someone to go to and that democratic movements from below needed to find a way to prevent the media from choosing who that person would be. "If you let it," he explained, "the news media will tell you who your leaders are instead of your telling the news media who your leaders are."[71]

Like Moses, Savio experienced his own stardom as a violation of the democratic ethos. After leading the successful struggle at Berkeley in 1964, he became active in the antiwar movement. He hated being treated like a star and dropped out of the movement. Some male veterans of the Berkeley Free Speech Movement could not believe that Savio, with his oratorical talent, willingly quit the antiwar movement; they blamed his wife. Savio himself, in a more genuine way, also invoked gender: he wondered afterwards whether he might have become an effective antiwar leader if the women's liberation movement, with its emphasis on the personal, had occurred earlier. "Maybe there would have been the possibility of talking about those feelings."[72] He might have been able to talk to fellow activists about his feelings regarding celebrity, work them through, and continue to be a leader.

Moses and Savio, with their tremendous talents, quit their leadership roles rather than become celebrities. Moses refused to be macho, to fight for power; he led not only by listening, but by crying. Savio, more confused, refused the traditional male role of the charismatic leader, but kept his feelings to himself. Baker, Carson, and Jacobs were able to work out more constructive and effective ways of handling celebrity. As women, they were not expected to be macho or dominant.

Moses made a symbolic statement about the relationship of power to gender as he retreated from the power struggle in SNCC. Among men in SNCC, he was already unusual for his grasp of women's issues; in 1964, Mary King noted that he understood "the connections between women and political struggle. . . . Bob is liberated in all the important ways."[73] Now, in February 1965, he renounced his father's name and adopted his mother's maiden name, Parris, asking people to call him Bob Parris.[74] Savio knew this. Trying to put "some degree of distance" between his own famous self and the man he wanted to be, Savio added a middle initial: Mario E. Savio. "E" was his mother's middle initial.[75] In their symbolic identification with women, Moses and Savio tried to escape traditional male celebrity.

Celebrity is power. Celebrity corrupts. The grassroots movements of the early sixties, and the decentralized women's liberation groups of the later sixties, grew in relative obscurity, out of the media spotlight, outside the mainstream, on the margins. The challenge for successful movements from below was—and still is—how to handle success.

Epilogue: 1970 and Beyond

Rachel Carson, Jane Jacobs, Betty Friedan, and Ella Baker helped build popular movements that challenged the rich and powerful. Together, the four women shaped the pattern of radical thought and action that characterized the sixties. But not in the same way. In the 1970s, it became clear that the work of the four women had different long-range implications, especially regarding capitalism.

The Environmental Movement and Capitalism

Rachel Carson viewed the drive for profit as the enemy of nature. Recognizing that commerce was winning the long battle with nature, she risked her peace, her closest friendship, and her reputation in the fight against DDT, the chemical industry, and agribusiness. She died in 1964. The grassroots movement that she joined, and briefly led, seemed to share her values, putting nature ahead of profit.

The movement won its first big victory in 1970. Laurie Otto, a housewife in a Milwaukee suburb, became disturbed when her village began regular spraying of mosquitoes in the late 1950s. Shy, not an activist, she felt helpless. "The robins were dying." She talked to other women, especially other birdwatchers, and began to feel less isolated. The day when the first installment of *Silent Spring* appeared in the *New Yorker* was "one of the happiest days in my life." Otto wrote to Carson, expressing gratitude. She was becoming an activist. When the Wisconsin Department of Agriculture resumed spraying elms in 1965, she went to the village office and slammed a basket of dead robins on the table. Echoing Carson's critique, she told a Milwaukee reporter, "Diversity and beauty are synonymous. We're taking all this from our lives for elm trees—or for money."[1]

While Dixie Larkin and other birdwatchers battled DDT in Wisconsin towns, Otto took the fight to the state level. She brought a dead robin and dead bats to the legislature in Madison in 1967 but got nowhere. In 1968, she changed tactics. She decided to sue Wisconsin. With an ornithologist from the University of Wisconsin, she flew to New York and asked the Environmental Defense Fund to take the case. The EDF formed in 1967 to file suit against DDT spraying on Long Island. The driving force in that case was a house-wife who lost a beloved lake to DDT and was following in the footsteps of Marjorie Spock and Polly Richards, who had lost their garden. The new Long Island case, like the old, ended without victory. But EDF was just get-ting started. In 1968, invited by Otto and sustained by her fundraising, EDF invaded Wisconsin.[2]

EDF brought scientific proof that DDT caused the long-term decline of birds. The precise causal connection between DDT and the eagles' decline was unclear when Carson wrote *Silent Spring*. After her death, several American wildlife biol-ogists and an English naturalist focused their research on another powerful bird of prey, the peregrine falcon. Like the eagle, the peregrine was at the top of the food chain, and like the eagle, it was in sharp decline. They found DDT did its greatest damage not to the central nervous system but to the hormonal system. By 1968, their studies demonstrated conclusively that the peregrine was declin-ing because DDT thinned its egg shells beyond the point where the eggs were viable. The hearings in Madison, from 1968 to 1969, gave the EDF the opportu-nity to offer, in evidence, the new studies on hormonal damage.[3]

In *Silent Spring*, Carson acted as a kind of public prosecutor, putting DDT's defenders on trial. By 1968, the environmental movement was becoming powerful enough to literally put DDT's scientific defenders on the stand. The Madison hearings gave EDF the opportunity to cross-examine the experts who had been defending DDT since the 1950s. Wayland Hayes, the key scien-tific witness for the defense in the original Long Island case, was the longtime chief toxicologist of the US Public Health Service and DDT's most prominent defender. Carson wanted to pounce on his 1950s experiments with prison-ers but held back in the book. Utilizing the new research on peregrines, EDF confronted Hayes: his study completely ignored DDT's long-term biochemi-cal and hormonal impact, and so proved nothing about its safety. Hayes, usu-ally confident and cool, was visibly shaken by the cross-examination.[4] Carson would have loved it.

The EDF also cross-examined Louis McLean, the attorney for the Velsicol Chemical Corporation who threatened to sue *Silent Spring*'s publisher in 1962. Carson was trying "to create the false impression that all business is grasping and immoral, and to reduce the use of agricultural chemicals . . . so that our supply of food will be reduced to east-curtain parity."[5] In 1967, he unleashed an even more violent attack in the journal *BioScience*, accusing Carson and the environmental movement of creating a climate of fear around the development and use of pesticides, thereby causing mass death by starvation and disease.[6] McLean's sensational claims were well suited to legislative hearings, where no one pushed back. But bullies rarely do well when people stand up to them. The cross-examination in Madison exposed McLean, who was leading the defense. EDF's lawyer read aloud from his article in *BioScience*, asking if he seriously believed this stuff. McLean tried to argue that "practical men" like himself knew more about DDT than mere "bird watchers" but was out of his depth. EDF used the peregrine studies, as well as the earlier work of wildlife biologists like Clarence Cottam, to prove the birdwatchers were right.[7]

As a result of the Madison hearings, Wisconsin moved toward completely banning DDT. In 1970, the ban became state law. It was a huge victory for the young environmental movement that Carson did so much to propel. During the long hearings in Madison, the Rachel Carson Fund of the National Audubon Society financially supported the fledgling EDF.[8] She was still contributing, still intervening.

The movement won a very different environmental victory in California in 1970. Caesar Chavez and Dolores Huerta founded the United Farm Workers in 1962 to fight for migrant field workers against California agribusiness. In 1968, the UFW began focusing on the effects of pesticides on the pickers. In 1969, the union called for a grape boycott and brought farmworkers to testify before the United State Senate about their experience of pesticide spraying: the headaches, nosebleeds, rashes, nausea, and seizures. EDF joined forces with UFW and sued the United States Department of Agriculture for allowing agribusiness to poison the pickers. Their victory in court in 1970 encouraged the newly established Environmental Protection Agency to recommend a ban on DDT in the United States.[9]

A further scientific discovery pushed Congress to enact the ban. Carson explored what pesticides did to humans, emphasizing the possibility that DDT caused cancer. In 1969, too late for the Madison hearings, the National Cancer Institute demonstrated that DDT gave cancer to mice. Now the possibility DDT gave cancer to people became a probability, and seventeen congressional representatives called for a ban.[10] The battle for public opinion, which Carson began, was finally won. As she foresaw, people who didn't much care about robins or eagles did care about humans. In 1972, a decade after *Silent Spring* was published, eight years after her death, two years after EDF's victory in Wisconsin and the UFW's victory in California, her book and her arguments finally led to the banning of DDT in the United States.

But the victory proved limited. California agribusiness shifted seamlessly from DDT and other chlorinated hydrocarbons to organic phosphates, which decompose more quickly. Organic phosphates kill more bugs than DDT but have less impact on the food chain, and therefore on consumers. Because organic phosphates are more toxic than DDT, they do even more damage to the people who pick the fruit.[11] In *Silent Spring*, Carson warned of "the danger to all workers applying the organic phosphates in fields, orchards, and vineyards" and cited Riverside, California, where "eleven out of thirty men picking oranges became violently ill."[12]

During the 1970s, the farm workers renewed their grape boycott, protesting the use of organic phosphates. Mainstream environmental groups refused to endorse the boycott. Unlike Carson, they were more concerned with the effect of pesticides on consumers than producers; they did not see the fight of migrant agricultural workers as their fight. The moment of 1969—when UFW and EDF, the activist labor movement and activist environmental movement, came together—did not last. According to a leader of EDF, their alliance was only a "marriage of convenience."[13] If environmental groups had fought for producers as much as consumers, they would have put themselves in direct opposition to corporate farming. Unlike Carson, they chose to avoid conflict with a powerful industry. The agricultural workers, and Carson, lost.

Carson's approach to cancer met a similar fate. In *Silent Spring*, she argued that waiting for a cure was passive; we should attack the causes of cancer by getting chemicals out of the environment, as the public health campaigns of the late nineteenth century attacked the causes of disease. After 1971, when President Nixon declared war on cancer, federal dollars flowed into cancer research, and searching for the cure became a big industry. The American Cancer Society focused on finding the cure rather than reducing chemicals in the air, water, and food chain. Carson died from breast cancer. Today we know that some chemicals (including some pesticides) mimic the female hormone and increase the risk of breast cancer. Her emphasis on prevention has been largely ignored by the cancer industry; preventing cancer is not so profitable.[14] Here too, Carson's distrust of capitalism continues to be cutting edge.

That's why her legacy has been challenged, and DDT itself is experiencing a revival of sorts in the court of public opinion. The chemical industry doesn't care about DDT anymore; it is no longer under patent, and newer pesticides are more profitable.[15] Today, the attack on Carson comes from people who are defending capitalism itself. The Competitive Enterprise Institute maintains a website called "Rachel Was Wrong," which echoes McLean's arguments: Carson was a mass murderer who deprived malaria victims, especially in Africa, of the protection that DDT offered; many people also die from starvation because she attacked industrial agriculture.[16] A piece in the *Huffington Post* repeats the charges. "Her rhetoric spawned a radical environmental movement that promotes unwarranted bans and restrictions on pesticides that otherwise could be used to make food more affordable and fight mosquito-transmitted diseases such as malaria, the Zika virus, the West Nile virus, and more."[17]

The continuing attack on Carson is not really about the facts concerning DDT but about the merits of free enterprise. The facts are clear. Carson did not call for a total ban on DDT in *Silent Spring*; she left room for exceptions. The eventual ban was only in the United States; it affected but did not prevent the use of DDT in the rest of the world, where it is still used (but never sprayed from the air) as one of the weapons against malaria. However, a big problem in using DDT to fight malaria, as Carson inconveniently pointed out, is that mosquitoes develop resistance. Another reason for malaria's persistence in Africa is a lack of consistent funding from wealthy nations, which have other priorities.[18]

Promoters of free enterprise are angry at Carson not because of malaria in Africa but because she incited citizens to demand that the government regulate capitalism. The older conservation movement did not threaten free enterprise; protected national parks existed side-by-side with big business. The new environmental movement Carson helped launch was, from the beginning, based on the assumption that capitalism would—if left to its own devices—destroy the environment.[19] That's why defenders of capitalism still hate Carson, still call her Rachel, still recycle all the arguments raised by the chemical companies and their apologists against her in the 1960s.

Their arguments are misleading, but their fundamental point is not wrong. Between capitalism and environmentalism, as shaped by Carson, there is a real conflict. *Since Silent Spring*, written in 1970 by Frank Graham, compared the "delaying action" of the tobacco industry against evidence its product caused cancer to the delaying action of the chemical industry regarding DDT.[20] Forty years later, *Merchants of Doubt*, by Erik Conway and Naomi Oreskes, connected the continuing attacks on Carson to the well-funded campaign to deny the science of climate change.[21] Naomi Klein's *This Changes Everything* (2014) carried Carson's logic to its conclusion: if capitalism cannot protect life on the planet, then capitalism must go.[22] There is a direct link from *Silent Spring* to *This Changes Everything*, and from pesticide denial to climate denial.

The large mainstream environmental organizations—The Nature Conservancy, The Natural Resources Defense Council, and, sadly, The

Environmental Defense Fund—have long since accepted corporate funding and made their peace with capitalism. Advocating market-friendly solutions to the problem of global warming, they see themselves as lobbies, pushing business and government to do the right thing.[23] But activist grassroots
groups—350.org, Greenpeace, Friends of the Earth, and others—embrace
Carson's commitment to nature over profits. The struggle which Carson did
so much to shape is ongoing.

Jane Jacobs and Capitalism

In 1970, in Wisconsin, speaking during the first celebration of Earth Day,
Jane Jacobs denounced automobiles as the enemy not only of cities but of the
environment. Cars "increasingly debase towns, shorelines and countrysides."
In 1961, she warned of the death of cities. Now, connecting the increased need
for oil to the increased reliance on cars, she warned of the death of nature.

> The destruction of city communities for the sake of expressways and destruc-
> tion of beaches by oil slicks in the frantic endeavor to get ever more oil to
> market are directly linked. The fragile ecology of a city neighborhood and the
> fragile ecology of the Arctic stand and fall together. Because a mounting prob-
> lem has gone unsolved in cities, in deference to the status quo, the outermost
> wilderness is finally threatened.[24]

In the late 1960s, Jacobs connected her urban movement to the new environmental movement. Speaking in London in 1967, she cited "air and water
pollution" as typical of the environmental problem which "comes to a head in
cities."[25] Her second book, *The Economy of Cities* (1969), advocated recycling
as a major urban industry. "Cities will become huge, rich and diverse mines of
raw materials."[26] Later, she defended cities against the charge of having oversized ecological footprints, pointing to the way cities recycle so much of what
they use and celebrating cities as incubators of green solutions: pesticide-free
gardens, composting, mobile kitchens which harvest local gardens.[27]

The connections she made between her urban movement and the environmental movement were rooted in her activism. During the long struggle
over the Lower Manhattan Expressway, proponents of LOMEX justified its
high cost by pointing to the greater amount of traffic it would carry. Jacobs
countered: "Carrying and generating increased traffic . . . implies horren-
dous damage to the environment." It was a winning argument. "The Lower
Manhattan Expressway fight was the first one, at least in New York, where the

citizens fighting it began to focus on" environmental damage. "That's partly because of the much greater awareness of what was happening to air quality than in the past."[28]

Nevertheless, Jacobs was ambivalent toward the environmental movement. Privately, from the beginning, she worried about its anticapitalist tendencies. She was glad that heightened environmental consciousness helped citizens defeat highways that would cut through their neighborhoods. She embraced environmentalism as one way to create new urban industries. She liked solar and wind power. But she never wanted government, in the name of protecting the environment, to control capitalist enterprise. In 1969, in *The Economy of Cities*, she praised cities as engines of economic growth. She wanted to free cities to play their historic role, not to further encumber them with government regulations and bureaucracy. Unlike Carson, she was committed to growing the economy. "Everybody is feeling good about the great outpouring of environmental concern during Earth Week," she wrote in an early draft of her 1970 talk. "I have my doubts. In some ways, it looks to me more like Accepting-and-Planning-for-Stagnation Week."[29]

Jacobs knew the environmental movement was identifying real problems. She was skeptical about governmental solutions. Her doubts about the federal government's ability to solve problems were not new. Critical of some New Deal programs, she opposed Roosevelt when he ran in 1940; in 1952, she said she no longer believed in "government-controlled medical insurance."[30] Later, as she developed her own line of thought, she didn't just object to new government programs but sought to dismantle old ones. In 1980, in Toronto, she helped found Energy Probe, which aimed at privatizing mail delivery, mass transportation, and energy. In 1998, Energy Probe succeeded in privatizing Ontario's electric utility. But the year before, in 1997, after sixteen years on the board, Jacobs quit Energy Probe because it was becoming increasingly tied to the libertarian right. People who saw her as right wing, she said, were "stupid." She wanted no part of right-wing attacks on the poor by Canadian versions of Margaret Thatcher or Ronald Reagan. She opposed the welfare state *and* the warfare state, which she saw as going hand and hand. She opposed higher levels of public spending for the same reason that she opposed public monopolies like transit systems—because they drew money away from the private sector and led, she believed, to economic stagnation.[31]

What she wanted was to empower ordinary people to solve their own problems. She denounced the World Bank, the International Monetary Fund, and all "bureaucratized economic and development agencies" as "part of the problem."[32] They were top down. It was small, unplanned, bottom-up enterprises which drove economic growth. "Giant corporations are not dependable cornucopias of work and income." By contrast, "small enterprises have been more fertile and innovating." A dual emphasis on small enterprise and grass-roots activism was characteristic of Jacobs. She valued capitalism when it was competitive and criticized it when it depended on government favors. During the fight to save the West Village, she criticized developers for making secret deals with the city government, avoiding accountability from citizens and markets. In 1984, she summed up her point of view: "The more that cities can make use of their own ordinary people's capacities for economic and social invention and experiment, the more useful and valuable cities become."³³

During the late sixties, Jacobs' anti-authoritarian, almost anarchic, tendencies tended to obscure her procapitalist beliefs. During a visit to New York in 1970, at the 92nd street YMHA, she urged her mostly young audience to "break at least one rule a day," suggesting draft-card burning and military desertion. Her advice was consistent with her deep opposition to the Vietnam war and her principled civil disobedience. But she also suggested that people ride the subway without paying, anticipating her opposition to public mass transit in Canada. The point was to undermine all top-down control. "Our first duty is to misbehave, and to keep on misbehaving in order to destroy authority." Easy to overlook, in this subversive talk, was her abiding emphasis on economic growth through competitive capitalism. "Ossified rules" and regulations led to economic stagnation, she told the young people.³⁴

After the dust cleared, after the movements of the sixties receded, what had always been true became clear: Jacobs was a passionate advocate of free enterprise. Regarding the environment, she took a market-based, small-business approach. What she liked about the environmental movement was that it offered help in defending cities against superhighways and opened up opportunities for small and diverse businesses. It could, however, lead to increased government regulation of the economy; that's what she didn't like.³⁵ Even at her most radical, it was capitalism she was advocating, and it was liberty she cherished. Liberty—the full assertion by all citizens, Black or white, female or male, of their unique powers—was what she loved. Equality did not excite her in the same way. She already felt equal to anyone.

Jacobs's response to the women's movement clarified where she stood on the question of equality. In 1963, the publisher of *The Feminine Mystique* sent her a pre-publication copy. In 1964, Jacobs and Friedan met. In 1966, having co-founding NOW, Friedan contacted Jacobs, hoping to involve her in the fledgling organization. Jacobs responded warmly. "Many many thanks for sending me the membership application for N.O.W. . . . . I, for one, am so glad you and the others are starting this. Just what is needed. . . . Your description of purposes & strategy is in accord with my ideas." She added a personal note: "How are you? I have been meaning to ask you down. . . . With very best regards—from Bob too." She joined NOW and apologized to Friedan for not attending an organizational meeting.[36]

Jacobs supported NOW's fight for the equality of women because she believed women were equal. By the same token, she never became active in the women's movement because the power of men did not much bother her. Like all ambitious women, she was subject to male dominance and male bullying. When she was young, her boss at a trade journal "attempted to embarrass me by sending me, as a work assignment, to a stag dinner and entertainment."[37] But Jacobs did not feel intimidated by gender rules. She went where she wanted to go, regardless of whether it was proper for women—for example, on fishing boats—and worked full-time, happily, as the mother of three young children. Jacobs responded positively to Friedan for encouraging women to trust their ambition and not feel guilty, as she herself encouraged women and men to not feel guilty for wanting to protect their neighborhoods. She recognized the destructive power of the feminine mystique. "In my generation women were made to feel guilty if they didn't stay home and devote themselves to being wives and mothers," she observed in 1970.[38]

But the mystique never got to her. "The male-domination things affected me externally, and I resented it," she later explained. "But I didn't resent it in this corrosive way because it wasn't affecting me internally." She attributed her confidence and inner freedom, characteristically, to the activism of others. "The years when I was growing up, in the 1920s, were not like the 1950s. Women had gotten the vote, there was an earlier wave of feminism, and I grew up with the idea that I could do anything."[39] In 1952, explaining her beliefs, she reached further back in the history of feminism: "I am proud . . . of a remoter relative, a Quaker, who, believing in women's rights and women's brains, set up her own printing press to publish her own works without a masculine nom de plume."[40] Over fifty years later, dismissing the "tissue of outright lies about the inferiority of women (and others who are not men of Western European descent)," she added: "I have not made this an overt cause, but have simply acted as if it is not true."[41] She felt and acted equal, as an individual, and encouraged other women to do the same.

Once, like Friedan, Jacobs hoped the labor movement would help women win equal pay. At the trade journal, around 1940, "I attempted to interest others in the union. Any arguments I used as to the benefits of union membership had solely to do with wages, particularly equalization of pay between men and women for similar work, and job security."[42] Her interest in unions faded. Like Friedan, Jacobs wanted ambitious women to achieve success. But whereas Friedan and NOW emphasized protest, lobbying, and legislation to destroy the glass ceiling, Jacobs emphasized the individual efforts of enterprising women. "When the ceiling does dissolve it does not do so . . . because legislation says it must." She was speaking to an audience of women. She entitled this 1994 talk "Women as Natural Entrepreneurs." Celebrating the fact that many women start small businesses, she urged them to keep control. "If you don't give away the shop once you've started it, in your lifetimes you will see how rapidly the glass ceiling dissolves."[43]

Jacobs's responses to the environmental and women's movements were complex and creative. Her engagement with the movement for racial equality was less so. Throughout her long career as an activist, she denounced the effects of segregation and redlining; she protested Negro removal from neighborhoods in general, and the removal of Black children from her neighborhood school in particular. In her 1970 talk at the Y, she emphasized the power of racism in the United States: any attempt at population control—which some environmentalists were advocating—could lead to genocide against Black people.[44] In her Earth Day talk, two months later, she explained: over-population might be a problem, but a public program of "population control . . . is a dreadfully dangerous answer. . . . Nothing in America works the same for blacks and whites."[45] Keenly aware of the destructive power of racism, she supported the demands of the civil rights movement, but without her usual creativity. Insofar as the movement looked to the federal government to enforce racial equality, it could not fully engage her. Individual freedom moved her. She urged individual women to dissolve the glass ceiling by acting as if it didn't exist. But what could she say to Black people? Could they, as individuals, ignore racism? If Friedan never grasped the power of coming out as lesbian, Jacobs, in her enthusiasm for individual freedom, never fully grasped the powerful experience of Black people, acting as a group, becoming themselves.

Her encounters with the environmental, women's, and Black movements reveal her faith in people and markets and her mistrust of government. As the sixties movements receded and reaction set in, she remained pretty much where she'd always been, fiercely committed to grassroots enterprise and protest. From time to time she returned to the West Village and witnessed how it had changed since the days when she and her neighbors fought to save it from urban renewal. "They are just gentrifying in the most ridiculous way," she said in 2000, six years before her death. "They are crowding out everybody except people with exorbitant amounts of money."[46] She blamed gentrification of her beloved Village on the inadequate supply of vital neighborhoods: there were too many people wanting to live in too few thriving neighborhoods, which drove up the price and drove out the people who were not rich. In *Death and Life*, in 1961, she explained how the diversity of a flourishing neighborhood could turn, through supply and demand, into its opposite. "Self-destruction of diversity is caused by success, not by failure.... The process is a continuation of the same economic processes that led to the success itself."[47]

Adam Gopnik, writing in 2016, made the same point, with a different emphasis. "The Jacobs street, a perfect reflection of the miracle of self-organizing systems that free markets create, becomes a perfect reflection of the brutal and unappeasable destruction that free markets enforce." Free-enterprise capitalism made Jacobs's West Village possible and then made it impossible. "The West Village may be unrecognizable today, but it is not because the underlying forces working upon it have changed. It is because they have remained exactly the same."[48] Jacobs's commitment to capitalism—competitive, local, unplanned— was both the strength and the limit of her thought.

Betty Friedan and Capitalism

Betty Friedan was conflicted about capitalism. As leader of the less radical wing of the women's movement, Friedan emphasized reforms that would level the playing field for women, enabling women to succeed within the capitalist system. But she never entirely lost the critical attitude toward capitalism to which she had been introduced by her professors in college. At times, depending on the historical moment, her criticisms came to the fore.

In the radical moment of 1970, when she led the one-day women's strike for equality, she revived her critique of capitalism. The strike was a mass action, driven not only by the professional women of NOW but also by the radical young women of the decentralized consciousness-raising groups. And it was national, with women marching in Boston, Baltimore, San Francisco, Miami, and New York. Friedan, who had just stepped down from NOW's presidency, called the strike on her own initiative. Addressing marchers in New York, she emphasized that the emergence of women was changing everything. As if thinking of Jacobs, she wondered what would happen when most women were no longer home, volunteering and watching the street. "What will happen to architecture, to city planning, when women are no longer the unpaid servants of the home?" Borne along by the popular uprising, Friedan went beyond the economic assumptions of NOW. "What will happen to the economy when women are no longer so mired in self-denigration from prenubility to late senility that they can be sold anything and everything in order to catch and keep a man?"[49] This was the anticapitalist note she had sounded in *The Feminine Mystique* but suppressed in NOW.

She complicated her critique in 1975, at a time of "immense resistance" toward and "reaction" against the women's movement. The tremendous energy of liberated women was giving new life to capitalism.

> If the women went home again, this whole inflated economy would collapse. Sure, sex discrimination was profitable—still is for some companies. But for the economy as a whole—yes, even under rotten old capitalism, which may or may not have the power to regenerate itself—equality between the sexes, participation of women, with all the rewards thereof, is becoming one of the main sources of new energy.[50]

In Friedan's mature view, articulated in this 1975 piece, working women, as they became integrated into the economy, greatly increased productivity. But at the same time, the integration of women opened up the possibility of a united labor movement. Before the modern women's movement, women were doubly exploited as consumers and as marginal workers. Now women were adding their energies to the economy as a whole, simultaneously strengthening it and exposing its vulnerability. "There is a pervasive threat to all corporate profiteers in eliminating that substratum of helpless, anonymous, unorganized female labor: . . . the virtually invisible women who quit when they got married or had kids and never stayed around long enough to fight for their rights or accumulate benefits."[51]

In 1976, during a time of layoffs and rising unemployment, she feared women would lose their gains. "Was the women's movement going to be pitted against the unions over seniority? Or accept, again, women last hired, first fired?" Her radical hope now—the hope of many feminists—was that women and men would join together to fight to make the work day shorter. "Weren't the real implications of sex-role equality shorter hours for everyone?"[52] Later, she expressed the hope that shorter hours would not only create more jobs, but would make it possible for both spouses to raise their children together.[53]

Friedan had no way to know, in the midseventies, that the historic tendency to a shorter working day, driven by the labor movement and lasting roughly a century and a half, would be halted and reversed around 1980. Unions—weakened by attacks over many decades, on the defensive, out-maneuvered and outgunned—have not been able to protect working people. Americans are forced to work longer and longer hours.

She lived long enough to see the defeat of her radical hopes. In 1996, more urgently, she advanced the same critique of capitalism and the same point about shorter hours. *The Feminine Mystique* had triggered a paradigm shift. "The new paradigm was simply the ethos of American democracy—equality of opportunity, our own voices in the decisions of our destiny—but applied to women." But something went wrong.

> While we weren't looking, something really dangerous was going on in America: the accumulation of more and more and obscenely more wealth and resources of this nation by those who are already rich. It is a dangerous income inequality. . . . Should we not—women, black, all of us—join with labor as Americans did fifty years ago when they fought for the forty-hour week, and fight for the thirty-hour week?[54]

As Americans did fifty years ago: in 1946, at the height of the old paradigm, organized working people led the charge for all, backed by almost the entire community. That was her story: class conflict for the common good, except the good of capitalists. Dismayed by the rising inequality, sensing that equality of opportunity was not enough, Friedan looked back for a moment toward the old paradigm of class.

She died in 2006, two months before Jacobs. The question she posed in 1975, as to whether "rotten old capitalism" would be able to regenerate itself, has been answered in the affirmative—at the expense not only of the environment, but of women and men who work longer and longer hours, and therefore of their children, too.

Ella Baker and Capitalism

Ella Baker was anticapitalist from the early 1930s, when she listened to Marxists in Harlem, to the day she died in 1986. She viewed capitalism as the enemy of Black and white people, of the working and middle class, of women and men. She never believed we could become truly equal, or fully human, under capitalism. That's why she pointed SNCC beyond lunch counters, "beyond a hamburger"; why she always focused on revolt from the bottom up; why she aimed at nothing less than the transformation of the whole society. Her work, her decades of organizing and reflecting, culminated in the uprisings of the 1960s. She lived to see the movements break open the closed societies of the Deep South, end the war, and give women voice—yet not break the power of capitalism itself.

Throughout the 1970s, as her strength declined, she searched for a way to reverse the decline of the mass movements that she, and SNCC, had done so much to foster. She was no longer so vital, but she could not give up. She remained in touch with many former SNCC activists and continued to mentor some. She participated in antiwar meetings and became active in the struggle for Puerto Rican independence. She also continued to encourage the emergence of women, speaking at two celebrations of International Women's Day.[55] As sixties movements receded, she participated in a long, fruitless attempt to build an anticapitalist political party. She joined with Arthur Kinoy (a Marxist civil rights lawyer) and others, in the Mass Party Organizing Committee, hoping, as always, to build from the ground up. At a meeting of the group in the late 1970s, an African American from the South made a theoretical Marxist point about the insufficient consciousness of the Black masses. Baker was listening quietly, as always. But now she was irked. She intervened, insisting that leftist rhetoric must never be used to make the people appear incompetent or powerless. Unsure where the next wave of uprisings would come from, or when, Baker never lost her faith in the capacity of people to rise.[56]

She died in 1986, on her eighty-third birthday. Twenty-seven years later, in 2013, three young Black women—Alicia Garza, Patrisse Cullors, and Opal Tometi—founded Black Lives Matter. Baker would have been delighted. Jelani Cobb, in an influential article on "The Matter of Black Lives," points to Baker, who "was emphatically adverse to the spotlight" and "came to be seen as a counter-model to the careers of leaders like Martin Luther King, Jr."[57] Keisha M. Blain adds: "What's interesting is the structure of Black Lives Matter, actually, in so many ways, encapsulates this idea of group central leadership, which is an idea that comes directly from Ella Baker."[58] Garza, Cullors, and Tometi acted on their anger against injustice and triggered a new mass movement for equality, as Baker knew would happen, though she didn't know how or when.

It wasn't only Baker—or Jacobs or Carson or Friedan—who transformed America. It was all the defiant, angry, idealistic women who spearheaded popular uprising. SNCC, founded by a woman, came into its own in Mississippi, where women played the leading role. Women led the movement to defend Washington Square Park, and the West Village, and lower Manhattan. Women were the local activists who fought for birds and gardens and communities against DDT. Women rebelled against inequality within the civil-rights and anti-war movement and drove perhaps the most transformative movement of all, the women's movement. This book is itself driven by the energy of women, not just the famous leaders, but the other women too, who set the famous leaders in motion and carried their ideas into action. These women remade

America: Marjorie Spock, Mary Richards, Rachel Carson, Dixie Larkin, Laurie Otto, Dolores Huerta; Shirley Hayes, Edith Lyons, Ellen Lurie, Jane Jacobs, Rachele Wall, Gloria Hamilton, Frances Golden; Mary King, Casey Hayden, Pauli Murray, Sonia Pressman, Betty Friedan, Kathie Sarachild; Rosa Parks, Ella Baker, Diane Nash, Fannie Lou Hamer, Alicia Garza. . . .

Like the four women featured in this book, millions of women entered history and changed its direction. As outsiders, many were able to question assumptions that limited the vision of leading men. They brought fresh energy and fresh eyes; they saw not only what was wrong but new possibilities of change. Also, as women, they tended to care about the living beings whom they were observing, or for whom they were advocating; they were perhaps less likely to get lost in abstractions. They tended also to be good listeners. By listening to each other, by insisting on their right to be equal to men, and to say what they saw, they challenged entrenched beliefs and institutions.

The radical wing of the civil rights movement, and the radical women's movement that grew out of it, did not prevail. The young radicals won victories; they opened up previously closed questions and closed systems. But insofar as Baker and SNCC and the radical women's movement were anti-capitalist, they were defeated. The formal and legal inequality of Blacks and women was overthrown. Actual inequality between rich and poor—that is, between a few rich white men and everyone else—has increased dramatically.

Later than Baker, Martin Luther King Jr. recognized the problem of economic inequality. He organized the Poor People's Campaign and was helping the Memphis garbage workers when he was murdered. King, like SNCC, could not turn the tide. The corporations and banks have proven flexible, adopting ideas they previously opposed like racial and gender diversity, mixed-use neighborhoods, recycling, and gay marriage, while simultaneously drawing a line in the sand where profits are concerned. It's not just the civil rights movement and the women's movement that hit the wall of capitalism and foundered. The environmental movement is in similar crisis. Its ideas have triumphed everywhere, except where they threaten profits. Capitalism—more and more aggressive, demanding sacrifices by everyone except capitalists—has emerged from behind the scenes as the question of the day. Especially since the Great Recession triggered by the financial collapse of 2008, capitalism itself has become an issue.

Today, new and radical movements, often led by young people, are contesting income inequality, racism, police violence, gun violence, global warming, and the role of money in politics. My hope is that this book about the movements of the sixties will be helpful to new, young activists as they lead a new anticapitalist movement. In contrast to the anticapitalist and anti-racist movements of the 1930s, an anti-capitalist, antiracist movement today will be aggressively feminist and environmentalist; young and old, we all stand on the shoulders of Betty Friedan and the women's movement and Rachel Carson and the environmental movement. Now Ella Baker's vision of a bottom-up movement, led by Black and white, young and old, working class and middle class, women and men—practicing the democracy we preach, listening to each other and learning to listen to others not yet part of the movement, always treating people as ends in themselves—has become more relevant than ever. Is it too much to hope as well, that young activists, as they struggle to save America and the planet, may channel Jane Jacobs' playful spirit?

Notes

Introduction

1. Rebecca Solnit, "Three Who Made a Revolution," *The Nation*, April 3, 2006, pp. 29–32. See also Sara F. Anderson, "The View from the Outside: How Three Women's Work Contributed to Changes Toward Equity and Human Rights: A Study of the Work of Rachel Carson, Jane Jacobs, and Betty Friedan," *New England Journal of History*, vol. 67, no. 1 (Fall 2010), pp. 4–18; Louis Menand, "Books as Bombs," *New Yorker*, January 24, 2011, p. 79; Andrea Barnet, *Visionary Women: How Rachel Carson, Jane Jacobs, Jane Goodall, and Alice Waters Changed Our World*. New York: HarperCollins, 2018.

2. Charles Payne, *I've Got the Light of Freedom: The Organizing Tradition and the Mississippi Freedom Struggle*. University of California Press: Berkeley, 1995.

3. Daniel Horowitz, *On the Cusp: the Yale College Class of 1960 and a World on the Verge of Change* (Amherst: University of Massachusetts Press, 2015), pp. 2, 20, 76, and 254.

4. David Halberstam, *The Fifties* (New York: Random House, 1993), pp. 592–98 and 799.

5. Fred Kaplan, *1959: The Year Everything Changed* (Hoboken, NJ: John Wiley & Sons, 2009), pp. 148, 233, and 245. An older study similarly locates the late 1950s as the turning point, citing the researches of Friedan and Carson. Douglas T. Miller and Marion Nowak, *The Fifties: The Way We Really Were* (Garden City, NY: Doubleday, 1957), p. 397.

6. David Farber, "The Radical Sixties," *Reviews in American History*, vol. 39, no. 4 (December 2011), pp. 712, 713, and 716. For an example of the long sixties approach, see his earlier work: David Farber, *The Age of Great Dreams: America in the 1960s* (New York: Hill and Wang, 1994), especially pp. 3–4.

Chapter One

1. EB, quoted by Joanne Grant, *Ella Baker: Freedom Bound* (New York: John Wiley & Sons, 1998), p. 25.

2. EB, Thrasher and Hayden, New York, April 19, 1977, typescript, p. 35, at http://docsouth .unc.edu/sohp/G-0008/G-0008.html/. See also Barbara Ransby, *Ella Baker and the Black Freedom Movement: A Radical Democratic Vision* (Chapel Hill: University of North Carolina Press, 2003), p. 68.

3. EB, Thrasher and Hayden interview, p. 40. See also Grant, *Ella Baker*, pp. 42–43.

4. EB, interviewed by John Britton, June 19, 1968, typescript, p. 12, at http://www.crmvet.org /nars/baker68.htm/.

5. Letter from the National Office, Young Negroes' Cooperative League, undated, quoted by Grant, *Ella Baker*, p. 34.

6. EB, Thrasher and Hayden interview, pp. 48–49. See also Grant, *Ella Baker*, p. 96; Charles M. Payne, *I've Got the Light of Freedom: The Organizing Tradition and the Mississippi Freedom Struggle* (Berkeley: University of California Press, 1995), p. 87.

7. EB, quoted by Grant, *Ella Baker*, p. 51.

8. EB, interviewed by Lenore Bredeson Hogan, New York, March 4, 1979, typescript, p. 21. Highlander Research and Education Center, New Market, Tenn.

9. EB, quoted by Ransby, *Ella Baker*, p. 112.

10. EB, quoted by Payne, *I've Got the Light of Freedom*, p. 85.

11. EB, Hogan interview, p. 40. The lawyer, William Hastie, was a graduate of Harvard Law School.

12. EB, Britton interview, p. 6.

13. EB, Hogan interview, p. 18.

14. EB, Hogan interview, p. 43. See also EB, Britton interview, pp. 28 and 31–32; EB, interview by Clayborne Carson, New York, May 5, 1972, typescript, p. 2; EB, in *Fundi: The Story of Ella Baker*," documentary film, directed by Joanne Grant (New York: Icarus Films, 1981).

15. EB, quoted by Ransby, *Ella Baker*, p. 133. See also EB, Thrasher and Hayden interview, p. 44.

16. Other leaders who developed a similar kind of bottom-up, democratic organizing were Septima Clark and Miles Horton. Payne, *I've Got the Light of Freedom*, p. 101.

17. EB, Thrasher and Hayden interview, p. 32.

18. EB, interviewed by Eugene Walker, Sept. 4, 1974, typescript, p. 62, at http://docsouth.unc.edu/sohp/G-0007/G-0007.html/ See also Ransby, *Ella Baker* pp. 148–51; Grant, *Ella Baker*, pp. 96–97.

19. EB, Britton interview, p. 11.

20. EB, Walker interview, pp. 3–4.

21. EB, Walker interview, pp. 8–9.

22. EB, column, "Shuttlesworth Says," *Pittsburgh Courier*, August 8, 1959, p. 4. See also "'Nothing is Too Dear To Pay for Freedom,' Miss Baker," *Birmingham World*, June 10, 1959, p. 6 (cont. from 1) and J. Todd Moye, *Ella Baker: Community Organizer of the Civil Rights Movement* (Lanham, Maryland: Rowman & Littlefield, 2013), p. 84.

23. EB, Hogan interview, p. 18. See also EB, Walker interview, p. 3.

24. Ransby, *Ella Baker*, pp. 82–94.

25. Rosa Parks, quoted by Douglas Brinkley, *Rosa Parks* (New York: Penguin Putnam, 2000), pp. 68–69, and by Moye, *Ella Baker*, p. 63. See also EB, Walker interview, p. 6; EB, Hogan interview, p. 19; Brinkley, *Rosa Parks*, p. 162.

26. EB, Hogan interview, p. 20. See also Ransby, *Ella Baker*, pp. 120 and 122–24.

27. EB, letter to Rev. Kilgore, February 26, 1956, in Ella Baker papers, Schomburg Center for Research in Black Culture, Box 10, folder 1.

28. Jeanne Theoharis, *The Rebellious Life of Mrs. Rosa Parks* (Boston: Beacon Press, 2013), pp. 25–26; Grant, *Ella Baker*, p. 102; Jeanne Theoharis, *A More Beautiful and Terrible History: The Uses and Misuses of Civil Rights History* (Boston: Beacon, 2018), p. 201.

29. EB, Walker interview, p. 10.

30. David J. Garrow, *Bearing the Cross: Martin Luther King, Jr., and the Southern Christian Leadership Conference* (New York: William Morrow, 1986), p. 84; Ransby, *Ella Baker*, pp. 167–68.

31. EB, Walker interview, pp. 12–15.

32. EB, Britton interview, p. 39.

33. EB, Thrasher and Hayden interview, p. 62. See also Ransby, *Ella Baker*, pp. 161–74.

34. EB, Thrasher and Hayden interview, p. 63. See also Taylor Branch, *Parting the Waters: America in the King years, 1954–1963* (New York: Simon & Schuster, 1988), p. 258.

35. EB, interview by Gerda Lerner, 1970, in Gerda Lerner, ed., *Black Women in White America: A Documentary History* (New York: Pantheon, 1972), p. 349.

36. EB, Lerner interview, p. 351.

37. Grant, *Ella Baker*, pp. 109–10; Ransby, *Ella Baker*, pp. 175–76 and 180; and Moye, *Ella Baker*, pp. 93–101.

38. EB, Britton interview, p. 16. See also Moye, *Ella Baker*, pp. 105–6. On Septima Clark's similar criticism of King, see Lynne Olson, *Freedom's Daughters: The Unsung Heroines of the Civil Rights Movement from 1930 to 1970* (New York: Scribner, 2001), p. 222.

39. EB, Britton interview, p. 16. See also Grant, *Ella Baker*, pp. 107–8; Branch, *Parting the Waters*, p. 247; and Pascal Robert, "Ella Baker and the Limits of Charismatic Masculinity," *Huffington Post*, December 6, 2017. https://www.huffingtonpost.com/pascal-robert/ella-baker-and-the-limits_b_2718608.html/.

40. EB, letter to Bayard Rustin and Stanley Levison, June 16, 1958, quoted by Garrow, *Bearing the Cross*, p. 650, note 4.

41. EB, Memorandum to Committee on Administration, "S.C.L.C. as a Crusade," October 23, 1959, p. 2. http://www.crmvet.org/docs/5910_sclc_baker-crusade.pdf/.

42. EB, Memorandum, "S.C.L.C. as a Crusade," p. 1. https://www.crmvet.org/docs/5910_sclc_baker-crusade.pdf/. See also Payne, *I've Got the Light of Freedom*, pp. 94–95.

43. Olson, *Freedom's Daughters*, pp. 74 and 146; Moye, *Ella Baker*, p. 109.

44. EB, Hogan interview, p. 3.

45. EB, interviewed by Clay Carson, NYC, May 5, 1972, typescript, p. 4. http://www.crmvet.org/nars/720505_baker_carson.pdf/.

46. EB, Hogan interview, p. 70. See also Ransby, *Ella Baker*, p. 195.

47. John Lewis, quoted by Clayborne Carson, *In Struggle: SNCC and the Black Awakening of the 1960s* (Cambridge: Harvard University Press, 1995 [first edition 1981]), p. 24.

48. EB, in *Fundi.*

49. EB, Lerner interview, p. 350.

50. EB, in *Fundi.* The other woman, not identified, was elderly, southern, and apparently white.

51. EB, in *Fundi.*

52. EB, interviewed by Anne Cooke Romaine, New York, 1967, typescript, p. 7, at http://www.crmvet.org/nars/6702_baker.pdf/.

53. EB, Carson interview, p. 8.

54. EB, Hogan interview, p. 4.

55. Jessica Gordon Nembhard, *Collective Courage: A History of African American Cooperative Economic Thought and Practice* (University Park: Pennsylvania State University, 2014), pp. 112–25, especially p. 119.

56. EB, Report of the Director to the Executive Board, May 15, 1959, p. 3, in the Boston University Howard Gotlieb Research Center, Dr. Martin Luther King Archive. See also EB, Walker interview, p. 20.

57. EB, Hogan interview, p. 3.

58. EB, Carson interview, p. 5.

59. EB, Hogan interview, p. 5.

60. EB Thrasher, and Hayden interview, p. 66; EB, Carson interview, pp. 6–7; EB, Hogan interview, p. 8.

61. EB, Hogan interview, p. 4. See also EB, Carson interview, p. 6.

62. EB, in *Fundi.*

63. EB, Hogan interview, p. 6.

64. EB, Hogan interview, p. 71. See also Grant, *Ella Baker*, p. 128.

65. Julian Bond, interviewed by Elizabeth Gritter, November 1 and 22, 1999, Southern Oral History Program Collection (#4007) in the Southern Historical Collection, Wilson Library, University of North Carolina at Chapel Hill.

66. Diane Nash, interview, in *Voices of Freedom: An Oral History of the Civil Rights Movement from the 1950s through the 1980s*, ed. Henry Hampton, Steve Fayer, and Sarah Flynn, paperback edition (New York, Bantam Books, 1991), pp. 61–62.

67. Diane Nash, quoted in Ransby, *Ella Baker*, p. 247.

68. EB, in *Fundi*.

69. EB, Walker interview, p. 70. See also Ransby, *Ella Baker*, p. 247.

70. EB, Britton interview, pp. 73–74.

71. EB, quoted by Ellen Cantarow and Susan Gushee O'Malley, "Ella Baker: Organizing for Civil Rights," in *Moving the Mountain: Women Working for Social Change*, ed. Ellen Cantarow, Susan Gushee O'Malley, and Sharon Hartman Strom (New York: Feminist Press, 1980), p.53.

72. EB, Hogan interview, p. 73.

73. EB, Lerner interview, p. 352.

74. James Lawson, quoted by Garrow, *Bearing the Cross*, p. 141.

75. Andrew Young, *An Easy Burden: The Civil Rights Movement and the Transformation of America* (New York: HarperCollins, 1996), p. 137.

76. EB, Britton interview, p. 34.

77. EB, Walker interview, p. 77.

78. EB, in *Fundi*.

79. EB, Walker interview, p. 19. See also Olson, *Freedom's Daughters*, pp. 141–46 and 149–50. For Septima Clark's strikingly similar criticism of SCLC's treatment of women, see Olson, *Freedom's Daughters*, p. 222.

80. EB, Britton interview, p. 37. See also EB, Romaine interview, p. 5.

81. EB, Britton interview, p. 60. See also Ransby, *Ella Baker*, p. 62 and pp. 357–62.

82. EB, Britton interview, 2nd interview session, July 19, 1969, p. 96.

83. Charles Payne, "Ella Baker and Models of Social Change," *Signs: Journal of Women in Culture and Society*, 1989, vol. 14, no. 4, pp. 892–93 and 897.

84. Ransby, *Ella Baker*, pp. 189 and 192; Moye, *Ella Baker*, pp. 107–8.

85. Payne, *I've Got the Light of Freedom*, pp. 91–94.

Chapter Two

1. Jane Jacobs, "Hitch-hiking with the Fish," unpublished MS, revised 1954, Jane Jacobs Papers, MS1995-29, John J. Burns Library, Boston College, Box 22, folder 8, p. 1. See also JJ, "Islands the Boats Pass By," *Harper's Bazaar*, July 1947, JJ Papers, Box 27, folder 1, pp. 77 and 79, and JJ interview, "The Way We Are: Jane Jacobs, critic of critics," *Toronto Star*, October 24, 1970, JJ Papers, Box 24, folder 5.

2. JJ, "Hitch-hiking," p. 1.

3. JJ, "Hitch-hiking, pp. 4 and 8.

4. JJ, "Hitch-hiking," p. 8.

5. JJ, "Hitch-hiking," p. 8.

6. JJ, "Hitch-hiking," p. 6.

7. JJ, letter to Miss Talmey, November 22, 1961, JJ Papers, Box 5, folder 3.

8. JJ, interviewed by Jim Kunstler, Part I, p. 5, at http://www.metropolismag.com/cities/jane-jacobs-godmother-of-the-american-city/. Originally in *Metropolis Magazine*, March 2001.

9. Robert Kanigel, *Eyes on the Street: The Life of Jane Jacobs* (New York: Penguin Random House, 2016), p. 38.

10. "Jade Writes Potpourri," *The Scranton Times*, March 22, 1995, in *Ideas That Matter: The Worlds of Jane Jacobs*, ed. Max Allen (Ontario: The Ginger Press, 2011), p. 17. Some of the pieces in *Ideas That Matter* are abridged.

11. Joe Berridge, "Real Cities," *Ideas That Matter*, p. 189.

12. JJ, Kunstler interview, *Metropolitan*, part I, p. 6. See also Peter L. Laurence, *Becoming Jane Jacobs* (Philadelphia: University of Pennsylvania, 2016), p. 128.

13. JJ, quoted by Jonathan Karp, "Jane Jacobs Doesn't Live Here Anymore," *Ideas That Matter*, p. 15.

14. JJ, "Caution Men Working," *CUE*, May 18, 1940, in *Vital Little Plans: The Short Works of Jane Jacobs* (New York: Random House, 2016), ed. Samuel Zipp and Nathan Storring, pp. 22–28.

15. JJ, Kunstler interview, *Metropolitan*, Part I, p. 6. For the "scale of things," JJ, quoted by Albert Amateau, "Jane Jacobs comes back to the Village She Saved," *The Villager*, vol. 74, no. 2, May 12–18, 2004. htttp://www.the villager_54Jjanejacobs.html, p. 2.

16. JJ, letter to Miss Talmey.

17. JJ, interviewed by Eve Auchincloss and Nancy Lynch, "Disturber of the Peace: Jane Jacobs," *Mademoiselle*, October 1962, in *Jane Jacobs: The Last Interview and Other Conversations* (Brooklyn: Melville House, 2016), p. 12. See also JJ, "Answers to Interrogatory for Jane Butzner Jacobs," July 22, 1949, JJ Papers, Box 5, folder 3, p. 1.

18. JJ, "Interrogatory," March 25, 1952, *Ideas That Matter*, p. 177.

19. Laurence, *Becoming Jane Jacobs*, pp. 55–62.

20. Alice Sparberg Alexiou, *Jane Jacobs: Urban Visionary* (Rutgers University Press, New Brunswick, NJ, 2006), pp. 33–34.

21. Laurence, *Becoming Jane Jacobs*, pp. 149 and 169–70. See also Kanigel, *Eyes on the Street*, pp. 125–26 and 131–32.

22. JJ, "The Missing Link in City Redevelopment," talk, the Conference on Urban Design at Harvard University, April 1956, *Ideas That Matter*, p. 39.

23. JJ, "The Missing Link," pp. 39–40.

24. JJ, "Downtown Is for People," *Fortune*, April 1958, in *The Exploding Metropolis*, ed. the editors of *Fortune* (Garden City, NY: Doubleday Anchor, 1958), pp. 140–41.

25. JJ, typescript of talk, April 20, 1958, New School Associates, New School for Social Research, New York, JJ Papers, Box 19, folder 3, p. 4.

26. "Downtown Is for People," p. 168.

27. New School talk, pp. 2–3.

28. Robert Moses, quoted in "Moses Scores Foes on Washington Square," *New York Times*, June 11, 1940, p. 27. See also Anthony Wood, *Preserving New York: Winning the Right to Protect a City's Landmarks* (New York: Routledge, 2008), pp. 169–71; Anthony Flint, *Wrestling with Moses: How Jane Jacobs Took on New York's Master Builder and Transformed the American City* (New York: Random House, 2009), pp. 73–74.

29. JJ, "Reason, Emotion, Pressure: There Is No Other Recipe," talk at Cooper Union, May 1957, *Vital Little Plans*, p. 82. See also Laurence, *Becoming Jane Jacobs*, pp. 162–63.

30. New School talk, p. 7.

31. New School talk, p. 8. See also Peter L. Laurence, "Jane Jacobs Before *Death and Life*," *Journal of the Society of Architectural Historians*, vol. 66, no. 1 (March 2007), p. 10, and Flint, *Wrestling with Moses*, pp. 65 and 75.

32. New School talk, p. 8.

33. JJ, "Candor Tactics," letter to the editor, *The Columbia Forum*, Fall 1972, in *Ideas That Matter*, p. 82.

34. JJ, *The Death and Life of Great American Cities* (New York: Random House, 1961), p. 105.

35. JJ, *Death and Life*, p. 361. Italics in the original. See also Laurence, *Becoming Jane Jacobs*, p. 162.

36. Edith Lyons, interviewed by Vicki Weiner, New York City, February 19, 1997 and July 3, 1998, in Greenwich Village Society for Historic Preservation, www.gvshp.org/_gvshp/resources /doc/lyons_transcript.pdf / See also "Traffic Ban is Aim in Washington Sq.," *New York Times*, June 4, 1952, p. 26.

37. Douglas Martin, "Shirley Hayes, 89; Won Victory over Road," *New York Times*, May 11, 2002, p. 25.

38. Sandra Knox, "Villagers Defeat New Traffic Plan," *New York Times*, May 28, 1952, p. 31.

39. JJ, quoted by Rebecca Gratz, *Battle for Gotham: New York in the Shadow of Robert Moses and Jane Jacobs* (Nation Books, New York, 2010), p. 77.

40. Robert Moses, quoted by Robert Fishman, "Revolt of the Urbs: Robert Moses and His Critics," in *Robert Moses and the Modern City*, ed. Hilary Ballon and Kenneth T. Jackson (New York: W. W. Norton, 2007), p. 122. See also Wood, *Preserving New York*, p. 183; Flint, *Wrestling with Moses*, p. 62.

41. JJ, quoted by Gratz, *Battle for Gotham*, p. 77.

42. JJ, "Pedalling Together," Speech, 1988 Spokespeople Conference, Toronto, *Ideas That Matter*, p. 123. The spelling is British.

43. JJ, interviewed by Leticia Kent, Toronto: 1997, p. 3. www.gvshp.org/_gvshp/resources/doc /jacobs_transcript.pdf.

44. JJ, Kent interview, p. 4.

45. JJ, Kent interview, p. 5.

46. Charles G. Bennett, "Showdown Looms in Washington Sq.," *New York Times*, Sept. 16, 1958, p. 29.

47. Mary Perot Nichols, "City Closed Square Saturday," *Village Voice*, November 5, 1958, p. 3; Flint, *Wrestling with Moses*, p. 87.

48. JJ, Kent interview, pp. 9 and 4–5. See also "Whitney North Seymour, Jr: An Oral History Interview," by Anthony C. Wood, July 29, 2006, at www.nypap.org/oral-history/whitney-north -seymour-jr/; Wood, *Preserving New York*, pp. 195–96, n. 65.

49. JJ, quoted by Jane Kramer, "All the Ranks and Rungs of Mrs. Jacobs' Ladder," *Village Voice*, December 20, 1962, p. 24 (cont. from p. 3).

50. JJ, quoted by Wayne Phillips, "Title I Slum Clearance Proves Spur to Cooperative Housing in City," *New York Times*, July 2, 1959.

51. JJ, interviewed by James Howard Kunstler, in *Jane Jacobs: The Last Interview and Other Conversations* (Brooklyn: Melville House, 2016), p. 64. Italics in the text.

52. JJ, Kent interview, p. 15. See also Jacobs, "Reason, Emotion, Pressure," p. 85; JJ, transcript of her comments, "A Symposium: Jane Jacobs and the New Urban Ecology," Boston College Law School," November 18, 2000, in JJ Papers, Box 20, folder 8, p. 5.

53. Laurence, *Becoming Jane Jacobs*, p. 207.

54. Fishman, "Revolt of the Urbs," pp. 128–29. See also Gratz, *Battle for Gotham*, pp. xxiii–xxiv; Laurence, "Jane Jacobs Before *Death and Life*," p. 12.

55. Ellen Lurie, quoted by Samuel Zipp, *Manhattan Projects: The Rise and Fall of Urban Renewal in Cold War New York* (New York: Oxford University Press, 2010), pp. 324–25. See also Kanigel, *Eyes on the Street*, pp. 179–80.

56. JJ, letter to Chadbourne Gilpatric, July 1, 1958, *Ideas That Matter*, p. 48. See also Laurence, *Becoming Jane Jacobs*, p. 164; Zipp, *Manhattan Projects*, pp. 303–61.

57. JJ, *Death and Life*, pp. 15–16. See also *Ibid.*, pp. 66 and 278; Alexiou, *Jane Jacobs*, pp. 43–49; and Laurence, *Becoming Jane Jacobs*, pp. 182–89.

58. JJ, letter to Grady Clay, March 3, 1959, quoted by Laurence, *Becoming Jane Jacobs*, pp. 269–70.

59. JJ, speech, Greenwich Village, May 7, 2004, quoted by Amateau, "Jane Jacobs comes back," p. 2, and by Alexiou, pp. 39–40; JJ, quoted by Christopher Hume, "Let's Hope Jane Jacobs Keeps Talking and That Movers and Shakers Listen," *Toronto Star*, Sept. 7, 1991, *Ideas That Matter*, p. 126.

60. JJ, quoted by Amateau, "Jane Jacobs comes back," p. 2.

61. JJ, Kunstler interview, *Metropolitan*, part II, p. 8. See also Lizabeth Cohen, *Saving America's Cities: Ed Logue and the Struggle to Renew Urban America in the Suburban Age* (New York: Farrer, Strauss and Giroux, 2019), p. 139.

62. JJ, Kunstler interview, *Metropolitan*, part II, p. 1.

63. JJ, quoted in (no author) "Greenwich Village Study Wants: More Housing, No Projects, Traffic to Bypass Square," *Village Voice*, November 20, 1957, p. 1.

64. JJ, quoted in Martin Arnold, "Housing Men Told Renewal Is Dying," *New York Times*, May 12, 1962, in JJ Papers, Box 23, folder 2. See also JJ, 1969 Seminar Report, Stratford (Ontario) Seminar in Civic Design, in *Ideas That Matter*, p. 60.

65. JJ, in "Meeting of Six Minds," slightly condensed transcript, National Housing Conference annual meeting, Washington DC, March 12, 1962, JJ Papers, Box 22, folder 12, p. 14.

66. JJ, quoted by Lucille Preuss, "Jane Jacobs Way of Life Fits Her Preaching," *The Milwaukee Journal*, Sunday July 8, 1962, Part 6, p. 15, JJ Papers, Box 23, folder 2. See also Laurence, *Becoming Jane Jacobs*, p. 256.

67. JJ, Auchincloss and Lynch interview, pp. 12–13. Italics in the original.

68. JJ, Kent interview, p. 24.

69. JJ, Kent interview, p. 18.

70. JJ commentary, *Ideas That Matter*, p. 71. See also Flint, *Wrestling with Moses*, p. 85; Alexiou, *Jane Jacobs*, p. 55.

71. JJ, Kent interview, p. 24.

72. JJ commentary, *Ideas That Matter*, p. 71.

73. JJ, *Death and Life*, p. 272, note.

74. JJ, quoted by Ed Zotti, "Eyes on Jane Jacobs," September 1986, *Ideas That Matter*, 61.

75. JJ, new forward to Modern Library Edition, *The Death and Life of Great American Cities* (New York: Random House, 1993), p. xii.

Chapter Three

1. Rachel Carson, letter to Hendrik Van Loon, 1937, quoted by Mark Hamilton Lytle, *The Gentle Subversive: Rachel Carson, Silent Spring, and the Rise of the Environmental Movement* (New York: Oxford University Press, 2007), p. 44.

2. RC, *Under the Sea-Wind* (London: Penguin, 2007), p. 3 (from Carson's 1941 forward.)

3. RC, *Under the Sea-Wind*, p. 65. See also Lytle, *The Gentle Subversive*, pp. 50–51 and 90.

4. William Souder, *On a Farther Shore: The Life and Legacy of Rachel Carson* (New York: Crown Publishers, 2012), p. 77. The pro-Hitler author was Henry Williamson.

5. Linda Lear, *Rachel Carson: Witness for Nature* (New York: Henry Holt, 1997), pp. 54–55 and 137.

6. RC, letter to Dr. William Beebe, September 6, 1948, in Rachel Carson Papers, Yale Collection of American Literature, Beinecke Rare Book and Manuscript Library, Yale University, New Haven, CT, Box 4, folder 67.

7. RC, "National Book Award Acceptance Speech," 1952, in Paul Brooks, *The House of Life: Rachel Carson at Work* (Boston: Houghton Mifflin, 1972), p. 129.

8. RC, "Of Man and the Stream of Time," 1962 speech at Scripps College, Claremont California, in *Literature and the Environment: A Reader on Nature and Culture*, ed. Lorraine Anderson, Scott Slovic, John P. O'Grady (New York: Longman, 1999), p. 313. See also Lear, *Rachel Carson*, p. 220.

9. RC, *The Sea around Us* (New York: Oxford University Press, 1951), pp. 92–93.

10. RC, *Under the Sea-Wind*, pp. 14–15.

11. RC, Speech to National Symphony Orchestra benefit lunch, September 25, 1951, in Linda Lear, ed., *Lost Woods: The Discovered Writings of Rachel Carson* (Boston: Beacon Press, 1998), p. 89.

12. RC, "Of Man and the Stream of Time," p. 312.

13. Lear, *Rachel Carson*, p. 180.

14. RC, letter to the Washington Post, April 22, 1953, in *Lost Woods*, pp. 99–100.

15. RC, "The Real World around Us," Matrix Table Dinner, Theta Sigma Phi, Columbus, Ohio, April 21,1954, in *Lost Woods*, pp. 161 and 163. See also Souder, *On a Farther Shore*, p. 126.

16. RC, "The Real World around Us," pp. 161–62.

17. RC, "The Real World around Us," pp. 151–52 and 161. Italics in the text. See also Lear, *Rachel Carson*, 167.

18. RC, letter to Edward Weeks, July 18, 1937, quoted by Lear, *Rachel Carson*, p. 87.

19. RC, typescript of speech, Book and Author Luncheon, October 16, 1951, in *Lost Woods*, p. 77. See also Brooks, *House of Life*, p.71, and Lytle, *Gentle Subversive*, p. 57.

20. RC, "National Book Award Acceptance Speech," *House of Life*, p. 128.

21. RC, letter to Paul Brooks, May 1957, quoted by Brooks, *House of Life*, p. 214.

22. RC, letter to Dorothy Freeman, February 3, 1956, in *Always, Rachel: The Letters of Rachel Carson and Dorothy Freeman, 1952–1964*, edited by Martha Freeman (Boston: Beacon Press, 1995), p. 151. See also Lear, *Rachel Carson*, pp. 236–37, 282–83, and 302; Lytle, *Gentle Subversive*, pp. 116–19.

23. Barbara McClintock, quoted by Evelyn Fox Keller, *A Feeling for the Organism: The Life and Work of Barbara McClintock* (New York: W. H. Freeman, 1983), p. 198. See also Vera L. Norwood, "The Nature of Knowing: Rachel Carson and the American Environment," *Signs*, vol. 12, no. 4 (summer 1987), pp. 759–60.

24. Rachel Carson, *The Edge of the Sea* (Boston: Houghton Mifflin, 1955), pp. 5 and 225.

25. Carson, *Edge of the Sea*, pp. 123 and 189.

26. RC, letter to Maria Rodell, Oct. 26, 1957, in *House of Life*, p. 215.

27. RC, letter to Paul Brooks [no date], quoted by Brooks, *House of Life*, p. 214. Italics in the text.

28. RC, "Our Ever-Changing Shore," *Holiday*, 1958, in *Lost Woods*, pp. 122–23.

29. Thomas R. Dunlap, *DDT: Scientists, Citizens, and Public Policy* (Princeton: Princeton University Press, 1981), p. 78.

30. Marjorie Spock, letter to RC, February 5, 1958, quoted by Lear, *Rachel Carson*, p, 318. See also John Paull, "The Rachel Carson Letters and the Making of *Silent Spring*," *Sage Open*, 3 (July 2013), pp. 1–12; Robert Musil, *Rachel Carson and Her Sisters* (New Brunswick, NJ: Rutgers University Press, 2014), p. 115; Lear, *Rachel Carson*, pp. 318, 335, and 552, note 75; and Brooks, *House of Life*, p. 238.

31. Lear, *Rachel Carson*, pp. 118–19.

32. Marjorie Spock with Mary Richards, "Rachel Carson: A Portrait," at http://www.rachel carsoncouncil.org/index.php?/mact=Printing,m2,printpage,1&m2returnid=215&page=215, p. 3.

33. Sandra Steingraber, "Silent Spring: A Father-Daughter Dance," in *Courage for the Earth: Writers, Scientists, and Activists Celebrate the Life and Writing of Rachel Carson*, ed. Peter Matthiessen (Boston: Houghton Mifflin, 2007), pp. 57–58.

34. RC, letter to Marjorie Spock, Sept. 15, 1958, quoted by Lear, *Rachel Carson*, p. 332.

35. RC, letter to Marjorie Spock, July 15, 1959, RC Papers, Box 44, folder 828. See also Paull, "The Rachel Carson Letters," pp. 6–7.

36. RC, letter to Marjorie Spock, December 4, 1958, RC Papers, Box 44, folder 828.

37. RC, letter to Marjorie Spock, May 7, 1958, RC papers, Box 44, folder 828.

38. Marjorie Spock, interview by Linda Lear, 1994, quoted by Lear, *Rachel Carson*, p. 319. See also Lytle, *Gentle Subversive*, pp. 140–41.

39. RC, letter to Dorothy Freeman, February 1, 1958, in *Always, Rachel*, pp. 248–49.

40. RC, letter to Dorothy Freeman, June 28, 1958, and RC, letter to Dorothy Freeman, July 5, 1958, in *Always, Rachel*, pp. 258–59 and 261.

41. Dunlap, *DDT*, pp. 76–77 and 292.

42. Clarence Cottam, letter to RC, November 21, 1958, quoted by Brooks, *House of Life*, p. 249.

43. Clarence Cottam, letter to RC, November 21, 1958, and RC, letter to Clarence Cottam, January 8, 1959, p. 249.

44. RC, letter to Clarence Cottam, October 30, 1959, quoted by Brooks, *House of Life*, p. 251.

45. Lear, *Rachel Carson*, pp. 14, 333–34, 344–45, and 356; Lytle, *Gentle Subversive*, p.1.

46. Carson, "Of Man and the Stream of Time," p. 315.

47. Vera Norwood, *Made from This Earth: American Women and Nature* (Chapel Hill: University of North Carolina Press, 1993), pp. 147–48, 154–55, 157–59, 163, and 167.

48. Olga Huckins, letter to *Boston Herald*, January 29, 1958, quoted by Brooks, *House of Life*, p. 232.

49. Musil, *Rachel Carson*, p. 54; Lear, *Rachel Carson*, pp. 181–82 and 343.

50. Dunlap, *DDT*, pp. 91–92. See also *Pesticides, a Love Story: American's Enduring Embrace of Dangerous Chemicals* (Lawrence: University Press of Kansas, 2015), pp. 114–19.

51. Dunlap, *DDT*, pp. 81 and 85. See also Maril Hazlett, "'woman vs. man vs. bugs': Gender and Popular Ecology in Early Reactions to *Silent Spring*," *Environmental History* 9 (October 2004), p. 714.

52. Dunlap, *DDT*, p. 85. The biologist was Joseph Hickey.

53. RC, letter to George J. Wallace, October 11, 1958, quoted by Brooks, *House of Life*, p. 252. See also Dunlap, *DDT*, pp. 83–84; Hazlett, "woman vs. man vs. bugs," p. 726, note 53.

54. Dixie Larkin, letter to unknown government official, July 29, 1957, reproduced in Bill Berry, *Banning DDT: How Citizen Activists in Wisconsin Led the Way* (Madison: Wisconsin Historical Society, 2014), p. 118. See also *Banning DDT*, pp. 20 and 117.

55. "Punchy Phrases Punctuate Hearing on DDT Spray," *Milwaukee Sentinel*, March 25, 1960, n.p., in RC Papers, Box 33, folder 576.

56. RC, letter to Mrs. F. L. Larkin, June 1, 1960, quoted by Brooks, *House of Life*, p. 263.

57. RC, *Silent Spring* (Boston: Houghton Mifflin, 2002), p. ix.

58. Maria Rodell, letter to RC, December 2, 1960, RC papers, Box 105, folder 1991; RC, letter to Dorothy Freeman, June 27, 1962, in *Always, Rachel*, p. 408. See also Frank Graham, Jr., *Since Silent Spring* (Boston: Houghton Mifflin, 1970), pp. 7 and 9.

59. RC, letter to Marjorie Spock, September 26, 1958, RC Papers, Box 44, folder 828.

60. "Vanishing Bald Eagle Gets Champion," *The Florida Naturalist*, April 1959, p. 64, typescript, RCP-BLYU, Box 33, folder 576. See also Charles L. Broley, "The Plight of the American Bald Eagle," *Audubon Magazine*, July–August 1958, pp. 162–63, in RC Papers, Box 33, folder 575.

61. Chad Montrie, *The Myth of* Silent Spring: *Rethinking the Origins of American Environmentalism* (Oakland: University of California Press, 2018), pp. 7–9, rightly points out that Carson didn't start the environmental movement, but misses her gratitude to the local activists who preceded and helped her.

62. Irston Barnes, letter to Ezra Taft Benson, March 23, 1959, quoted by Lear, *Rachel Carson*, p. 343.

63. RC, letter to *Washington Post*, April 10, 1961, in *Lost Woods*, pp. 190–91. She took the phrase "rain of death" from British ecologist Charles Elton.

64. RC, letter to Marjorie Spock, June 3, 1959, in RC Papers, Box 44, folder 828.

65. RC, letter to Marjorie Spock, June 19, 1959, in RC Papers, Box 44, folder 828.

66. RC, letter to Paul Brooks, June 26, 1961, in *House of Life*, p. 268.

67. RC, quoted by Lear, *Rachel Carson*, p. 358.

68. RC, letter to Dorothy Freeman, October 18, 1959, in *Always, Rachel*, p. 287.

69. Musil, *Rachel Carson and Her Sisters*, pp. 91 and 121; Lear, *Rachel Carson*, pp. 404–6; Lytle, The *Gentle Subversive*, pp. 7–8, 147–48 and 164–65.

70. RC, letter to Dorothy Freeman, January 6, 1962, in *Always, Rachel*, p. 391.

71. Lytle, *Gentle Subversive*, pp. 236–37. Lytle acknowledges that "gentle" is not an exact fit. See ibid., pp. 238–39.

72. Mrs. Thomas Duff (formerly Betty Haney), letter to Paul Brooks, February 24, 1969, quoted by Brooks, *House of Life*, p. 259.

73. RC, letter to Edwin Way Teale, October 12, 1958, quoted by Lear, *Rachel Carson*, p. 334. See also Dunlap, *DDT*, pp. 70 and 88; Souder, *On a Farther Shore*, p. 284; Frederick Rowe Davis, *BANNED: A History of Pesticides and the Science of Technology* (New Haven: Yale University Press, 2014), pp. 69–69 and 129; and Edmund Russell, *War and Nature: Fighting Humans and Insects with Chemicals from World War I to* Silent Spring (New York: Cambridge University Press, 2001), p. 219.

74. RC, *Silent Spring*, p.193.

75. RC, letter to Marjorie Spock, February 24, 1960, RC Papers, Box 44, folder 829.

76. RC, letter to Dorothy Freeman, November 19, 1959, in *Always, Rachel*, p. 290.

77. RC, letter to Dr. Edward O. Wilson, November 6, 1958, RC Papers, Box 44, folder 841.

78. RC, letter to Marjorie Spock, April 7, 1959, RC Papers, Box 44, folder 129.

79. RC, letter to Paul Brooks, December 3, 1959, quoted by Brooks, *House of Life*, p. 258.

80. Clarence Cottam, letter to RC, February 26, 1962, RC Papers, Box 42, folder 774.

81. Marie Rodell, letter to RC, December 2, 1960, RC Papers, Box 105, folder 1991.

82. RC, letter to Lois Crisler, February 8, 1962, quoted by Brooks, *House of Life*, p. 13.

83. RC, letter to Paul Brooks, December 3, 1959, quoted by Lear, *Rachel Carson*, p. 357.

84. RC, letter to Paul Brooks, December 27, 1960, quoted by Lear, *Rachel Carson*, p. 368.

85. RC, letter to Marjorie Spock, April 12, 1960, RC Papers, Box 44, folder 129.

86. RC, letter to George Crile, December17, 1960, quoted by Lear, *Rachel Carson*, p. 380.

87. Dorothy Freeman, quoted by Lytle, *Gentle Subversive*, p. 127.

88. RC, letter to Marjorie Spock, July 11, 1960, RC Papers, Box 44, folder 129.

89. Dunlap, *DDT*, pp. 78–79.

90. Dunlap, *DDT*, p. 141.

91. RC, *Silent Spring*, pp. 227–28. See also Musil, *Rachel Carson*, p. 6.

Chapter Four

1. Lillian Stone, aka Betty Goldstein, "New Day in Stamford," *The New Masses*, vol. 57, no. 4 (January 22, 1946), in Betty Friedan Papers, Arthur and Elizabeth Schlesinger Library on the History of Women in America, Radcliffe Institute for Advanced Study at Harvard University, Cambridge, Mass., Box 23, folder 345b, p. 3.

2. "Stamford Unions Stage Short General Strike," *Life*, January 14, 1946, p. 31. The article was unsigned.

3. Betty Goldstein, "UE Strikers Fighting for Us, say people of Bloomfield," *Federated Press*, Jan. 16, 1946, Betty Friedan papers, Box 23, folder 329. See also David Jackovino, "Labor unrest results in strikes in post-war Bloomfield," *The Independent Press and Glen Ridge Paper*, October 3, 2013, p. 6.

4. Richard Lynch, quoted by Goldstein, "UE Strikers Fighting for Us."

5. Ella Baker, quoted by *Atlanta Daily World*, January 2, 1947, in Joanne Grant, *Ella Baker: Freedom Bound* (New York: John Wiley & Sons, 1998), p. 91.

6. Betty Goldstein, "Family Day on Westinghouse Picketline," *Federated Press*, April 24, 1946, BF papers, Box 23, folder 329.

7. Betty Goldstein, "A Tale of Sacrifice: A Story of Equality in the United States, 1951," *March of Labor*, no. 4, May, 1951, BF papers, Box 23, folder 334, p. 16. See also Betty Goldstein, "Shadows over Lawrence: Textile Town's Troubles are Warning for Labor," *March of Labor*, no. 3, March 1952, BF papers, Box 23, folder 334, p. 28.

8. Goldstein, "A Tale of Sacrifice," p. 16.

9. BF, Introduction to Part I, *It Changed My Life: Writings on the Women's Movement* (New York: Random House, 1976), p. 6.

10. Joy James, "Ella Baker, 'Black Women's Work and Activist Intellectuals," *The Black Scholar*, vol. 24, no. 4 (Fall 1994), pp. 10–13; J. Todd Moye, *Ella Baker: Community Organizer of the Civil Rights Movement* (Lanham, MD: Rowman & Littlefield, 2013), pp. 37–39.

11. Betty Goldstein, "Well-Healed White Collar League Seen as Disguised Native Fascist Threat," *Federated Press*, March 16, 1944, BF papers, Box 22, folder 328.

12. BF, "The Way We Were—1949," 1974, in *It Changed My Life*, p. 12; Daniel Horowitz, *Betty Friedan and the Making of the Feminine Mystique: The American Left, the Cold War, and Modern Feminism* (Amherst: University of Massachusetts Press, 1998), p. 80.

13. JJ, "Chilton Boss Says He Won't Do It Again," no date, clipping, JJ Papers, Box 27, folder 1; Peter L. Laurence, *Becoming Jane Jacobs* (Philadelphia: University of Pennsylvania Press, 2016), pp. 55–56.

14. Betty Goldstein, "Pretty Posters Won't Stop the Turnover of Women in Industry," *Federated Press*, October 26, 1943, BF papers, Box 22, folder 328.

15. Horowitz, *Betty Friedan*, pp. 52–53. The professor was Dorothy Wolff Douglas.

16. Betty Goldstein, "NAM Honors War Workers," *Federated Press*, December 8, 1943, BF papers, Box 22, folder 328. The piece was signed bg-rt.

17. Betty Goldstein, "UE Fights for Women Workers," in *Public Women, Public Worlds: A Documentary History of American Feminism*, ed. Dawn Keetley and John Pettegrew (Lanham, Maryland: Rowman & Littlefield, 2002), pp. 434, 437–38, 439, and 445. The pamphlet was published without an identified author, but Friedan, Horowitz, and the UE agree it was her. Betty Friedan, *Life So Far: A Memoir* (New York: Simon & Schuster, 2000), p. 65; Horowitz, *Betty Friedan*, p. 298, note 41.

18. Bettye Goldstein, "Clerks Tell Students How They Doubled Their Pay," *Federated Press*, Sept. 3, 1941, BF Papers, Box 22, folder 328.

19. Betty Goldstein, quoted by Horowitz, *Betty Friedan*, p. 101. See also *Interviews with Betty Friedan* (Jackson: University Press of Mississippi, 2002), p. xix.

20. BF, "The Way We Were," pp. 13 and 14.

21. BF, Introduction to Part I, *It Changed My Life*, p. 6.

22. BF, "The Way We Were," p. 16. See also Horowitz, *Betty Friedan*, pp. 141–42.

23. BF, "The Way We Were," p. 15. (Italics in the original.)

24. BF, Introduction to "The Crisis in Women's Identity," *It Changed My Life*, p. 59.

25. BF, "The Way We Were," p. 15.

26. BF, "Was Their Education UnAmerican?," typescript, c. 1953, BF papers, Box 31, folder 416. See also Friedan, *Life So Far*, p. 71; Daniel Horowitz, "Rethinking Betty Friedan and *The Feminine Mystique*: Labor Union Radicalism and Feminism in Cold War America," *American Quarterly*, vol. 48, no. 1 (March 1996), p. 9.

27. BF, "I Went Back to Work," *Charm*, April 1955, pp. 145 and 200, in BF papers, Box 29, folder 403.

28. BF, "I Went Back to Work," pp. 200–201.

29. Horowitz, *Betty Friedan*, pp. 180–81.

30. BF, "You Can Go Home Again," typescript, c. 1954, BF Papers, Box 29, folder 397, pp. 2 and 5.

31. BF, "You Can Go Home Again, pp, 6–7.

32. EB, interviewed by Urban Review editors, *Urban Review* 4, no. 3 (May 1970), p. 21.

33. BF, "More than a Nosewiper: Housing Project Mothers Make a Backyard Camp for their Kids," typescript, c. 1956, BF Papers, Box 26, folder 378, pp. 4 and 6.

34. BF, "More than a Nosewiper, pp. 7 and 20.

35. BF, "More than a Nosewiper, p. 9.

36. BF, "They Found Out Americans Aren't So Awful After All," typescript, c. 1955, quoted by Sylvie Murray, *The Progressive Housewife: Community Activism in Suburban Queens, 1945–1965* (Philadelphia: University of Pennsylvania Press, 2003), p. 144.

37. BF, "The Way We Were," pp. 15–16.

38. Horowitz, *Betty Friedan*, pp. 191–92.

39. Betty Goldstein Friedan, "If One Generation Can Ever Tell Another: A Woman Is a Person Too," *Smith Alumnae Quarterly*, vol. 52, no. 2 (Winter 1961), pp. 68–69.

40. BF, "If One Generation Can Ever Tell Another," p. 69.

41. BF, "If One Generation Can Ever Tell Another," p. 70.

42. BF, *The Feminine Mystique* (New York: Dell, 1963), p. 7. See also Horowitz, *Betty Friedan*, pp. 193 and 209–13.

43. BF, *The Feminine Mystique*, pp. 346 and 347.

44. BF, *The Feminine Mystique*, p. 31.

45. EB, quoted by Grant, *Ella Baker*, p. 108. See also Barbara Ransby, *Ella Baker & The Black Freedom Movement* (Chapel Hill: University of North Carolina Press, 2003), p. 184.

46. See especially Joanne Meyerowitz, "Beyond the Feminine Mystique: A Reassessment of Postwar Mass Culture, 1946–1958," *Journal of American History* 79 (March 1993), pp. 1455–82. A good balance is struck by Stephanie Coontz, *A Strange Stirring: The Feminine Mystique and American Women at the Dawn of the 1960s* (New York: Basic Books, 2011), pp. 56–57, 67, and 74.

47. BF, *The Feminine Mystique*, p. 361.

48. Betty Goldstein, quoted by Goldstein, "Shadows over Lawrence," p. 28; Horowitz, *Betty Friedan*, p. 150.

49. Horowitz, *Betty Friedan*, pp. 92–93, 145–49, 177–78, and 242–43. See also Horowitz, "Rethinking Betty Friedan," p. 17.

50. BF, "Insert–left wing thought," BF papers, Box 46, folder 597, no pages.

51. Ella Baker, interviewed by Anne Cooke Romaine, New York, 1967, typescript, p. 7, at http://www.crmvet.org/nars/6702_baker.pdf/.

52. EB, interviewed by Clay Carson, NYC, May 5, 1972, p. 3, at http://www.crmvet.org/nars/720505_baker_carson.pdf/.

53. EB, interviewed by Eugene Walker, 1974, typescript, p. 57, at http://docsouth.unc.edu/sohp/G-0007/G-0007.html/; Ransby, *Ella Baker*, p. 175.

54. EB, Minutes of the Administrative Committee, July 3, 1958, quoted by Grant, *Ella Baker*, p. 109.

55. EB quoted by Grant, *Ella Baker*, p. 99. See also Ransby, *Ella Baker*, pp. 160–61.

56. JJ, Forward to Interrogatory, March 25, 1952, in *Ideas That Matter: The Worlds of Jane Jacobs*, edited by Max Allen (Owen Sound, Ontario: Ginger Press, 2011), p. 169.

57. JJ, Interrogatory for Jane Butzner Jacobs, in *Ideas That Matter*, pp. 172 and 175. See also Laurence, *Becoming Jane Jacobs*, pp. 84–91.

58. Ransby, *Ella Baker*, pp. 160 and 234.

59. John Paull, "The Rachel Carson Letters and the Making of *Silent Spring*," *Sage Open*, 3 (July 2013), pp. 7–8; William Souder, *On a Farther Shore: The Life and Legacy of Rachel Carson* (New York: Crown Publishers, 2012), p. 406, note 15; Linda Lear, *Rachel Carson: Witness for Nature* (New York: Houghton Mifflin, 1997), pp. 409 and 429; Robert Musil, *Rachel Carson and Her Sisters* (New Brunswick, NJ: Rutgers University Press, 2014), pp. 111–13; Priscila Coit Murphy, *What a Book Can Do: The Publication and Reception of* Silent Spring (Amherst: University of Massachusetts Press, 2005), p. 45 and p. 228, n.78.

Chapter Five

1. Ella Baker, quoted by Aldon Morris, *The Origins of the Civil Rights Movement: Black Communities Organizing for Change* (New York: Free Press, 1984), p. 201. See also Joanne Grant, *Ella Baker: Freedom Bound* (New York: John Wiley & Sons, 1998), p. 127. Christopher W. Schmidt, *The Sit-ins: Protest & Legal Change in the Civil Rights Era* (Chicago: University of Chicago, 2018), emphasizes that without lawyers and politicians, no legal change would have occurred. He is not wrong. But my focus, like Ella Baker's, is on the uprising from below.

2. EB, quoted by Ellen Cantarow and Susan Gushee O'Malley, "Ella Baker: Organizing for Civil Rights," in *Moving the Mountain: Women Working for Social Change*, ed. Ellen Cantarow, Susan Gushee O'Malley, and Sharon Hartman Strom (New York: Feminist Press, 1980), p. 83.

3. "Youth Leadership Meeting," flyer, Shaw University, Raleigh, NC, April 15–17, at https:// digitalcollections.nypl.org/items/35f9cc00-dd04-0130-f3c6-58d385a7b928.

4. EB, interviewed by John Britton, June 19, 1968, typescript, pp. 40–41, at http://www.crmvet .org/nars/baker68.htm/.

5. EB, letter to Anne Braden, March 21, 1960, in Ella Baker papers, Schomburg Center for Research in Black Culture, Box 5, folder 1. See also EB, interviewed by Eugene Walker, Sept. 4, 1974, typescript, p. 94, at http://docsouth.unc.edu/sohp/G-0007/G-0007.html/; EB, Britton interview, 1968, p. 41; EB, interviewed by Sue Thrasher and Casey Hayden, New York, April 19, 1977, typescript, p. 65, at http://docsouth.unc.edu/sohp/G-0008/G-0008.html/.

6. EB, "Youth Leadership Retreat Planned," Press Release, March 2, 1960, EB Papers, Box 5, folder 1.

7. EB, Britton interview, p. 41; EB, "Expenditures made in connection with trip to Raleigh-Durham, N. C., March 16–18, 1960," Memorandum, EB Papers, Box 5, folder 2. See also Barbara Ransby, *Ella Baker and the Black Freedom Movement: A Radical Democratic Vision* (Chapel Hill: University of North Carolina Press, 2003), p. 240; Dorothy Dawson Burlage, "Truth of the Heart," in *Deep in Our Hearts: Nine White Women in the Freedom Movement* (Athens, Georgia: University of Georgia Press, 2000), p. 107.

8. Glenford Mitchell, "College Students Take Over," in Glenford Mitchell and William Peace, ed., *The Angry Black South* (New York: Corinth Books, 1962), pp. 75, 76, and 82–83. See also *Raleigh News and Observer*, February 10, 1960; *Raleigh Times*, February 10, 1960; William Peace, "The South Reacts," in *The Angry Black South*, p. 103.

9. Mitchell, "College Students Take Over," pp. 82 and 87–88.

10. Report from Ella J. Baker to Dr. Martin L King, Jr. and Rev. Ralph Abernathy, March 23, 1960, at https://kinginstitute.stanford.edu/king-papers/documents/ella-j-baker-6/.

11. Letter to Crusader for Freedom, March 25, 1960, EB Papers, Box 5, folder 9.

12. Letter to Student Leader, April 8, 1960, EB Papers, Box 5, folder 9.

13. "Delegates to Youth Leadership Conference Shaw University–Raleigh, NC, April 15–17," in EB Papers, Box 5, folder 7. The Student Non-Violent Coordinating Committee, "Report of the Raleigh Conference," EB Papers, Box 7, folder 5, p. 1, said there were 126 southern students. See also Martin Oppenheimer, *The Sit-In Movement of 1960* (Brooklyn: Carlson, 1989

[reprinted from 1963]), pp. 43 and 90–91; Delegates to Youth Leadership Conference, Shaw University, Raleigh, N.C., p. 3, at http://www.crmvet.org/docs/6004_shaw_delegates-r.pdf.

14. EB, interviewed by Emily Stoper, December 27, 1966, in Emily Stoper, *The Student Nonviolent Coordinating Committee: The Growth of Radicalism in a Civil Rights Organization* (Brooklyn: Carlson, 1989), p. 265.

15. EB, Britton interview, p. 43. See also EB, interviewed by Clay Carson, NYC, May 5, 1972, typescript, p. 9, at http://www.crmvet.org/nars/720505_baker_carson.pdf/.

16. EB, "News Alert to: Press, Radio and Television Media," April 11, 1960, EB Papers, Box 5, folder 9.

17. EB, Britton interview, p. 43.

18. Charles Payne, "Ella Baker and Models of Social Change," *Signs: Journal of Women in Culture and Society*, 1989, vol. 14, no. 4, p. 897; Ransby, *Ella Baker*, pp. 244–45.

19. Student Non-Violent Coordinating Committee, "Report of the Raleigh Conference," p. 1.

20. Newspaper fragment, in EB papers, Box 5, folder 6; Andrew Maguire, "Veterans of the Civil Rights Movement," at https://www.crmvet.org/vet/maguirea.htm.

21. EB, Britton interview, p. 45. See also EB, quoted by Ellen Cantarow and Susan Gushee O'Malley, "Ella Baker: Organizing for Civil Rights," in *Moving the Mountain*, p. 84.

22. EB, Britton interview, 1968, p. 44. See also EB, Thrasher and Hayden interview, 1977, p. 67.

23. EB, quoted by Cantarow and O'Malley, "Ella Baker," p. 84.

24. EB, in *Fundi: The Story of Ella Baker*, documentary film, directed by Joanne Grant (New York: Icarus Films, 1981).

25. EB, Walker interview, pp. 73–74.

26. EB, quoted by Cantarow and O'Malley, "Ella Baker," p. 84. See also EB, Carson interview, pp. 8–9; Grant, *Ella Baker*, pp. 128–29; Ransby, *Ella Baker*, pp. 242–43. Ransby suggests King may not have been as determined to annex the student movement as Baker thought he was.

27. Bernard Lee, quoted by David J. Garrow, *Bearing the Cross: Martin Luther King, Jr., and the Southern Christian Leadership Conference* (New York: William Morrow, 1986), p. 133.

28. Septima P. Clark, letter to Ella Baker, March 24, 1960, in EB papers, Box 5, folder 1; Taylor Branch, *Parting the Waters: America in the King years, 1954–1963* (New York: Simon & Schuster, 1988), p. 290.

29. Mitchell, "College Students Take Over," p. 90.

30. EB, Britton interview, 1968, p. 46.

31. Ella Baker, "Bigger Than a Hamburger," *Southern Patriot*, May 1960, vol. 18, no. 5 (June 1960), p. 4. The article carried a Raleigh dateline.

32. EB, Stoper interview, p. 266.

33. Julian Bond, interview, in Henry Hampton and Steve Fraser, ed., *Voices of Freedom: An Oral History of the Civil Rights Movement from the 1950s through the 1980s* (New York: Bantam Books, 1990), p. 63.

34. Julian Bond, in *Fundi*.

35. Julian Bond, in *Voices of Freedom*, p. 64. See also EB, Carson interview, p. 8; Recommendations of the Finding and Recommendations Committee, April, 1960. Youth Leadership Conference, Shaw College, Raleigh, NC, at https://www.crmvet.org/docs/shawdocs.htm; Constance Curry, "Wild Geese to the Past," in *Deep in Our Hearts*, p. 15.

36. Student Non-Violent Coordinating Committee, "Report of the Raleigh Conference," p. 1.

37. Ella Baker, "After the Sit-Ins, What?," transcript of remarks, EB Papers, Box 6, folder 5. See also Britton interview, p. 54.

38. EB, Stoper interview, p. 268.

39. Ella Baker, quoted by Howard Zinn, *SNCC: The New Abolitionists* (Haymarket Books: Chicago, 2013), p. 106.

40. EB, quoted by Cantarow and O'Malley, "Ella Baker," pp. 86–87.

41. EB, Britton interview, p. 57.

42. Cantarow and O'Malley, "Ella Baker," p. 86.

43. EB, quoted by Cantarow and O'Malley, "Ella Baker," p. 87.

44. EB, Britton interview, p. 56.

45. Julian Bond, quoted by Charles M. Payne, *I've Got the Light of Freedom: The Organizing Tradition and the Mississippi Freedom Struggle* (Berkeley: University of California Press, 1995), pp. 104–5.

46. EB, Britton interview, p. 57.

47. EB, Walker interview, p. 68.

48. EB, Britton interview, p. 57.

49. EB, Walker interview, p. 69.

50. EB, quoted by Cantarow and O'Malley, "Ella Baker," p. 87. See also EB, Romaine interview, p. 2; EB, Britton interview, p. 60.

51. EB, quoted by Cantarow and O'Malley, "Ella Baker," p. 87.

52. EB, Walker interview, 1974, p. 23.

Chapter Six

1. Jane Jacobs, *The Death and Life of Great American Cities* (New York: Random House, 1961), p. 268.

2. *Death and Life*, acknowledgment page; Robert Kanigel, *Eyes on the Street: The Life of Jane Jacobs* (New York: Penguin Random House, 2016), pp. 200–201.

3. JJ, Foreword to the Japanese edition of *Cities and the Wealth of Nations*, April 1986, in *Ideas That Matter: The Worlds of Jane Jacobs*, ed. Max Allen (Ontario: Ginger Press, 2011), p. 108. Some pieces in *Ideas That Matter* are abridged.

4. Samuel R. Mozes and Jane Jacobs, quoted in "Big Cities, Big Problems: Planning: Waste or Wisdom," *National Observer*, Sunday, April 22, 1962, p. 12, JJ Papers, Box 22, folder 12.

5. Penny Fox, "Suburbs Do Not Suit Citified Author," *Newsday*, clipping, JJ Papers, Box 23, folder 1. See also JJ, interviewed by Eve Auchincloss and Nancy Lynch, "Disturber of the Peace: Jane Jacobs," *Mademoiselle*, October 1962, reprinted in *Jane Jacobs: The Last Interview and Other Conversations* (Brooklyn: Melville House, 2016), p. 18.

6. JJ, draft of a letter to Frank Rudman, December 1964, in *Ideas That Matter*, pp. 59–60.

Chapter Seven

1. Rachel Carson, *Silent Spring* (Boston: Houghton Mifflin, 2002), p. 189.

2. Robert K. Musil, *Rachel Carson and Her Sisters* (New Brunswick, NJ: Rutgers University Press, 2014), pp. 124–29; Edmund Russell, *War and Nature: Fighting Humans and Insects with Chemicals from World War I to* Silent Spring (New York: Cambridge University Press, 2001), p. 210.

3. Russell, *War and Nature*, p. 211.

4. RC, letter to Marjorie Spock, September 26, 1958, in Rachel Carson Papers, Yale Collection of American Literature, Beinecke Rare Book and Manuscript Library, Yale University, New Haven, CT, Box 44, folder 828; Frank Graham, Jr., *Since* Silent Spring (Boston: Houghton Mifflin, 1970), pp. 28–29: Linda Lear, *Rachel Carson: Witness for Nature* (New York: Henry Holt, 1997), pp. 398, 402, and 566, note 18.

5. Daniel Horowitz, *The Anxieties of Affluence: Critiques of American Consumer Culture, 1939-1979* (Amherst: University of Massachusetts Press, 2004), p. 157; Michelle Mart, *Pesticides,*

a Love Story: American's Enduring Embrace of Dangerous Chemicals (Lawrence: University Press of Kansas, 2015), pp. 71–73.

6. Russell, *War and Nature*, pp. 225–27.

7. Musil, *Rachel Carson and Her Sisters*, p. 227.

8. Jane Jacobs, *The Death and Life of Great American Cities* (New York: Random House, 1961), p. 391. See also David Kinkela, "The Ecological Landscapes of both Jane Jacobs and Rachel Carson," *American Quarterly*, vol. 61, no. 4 (December 2008), pp. 905–28.

9. RC, application for a Guggenheim fellowship, quoted by Lear, *Rachel Carson*, p. 187.

10. RC, letter to Edward O. Wilson, November 6, 1958, in RC Papers, Box 44, folder 841. See also Donald Worster, *Nature's Economy: A History of Ecological Ideas* (Cambridge: Cambridge University Press, 1977), pp. 294–301.

11. JJ, *Death and Life*, p. 433. See also Peter L. Laurence, *Becoming Jane Jacobs* (Philadelphia: University of Pennsylvania Press, 2016), pp. 57–59; Peter Laurence, "Jane Jacobs Before *Death and Life*," *Journal of the Society of Architectural Historians* (March, 2007), pp. 5 and 7–8.

12. JJ, *Death and Life*, pp. 438–39. See also Robert Fulford, "Abbatoir for Sacred Cows: Three Decades in the Life of a Classic," 1991, in *Ideas That Matter, The Worlds of Jane Jacobs*, edited by Max Allen (The Ginger Press: Owen Sound, Ontario, 2011), p. 7; Rebecca Gratz, *Battle for Gotham: New York in the Shadows of Robert Moses and Jane Jacobs* (New York: Nation Books, 2010), p. xxiv.

13. JJ, new forward to Modern Library Edition, *The Death and Life of Great American Cities* (New York: Random House, 1993), p. xvi.

14. JJ, interviewed by Joseph Plummer, "The Curious Island," *Jubilee*, January, 1962, JJ Papers, Box 22, folder 12. See also Andrea Barnet, *Visionary Women: How Rachel Carson, Jane Jacobs, Jane Goodall, and Alice Waters Changed Our World* (New York: HarperCollins, 2018), pp. 197–98.

15. JJ, interviewed by Plummer.

16. JJ, quoted by Lucille Preuss, "Jane Jacobs' Way of Life Fits Her Preaching," *The Milwaukee Journal*, June 8, 1962, part 6, p. 15, JJ Papers, Box 23, folder 2.

Chapter Eight

1. Betty Friedan, *The Feminine Mystique* (New York: Dell, 1963), p. 15.

2. BF, interviewed by Barbara Mantz Drake, 1999, in *Interviews with Betty Friedan*, ed. Janann Sherman (Jackson: University Press of Mississippi, 2002), p. 182. See also Daniel Horowitz, *Betty Friedan and the Making of the Feminine Mystique: The American Left, the Cold War, and Modern Feminism* (Amherst: University of Massachusetts Press, 1998), p. 22.

3. Betty Friedan, *Life So Far: A Memoir* (New York: Simon & Schuster, 2000), p. 111. See also Horowitz, *Betty Friedan*, pp. 110–11.

4. BF, "The Sexual Counter-Revolution," typescript, in Betty Friedan Papers, Arthur and Elizabeth Schlesinger Library on the History of Women in America, Radcliffe Institute for Advanced Study at Harvard University, Cambridge, MA, Box 40, folder 527, p. 1. The larger manuscript, of which this is part, is called "Togetherness Women."

5. Friedan, "The Sexual Counter-Revolution," p. 15. The professor was John P. Mallan. It is not clear from Friedan's manuscript which words are his, and which are hers. My guess is that the ideas are his, and the words are hers.

6. BF, "Insert–left wing thought," BF papers, Box 46, folder 597.

7. BF, "The Way We Were—1949," 1974, in *It Changed My Life: Writings on the Women's Movement* (New York: Random House, 1976), pp. 13–14.

8. BF, "The Sexual Counter-Revolution," p. 2.

9. BF, *Life So Far*, p. 65.

10. BF, "Togetherness women/ Mystique," BF Papers, Box 40, folder 527.

11. Gerda Lerner, letter to Betty Friedan, February 6, 1963, Box 57, folder 715, pp. 1–2, BF Papers. See also Horowitz, *Betty Friedan*, p. 213.

12. Friedan, *Life So Far*, p. 131. Italics in the text.

13. Linda Gordon, "Gerda Lerner, 1920–2013," *Solidarity*, at https://www.solidarity-us.org /node/3818.

14. Joanne Meyerowitz, "Beyond the Feminine Mystique: A Reassessment of Postwar Mass Culture, 1946–1958," *Journal of American History*, vol. 79 (March 1993), p. 1481.

15. Jessica Mitford, "The Indignant Generation," *The Nation*, May 27, 1961, pp. 451 and 453.

16. BF, Introduction to "Angry Letters, Relieved Letters," *It Changed My Life*, p. 17.

17. BF, *Life So Far*, p. 108.

18. BF, Introduction, *It Changed My Life*, p. xv. See also BF, *Life So Far*, p. 134.

19. BF, interviewed by Ben J. Wattenberg, "The First Measured Century," PBS documentary, 2000. See Stephanie Coontz, *A Strange Stirring: The Feminine Mystique and American Women at the Dawn of the 1960s* (New York: Basic Books, 2011), pp. 33 and 150–52.

20. Coontz, *A Strange Stirring*, pp. 66 and 142–44.

21. Coontz, *A Strange Stirring*, pp. 30–31.

22. BF, *Life So Far*, p. 138. See Linda Lear, *Rachel Carson: Witness for Nature* (New York: Henry Holt, 1997), pp. 377–78 and 398.

23. BF, "The Way We Were—1949," 1974, in *It Changed My Life*, p. 15. Italics in the original.

24. Typescript, "interview with female psychiatrist," n.d., BF papers, Box 159, folder 2015. The typescript is in a folder with fragments from the Smith 1957 questionnaire, so this woman may have been a 1942 Smith graduate.

25. Jeri G., Janice K., Constance Ahrons, and Glenda Schilt Edwards, quoted by Coontz, *A Strange Stirring*, pp. 81, 83, and 87.

Chapter Nine

1. Barbara Ransby, *Ella Baker & the Black Freedom Movement: A Radical Democratic Vision* (Chapel Hill: University of North Carolina Press, 2003), p. 249.

2. Ella Baker, interviewed by Emily Stoper, December 27, 1966, in Emily Stoper, *The Student Nonviolent Coordinating Committee: The Growth of Radicalism in a Civil Rights Organization* (Brooklyn: Carlson, 1989), p. 270. See also Tanisha C. Ford, *Liberated Threads: Black Women, Style, and the Global Politics of Soul* (Chapel Hill: University of North Carolina Press, 2015), pp. 67–76; Ransby, *Ella Baker*, pp. 259 and 278.

3. Charles McDew, quoted in Peter Dreier, "Ella Baker, Ferguson, and 'Black Mothers' Sons'" (2014). UEP Faculty & UEPI Staff Scholarship, at http://scholar.oedu/uep_faculty/835.

4. Courtland Cox, in *Fundi: The Story of Ella Baker*, documentary film, directed by Joanne Grant (New York: Icarus Films, 1981).

5. Mary King, *Freedom Song: A Personal Story of the 1960s Civil Rights Movement* (New York: William Morrow, 1987), p. 61.

6. EB, Stoper interview, p. 269.

7. Rick Manning, personal communications to me, May 4, 2015. Manning, who worked in the Atlanta office of SNCC from 1963 to 1965, was more aware of the importance of Moses than of the importance of Baker.

8. Howard Zinn, *SNCC: The New Abolitionists* (Chicago: Haymarket Books, 2013), dedication and pp. iii, 32–34 and 63–64. (Originally published in 1964.) A historian of popular movements who makes no mention of Baker is Michael Kazin, *American Dreamers: How the Left Changed America* (New York: Knopf, 2011.)

9. Robert P. Moses and Charles E. Cobb, Jr., *Radical Equations: Civil Right from Mississippi to the Algebra Project* (Boston: Beacon Press, 2001), pp. 3 and 26. See also Laura Visser-Maessen, *Robert Parris Moses: A Life in Civil Rights and Leadership at the Grassroots* (Chapel Hill: University of North Carolina Press, 2016), pp. 33–35; Zinn, *SNCC*, p. 17.

10. Moses, *radical equations*, p. 32.

11. Bob Moses, interviewed by Clayborne Carson, June 19, 1970, p. 1, at http://king encyclopedia.stanford.edu/primarydocuments/Interview_Bob_Moses.pdf/ See also Visser-Maessen, *Robert Parris Moses*, pp. 46–47 and 119.

12. Moses, *radical equations*, p. 32.

13. Bob Moses, quoted by Joanne Grant, *Ella Baker: Freedom Bound* (New York: John Wiley, 1988), p. 121.

14. EB, "Organizing for Civil Rights," in *Moving the Mountain: Women Working for Social Change*, ed. Ellen Cantarow, Susan Gushee O'Malley, and Sharon Hartman Strom (New York: Feminist Press, 1980), p. 89.

15. Bob Moses, letter to Jane Stembridge, August 1960, quoted by Taylor Branch, *Parting the Waters: America in the King years, 1954–1963* (New York: Simon and Schuster, 1989), p. 330.

16. Moses, quoted in Visser-Maessen, *Robert Parris Moses*, p. 56.

17. Bob Moses, "The Transformation of People," in *Debating the Civil Rights Movement, 1945—1968* (Lanham, Maryland: Rowman & Littlefield, 2006, 2nd ed.), p. 182.

18. Moses, *radical equations*, p. 38.

19. Grant, *Ella Baker*, p. 134.

20. Moses, radical equations, p. 44. Italics in the text.

21. Moses, radical equations, p. 57.

22. Charles Payne, *I've Got the Light of Freedom: The Organizing Tradition and the Mississippi Freedom Struggle* (University of California Press: Berkeley, 1995), p. 177. See also pp. 157–58 and 199.

23. Moses, radical equations, p. 68. Italics in the original.

24. Moses, *radical equations*, p. 65.

25. Worth Long, quoted by Payne, *I've Got the Light*, p. 334.

26. Moses, *radical equations*, p. 16.

27. Moses, *radical equations*, p. 87. In Mississippi, SNCC formed an umbrella organization with the Congress on Racial Equality and the NAACP, called the Council of Federated Organizations. SNCC staff dominated COFO; Moses was its program director.

28. Moses, *radical equations*, table of contents and p. 23.

29. Bob Moses, quoted by Ransby, *Ella Baker*, p. 330. See also Moses quoted in ibid., p. 303, and in Payne, *I've Got the Light of Freedom*. p. 236.

30. EB, Speech to SNCC Conference, Washington, DC, December 1963, in Davis W. Houck and David E. Dixon, *Women and the Civil Rights Movement, 1954–1965* (Jackson: University Press of Mississippi, 2009), pp. 246–50.

31. Grant, *Ella Baker*, p. 163; Ransby, *Ella Baker*, p. 333; Joanne Grant, "Mississippi Politics—A Day in the Life," in *The Black Woman: An Anthology*, ed. Toni Cade Bambara (New York: Washington Square Press, 2005), p. 68. The first edition was published in 1970.

32. Nelson Lichtenstein, *The Most Dangerous Man in Detroit: Walter Reuther & the Fate of American Labor* (New York: Basic Books, 1995), pp. 392–95; Ransby, *Ella Baker*, p. 333.

33. Moses, *radical equations*, p. 82. See also Ransby, *Ella Baker*, pp. 339–40.

34. Fannie Lou Hamer, quoted by Payne, *I've Got the Light*, p. 332.

35. EB, Stoper interview, p. 271. Italics in the text. See also Ransby, *Ella Baker*, p. 341, and Grant, *Ella Baker*, p. 173.

36. Maria Varela, "Time to Get Ready," in *Hands on the Freedom Plow*, p. 562. Varela was a SNCC organizer in Alabama and Mississippi. Baker used the identical words in a speech in Atlanta in 1969. EB, "The Black Woman in the Civil Rights Struggle," speech, Atlanta, 1969, excerpted in Grant, *Ella Baker*, p. 230.

37. Moses, Carson interview, p. 9.

38. Julian Bond, quoted by Payne, *I've Got the Light*, 104–5.

39. Anne Braden, in *Fundi*. See also Catherine Fosl, *Subversive Southerner: Anne Braden and the Struggle for Racial Justice in the Cold War South* (New York: Palgrave Macmillan, 2002), pp. 285–86.

40. EB, quoted by Grant, *Ella Baker*, p. 157.

41. Clayborne Carson, *In Struggle: SNCC and the Black Awakening of the 1960s* (Cambridge: Harvard University Press, 1995 [first edition 1981]), pp. 180–83. See also Ransby, *Ella Baker*, pp. 129; 403, note 2; and 404, n. 23.

42. EB, quoted by Grant, "Mississippi Politics," p. 72.

43. Ransby, *Ella Baker*, p. 290.

44. Moses, Carson interview, p 10. See also Visser-Maessen, *Robert Parris Moses*, p. 47.

45. Bob Moses, quoted by Zinn, *SNCC*, pp. 226–27.

46. Personal reminiscence of the author.

47. Jane Jacobs, interviewed by James Howard Kunstler, "Godmother of the American City," *Metropolis*, March 2001, in *Jane Jacobs: The Last Interview and Other Conversations* (Brooklyn: Melville House, 2016), pp. 61–62 and 64–65.

48. Jane Jacobs, interviewed by Leticia Kent, Toronto, 1997, p. 45.

49. Carson, *In Struggle*, pp. 111–303, especially 127–28, 133, 138, 149–50, and 153.

50. Payne, *I've Got the Light of Freedom*, pp. 315–16 and 365–78.

51. EB, Stoper interview, p. 266.

52. Ransby, *Ella Baker*, pp. 347 and 351.

53. EB, Stoper interview, p. 272.

54. EB, interviewed by *Urban Review* editors, *Urban Review* 4, no. 3 (May 1970), p. 23.

55. Peter Dreier, "What Can We Learn from Ella Baker in A Post-Ferguson Era," *Café*, December 26, 2014; Barbara Ransby, "Ella Baker's Radical Democratic Vision," *Jacobin*, June 18, 2015; Irv Randolph, "The work and wisdom of Ella Baker," *The Philadelphia Tribune*. March 2, 2019; Jelani Cobb, "The Matter of Black Lives," *New Yorker*, March 14, 2016, at https://www.newyorker.com/magazine/2016/03/14/where-is-black-lives-matter-headed/.

Chapter Ten

1. Jane Jacobs, quoted by Rebecca Gratz, *Battle for Gotham: New York in the Shadows of Robert Moses and Jane Jacobs* (New York: Nation Books, 2010), p. 101.

2. John Sibley, "Two Blighted Downtown Areas Are Chosen for Urban Renewal," *New York Times*, Feb. 21, 1961, p. 37; JJ, interviewed by Leticia Kent, Toronto, 1997, p. 118, at www.gvshp.org/_gvshp/resources/doc/jacobs_transcript.pdf.

3. JJ, Kent interview, p. 19.

4. Priscilla Chapman, "City Critic in Favor of Neighborhoods," *New York Herald Tribune*, March 4, 1961, in *Ideas that Matter: The Worlds of Jane Jacobs*, ed. by Max Allen (Owen Sound, Ontario: Ginger Press, 2011), p. 49. Some pieces in *Ideas That Matter* are abridged.

5. JJ, Kent interview, pp. 19–20.

6. JJ, Kent interview, pp. 25–26; "'Villagers Seek to Halt Renewal," *New York Times*, March 4, 1961, p. 11.

7. JJ, Kent interview, p. 26.

8. JJ, Kent interview, p. 20; Amateau, "Jane Jacobs comes back."

9. Committee to Save the West Village newsletter, quoted by Kanigel, *Eyes on the Street*, p. 235.

10. JJ, Kent interview, pp. 29 and 30. See also JJ, interviewed by Roberta Brandes Gratz, "How Westway Will Destroy New York," February 6, 1979, in *Jane Jacobs: The Last Interview and Other Conversations* (Brooklyn: Melville House, 2016), p. 26.

11. JJ, Kent interview, pp. 27–28. See also "City Gives Up Plan for West Village," *New York Times*, February 1, 1962, p. 33, and cont. p. 35.

12. JJ, Kent interview, p. 31. See also Alice Sparberg Alexiou, *Jane Jacobs: Urban Visionary* (Rutgers University Press: New Brunswick, NJ, 2006), p. 103.

13. Sam Pope Brewer, "'Villagers' Seek to Halt Renewal," *New York Times*, March 4, 1961, p. 11.

14. Chapman, "City Critic in Favor of Neighborhoods," pp. 48–49.

15. JJ, letter to Arnold Nicholson, October 20, 1961, Jane Jacobs Papers, MS1995-29, John J. Burns Library, Boston College, Box 5, folder 3; JJ, quoted by Larrabee, "In Print: Jane Jacobs," p. 50.

16. JJ, "Candor Tactics," Letter to the Editor, *The Columbia Forum*, Fall, 1972, in *Ideas That Matter*, p. 82.

17. J. Clarence Davis, Jr., quoted by "Renewal Chief Sets 7 Projects for 1961," *New York Times*, Feb. 17, 1961, p. 5. See also Alexiou, *Jane Jacobs*, p. 99.

18. Robert Moses, quoted by Sam Roberts, "METRO MATTERS: Consensus is a New Westway Route," *New York Times*, May 25, 1992, at http://www.nytimes.com/1992/05/25/ny region/metro-matters-consensus-is-a-new-westway-route.html.

19. JJ, Kent interview, p.35.

20. JJ, Kent interview, p. 34.

21. JJ, "Candor Tactics," p. 82.

22. JJ, interviewed by Susan Fickel, Nancy Cooke, and Elaine Reuben, *Mademoiselle*, August 1962, p. 251.

23. JJ, Kent interview, p. 35.

24. "Village Group Wins Court Stay," *New York Times*, April 28, 1961, p. 34.

25. "Plan Board Votes Village Project," *New York Times*, Oct. 19, 1961, p. 30 (cont. from p. 1).

26. "Plan Board Votes Village Project," pp. 1 and 30.

27. "Plan Board Votes Village Project," pp. 1 and 30.

28. JJ, Kent interview, pp. 45–46.

29. JJ, Kent interview, p. 46; "City Gives Up Plan for West Village, *New York Times*, February 1, 1962, p. 33; Alexiou, *Jane Jacobs*, p. 106.

30. Jane Kramer, "All the Ranks and Rungs of Mrs. Jacobs' Ladder," *Village Voice*, December 20, 1962, p. 24.

31. Eric Larrabee, "In Print: Jane Jacobs," *Horizon* magazine, summer 1962, in *Ideas That Matter*, p. 50.

32. Mary Perot Nichols, "Mario's Not Afraid of the Bulldozer," *Village Voice*, August 14, 1969, p. 11.

33. Anthony Flint, *Wrestling with Moses: How Jane Jacobs Took on New York's Master Builder and Transformed the American City* (New York: Random House, 2009), pp. 103–21; the documentary film, *Citizen Jane: Battle for the City*, directed by Matt Tyrnauer (Altimeter Films, 2016).

34. JJ, quoted by Albert Amateau, "Jane Jacobs Comes Back to the Village She Saved," *The Villager*, vol. 74, no. 2 (May 12–18, 2004).

35. JJ, letter to Miss Talmey, November 22, 1961, JJ Papers, Box 5, folder 3.

36. JJ, Kent interview, p. 35.

37. JJ, quoted by Kramer, "All the Ranks," p. 24 (cont. from p. 3).

38. "Advocates Rejection of Urban Renewal Program for City," *Woodbury Daily Times*, p.2 (cont. from 1); JJ Papers, Box 23, folder 1; "Authority Raps Filling of Cove," *West Palm Beach/Miami Herald*, March 18, 1962, p. 1, JJ Papers, Box 23, folder 1; Robert J. Einhorn, "Jacobs Call Urban Renewal Irrelevant to Ithaca Solution," *The Cornell Daily Sun*, May 15, 1962, p.1, JJ Papers, Box 23, folder 1; William Allan, "Planning Critic Gets Roasting Reply," *Pittsburgh Press*, February 22, 1962, in *Ideas That Matter*, p. 51.

39. JJ, quoted by Lucille Preuss, "Jane Jacobs' Way of Life Fits Her Preaching," *The Milwaukee Journal*, July 8, 1962, part 6, p. 17 (cont. from p.15), JJ Papers, Box 23, folder 1.

40. JJ, quoted by Georgie Ann Guyer, "Lambastes Urban Renewal Plan," *Chicago Daily News*, March 15, 1962, JJ Papers, Box 23, folder 1.

41. Arnold Nicholson, letter to Jane Jacobs, April 4, 1962, in JJ Papers, Box 5, folder 3.

42. JJ, interviewed by Eve Auchincloss and Nancy Lynch, "Disturber of the Peace: Jane Jacobs," *Mademoiselle*, October 1962, reprinted in *Jane Jacobs: The Last Interview*, p. 5.

43. Rudolph Flesch, "History-Changing Book Decries City Planning," *Register and Tribune Newspaper Syndicate Release*, April 1, 1962, in *Ideas That Matter*, p. 51.

44. JJ, quoted by Frederick Pillsbury, "'I Like Philadelphia' . . . with some big Ifs and BUTS," *The Sunday Bulletin Magazine* [Philadelphia], June 24, 1962, pp. 4–5, JJ Papers, Box 22, folder 12.

45. JJ, quoted by Preuss, "Jane Jacobs' Way," p. 17.

46. JJ, quoted by Susan Brownmiller, "Jane Jacobs, Civic Battler," *Vogue*, May 1969, p. 180, JJ Papers, Box 24, folder 2.

47. Remarks of Jane Jacobs, at the Fifth Monthly Women Doers Luncheon Sponsored by Mrs. Lyndon B. Johnson at the White House, June 16, 1964, in *Ideas That Matter*, pp. 58–59.

48. Alexiou, *Jane Jacobs*, pp. 7, 115–16 and 135–39; Kanigel, *Eyes on the Street*, pp. 221–22; Gina Bellafante, "Fighting the Power Broker," *New York Times Book Review*, Oct. 9, 2016. p. 17; Marshall Berman, *All That Is Solid Melts into Air: The Experience of Modernity* (New York: Simon and Schuster, 1982), p. 324; Scott Larson, *"Building Like Moses with Jacobs in Mind:" Contemporary Planning in New York City* (Philadelphia: Temple University Press, 2013), pp. 105–7. But see Peter Laurence, "The Blind Claims of Jane Jacobs' Race-Blindness, News & Tweets—Becoming Jane Jacobs," at http://becomingjanejacobs.com/blog/2016/10/2/the-blindness-of-claims-of-jacobs-race-blindness.

49. JJ, *The Death and Life of Great American Cities* (New York: Random House, 1961), pp. 71 and 283–84.

50. JJ, quoted in "Author Cites Some Urban Renewal Planning Errors," *Germantown [PA] Courier*, May 3, 1962, p. 11 (cont. from 1), JJ Papers, Box 23, folder 2.

51. JJ, quoted by Daisy Cleveland, "City Amenities Neglected, First Lady's Doers' Hear," *The [Washington DC] Evening Star*, June 17, 1964, JJ Papers, Box 23, folder 6. See also Peter L. Laurence, *Becoming Jane Jacobs* (Philadelphia: University of Pennsylvania Press, 2016), p. 71.

52. JJ, quoted by "Writer Sees Blacklist in Negro Home Loans," *Philadelphia Inquirer*, Oct. 23, 1962, p. 42, JJ Papers, Box 22, folder 12.

53. JJ, *Death and Life*, p. 407.

54. JJ, quoted by Jeanne Barnes, *Dallas Morning News*, May 9, 1962, p. 3, JJ Papers, Box 23, folder 2.

55. JJ, quoted by Stephanie Gervis Harrington, "Private or Public Schools: Challenge of Integration," *Village Voice*, February 20, 1964, p. 1.

56. P.S. 41 Education Committee, "Village Picket Protesting Shift of Negro Pupils," September 1963, in *Ideas That Matter*, p. 72.

57. "Negro Pupil Shift Fought in Village," *New York Times*, June 13, 1963, p. 15.

58. Stephanie Gervis Harrington, "Boycott Strips Schools, Over Half Pupils Out," *Village Voice*, February 6, 1964, p. 15 (cont. from p. 1). See also Jeanne Theoharis, *A More Beautiful and Terrible History: The Uses and Misuses of Civil Rights History* (Boston: Beacon, 2018), pp. 35–48.

59. JJ, quoted in "Private or Public Schools," pp. 15–16 (cont. from p. 1).

60. Roger Starr, quoted by Alexiou, *Jane Jacobs*, p. 115. For an example of Black activists fighting successfully to protect their neighborhoods, see Karilyn Crockett, *People Before Highways: Boston Activists, Urban Planners, and a New Movement for City Making*. (Amherst: University of Massachusetts Press, 2018).

61. Mindy Thompson Fullilove, *Root Shock: How Tearing Up City Neighborhoods Hurts America, and What We Can Do About It* (New York: Ballantine, 2005), pp. 19–20.

62. Fullilove, *Root Shock*, pp. 44 and 45.

63. JJ, in Fullilove, *Root Shock*, Paperback (New York: One World/Ballantine, 2005), front matter.

Chapter Eleven

1. John M. Lee, "'Silent Spring' Is Now Noisy Summer," *New York Times*, July 22, 1962, Business and Financial Section, p. 1.

2. "Industry Maps Defense to Pesticide Criticisms," *Chemical and Engineering News*, vol. 40, no. 33, August 13, 1962, p. 25. See also Priscilla Coit Murphy, *What a Book Can Do: The Publication and Reception of* Silent Spring (Amherst: University of Massachusetts Press, 2005), pp. 98–100.

3. Dr. Arthur Rose, quoted in "Industry Maps Defense," p. 25. Ellipses in original.

4. Dr. George C. Decker, quoted in "Industry Maps Defense," p. 25.

5. "The Desolate Year," *Monsanto Magazine*, October 1962, pp. 5–7.

6. Louis A. McLean, quoted by Linda Lear, *Rachel Carson: Witness for Nature* (New York: Henry Holt, 1997), p. 417. See also Murphy, *What a Book Can Do*, pp. 64–65; Lear, *Rachel Carson*, p. 418.

7. Lear, *Rachel Carson*, pp. 420 and 428.

8. Hobert O. Thomas, quoted and then paraphrased, in "Industry Maps Defense," p. 25. See also Murphy, *What a Book Can Do*, p. 98.

9. "USDA Official Byron T. Shaw Dies," *Washington Post*, July 14, 2001, p. B06; William Souder, *On a Farther Shore: The Life and Legacy of Rachel Carson* (New York: Crown Publishers, 2012), pp. 15–16 and 340–43.

10. "How to Answer Rachel Carson," National Agricultural Chemical Association booklet, p. 2, Rachel Carson Papers, Yale Collection of American Literature, Beinecke Rare Book and Manuscript Library, Yale University, New Haven, CT, Box 66, folder 1192.

11. Dr. David H. Marsden, "could we SURVIVE without pesticides?" *Eastern States Cooperator*, November–December 1962, pp. 8–9. See also Mark Hamilton Lytle, *The Gentle Subversive: Rachel Carson, Silent Spring, and the Rise of the Environmental Movement* (New York: Oxford University Press, 2007), p. 166.

12. V. H. Freed, "Agricultural Chemicals–Boon or Bane?", *Oregon's Agricultural Progress*, vol. 9, no. 2 (Summer 1962), reprinted in *NAC News and Pesticide Review*, vol. 21, no. 2, December 1962, pp. 3–4. See also Fredrick J. Stare, "On *Silent Spring*," *Nutrition Reviews*, vol. 21, no. 1 (January 1963), p. 1.

13. "Pesticides: The Price for Progress," *Time*, vol. 80, no. 13 (September 28, 1962), pp. 45–48.

14. L. R. Gardner, "The Silence in 'Silent Spring,'" in National Agricultural Chemical Association booklet, RC Papers, Box 66, folder 1192. Italics in the text.

15. Edwin Diamond, "The myth of the 'Pesticide Menace,'" *Saturday Evening Post*, Sept. 28, 1963, pp. 16 and 18.

16. Dr. Edgar M. Adams, quoted in "Industry Maps Defense," p. 25.

17. Monroe Bush, SILENT SPRING..noisy autumn," *American Forests*, Oct. 1962, pp. 12, 52, and 53.

18. I. L. Baldwin, "Chemicals and Pests," *Science*, vol. 137, no. 3535 (Sept. 28, 1962), pp. 1042–43.

19. Anonymous author, "CONFIDENCE IN OUR LEADERSHIP: For Sale for Thirty Pieces of Silver," pp. 1–2, in RC Papers, Box 66, folder 1191. See also Murphy, *What a Book Can Do*, pp. 106–7.

20. William J. Darby, "Silence, Miss Carson!" *Chemical and Engineering News*, Oct. 1, 1962, pp. 62–63. See also Frank Graham, Jr., *Since* Silent Spring (Boston: Houghton Mifflin, 1970), p. 56; F. A. Soraci, Director of the New Jersey Department of Agriculture, quoted in Clarence Cottam, "A Noisy Reaction to Silent Spring," *Sierra Club Bulletin*, vol., 48, no. 1 (January 1963), p. 5. See also Stare, "On *Silent Spring*," p. 1.

21. William B. Bean, "The Noise of Silent Spring," *Archives of Internal Medicine*, Vol. 112 (1963), no. 3, pp. 308–11. Italics in the original. See also Maril Hazlett, "Voices from the Spring," *Seeing Nature Through Gender*, ed. by Virginia Scharff (Lawrence: University of Kansas Press, 2003), p. 116; Michael B. Smith, "'Silence, Miss Carson!' Science, Gender, and the Reception of 'Silent Spring,' *Feminist Studies*, vol. 27, no. 3 (Autumn, 2001), pp. 738–42; H. Patricia Hynes, *The Recurring Silent Spring* (New York: Pergamon Press, 1989), pp. 116–20; and Lear, *Rachel Carson*, p. 430.

22. Diamond, "The Myth of the Pesticide Menace," p. 16.

23. Quoted by Lear, *Rachel Carson*, p. 429. It is not certain which government official made the remark. See ibid., p. 573, note 4; Graham, *Since* Silent Spring, pp. 49–50.

24. Elaine Tyler May, *Homeward Bound: American Families in the Cold War Era* (New York: Basic Books, 2008), pp. 30 and 209. (The first edition was published in 1988.)

25. RC, "What's the Reason Why," Symposium, *New York Times Book Review*, December 2, 1962, p. 3.

26. Rachel Carson, Speech to the Women's National Press Club, December 5, 1962, in *Lost Woods: The Discovered Writing of Rachel Carson*, ed. by Linda Lear (Boston: Beacon Press, 1998), pp. 202–3 and 207.

27. Lear, *Rachel Carson*, p. 435; Murphy, *What a Book Can Do*, p. 173.

28. Lear, *Rachel Carson*, pp. 423 and 460–61. See also Murphy, *What a Book Can Do*, pp. 38–39.

29. Rachel Carson, Address to the Women of the Garden Club of America, January 1963, in *Lost Woods*, pp. 214, 217, 218, and 220. See also Edmund Russell, *War and Nature: Fighting Humans and Insects with Chemicals from World War I to* Silent Spring (New York: Cambridge University Press, 2001), p. 214; Michelle Mart, *Pesticides, a Love Story: American's Enduring Embrace of Dangerous Chemicals* (Lawrence: University Press of Kansas, 2015), p. 68.

30. Carson, Speech to the Women's National Press Club, pp. 208–10. See also Lear, *Rachel Carson*, p. 426; Paul Brooks, *The House of Life: Rachel Carson at Work* (Boston: Houghton Mifflin, 1972), p. 297; Cottam, "A Noisy Reaction," p. 15.

31. Carson, quoted by Brooks, *House of Life*, p. 319. See also Lear, *Rachel Carson*, pp. 448 and 450; Murphy, *What a Book Can Do*, p. 116.

32. Eric Sevareid, quoted by Lear, *Rachel Carson*, p. 452. See also Zuoyue Wang, "Responding to *Silent Spring*: Scientists, Popular Science Communication, and Environment Policy in the Kennedy Years," *Science Communication*, vol. 19, no. 2 (1997), pp. 147–51 and 154–58.

33. Hynes, *The Recurring Silent Spring*, p. 45.

34. Robert Moses, letter to Bennet Cerf, New York, November 15, 1961, in *Ideas That Matter: The Worlds of Jane Jacobs*, ed. Max Allen (Ontario: Ginger Press, 2011), p. 97. Some pieces in *Ideas That Matter* are abridged.

35. Dennis Harrow, "Jacobin Revival," *American Society of Planning Officials Newsletter*, Feb. 1962, in *Ideas That Matter*, p. 9. See also "Barnes Sails into Troubled Water," *Village Voice*, Jan. 3, 1963, in *Ideas That Matter*, p. 70.

36. Roger Starr, "Adventure in Mooritania: review of The Death and Life of Great American Cities," *Newsletter of the Citizens' Housing and Planning Council of New York, Inc.*, January 1962, in *Ideas That Matter*, pp. 53–54.

37. "Book Review: Death and Life," *American City Magazine*, May 1962, in *Ideas That Matter*, p. 51.

38. Alfred L. Tronzo, quoted by William Allan, "City Planning Critic Gets Roasting Reply," *Pittsburgh Press*, Feb. 22, 1962, in *Ideas That Matter*, p. 52.

39. Jane Jacobs, quoted by Clark Whelton, "'Great American Cities': Won't you come home, Jane Jacobs?" *Village Voice*, July 6, 1972, p. 26.

40. Robert Kanigel, *Eyes on the Street: The Life of Jane Jacobs* (New York: Penguin Random House, 2016), p. 175. See also Peter L. Laurence, *Becoming Jane Jacobs* (Philadelphia: University of Pennsylvania Press, 2016), pp. 248 and 252.

41. Lewis Mumford, letter to Jane Jacobs, Amenia New York, 22 July 1958, p. 2, JJ Papers, Box 2, folder 2.

42. JJ, *The Death and Life of Great American Cities* (New York: Random House, 1961), p. 20.

43. Lewis Mumford, letter to Mr. Wensberg, Oct. 18, 1961, in *Ideas That Matter*, p. 96.

44. Lewis Mumford, "Mother Jacobs' Home Remedies," *New Yorker*, December 1, 1962, p. 158.

45. Mumford, "Mother Jacobs' Home Remedies," pp. 158, 163, 168, 173–74, and 178–79.

46. Lewis Mumford, quoted in Alexiou, Alice Sparberg, *Jane Jacobs: Urban Visionary* (New Brunswick: Rutgers University Press, 2006). p. 93.

47. JJ, interviewed by Jim Kunstler, Part II, pp. 12–13, at http://www.metropolismag.com/cities/jane-jacobs-godmother-of-the-american-city/. Originally in *Metropolis Magazine*, March 2001.

48. "New York's Little Italy Beats the Bulldozers," *National Observer*, December 24, 1962, JJ Papers, Box 23, folder 2; JJ, interviewed by Claire Parin, Toronto, May 28, 1999, transcript of translation, p. 2; Jane Jacobs Papers, MS1995–29, John J. Burns Library, Boston College, Box 22, folder 32; Parin interview, pp. 3–4; Kanigel, *Eyes on the Street*, p. 265; Alexiou, *Jane Jacobs*, p. 109.

49. JJ, "Small Improvements," *Canadian Heritage magazine*, May/June 1987, in *Ideas That Matter*, p. 27.

50. Jacobs, Kunstler interview, Part II, pp. 12–13.

51. Jane Jacobs, quoted by Kanigel, *Eyes on the Street*, p. 392; see also p. 218.

52. Sara F. Anderson, "The View from the Outside: How Three Women's Work Contributed to Changes toward Equity and Human Rights: A Study of the Work of Rachel Carson, Jane Jacobs, and Betty Friedan," *New England Journal of History*, vol. 67, no. 1 (Fall 2010), p. 13.

53. Harrow, "Jacobin Revival," p. 10; W. E. McCauley, "On 'Silent Spring,'" *Service Letter Special G*, National Pest Control Association, Appendix I, p. 61, RC Papers, Box 66, folder 1192.

Chapter Twelve

1. Charles Payne, review, "Ella Baker and the Black Freedom Movement: A Radical Democratic Vision, "*Southern Culture*, vol. 10, no. 3 (Fall 2004), p. 106.

2. Aldon D. Morris, *Origins of the Civil Rights Movement: Black Communities Organizing Change* (New York: Free Press, 1964), p. 223.

3. Tom Hayden, "Participatory Democracy: from Port Huron to Occupy Wall Street," *The Nation*, April 16, 2012, p. 12. See also Tom Hayden, "Revolution in Mississippi," pamphlet, Students for a Democratic Society, January 1962; Wesley Hogan, "Freedom Now!: SNCC

Galvanizes the New Left," in *Rebellion in Black and White: Southern Student Activism in the 1960s*, ed. Robert Cohen and David J. Snyder (Baltimore: John Hopkins University Press, 2013), pp. 43–58; and Gregory Nevala Calvert, *Democracy from the Heart: Spiritual Values, Decentralism, and Democratic Idealism in the Movement of the 1960s* (Eugene, OR: Communitas Press, 1991), pp. 88–90 and 96–97.

4. Sara Evans, *Personal Politics: The Roots of the Women's Liberation Movement in the Civil Rights Movement & the New Left* (New York: Alfred A. Knopf, 1979).

5. Linda Gordon, "Social Movements, Leadership, and Democracy: Toward More Utopian Mistakes," *Journal of Women's History*, vol. 14, no. 2, (Summer 2002), p. 108. See also Myra Marx Ferree and Beth B. Hess, *Controversy and Coalition: The New Feminist Movement across Three Decades of Change* (New York: Routledge, 1995), third edition, p. 56.

6. EB, Memorandum to Committee on Administration, "S.C.L.C. as a Crusade," October 23, 1959, in Wisconsin Historical Society, Ella Baker Papers, Freedom Summer Digital Collection, pp. 2 and 3, at http://content.wisconsinhistory.org/cdm/ref/collection/p15932coll2/id/18105. See also Morris, *The Origins of the Civil Rights Movement*, p. 113.

7. Barbara Ransby, *Ella Baker & the Black Freedom Movement* (Chapel Hill: University of North Carolina Press, 2003), pp. 6 and 297. See also ibid., pp. 293–94.

8. Ella Baler, interviewed by Lenore Bredeson Hogan, New York, March 4, 1979, typescript, p. 72. Highlander Research and Education Center, New Market, Tenn.

9. Martha Prescod Norman Noonan, "Captured by the Movement," in *Hands on the Freedom Plow: Personal Accounts by Women in SNCC*, ed. Faith S. Holsaert, Martha Prescod Norman Noonan, Judy Richardson, Betty Garman Robinson, Jean Smith Young and Dorothy M. Zellner (Champaign: University of Illinois Press, 2010), p. 486.

10. Lawrence Guyot, quoted by Charles Payne, *I've Got the Light of Freedom: The Organizing Tradition and the Mississippi Freedom Struggle* (University of California Press: Berkeley, 1995), p. 271. Guyot organized in Mississippi.

11. Stokely Carmichael, quoted by Ransby, *Ella Baker*, p. 310. Carmichael's infamous joke about the position of women in the movement has obscured his recognition of powerful women in SNCC.

12. Casey Hayden, "Ella Baker as I Knew Her: She Trusted Youth!," *Social Policy*, vol. 34, no. 3, (Spring 2004), p. 103.

13. Hayden "Ella Baker as I Knew Her," pp. 101 and 102.

14. Hayden, "Ella Baker as I Knew Her," pp. 101–2.

15. Hayden "Ella Baker as I Knew Her," p. 102. See also Casey Hayden, "Fields of Blue," in *Deep in Our Hearts: Nine White Women in the Freedom Movement*, ed. Constance Curry et al., (Athens: University of Georgia Press, 2000), p. 345.

16. Mary King, *Freedom Song: A Personal Story of the 1960s Civil Rights Movement* (New York: Quill/ William Morrow, 1987), pp. 60 and 455.

17. King, *Freedom Song*, p. 455. See also Ransby, *Ella Baker*, p. 102; Joanne Grant, *Ella Baker: Freedom Bound* (New York: John Wiley & Sons, 1998), p. 40; EB, interviewed by Sue Thrasher and Casey Hayden, New York, 1977, pp. 57–60, at http://docsouth.unc.edu/sohp/G-0008/G-0008.html/.

18. Hayden, "Ella Baker as I Knew Her," p. 102.

19. King, *Freedom Song*, p. 456.

20. Hayden, "Fields of Blue," p. 352; Emmie Schrader Adams, "From Africa to Mississippi," in *Deep in Our Hearts*, p. 325.

21. Hayden, "Fields of Blue," p. 363.

22. Hayden, "Fields of Blue, p. 365.

23. King, *Freedom Song*, pp. 444–45.

24. Winifred Breines, *The Trouble between Us: An Uneasy History of White and Black Women in the Feminist Movement* (Oxford: Oxford University Press, 2006), p. 206, note 10.

25. Mary King and Casey Hayden, Untitled SNCC Position Paper, November 1964, reprinted in King, *Freedom Song*, pp. 567 and 568.

26. Untitled SNCC Position Paper, p. 568.

27. Untitled SNCC Position Paper, p. 569.

28. Adams, "From Africa to Mississippi," p. 325.

29. King, *Freedom Song*, p. 471.

30. Casey Hayden, "Preface" to King, *Freedom Song*, p. 9.

31. Untitled SNCC Position Paper, p. 568.

32. Untitled SNCC Position Paper, p, 569.

33. King, *Freedom Song*, pp. 450 and 462.

34. Cynthia Washington, letter to "Southern Exposure," 1977, excerpts reprinted in Evans, *Personal Politics*, p. 238.

35. Gloria Wade Gayles, quoted by Breines, *The Trouble between Us*, p. 45.

36. Washington, letter to "Southern Exposure," p. 239.

37. Breines, *The Trouble between Us*, pp. 39–40 and 48. See chapter 1: "Together and Apart: Women and SNCC." See also Clayborne Carson, *In Struggle: SNCC and the Black Awakening of the 1960s* (Cambridge MA: Harvard University Press, 1981), p. 148.

38. Annie Pearl Avery, "There Are No Cowards in My Family," *Hands on the Freedom Plow*, p. 459.

39. Penny Patch, "Sweet Tea at Shoney's," in *Deep in Our Hearts*, p. 166.

40. Jean Wiley, "Letter to My Adolescent Son," *Hands on the Freedom Plow*, p. 521.

41. King, *Freedom Song*, p. 455.

42. Casey Hayden and Mary King, "A KIND OF MEMO FROM CASEY HAYDEN AND MARY KING TO A NUMBER OF OTHER WOMEN IN THE PEACE AND FREEDOM MOVEMENT," November 18, 1965 reprinted in King, *Freedom Song*, p. 571, pp. 571 and 574. The memo is sometimes called "Sex and Caste: A Kind of Memo."

43. Hayden and King, "A KIND OF MEMO," p. 573.

44. King, *Freedom Song*, p. 458. See also Evans, *Personal Politics*, p. 189.

45. Evans, *Personal Politics*, pp. 141–51.

46. Heather Tobis, quoted by Evans, *Personal Politics*, p. 163. Tobias is describing a subgroup of the workshop.

47. Evans, *Personal Politics*, p. 166. See also Ruth Rosen, *The World Split Open: How the Modern Women's Movement Changed America* (New York: Viking, 2000), pp. 121–24.

48. Alice Echols, *Daring to Be Bad: Radical Feminism in America 1967–1975* (Minneapolis: University of Minnesota Press, 1989), pp. 131–34; Evans, *Personal Politics*, pp. 190, 192, 201, and 211; Linda Gordon, "Participatory Democracy from SNCC through Port Huron to Women's Liberation to Occupy: strengths and problems of prefigurative politics," pp. 9–16, at http://www.lindagordonhistorian.org/files/Porthuron.Nation.doc/.

49. Kathie Sarachild, "A Program for Feminist 'Consciousness Raising,'" in *Notes from the Second Year: Women's Liberation: Major Writings of Radical Women*, ed. Shulamith Firestone and Anne Koedt (New York: Radical Feminism,1970), pp. 78–79. Ellipses and italics in the text. See also Echols, *Daring to Be Bad*, pp. 83–88.

50. Kathie Sarachild, "Consciousness Raising: A Radical Weapon," talk to the First National Conference of Stewardesses for Women's Rights," March 12, 1973, expanded and reprinted in *Feminist Revolution* (New York: Random House, 1978), pp. 144–50, at https://organizingforwomensliberation.wordpress.com/ . . . /consciousness-raising-a-radic . . . /.

51. Carol Hanisch, "The Personal Is Political," published in *Notes from the Second Year*, p. 4, at http://webhome.cs.uvic.ca/~mserra/AttachedFiles/PersonalPolitical.pdf/.

52. Echols, *Daring to Be Bad*, pp. 72–73 and 379.

53. Rosen, *The World Split Open*, p. 197.

54. Gordon, "Participatory Democracy," p. 8. See also Gordon, "Social Movements, Leadership, and Democracy," pp. 102–7.

55. Pat Cody, quoted by Rosen, *The World Split Open*, p. 200.

56. Unknown FBI informant's report, quoted by Rosen, *The World Split Open*, p. 242.

57. BF, "Chapter Outline: The New Woman," typescript, Betty Friedan Papers, Arthur and Elizabeth Schlesinger Library on the History of Women in America, Radcliffe Institute for Advanced Study at Harvard University, Cambridge, Mass., Box 67, folder 813.

58. Pauli Murray, *The Autobiography of a Black Activist, Feminist, Lawyer, Priest, and Poet* (Knoxville: University of Tennessee Press, 1989), p. 285. See also Edith Evans Asbury, "Protest Proposed on Woman's Jobs," *New York Times*, October 13, 1965, p. 32.

59. BF, "The Day the Men Stopped Laughing," typescript, pp. 67, 70, and 72, BF Papers, Box 68, folder 821. See also Rosalind Rosenberg, *Jane Crow: The Life of Pauli Murray* (New York: Oxford University Press, 2017), pp. 190–91.

60. Sonia Pressman, quoted by BF, *It Changed My Life: Writings on the Women's Movement* (New York: Random House, 1976), p. 80. See also Betty Friedan, *Life So Far: A Memoir* (New York: Simon & Schuster, 2000), pp. 164–65 and 167–68.

61. Sonia Pressman Fuentes, "Statement," in Jewish Women's Archive: Sharing Stories, Inspiring Change, p. 3, at http://jwa.org/feminism/fuentes-sonia-pressman/.

62. BF, quoted by Cynthia Fuchs Epstein, "Betty Friedan: An Appreciation," p. 1, at http://www.asanet.org/sites/default/files/savvy/footnotes/maro6/indextwo.html/.

63. BF, "The First Year," President's Report to NOW, 1967, in BF, *It Changed My Life*, p. 97.

64. BF, interviewed by Barbara Mantz Drake, 1999, in *Interviews with Betty Friedan*, pp. 186–87.

65. NOW, "Statement of Purpose," pp. 1 and 2–3, at https://archive.org/details/NOW StatementOfPurpose/.

66. Betty Friedan, "Human . . . Not Class!" *Social Policy*, March/ April 1973, BF Papers, Box 84, folder 959. See also BF, interviewed by Kathleen Erickson, 1994, in *Interviews with Betty Friedan*), pp. 153–55 and 158.

67. King, *Freedom Song*, pp. 77–78. See also Hayden, "Fields of Blue," p. 351.

68. EB, interviewed by Emily Stoper, December 27, 1966, in Emily Stoper, *The Student Nonviolent Coordinating Committee: The Growth of Radicalism in a Civil Rights Organization* (Brooklyn: Carlson, 1989), pp. 265 and 268. Italics in the text.

69. EB, "The Black Woman in the Civil Rights Struggle," speech, Atlanta, 1969, excerpted in Grant, *Ella Baker*, p. 228.

70. BF, Introduction to "Call to Women's Strike for Equality," *It Changed My Life*, p. 139. See also BF, *Life So Far*, p. 171.

71. BF, *Life So Far*, p. 176.

72. NOW, "Statement of Purpose," p. 2. See also Rosenberg, *Jane Crow*, p. 300.

73. BF, Introduction to Part II, *It Changed My Life*, pp. 80–81.

74. BF, letter to Miss Charlotte Roe, Sept. 27, 1966, p. 2, BF Papers, Box 122, folder 1496.

75. BF, Introduction, *It Changed My Life*, p. xviii.

76. EB, "The Black Woman," in Grant, *Ella Baker*, p. 229. See also Rosenberg, *Jane Crow*, pp. 81–95; Sara M. Evans, *Tidal Wave: How Women Changed America at Century's End* (New York: The Free Press, 2003), pp. 25–26.

77. BF, Introduction to Part II, *It Changed My Life*, pp. 77–78 and 81.

78. Rosenberg, *Jane Crow*, p. 204; Daniel Horowitz, *Betty Friedan and the Making of the Feminine Mystique: The American Left, the Cold War, and Modern Feminism* (Amherst: University of Massachusetts Press, 1998), p. 212. See also https://paulimurrayproject.org/pauli-murray /timeline/.

79. Murray, quoted by Rosenberg, *Jane Crow*, p. 309; Susan M. Hartmann, "Pauli Murray and the 'Juncture of Women's Liberation and Black Liberation,'" *Journal of Women's History*, vol. 14, no. 2 (Summer 2002), p. 76.

80. Jennifer Scanlon, *Until There Is Justice: The Life of Anna Arnold Hedgeman* (New York: Oxford University Press, 2016), pp. 208–12.

81. Friedan, Introduction to "The First Year," *It Changed My Life*, p. 96.

82. Breines, *The Trouble between Us*, pp. 94 and 137–48; Evans, *Tidal Wave*, p. 32.

83. Gerda Lerner, letter to Betty Friedan, February 6, 1963, BF Papers, Box 57, folder 715, p. 2.

84. Betty Friedan, "UE Fights for Women Workers," in *Public Women, Public Worlds: A Documentary History of American Feminism*, ed. Dawn Keetley & John Pettegrew (Lanham, Maryland: Rowman & Littlefield, 2002), p. 441.

85. Quoted by Elaine Tyler May, *Homeward Bound: American Families in the Cold War Era* (New York: Basic Books, 2008), p. 203. (First edition, 1988.)

86. BF, *It Changed My Life*, pp. xvi and 60.

87. BF, handwritten notes, no date, no page numbers, BF Papers, Box 70, folder 832.

88. BF, Introduction to "Our Revolution is Unique," *It Changed My Life*, p. 108.

89. BF, *Life So Far*, p. 189.

90. Meredith Tax, quoted by Rosen, *The World Split Open*, p. 84.

91. EB, "The Black Woman in the Civil Rights Struggle," pp. 227 and 230.

92. EB, Interviewed by John Britton, June 19, 1968, transcript, p. 78.

93. Ibid., p. 88.

Chapter Thirteen

1. Jane Jacobs, interviewed by Leticia Kent, 1997, pp. 48 and 49, at www.gvshp.org/_gvshp /resources/doc/jacobs_transcript.pdf. See also Anthony Flint. *Wrestling with Moses: How Jane Jacobs Took on New York's Master Builder and Transformed the American City* (Random House: New York, 2009), pp. 147–55.

2. JJ, Kent interview, p. 49. See also JJ, interviewed by Roberta Brandes Gratz, "How Westway Will Destroy New York," February 6, 1979, in *Jane Jacobs: The Last Interview and Other Conversations* (Brooklyn: Melville House, 2016), pp. 26–27.

3. Stephanie Gervis, "Artists, Politicians, People Join Fight for Little Italy," *Village Voice*, August 30, 1962, p. 6); Flint, *Wrestling with Moses*, pp. 157–58.

4. Lisa Shapiro, "American Writer: Canadian Cities Can Be Saved," *The Ottawa Journal*, March 21, 1970, Jane Jacobs Papers, MS1995–29, John J. Burns Library, Boston College, Box 24, folder 3, p. 19,

5. Mario Savio, quoted by Robert Cohen, *Freedom's Orator: Mario Savio and the Radical Legacy of the 1960s* (New York: Oxford University Press, 2009), p. 50.

6. Cohen, *Freedom's Orator*, p. 76. See also Waldo Martin, "Holding One Another: Mario Savio and the Freedom Struggle in Mississippi and Berkeley," in *The Free Speech Movement: Reflections on Berkeley in the 1960s*, ed. Robert Cohen and Reginald E. Zelnik (Berkeley: University of California Press, 2002), pp. 92–93 and 95.

7. Savio, quoted by Cohen, *Freedom's Orator*, p. 95. See also Laura Visser-Maessen, *Robert Parris Moses: A Life in Civil Rights and Leadership at the Grassroots* (Chapel Hill: University of North Carolina Press, 2016), pp. 206–7.

8. Mario Savio, quoted by Hal Draper, *Berkeley: The New Student Revolt* (New York: Grove Press, 1965), p. 124.

9. Savio, quoted by Cohen, *Freedom's Orator*, p. 212. (Italics and ellipsis in the text.)

10. JJ, *The Death and Life of Great American Cities* (New York: Random House, 1961), p. 406.

11. JJ, Kent interview, p. 55.

12. JJ, quoted in Leticia Kent, "Persecution of the City Performed by its Inmates," *The Village Voice*, April 18, 1968, in *Ideas That Matter: The Worlds of Jane Jacobs*, ed. Max Allen (Owen Sound, Ontario: Ginger Press 2011), p. 73. Some pieces in *Ideas That Matter* are abridged.

13. JJ, quoted in Kent, "Persecution of the City," p. 74.

14. JJ, "The Hearing," April 30, 1968, in *Ideas That Matter*, pp. 76–77.

15. JJ, quoted by Jay Levin, "Jane Jacobs Seized at Roadway Protest," *New York Post*, April 11, 1968, clipping in JJ Papers, Box 21, folder 14; JJ, quoted in Kent, "Persecution of the City," p. 74.

16. JJ, note added to Levin, "Jane Jacobs Seized."

17. Peter Blake, "About Mayor Lindsay, Jane Jacobs, and James Bogardus," *New York Magazine*, May 6, 1968, p. 42. Italics in the original.

18. JJ, quoted by Gratz, *Battle for Gotham: New York in the Shadows of Robert Moses and Jane Jacobs* (Nation Books, New York, 2010), p. 317. Some blame Jacobs for destroying the tape. See Alice Sparberg Alexiou, *Jane Jacobs: Urban Visionary* (New Brunswick: Rutgers University, 2006), pp. 131–32; Flint, *Wrestling with Moses*, p. 174.

19. Richard Serra, "Mrs. Jacobs's Protest Results in a Riot Charge," *New York Times*, April 18, 1968, p. 49.

20. JJ, quoted by Mike Pearl, "Jane Jacobs Charges a 'Gag' Order," *New York Post*, April 18, 1968, in JJ Papers, Box 21, folder 19.

21. JJ, quoted by Gratz, *The Battle for Gotham*, p. 318.

22. JJ, Kent interview, part II, p. 4. See also Alexiou, pp. 149–50; JJ, Kent interview, p. 59.

23. JJ, quoted by "The Way We Are: Jane Jacobs, critic of critics," *Toronto Star*, October 24, 1970, JJ Papers, Box 24, folder 5.

24. JJ, typescript on civil disobedience, unpublished correspondence with the *New York Times Magazine*, JJ Papers, Box 22, folder 13, p. 1.

25. JJ, quoted by Mark Feeney, "City Sage," *Boston Globe*, November 14, 1993, in *Ideas That Matter)*, p. 11, and by Samuel Zipp and Nathan Storring, editors, *Vital Little Plans: The Short Works of Jane Jacobs* (New York: Random House, 2016), p. 162.

26. JJ, typescript on civil disobedience," p. 2.

27. Sally Kempton, "Dawn's Early Light at Whitehall Street," *Village Voice*, December 7, 1967, p. 1.

28. C. Gerald Fraser, "Writers and Editors to Protest War by Defying Taxes," *New York Times*, January 31, 1968, clipping in JJ Papers, Box 23, folder 7; Betty Friedan, Introduction to "The National Women's Political Caucus," *It Changed My Life: Writings on the Women's Movement* (New York, Random House, 1976), p. 165.

29. JJ, quoted by Clark Whelton, "'Great American Cities': Won't you come home, Jane Jacobs," *Village Voice*, July 6, 1972, p. 28.

30. JJ, quoted by Gerald Clark, "The Fleecing of America," *Weekend Magazine*, Oct. 30, 1971, p. 13, JJ papers, Box 26, folder 1.

31. "Jane Jacobs and the New Urban Ecology," symposium transcript, Boston College, November 18, 2000, in JJ Papers, Box 32, Folder 30, pp. 13 and 15–16.

32. Michael Valpy, untitled, in *Ideas That Matter*, p. 202.

33. Alexiou, *Jane Jacobs*, p. 164. See also Robert Kanigel, *Eyes on the Street: The Life of Jane Jacobs* (New York: Penguin Random House, 2016), pp. 313–14.

34. David Crombie, quoted by Kanigel, *Eyes on the Street*, p. 317. See also Alexiou, *Jane Jacobs* pp. 285–89.

35. BF, "Our Revolution Is Unique," Report of the President to NOW, 1968, in *It Changed My Life*, pp. 112–13.

36. BF, "Betty Friedan's Notebook," in *It Changed My Life*, p. 248.

37. Sara Evans, *Personal Politics: The Roots of the Women's Liberation Movement in the Civil Rights Movement & the New Left* (Alfred A. Knopf: New York, 1979), p. 225; Alice Echols, *Daring to Be Bad: Radical Feminism in America 1967–1975* (Minneapolis: University of Minnesota Press, 1989), p. 199.

38. BF, "Betty Friedan's Notebook," pp. 191–92.

39. Sara M. Evans, *Tidal Wave: How Women Changed America at Century's End* (New York: The Free Press, 2003), pp. 49 and 56.

40. BF, "Critique of Sexual Politics," *Social Policy* Magazine, November 1970, in *It Changed My Life*, p. 163.

41. BF, Introduction to "Abortion: A Woman's Civil Right," *It Changed My Life*, p. 120.

42. BF, Introduction to "Call to Women's Strike for Equality," *It Changed My Life*, p. 139.

43. BF, letter to Miss Charlotte Roe, September 27, 1966, Betty Friedan Papers, Arthur and Elizabeth Schlesinger Library on the History of Women in America, Radcliffe Institute for Advanced Study at Harvard University, Cambridge, Mass., Box 122, Folder 1496, p. 1.

44. BF, Introduction to "Call to Women's Strike for Equality," pp. 137–38.

45. BF, "Critique of Sexual Politics," p. 163; BF, "Strike Day, August 26, 1970," in *It Changed My Life*, p. 153. See also BF, *Life So Far: A Memoir* (New York: Simon & Schuster, 2000), p.223.

46. Joanne Grant, *Ella Baker: Freedom Bound* (New York: John Wiley & Sons, 1998), p. 194.

47. BF, *It Changed My Life*, pp. 140–41. Pauli Murray, who was gay, shared Friedan's fear that NOW would be taken over by young radical lesbians. Rosalind Rosenberg, *Jane Crow: The Life of Pauli Murray* (New York: Oxford University Press, 2017), p. 336.

48. BF, *The Feminine Mystique* (New York: Dell, 1963), p. 265.

49. BF, *It Changed My Life*, pp. 158–59.

50. BF, "An Open Letter to the Women's Movement—1976," in *It Changed My Life*, p. 374.

51. BF, interviewed by Nathan Gardels, 1998, in *Interviews with Betty Friedan*, ed. Janann Sherman (Jackson: University Press of Mississippi, 2002, p. 178.

52. Echols, *Daring to Be Bad*, p. 219; Rosen, *The World Split Open*, p. 253; Lillian Faderman, *Odd Girls and Twilight Lovers: A History of Lesbian Life in 20th-Century America* (New York: Columbia University Press, 1991), p. 212.

53. JJ, *Death and Life*, p. 97. See also Kanigel, *Eyes on the Street: The Life of Jane Jacobs*, p. 249.

54. Barbara Ransby, *Ella Baker & the Black Freedom Movement: A Radical Democratic Vision* (Chapel Hill: University of North Carolina Press, 2003), pp. 4, 106, 110, and 255–56.

55. Priscilla Coit Murphy, *What a Book Can Do: The Publication and Reception of Silent Spring* (Amherst: University of Massachusetts Press, 2005), p. 226, note 17; Jill Lepore, "The Right Way to Remember Rachel Carson," at www.newyorker.com/magazine/2018/03/26/the-right-way-to-remember-rachel-carson; Martha Freeman, ed., *Always, Rachel: The Letters of Rachel Carson and Dorothy Freeman, 1952–1964* (Boston: Beacon Press, 1995), p. xvi; Linda Lear, *Rachel Carson: Witness for Nature* (New York: Henry Holt, 1997), pp. 262–63 and p. 535, note 53; William Souder, *On a Farther Shore: The Life and Legacy of Rachel Carson* (New York: Crown Publishers, 2012), pp. 181 and 199.

56. JJ, quoted in Adele Freedman, "Jane Jacobs," *The Globe and Mail*, June 9, 1984, in *Ideas That Matter*, p. 26.

57. EB, quoted by Ransby, *Ella Baker*, p. 191. See also Charles Payne, "Ella Baker and Models of Social Change," *Signs: Journal of Women in Culture and Society*, vol. 14, no. 4 (1989), p. 896.

58. BF, "Betty Friedan's Notebook," in *It Changed My Life*, pp. 253–54. See also BF, "Human . . . Not Class!" *Social Policy*, March/April 1973, BF Papers, Box 84, number 959.

59. BF, "Female Chauvinism is Dangerous," in *It Changed My Life*, p. 245.

60. BF, *It Changed My Life*, p. xiii.

61. Stephanie Coontz, *A Strange Stirring: The Feminine Mystique and American Women at the Dawn of the 1960s* (New York: Basic Books, 2011), pp. 149–52.

62. Horowitz, *Betty Friedan*, pp. 222–23.

63. Friedan, *Life So Far*, p. 140.

64. Betty Rollin, quoted by Lyn Tornabene, 1971, in *Interviews with Betty Friedan*, p. 26.

65. Milton Meltzer, *Betty Friedan: A Voice for Women's Rights* (New York: Viking Penguin, 1985), p. 50.

66. BF, "A Dialogue with Simone De Beauvoir," in *It Changed My Life*, p. 310.

67. Simone de Beauvoir, quoted by BF, "A Dialogue with Simone De Beauvoir," p. 310. See also Linda Gordon, "Social Movements, Leadership, and Democracy: Toward More Utopian Mistakes," *Journal of Women's History*, vol. 14, no. 2 (Summer 2002), pp. 313–14.

68. Bob Moses, interviewed by Charles Payne, 1993, in *Debating the Civil Rights Movement* (Lanham, MD: Rowman and Littlefield, 2006), p. 179.

69. Richard Manning, personal communications to me, 1965 and May 4, 2015. Manning was a SNCC staffer from 1963–1965, and was present when Moses spoke to the staff.

70. Bob Moses, Payne interview, p.179. See also Mary King, *Freedom Song: A Personal Story of the 1960s Civil Rights Movement* (New York: William Morrow, 1987), p. 476; Clayborne Carson, *In Struggle: SNCC and the Black Awakening of the 1960s* (Cambridge: Harvard University Press, 1995 [first edition 1981]), pp. 139–40 and 156–57.

71. Bob Moses, quoted by King, *Freedom Song*, p. 473.

72. Mario Savio, quoted by Cohen, *Freedom's Orator*, pp. 135–36. See also pp. 10 and 256.

73. Mary King, note to herself, December 28, 1964, quoted by King, *Freedom Song*, p. 468. See also Visser-Maessen, *Robert Parris Moses*, p. 149.

74. Visser-Maessen, *Robert Parris Moses*, pp. 278–79.

75. Savio, quoted by Cohen, *Freedom's Orator*, p. 290.

Epilogue

1. Laurie Otto, interviewed by Dick Gordon, "A Fight for the Robins," *The Story*, at www.thestory.org/stories/2008–08/fight-robins; Laurie Otto, quoted by Bill Berry, *Banning DDT: How Citizen Activists in Wisconsin Led the Way* (Madison: Wisconsin Historical Society, 2014), p. 123.

2. Thomas R. Dunlap, *DDT: Scientists, Citizens, and Public Policy* (Princeton, Princeton University Press, 1981), pp. 82 and 152; Berry, *Banning DDT*, pp. 82–85 and 123–24; "'Nature Lady' Otto helped lead DDT fight," at https://archive.jsonline.com/news/obituaries/95479219.html/.

3. Dunlap, *DDT*, pp. 137–39.

4. Dunlap, *DDT*, pp. 180–82; Berry, *Banning DDT*, pp. 184 and 193.

5. Louis A McClean, letter to William E. Spaulding, President Houghton Mifflin Company, August 2, 1962, quoted by Linda Lear, *Rachel Carson: Witness for Nature* (New York: Henry Holt, 1997), p. 417.

6. Louis A. McLean, "Pesticides and the Environment," *BioScience*, vol. 17, no. 9 (Sept. 1967), p. 613. See also Frank Graham, Jr., *Since Silent Spring* (Boston: Houghton Mifflin, 1970), p. 163.

7. Dunlap, *DDT*, pp. 159, 161–62, and 167.

8. Dunlap, *DDT*, pp. 179 and 197. Michigan, where EDF was also active, passed a not-quite total ban in 1969.

9. Robert Gordon, "Poisons in the Fields: The United Farm Workers, Pesticides, and Environmental Politics," *Pacific Historical Review*, vol. 68, no. 1 (1999), pp. 56–60; Linda Nash, "The Fruits of Ill-Health: Pesticides and Workers' Bodies in Post–World War II California," *Osiris*, 2nd Series, vol. 19 (2004), pp. 216–18.

10. Dunlap, *DDT*, pp. 202–3.

11. Gordon, "Poisons in the Fields," pp. 61 and 67; Michelle Mart, *Pesticides, a Love Story: American's Enduring Embrace of Dangerous Chemicals* (Lawrence: University Press of Kansas, 2015), pp. 9 and 57. See also Frederick Rowe Davis, *BANNED: A History of Pesticides and the Science of Technology* (New Haven: Yale University Press, 2014), p. 206.

12. RC, *Silent Spring* (Boston: Houghton Mifflin, 1962), p. 30. See also Lawrence Buell, "Toxic Discourse," *Critical Inquiry*, vol. 24, no. 3 (1998), pp. 652–53; Davis, *BANNED*, pp. 186–90.

13. Charles Wurster, quoted by Robert Gottlieb, *Forcing the Spring: The Transformation of the American Environmental Movement* (Washington, DC: Island Press, 1993), pp. 242–43. Chad Montrie rightly criticizes EDF and other environmental groups for keeping their distance from Huerta and Chavez and the UFW, but somehow he blames Carson for EDF's failure. Chad Montrie, *The Myth of Silent Spring: Rethinking the Origins of American Environmentalism* (Oakland: University of California Press, 2018), pp. 17–18 and 103.

14. Robert Musil, *Rachel Carson and Her Sisters* (New Brunswick, NJ: Rutgers University Press, 2014), pp. 218–19; H. Patricia Hynes, *The Recurring Silent Spring* (New York: Pergamon Press, 1989), pp. 103–5.

15. Mark Hamilton Lytle, The *Gentle Subversive: Rachel Carson*, Silent Spring, *and the Rise of the Environmental Movement* (New York: Oxford University Press, 2007), p. 224.

16. https://cei.org/issue-analysis/rachel-was-wrong.

17. Angela Logomasini, "Activists Celebrate Carson's Dangerous Anti-Chemical Legacy," *Huffington Post*, November 30, 2016. See also Henry I. Miller, "Rachel Carson's 'Heedless and Destructive Acts,'" *Forbes*, January 4, 2017, at https://www.heartland.org/publications-resources/publications/raochel-carsons-deadly-fantasies/; Lytle, *The Gentle Subversive*, pp. 222–23.

18. RC, *Silent Spring*, pp. 9 and 12; Erik M. Conway and Naomi Oreskes, *Merchants of Doubt: How a Handful of Scientists Obscured the Truth on Issues from Tobacco Smoke to Global Warming* (New York: Bloomsbury Press, 2010), pp. 216–39. See also John Quiggin and Tim Lambert, "Rehabilitating Carson," *Prospect Magazine*, May 24, 2008, pp. 3–4, at https://www.prospectmagazine.co.uk/magazine/rehabilitatingcarson/

19. Dunlap, DDT, p. 141. See also Lytle, *Gentle Subversive*, p. 227.

20. Graham, *Since* Silent Spring, p. 157.

21. Conway and Oreskes, *Merchants of Doubt*, pp. 223–24. See also Quiggin and Lambert, "Rehabilitating Carson," p. 4.

22. Naomi Klein, *This Changes Everything* (New York: Simon & Schuster, 2014).

23. Klein, *This Changes Everything*, pp. 83–85, 191–98, 213–17, and 225–29. See also John Stauber and Sheldon Rampton, *Toxic Waste Is Good for You! Lies, Damn Lies, and the Public Relations Industry* (Monroe, Maine: Common Courage Press, 1995), pp. 126–30.

24. JJ, "The Real Problem of Cities," speech at Milwaukee Technical College, 1970, in Samuel Zipp and Nathan Storring, ed., *Vital Little Plans: The Short Works of Jane Jacobs* (New York: Random House, 2016), pp. 199 and 203. See also Gottlieb, *Forcing the Spring*, pp. 105–14.

25. JJ, "The Self-generating Growth of Cities," speech, London, February 7, 1967, in *Ideas That Matter, The Worlds of Jane Jacobs*, ed. Max Allen (Owen Sound, Ontario: Ginger Press, 2011), p. 92. Some pieces in *Ideas That Matter* are abridged.

26. JJ, *The Economy of Cities* (New York: Vintage, 1970), p. 110. See also Jesse Walker, "Jacobean Tragedy: The Gross Misinterpretation of an Intellectual Icon," *Reason Magazine*, July 1998, p. 5.

27. JJ, "Jacobs Tape," Jane Jacobs Papers, MS1995–29, John J. Burns Library, Boston College, Box 22, folder 5; Rebecca Gratz, *Battle for Gotham: New York in the Shadows of Robert Moses and Jane Jacobs* (Nation Books, New York, 2010), p. 258.

28. JJ, quoted by Gratz, *Battle for Gotham*, pp. 221–22.

29. JJ, "The Real Problem of Cities," p. 201, note. See also JJ, interviewed by James Howard Kunstler, in *Jane Jacobs: The Last Interview and Other Conversations* (Brooklyn: Melville House, 2016), p. 88. The interview was in 2000.

30. JJ, "Forward to Interrogatory," March 25, 1952, in *Ideas That Matter*, p. 175. See also Peter L. Laurence, *Becoming Jane Jacobs* (Philadelphia: University of Pennsylvania Press, 2016), p. 62; Alice Sparberg Alexiou, *Jane Jacobs: Urban Visionary* (New Brunswick, NJ: Rutgers University Press, 2006), p. 190.

31. JJ, quoted by James Cook, "Cities and the Wealth of Nations: A Conversation with Jane Jacobs," *Forbes Magazine*, July 30, 1984, in *Ideas That Matter*, p. 111; Colin Ward, "Jane's Fighting Cities," *New Society*, January 31, 1985, in *Ideas That Matter*, p. 110. See also Zipp and Storring, ed., *Vital Little Plans*, pp. 245–48; Howard Husock, "Urban Iconoclast: Jane Jacobs Revisited," *City Journal* (Winter 1994), in *Ideas That Matter*, pp. 84–85; Laurence, *Becoming Jane Jacobs*, pp. 296–97; Alexiou, *Jane Jacobs*, p. 187.

32. JJ, "Encyclopedia Britannica Awards Statement," February 17, 1988, in *Ideas That Matter*, p. 28.

33. JJ, "The Responsibilities of Cities," speech, Amsterdam, September 12, 1984, in *Vital Little Plans*, pp. 252, 254, and 266.

34. JJ, quoted by David Noble, "Population Controll [*sic*]: Black Genocide Says Jane Jacobs," *Eastside News*, February 4, 1970, pp. 1 and 12, in Union Settlement Association Records, Butler Library, Columbia University, Series II, Box 14, folder 2. See also Alexiou, *Jane Jacobs*, p. 167.

35. Adam Gopnik, "Street Cred," *New Yorker*, Sept. 26, 2016, p. 69. See also Robert Kanigel, *Eyes on the Street: The Life of Jane Jacobs* (New York: Penguin Random House, 2016), pp. 296–97.

36. JJ, letter to Betty Friedan, Oct. 15, 1966, pp. 1–2, BF Papers, Box 122, folder 1496. See also *The Feminine Mystique*, BF Papers, Box 57, folder 713; Kanigel, *Eyes on the Street*, p. 248.

37. JJ, "Answers to Interrogatory for Jane Butzner Jacobs," July 22, 1949, JJ Papers, Box 5, folder 3, p. 1.

38. JJ, quoted by Leticia Kent, "More Babies Needed, Not Fewer," *Vogue*, August 15, 1970, in *Ideas That Matter*, p. 23.

39. JJ, quoted by Mark Feeney, "City Sage," *The Boston Globe*, November 14, 1993, in *Ideas That Matter*, pp. 11–13. See also Alexiou, *Jane Jacobs*, pp. 30 and 118–19.

40. JJ, "Forward to Interrogatory," p. 170.

41. JJ, quoted by Kanigel, *Eyes on the Street*, p. 394.

42. JJ, "Answers to Interrogatory," p. 1. See also Kanigel, *Eyes on the Street*, p. 13.

43. JJ, "Women as Natural Entrepreneurs," typescript, October 29, 1994, JJ Papers, Box 22, folder 24.

44. Jacobs, quoted by Noble, "Population Controll," p. 12.

45. Jacobs, "The Real Problem of Cities," p. 222.

46. JJ, Kunstler interview, p. 98.

47. JJ, *The Death and Life of Great American Cities* (New York: Vintage, 1961), p. 251.

48. Gopnik, "Street Cred," p. 74.

49. BF, "Strike Day, August 26, 1970," in *It Changed My Life: Writings on the Women's Movement* (New York: Random House, 1976, pp. 153–54.

50. BF, "An Open Letter to the Women's Movement," 1975, in *It Changed My Life*, p. 384; see also pp. 372 and 373.

51. BF, "An Open Letter to the Women's Movement," pp. 372–73. See also Kirsten Swinth, *Feminism's Forgotten Fight: The Unfinished Struggle for Work and Family* (Cambridge: Harvard University Press, 2018), pp. 70–96.

52. BF, Introduction to Part IV, *It Changed My Life*, p. 261. See also Swinth, Kirsten, *Feminism's Forgotten Fight: The Unfinished Struggle for Work and Family* (Cambridge: Harvard University Press, 2018).

53. BF, "History's Geiger Counter," in *Audacious Democracy: Labor, Intellectuals, and The Social Reconstruction of America*, ed. Steven Fraser and Joshua B. Freeman (Boston: Houghton Mifflin, 1997), p. 31.

54. BF, "History's Geiger Counter," pp. 25 and 31.

55. Barbara Ransby, *Ella Baker and the Black Freedom Movement: A Radical Democratic Vision* (Chapel Hill: University of North Carolina, 2003), pp. 354–56.

56. Ted Glick, "Ella Baker and the Process of Social Change," at https://tedglick.com/future-hope-columns/ella-baker-and-the-process-of-social-change/ See also Ransby, *Ella Baker*, p. 354.

57. Jelani Cobb, "The Matter of Black Lives," *New Yorker*, March 14, 2016, at https://www.newyorker.com/magazine/2016/03/14/where-is-black-lives-matter-headed/.

58. Keisha M. Blain, at https://www.vox.com/2020/7/6/21311171/black-lives-matter-legacy/.

Bibliography

The Papers of Baker, Jacobs, Carson, and Friedan

Ella Baker Papers, Schomburg Center for Research in Black Culture, New York Public Library, NY.

Jane Jacobs Papers, John J. Burns Library, Boston College, Chestnut Hill, MA.

Rachel Carson Papers, Yale Collection of American Literature, Beinecke Rare Book and Manuscript Library, Yale University, New Haven, CT.

Betty Friedan Papers, Arthur and Elizabeth Schlesinger Library on the History of Women in America, Radcliffe Institute for Advanced Study at Harvard University, Cambridge, MA.

Baker, Jacobs, Carson, Friedan: Books, Articles, Speeches, Interviews

Baker, Ella, flyer, "Youth Leadership Meeting," Shaw University, Raleigh, N.C, April 15–17, at https://digitalcollections.nypl.org/items/35f9cc00-dd04-0130-f3c6-58d385a7b928.

Baker, Ella, interview by John Britton, Washington, June 19, 1968, typescript, The Civil Rights Organizing Project.

Baker, Ella, interview by Lenore Bredeson Hogan, NY, March 4, 1979, typescript.

Baker, Ella, interview by Gerda Lerner, 1970, in Gerda Lerner, ed., *Black Women in White America: A Documentary History*, pp. 345–51. NY: Pantheon, 1972.

Baker, Ella, interview by Anne Cooke Romaine, New York, 1967, typescript, at http://www.crmvet .org/nars/6702_baker.pdf/.

Baker, Ella, interview by Emily Stoper, Dec. 27, 1966, in Stoper, *The Student Nonviolent Coordinating Committee: The Growth of Radicalism in a Civil Rights Organization*. Brooklyn: Carlson, 1989.

Baker, Ella, interview by Sue Thrasher and Casey Hayden, New York, April 19, 1977, typescript, at http://docsouth.unc.edu/sohp/G-0008/G-0008.html/.

Baker, Ella, interview by Eugene Walker, Sept. 4, 1974, typescript, at http://docsouth.unc.edu /sohp/G-0007/G-0007.html/.

Baker, Ella, interview by Urban Review editors, *The Urban Review*, vol. 4, no. 3 (May 1970), pp. 19–23.

Baker, Ella, Memorandum to Committee on Administration, "S.C.L.C. as a Crusade," Oct. 23, 1959, p. 2. http://www.crmvet.org/docs/5910_sclc_baker-crusade.pdf/.

Baker, Ella, Memorandum, "S.C.L.C. as a Crusade," at https://www.crmvet.org/docs/5910_sclc _baker-crusade.pdf/.

Baker, Ella, newspaper article, "Bigger Than a Hamburger," *Southern Patriot*, May 1960, vol. 18, no. 5 (June 1960), p. 4.

Baker, Ella, newspaper column, "Shuttlesworth Says," *Pittsburgh Courier*, Aug. 8, 1959, p. 4.

Baker, Ella, Report of the Director to the Executive Board, May 15, 1959, in the Boston University Howard Gotlieb Research Center, Dr. Martin Luther King Archive.

Baker, Ella, Report to Dr. Martin L King, Jr. and Rev. Ralph Abernathy, March 23, 1960, at https://kinginstitute.stanford.edu/king-papers/.

Baker, Ella, Speech, The Black Woman in the Civil Rights Struggle," Atlanta, 1969, in Joanne Grant, *Ella Baker: Freedom Bound*, pp. 227–31. NY: John Wiley, 1998.

Baker, Ella, Speech to SNCC Conference, Washington, DC, Dec. 1963, in Davis W. Houck and David E. Dixon, *Women and the Civil Rights Movement, 1954–1965*, pp. 246–50. Jackson: University Press of Mississippi, 2009.

Carson, Rachel, *The Edge of the Sea*. Boston: Houghton Mifflin, 1955.

Carson, Rachel, *Lost Woods: The Discovered Writing of Rachel Carson*, ed. Linda Lear. Boston: Beacon, 1998.

Carson, Rachel, "National Book Award Acceptance Speech," 1952, in *The House of Life: Rachel Carson at Work*. ed. Paul Brooks, pp. 127–29. Boston: Houghton Mifflin, 1972.

Carson, Rachel, "Of Man and the Stream of Time," Speech, Scripps College, Claremont CA, 1962, in *Literature and the Environment: A Reader on Nature and Culture*, ed. Lorraine Anderson, Scott Slovic, John P. O'Grady, pp. 310–15. NY: Longman, 1999.

Carson, Rachel, "What's the Reason Why," in Symposium, *New York Times Book Review*, Dec. 2, 1962, p. 3.

Carson, Rachel, *The Sea around Us*. NY: Oxford University, 1951.

Carson, Rachel, *Silent Spring*. NY: Houghton Mifflin, 1962.

Carson, Rachel, *Under the Sea-Wind*. London: Penguin, 2007.

Carson, Rachel, and Dorothy Freeman, *Always, Rachel: The Letters of Rachel Carson and Dorothy Freeman, 1952–1964*, ed. Martha Freeman. Boston: Beacon, 1995.

Friedan, Betty, *The Feminine Mystique*. NY: Dell, 1963.

Friedan, Betty, "History's Geiger Counter," in *Audacious Democracy: Labor, Intellectuals, and The Social Reconstruction of America*, ed. Steven Fraser and Joshua B. Freeman (Boston: Houghton Mifflin, 1997), pp. 22–31.

Friedan Betty, *Interviews with Betty Friedan*, ed. Janann Sherman Jackson: University Press of Mississippi, 2002.

Friedan, Betty, *It Changed My Life: Writings on the Women's Movement*. NY: Random House, 1976.

Friedan, Betty, *Life So Far: A Memoir*. NY: Simon & Schuster, 2000.

[Friedan, Betty], "UE Fights for Women Workers," in *Public Women, Public Worlds: A Documentary History of American Feminism*, Vol. II, ed. Dawn Keetley & John Pettegrew, (Lanham, MD: Rowman & Littlefield: 2002), pp. 433–45.

Friedan, Betty Goldstein, "If One Generation Can Ever Tell Another: A Woman Is a Person Too," *Smith Alumnae Quarterly*, vol. 52, no. 2 (Winter 1961) pp. 68–70.

Jacobs, Jane, *The Death and Life of Great American Cities*. NY: Random House, 1961.

Jacobs, Jane, "Downtown Is for People," *Fortune*, April 1958, in *The Exploding Metropolis*, ed. the editors of *Fortune*. Doubleday Anchor, Garden City, NY, 1958, pp. 140–68.

Jacobs, Jane, *The Economy of Cities*. NY: Vintage, 1970.

Jacobs, Jane, *Ideas That Matter: The Worlds of Jane Jacobs*, ed. Max Allen. Owen Sound, Ontario: The Ginger Press, 2011.

Jacobs, Jane, interview by Eve Auchincloss and Nancy Lynch, Mademoiselle, Oct. 1962, p. 142 and 163–67.

Jacobs, Jane, interview by Leticia Kent, Toronto, 1997, at www.gvshp.org/gvshp/resources/doc/jacobs_transcript.pdf

Jacobs, Jane, interview by Susan Fickel, Nancy Cooke, and Elaine Reuben, *Mademoiselle*, Aug. 1962, pp. 250–51 and 361.

Jacobs, Jane, *The Last Interview and Other Conversations*. Brooklyn: Melville House, 2016.

Jacobs, Jane, *Vital Little Plans: The Short Works of Jane Jacobs*, ed. Samuel Zipp and Nathan Storring. NY: Random House, 2016.

Newspaper Archives

New York Times.
The Village Voice.

Books and Articles

Albert Amateau, "Jane Jacobs comes back to the Village she saved," *The Villager*, vol. 74, no. 2 (May 12–18, 2004).

Alexiou, Alice Sparberg, *Jane Jacobs: Urban Visionary*. New Brunswick: Rutgers, 2006.

Anderson, Sara F., "The View from Outside: How Three Women's Work Contributed to Changes Toward Equity and Human Rights: A Study of the Work of Rachel Carson, Jane Jacobs, and Betty Friedan, *New England Journal of History*, vol. 67, no. 1 (Fall 2010), pp. 4–18.

Baldwin, I.L., "Chemicals and Pests," *Science*, vol. 137, no. 3535 (Sept. 28, 1962), pp. 1042–1043.

Barnet, Andrea, *Visionary Women: How Rachel Carson, Jane Jacobs, Jane Goodall, and Alice Waters Changed Our World*. NY: HarperCollins, 2018.

Bean, William B., "The Noise of Silent Spring," *Archives of Internal Medicine*, vol. 112, no. 3, (1963), pp. 308–11.

Berman, Marshall, *All That Is Solid Melts into Air: The Experience of Modernity*. NY: Simon and Schuster, 1982.

Berry, Bill, *Banning DDT: How Citizen Activists in Wisconsin Led the Way*. Madison, WI: Wisconsin Historical Society, 2014.

Blake, Peter, "About Mayor Lindsay, Jane Jacobs, and James Bogardus," *New York Magazine*, May 6, 1968, pp. 42–45.

Bond, Julian, interview by Elizabeth Gritter, Nov. 1 and 22, 1999, Southern Oral History Program Collection (#4007) in the Southern Historical Collection, Wilson Library, University of North Carolina at Chapel Hill.

Branch, Taylor, *Parting the Waters: America in the King Years*. NY: Simon & Schuster, 1988.

Breines, Wini, *The Trouble between Us*. Oxford: Oxford University, 2006.

Brinkley, Douglas, *Rosa Parks*. NY: Penguin Putnam, 2000.

Brooks, Paul, *The House of Life: Rachel Carson at Work*. Boston: Houghton Mifflin, 1972.

Brooks, Paul, *Speaking for Nature: How Literary Naturalists from Henry Thoreau to Rachel Carson Have Shaped America*. Boston: Houghton Mifflin, 1980.

Bush, Monroe, SILENT SPRING..noisy autumn," *American Forests*, Oct. 1962, pp. 12 and 52–54.

Calvert, Gregory Nevala, *Democracy from the Heart: Spiritual Values, Decentralism, and Democratic Idealism in the Movement of the 1960s*. Eugene, OR: Communitas Press, 1991.

Cantarow, Ellen and Susan Gushee O'Malley, "Ella Baker: Organizing for Civil Rights," in *Moving the Mountain: Women Working for Social Change*, ed. Cantarow, O'Malley, and Sharon Hartman Strom. New York: Feminist Press, 1980.

Caro, Robert A., *The Power Broker: Robert Moses and the Fall of New York*. NY: Vintage, 1975.

Carson, Clayborne, *In Struggle: SNCC and the Black Awakening of the 1960s.* Cambridge, MA: Harvard University, 1981.

Cobb, Jelani, "The Matter of Black Lives," *New Yorker,* March 14, 2016.

Cobble, Dorothy Sue, *The Other Woman's Movement: Workplace Justice and Social Rights in America.* Princeton: Princeton University, 2004.

Cohen, Lizabeth, *A Consumer's Republic: The Politics of Mass Consumption in Postwar America.* NY: Alfred Knopf, 2003.

Cohen, Lizabeth, *Saving America's Cities: Ed Logue and the Struggle to Renew Urban America in the Suburban Age.* NY: Farrer, Strauss and Giroux, 2019.

Conway, Erik M. and Naomi Oreskes, *Merchants of Doubt: How a Handful of Scientists Obscured the Truth on Issues from Tobacco Smoke to Global Warming.* NY: Bloomsbury, 2010.

Coontz, Stephanie, *A Strange Stirring: The Feminine Mystique and American Women at the Dawn of the 1960s.* NY: Basic, 2011.

Cottam, Clarence, "A Noisy Reaction to Spring," *Sierra Club Bulletin,* vol., 48, no. 1 (Jan. 1963), pp. 4–5 and 14–15.

Crockett, Karilyn, *People Before Highways: Boston Activists, Urban Planners, and a New Movement for City Making.* Amherst: University of Massachusetts, 2018.

Curry, Constance et al., *Deep in Our Hearts: Nine White Women in the Freedom Movement.* Athens: University of Georgia, 2002.

Darby, William J., "Silence, Miss Carson!" *Chemical & Engineering News,* Oct. 1, 1962, pp. 60–62.

Davis, Frederick Rowe, Banned: A History of Pesticides and the Science of Toxicology. New Haven, Yale University, 2014.

DeLaure, Marilyn Bordwell, "Planting Seeds of Change: Ella Baker's Radical Rhetoric," *Women's Studies in Communication,* vol. 31, no. 1, pp. 1–28.

Diamond, Edwin, "The myth of the 'Pesticide Menace,'" *Saturday Evening Post,* Sept. 28, 1963 vol. 236, no. 33, pp. 16–18.

Draper, Hal, *Berkeley: The New Student Movement.* NY: Grove, 1965.

Dreier, Peter, "Ella Baker, Ferguson, and 'Black Mothers' Sons'" (2014). *UEP Faculty & UEPI Staff Scholarship,* at http://scholar.oedu/uep_faculty/835.

Dreier, Peter, "What We Can Learn from Ella Baker in a Post- Ferguson Era," *Café,* Dec. 26, 2014.

Echols, Alice, *Daring to Be Bad: The Radical Feminism in America, 1967–1975.* Minneapolis: University of Minnesota, 1989.

Evans, Sara, *Personal Politics: The Roots of Women's Liberation in the Civil Rights Movement & the New Left.* NY: Alfred Knopf, 1979.

Evans, Sara, *Tidal Wave: How Women Changed America at Century's End.* NY: Free Press, 2003.

Fadiman, Lillian, *Odd Girls and Twilight Loves: A History of Lesbian Life in Twentieth Century America.* NY: Columbia University, 1991.

Farber, David, *The Age of Great Dreams: America in the 1960s.* NY: Hill and Wang, 1994.

Farber, David, "The Radical Sixties," *Reviews in American History,* vol. 39, no. 4 (December 2011), pp. 712–17.

Ferree, Myra Marx, and Beth B. Hess, *Controversy and Coalition: The New Feminist Movement across Three Decades of Change.* New York: Routledge, 1995.

Fishman, Robert, "Revolt of the Urbs: Robert Moses and His Critics," in *The Transformation of New York,* ed. Hilary Ballon and Kenneth T Jackson, pp. 122–29. NY: W. W. Norton, 2007.

Flint, Anthony, *Wrestling with Moses: How Jane Jacobs Took on New York's Master Builder and Transformed the American City.* Random House, NY, 2009.

Ford, Tanisha C., *Liberated Threads: Black Women, Style, and the Global Politics of Soul.* Chapel Hill: University of North Carolina Press, 2015.

Fosl, Catherine, *Subversive Southerner: Anne Braden and the Struggle for Racial Justice in the Cold War South*. NY: Palgrave Macmillan, 2002.

Fullilove, Mindy Thompson, *Root Shock: How Tearing Up City Neighborhoods Hurts America and What We Can Do About It*. NY: One World/ Ballantine (Random House), 2005.

Garrow, David, *Bearing the Cross: Martin Luther King, Jr., and the Southern Christian Leadership Conference*. NY: William Morrow, 1986.

Gilmore, Stephanie, *GROUNDSWELL: Grassroots Feminist Activism in Postwar America*. NY: Routledge, 2013.

Glick, Ted, "Ella Baker and the Process of Social Change," at https://tedglick.com/future-hope-columns/ella-baker-and-the-process-of-social-change/.

Gopnik, Adam, "Street Cred," *New Yorker*, Sept. 26, 2016, pp. 69–75.

Gordon, Linda, "Participatory Democracy from SNCC through Port Huron to Women's Liberation to Occupy: Strengths and Problems of Prefigurative Politics," pp. 9–16, at http://www.lindagordonhistorian.org/files/Porthuron.Nation.doc/.

Gordon, Linda, "Social Movements, Leadership, and Democracy: Toward More Utopian Mistakes," *Journal of Women's History*, vol. 14, no. 2 (2002), pp. 102–17.

Gordon, Robert, "Poisons in the Fields: The United Farm Workers, Pesticides, and Environmental Politics," *Pacific Historical Review*, Vol. 68, No. 1 (Feb. 1999), pp. 51–77.

Gosse, Van, *Rethinking the New Left: An Interpretive History*. NY: Palgrave Macmillan US, 2005.

Gottlieb, Robert, *Forcing the Spring: The Transformation of the American Environmental Movement*. Washington DC: Island Press, 1993.

Graham, Frank Jr., *Since Silent Spring*. Boston: Houghton Mifflin, 1970.

Grant, Joanne, *Ella Baker: Freedom Bound*. NY: John Wiley, 1998.

Grant, Joanne, director, *Fundi: The Story of Ella Baker*. Icarus Films, 1981.

Grant, Joanne, "Mississippi Politics: A Day in the Life of Ella Baker," in *The Black Woman: An Anthology*, ed. Toni Cade Barbara, pp. 65–73. NY: New American Library, 2005.

Gratz, Roberta Brandes, *The Battle for Gotham: New York in the Shadow of Robert Moses and Jane Jacobs*. NY: Nation Books, 2010.

Halberstam, David, *The Fifties*. New York: Random House, 1993.

Hampton, Henry and Steve Fraser, ed., *Voices of Freedom: An Oral History of the Civil Rights Movement from the 1950s through the 1980s*. NY: Bantam Books, 1990.

Hanisch, Carol, "The Personal Is Political," in *Notes from the Second Year*, at http://webhome.cs.uvic.ca/~mserra/AttachedFiles/PersonalPolitical.pdf/.

Hartman, Susan M., "Pauli Murray and the 'Juncture of Women's Liberation and Black Liberation,'" *Journal of Women's History*, vol. 14, no. 2 (Summer 2002), pp. 74–77.

Hayden, Casey, "Ella Baker as I Knew Her: She Trusted Youth!," *Social Policy*, vol. 34, no. 3 (2004), pp. 101–3.

Hayden, Tom, "Participatory Democracy: from Port Huron to Occupy Wall Street," *The Nation*, April 16, 2012, p. 12.

Hayden, Tom, *Revolution in Mississippi*. Pamphlet. NY: Students for a Democratic Society, 1962.

Hazlett, Maril, "Voices from the Spring: *Silent Spring* and the Ecological Turn in American Health," in *Seeing Nature Through Gender*, ed. Virginia Scharff, pp. 103–28. Lawrence: University of Kansas, 2003.

Hazlett, Maril, "'Woman vs. Man vs. Bugs': Gender and Popular Ecology in Early Reactions to Silent Spring," *Environmental History*, vol. 9, no. 4 (Oct., 2004), pp. 701–29.

Henderson, Margaret, "Betty Friedan, 1921–2006," *Australian Feminist Studies*, vol. 22, no. 53 (July 200) 7, pp. 163–66.

Hogan, Wesley, "Freedom Now!: SNCC Galvanizes the New Left," in *Rebellion in Black and White: Southern Student Activism in the 1960s*, ed. Robert Cohen and David J. Snyder, pp. 43–58. Baltimore: John Hopkins University Press, 2013.

Holsaert, Faith et al., *Hands on the Freedom Plow: Personal Accounts by Women in SNCC.* Champaign, IL: University of Illinois, 2010.

Horowitz, Daniel, *The Anxieties of Affluence: Critiques of American Consumer Culture, 1929–1979.* Amherst: University of Massachusetts Press, 2004.

Horowitz, Daniel, *Betty Friedan and the Making of* The Feminine Mystique: *The American Left, The Cold War, and Modern Feminism.* Amherst: University of Massachusetts Press, 2004.

Horowitz, Daniel, *On the Cusp: the Yale College Class of 1960 and a World on the Verge of Change.* Amherst: University of Massachusetts Press, 2015.

Hynes, H. Patricia, *The Recurring Silent Spring.* NY, Pergamon Press, 1989.

James, Joy, "Ella Baker, 'Black Women's Work' and Activist Intellectuals," *Black Scholar*, vol. 24, no. 4 (Fall, 2003), pp. 8–15.

Kanigel, Robert, *Eyes on the Street: The Life of Jane Jacobs.* NY: Knopf, 2016.

Kaplan, Fred, *1959: The Year Everything Changed.* Hoboken, NJ: John Wiley & Sons, 2009.

Kazin, Michael, *American Dreamers: How the Left Changed a Nation.* NY: Knopf, 2011.

Keller, Evelyn Fox *A Feeling for the Organism: The Life and Work of Barbara McClintock.* NY: W. H. Freeman, 1983.

King, Mary, *Freedom Song: A Personal Story of the 1960s Civil Rights Movement.* NY: William Morrow, 1987.

Kinkela, David, "The Ecological Landscapes of Jane Jacobs and Rachel Carson," *American Quarterly*, vol. 61, no. 4 (Dec. 2009), pp. 905–28.

Klein, Naomi, *This Changes Everything.* NY: Simon & Schuster, 2014.

Larson, Scott, *"Building Like Moses with Jacobs in Mind:" Contemporary Planning in New York City* (Philadelphia: Temple University Press, 2013)

Laurence, Peter L., *Becoming Jane Jacobs.* Philadelphia: University of Pennsylvania, 2016.

Laurence, Peter L., "Jane Jacobs Before *Death and Life*," *Journal of the Society of Architectural Historians*, vol. 66, no. 1 (March 2007), pp. 5–16.

Lear, Linda, *Rachel Carson: Witness for Nature.* NY: Henry Holt, 1998.

Lepore, Jill, "The Right Way to Remember Rachel Carson," at www.newyorker.com/magazine/2018/03/26/the-right-way-to-remember-rachel-carson

Lepore, Jill, "The Shorebird: Rachel Carson and the Rising of the Seas," *New Yorker*, March 26, 2018, pp. 64–66 and 68–72.

Lichtenstein, Nelson, *The Most Dangerous Man in Detroit: Walter Reuther and the Fate of American Labor.* NY: Basic Books, 1995.

Lytle, Mark Hamilton, *The Gentle Subversive: Rachel Carson,* Silent Spring, *and the Rise of the Environmental Movement.* NY: Oxford, 2007.

MacGillivray, Alex, *Understanding Rachel Carson's* Silent Spring. NY: Rosen, 2010.

Mart, Michelle, *Pesticides, A Love Story: America's Enduring Embrace of Dangerous Chemicals.* Lawrence: University of Kansas, 2015.

Martin, Waldo, "Holding One Another: Mario Savio and the Freedom Struggle in Mississippi and Berkeley," in *The Free Speech Movement: Reflections on Berkeley in the 1960s*, ed. Robert Cohen and Reginald E. Zelnik, pp. 83–102. Berkeley: University of California Press, 2002.

May, Elaine, *Homeward Bound: American Families in the Cold War Era.* NY: Basic Books, 1988.

McLean, Louis A., "Pesticides and the Environment," *BioScience*, vol. 17, no. 9 (Sept. 1967), pp. 613–17.

Meltzer, Milton, *Betty Friedan: A Voice for Women's Rights.* NY: Viking Penguin, 1985.

Meyerowitz, Joanne, "Beyond the Feminine Mystique: A Reassessment of Postwar Mass Culture, 1946–1958, *Journal of American History*, vol. 79, no. 4 (March 1993), pp. 1455–82.

Miller, Douglas T., and Marion Nowak, *The Fifties: The Way We Really Were*. Garden City, NY: Doubleday, 1957.

Mitchell, Glenford, "College Students Take Over," in *The Angry Black South*, ed. Glenford E. Mitchell and William H. Peace III, pp. 73–95. NY: Corinth, 1962.

Montrie, Chad, *The Myth of Silent Spring: Rethinking the Origins of American Environmentalism*. Oakland: University of California Press, 2018.

Morris, Aldon, *Origins of the Civil Rights Movement*. NY: Free Press, 1984.

Moses, Bob, interview by Clayborne Carson, June 19, 1970, at http://kingencyclopedia.stanford .edu/primarydocuments/InterviewBob_Moses.pdf/.

Moses, Bob, "This Transformation of People" (interview), in *Debating the Civil Rights Movement*, ed. Steven F. Lawson and Charles Payne, pp. 170–87. Lanham, MD: Rowman & Littlefield, 2006.

Moses, Robert P., and Charles E. Cobb Jr., *Radical Equations: Civil Rights from Mississippi to the Algebra Project*. Boston: Beacon, 2001.

Moye, J. Todd, *Ella Baker: Community Organizer of the Civil Rights Movement*. Lanham, MD: Rowman & Littlefield, 2013.

Mueller, Carol, "Ella Baker and the Origins of 'Participatory Democracy,'" in *Women in the Civil Rights Movement: Trailblazers and Torchbearers, 1941–1965*, ed. Vicki L. Crawford, Jacqueline Anne Rowe, and Barbara Woods, pp. 51–70. Bloomington, Indiana University, 1990.

Murphy, Priscilla Coit, *What a Book Can Do: The Publication and Reception of Silent Spring*. Amherst: University of Massachusetts, 2005.

Murray, Pauli, *The Autobiography of a Black Activist, Feminist, Lawyer, Priest, and Poet*. Knoxville: University of Tennessee, 1989.

Murray, Sylvia, *The Progressive Housewife: Community Activism in Suburban Queens, 1945–1965*. Philadelphia: University of Pennsylvania, 2003.

Musil, Robert K., *Rachel Carson and Her Sisters*. New Brunswick: Rutgers University, 2014.

Nash, Linda, "The Fruits of Ill-Health: Pesticides and Workers' Bodies in Post–World War II California," *Osiris*, second series, vol. 19 (2004), pp. 203–19.

Nembhard, Jessica Gordon, *Collective Courage: A History of African American Cooperative Economic Thought and Practice*, University Park: Pennsylvania State University Press, 2014.

(No Author), "The Desolate Year," *Monsanto Magazine*, Oct. 1962, pp. 5–7.

(No Author), "Industry Maps Defense to Pesticide Criticisms," *Chemical and Engineering News*, vol. 40, no. 33 (Aug. 13, 1962), pp. 23–25.

(No Author), "Pesticides: The Price for Progress," *Time*, vol. 80, no. 13 (September 28, 1962), pp. 45–48.

Norwood, Vera, *Made from This Earth: American Women and Nature*. Chapel Hill: University of North Carolina, 1993.

Norwood, Vera, "The Nature of Knowing: Rachel Carson and the American Environment," *Signs*, vol. 12, no. 4 (Summer 1987), pp. 740–61.

Olson, Lynne, *Freedom's Daughters: The Unsung Heroes of the Civil Rights Movement*. NY: Scribner, 2002.

Oppenheimer, Martin, *The Sit-in Movement of 1960*. Brooklyn: Carlson, 1989 (reprinted from 1963).

Paull, John, "The Rachel Carson Letters and the Making of *Silent Spring*," *Sage*, vol. 3, no. 3 (July 2013), pp. 1–12.

Payne, Charles M., "Ella Baker and the Black Freedom Movement: A Radical Democratic Vision," *Southern Culture*, vol. 10, no. 3 (Fall 2004), pp. 106–8.

Payne, Charles, "Ella Baker and Models of Social Change," *Signs*, vol. 14, no. 4 (Summer, 1989). pp. 885–99.

Payne, Charles, "Men Led, but Women Organized," in *Women in the Civil Rights Movement: Trailblazers and Torchbearers, 1941–1965*, ed. Vicki L. Crawford, Jacqueline Anne Rowe, and Barbara Woods, pp. 1–11. Bloomington: Indiana University Press, 1990.

Payne, Charles M., *I've Got the Light of Freedom: The Organizing Tradition and the Mississippi Freedom Struggle*. Berkeley: University of California Press, 1995.

Pease, William H. III, "The South Reacts," in *The Angry Black South*, ed. Glenford E. Mitchell and William H. Peace III, pp. 96–127. NY: Corinth, 1962.

Quiggin, John, and Tim Lambert, "Rehabilitating Carson," *Prospect Magazine*, May 24, 2008, pp. 3–4, at https://www.prospectmagazine.co.uk/magazine/rehabilitatingcarson/.

Randolph, Irv, "The Work and Wisdom of Ella Baker," *The Philadelphia Tribune*, March 2, 2019.

Ransby, Barbara, *Ella Baker & the Black Freedom Movement: A Radical Democratic Vision*. Chapel Hill: University of North Carolina Press, 2003.

Ransby, Barbara, "Ella Baker's Radical Democratic Vision," *Jacobin*, June 18, 2015.

Robert, Pascal, "Ella Baker and the Limits of Charismatic Masculinity," *Huffington Post*, The Blog, April 23, 2013.

Rosen, Ruth, *The World Split Open: How the Modern Women's Movement Changed America*. NY: Penguin, 2000.

Rosenberg, Rosalind, *Jane Crow: The Life of Pauli Murray*. NY: Oxford, 2017.

Russell, Edmund, *War and Nature: Fighting Humans and Insects with Chemicals from World War I to Silent Spring*. NY: Cambridge University, 2001.

Sarachild, Kathie, "A Program for Feminist 'Consciousness Raising,'" in *Notes from the Second Year: Women's Liberation: Major Writings of Radical Women*, ed. Shulamith Firestone and Anne Koedt (NY: Radical Feminism, 1970), pp. 78–80.

Scanlon, Jennifer, *Until There Is Justice: The Life of Anna Arnold Hedgeman*. NY: Oxford University, 2016.

Schmidt, Christopher W, *The Sit-Ins: Protest & Legal Change in the Civil Rights Era*. Chicago: University of Chicago Press, 2018.

Smith, Michael B., "'Silence, Miss Carson!' Science, Gender, and the Reception of *Silent Spring*," *Feminist Studies*, vol. 27, no. 3 (Fall 2001), pp. 733–52.

Solnit, Rebecca, "Three Who Made a Revolution," *The Nation*, April 3, 2006, pp. 29–32.

Souder, William, *On a Farther Shore: The Life and Legacy of Rachel Carson*. NY: Crown, 2012.

Stare, Fredrick J., "On *Silent Spring*," *Nutrition Reviews*, vol. 21, no. 1 (Jan. 1963), pp. 1–4.

Stauber, John, and Sheldon Rampton, *Toxic Waste Is Good for You! Lies, Damn Lies, and the Public Relations Industry*. Monroe, ME: Common Courage, 1995.

Steingraber, Sandra, "*Silent Spring*: A Father-Daughter Dance," in *Courage for the Earth: Writers, Scientists and Activists Celebrate the Life and Writing of Rachel Carson*, ed. Peter Matthiessen, pp. 49–61. Boston: Houghton Mifflin, 2007.

Swinth, Kirsten, *Feminism's Forgotten Fight: The Unfinished Struggle for Work and Family*. Cambridge: Harvard University Press, 2018.

Theoharis, Jeanne, *A More Beautiful and Terrible History: The Uses and Misuses of Civil Rights History*. Boston: Beacon, 2018.

Theoharis, Jeanne, *The Rebellious Life of Mrs. Rosa Parks*. Boston: Beacon, 2013.

Tyrnauer, Matt, director, *Citizen Jane: Battle for the City*. Altimeter Films, 2016.

Visser-Maessen, Laura, *Robert Parris Moses: A Life in Civil Rights and Leadership at the Grassroots*. Chapel Hill: University of North Carolina Press, 2016.

Wang, Zuoyue, "Responding to Silent Spring: Scientists, Popular Science Communication, and Environmental Policy in the Kennedy Years," *Science Communication*, vol. 19, no. 2 (1997), pp. 141–63.

Wood, Anthony G., *Preserving New York: Winning the Right to Protect a City's Landmarks*. NY: Routledge, 2008.

Worster, Donald, *Nature's Economy: A History of Ecological Ideas*. Cambridge: Cambridge University, 1977.

Young, Andrew, *An Easy Burden: The Civil Rights Movement and the Transformation of America*. NY: HarperCollins 1996.

Zinn, Howard, *SNCC: The New Abolitionists*. Chicago: Haymarket, 2013.

Zipp, Samuel, *Manhattan Projects: The Rise and Fall of Urban Renewal in Cold-War New York*. NY: Oxford University, 2010.

Index

Abernathy, Ralph, 84, 86

Adams, Emmie Schrader, 185

advertising and propaganda: Carson on, 113–15, 175; Friedan on, 66, 126–27, 128–29, 224–25

Allen, Pam, 189

anti-communism: and Baker, 13, 76–77, 149–52; and Carson, 77; and Friedan, 66–67, 76, 196–97; and Jacobs, 37, 77, 152

Avery, Annie Pearl, 187

Bacon, Edmund, 35

Baker, Ella: on anti-communism, 13, 76–77, 149–52; Blain on, 227; Bond on, 15, 88, 91, 150; Braden on, 150; and Brotherhood of Sleeping Car Porters, 6, 8; on Brown decision, 7; Carmichael on, 182; Casey Hayden on, 183–84; on celebrity, 13, 17, 85, 209–10, 211, 212; character traits of, xii; class analysis by, 4, 63, 153, 196; class and race combined, 3–4, 6–7, 130, 153; and CIO, 6, 148; Cobb on, 227; and cooperatives, 5, 13, 144; Cox on, 142; Evans on, 181–82; and FBI, 150; on gender, 16, 17–20, 147, 198–99; Gordon on, 182; in Greenwich Village, 4, 29, 152; Guyot on, 182; and Hamer, 146, 149; in Harlem, 4, 5, 8; against hierarchy, 5–6, 9, 17–18, 24, 84; at Highlander Conference, 90–92, 145; influence of, 18–20, 92–93, 143, 153, 181–84, 197, 227; and In Friendship, 9, 11, 144; as investigative reporter, 64; and Jacobs, 24–25, 106, 158–59; and Lawson, 17, 86; leadership style of, 11–20, 96–97, 141–44, 201; and Levinson, 9, 11; Lewis on, 12; Long on, 146; marriage and divorce of, 183–84; and Martin Luther King Jr., 9–11, 14–15, 17–19, 82, 85, 86–88, 143, 244n26; and Mary King, 142, 183–84; McDew on, 142; as mentor of SNCC women, 182–84, 187, 188; and Mississippi, 11, 18, 89–92, 142, 144–51; and Mississippi Freedom Democratic Party, 148–51; on Montgomery bus boycott, 7–10, 89; and Moore, 143–45; Moye on, 19; and NAACP, 5–7, 63, 76–77, 149, 194; Nash on, 16, 90–91; and Nixon, 8; Norman on, 182; and Parks, 8, 12, 20; Payne on, 19, 181; and Raleigh Conference, 12–16, 82–88, 141; Ransby on, 19, 182; and Robert Moses, 90–92, 143–53; and Rustin, 9, 11, 165; and SCLC, 9–11, 14–15, 17, 18, 76, 81, 82, 86–88, 144; and SDS, 181; sexuality of, 209; at Shaw University, 3, 14–16, 82; and sit-ins, 11–16, 81–89; and SNCC, 11–20, 77, 81–93, 144–51; Tom Hayden on, 181; on whites in the movement, 85–86, 147–48, 153; and the women's liberation movement, 181–84, 188–90, 197, 198–99, 208, 227; Young on, 17; and young people, 11–13, 16, 82; Zinn on, 142

Blain, Keisha M., 227

Bond, Julian, 15, 20, 88, 91, 150

Boston, 35, 102, 103, 162, 177

Braden, Anne, 150

Broley, Charles, 53

Brooks, Paul, 54, 57, 58

Brotherhood of Sleeping Car Porters, 6, 8

capitalism: Baker on, 226, 227; Carson on, 214, 217–18; Friedan on, 197, 224–26; Jacobs on, 220–21, 223–24

Carmichael, Stokely, 182, 210, 255n11
Carson, Rachel: as activist, 48–60, 77, 108,
    110, 174–76, 216; on advertising and
    propaganda, 113–15, 175; against Ameri-
    can Medical Association, 56, 175; anger
    of, 55–58; and Arthur Flemming, 56–57;
    and Audubon Society, 51–52, 53, 55, 169,
    175, 216; and Baker, 45, 60; on biological
    control, 112; and birdwatchers, 50–52, 214;
    and Brooks, 54; and cancer, 58–59, 115–16,
    216, 217; as Cassandra, 46–47; and CBS,
    168, 175–76; on celebrity, 209, 211; charac-
    ter traits of, xii; childhood of, 41; on com-
    merce as destroyer of nature, 41, 43–44,
    59, 109, 110, 111–12, 214; and Cottam, 50,
    54, 57; as counter attacker, 174–76, 189;
    and DDT, 47–60, 215, 216, 217–18; and
    eagles, 53, 59, 109, 215; and ecology, 45–46,
    107; The Edge of the Sea, 45–46; and
    Elton, 117–18; and Environmental Protec-
    tion Agency, 176, 216; family obligations
    of, 45; on Flemming, 56–57; and Freeman,
    49–50, 55, 59; and Friedan, 113, 121, 174;
    and Garden Club, 175; and Huckins, 51;
    human life as threatened, 54, 60, 107–8,
    176, 216; and Jacobs, 44, 47, 50, 60, 116–20,
    176–80; and Larkin, 52; and Marjorie
    Spock, 47–49, 56, 59, 77, 113; and McLean,
    169; and National Agricultural Chemical
    Association, 169, 170; nuclear war, 43, 108;
    ocean as comfort and cure, 41–42, 46;
    on progress, 46–47, 109–10, 113, 118, 170,
    174; as public prosecutor, 108, 112, 214; on
    resistance of insects to pesticides, 54, 115;
    on scientists corrupted by money, 112–13,
    172, 174; and the chemical industry, 109,
    112–16, 119, 135, 168–76; The Sea around
    Us, 41–42, 168; sexuality of, 209; Silent
    Spring, 48–60, 77, 107–20, 168–74, 217;
    Under the Sea-Wind, 41, 42–43; against
    US Department of Agriculture, 47, 53, 57,
    113, 114, 119, 170, 171, 176; at US Fish and
    Wildlife Service, 43, 44, 47, 50; and Wal-
    lace, 52; and Wayland Hayes, 56; women
    as deepest allies, 55; on women held back
    in science, 44–45, 173; on WWII as turn-
    ing point, 42–43, 48
celebrity, 209–13. See also Baker, Ella; Carson,
    Rachel; Friedan, Betty; Jacobs, Jane

change from below: Baker on, 5–6, 8–9,
    11–20, 63, 92–93, 134, 149, 194, 227; Carson
    on, 108, 134, 175; Friedan on, 62–63, 133;
    Jacobs on, 36, 134, 99–100, 106, 160–61
Chavez, Caesar, 216
CIO, 6, 63–64, 147, 194
Clark, Septima, 232n16
class analysis: by Baker, 4, 63, 153; by Friedan,
    30, 61–66
Cobb, Jelani, 227
Cold War, 64, 67, 76–77, 196–97
contempt for outspoken women: for Baker,
    17–18; for Carson, 169–74, 179–80; for
    Friedan, 132–33, 134–35, 184; for Jacobs,
    176–80; for women's liberation activists,
    184, 189
Conway, Erik, 218
Coontz, Stephanie, 137
Cottam, Clarence, 50, 54, 57, 216
Cox, Courtland, 142
Cullors, Patrisse, 227

Death and Life of Great American Cities, The,
    29, 33–39, 94–110, 116–20
de Beauvoir, Simone, 134, 193, 211
Democratic Party, 148–49, 152
De Sapio, Carmine, 31–32
DDT, 47–60, 107–20, 214–18
Dichter, Ernst, 128–29
diversity, value of: Baker, 153, 198, 229; Carson,
    44, 117–18; Jacobs, 96–98, 101–2, 118, 164

East Harlem, 25–26, 34–35
ecology: Carson, 45–46, 107, 117–18; Jacobs,
    104, 117–18
EDF (Environmental Defense Fund), 215–17,
    218–19
Edge of the Sea, The, 45–46
Eisenhower, Dwight D., 43, 51, 112, 128
Eisner, Lester, 155–56, 157
Elton, Charles, 117–18
environmental movement, 175–76, 214–19
Environmental Protection Agency, 176, 216
Evans, Sara, 181–82, 189

Farnham, Marynia, 123–24, 125–26
FBI: and Baker, 77, 150; and Carson, 77;
    and Friedan, 76; and Jacobs, 24, 77; and
    women's liberation groups, 191

About the Author

Photo by Jim Werkowski

Steve Golin taught history at Kansas State University and Bloomfield College (NJ). As a scholar, he combines his training in the history of ideas with his interest in social history. A life-long activist, he focuses his writing on social movements.